Copyright Law
for Librarians and
Educators

Copyright Law
for Librarians *and* Educators

Creative Strategies and Practical Solutions

FOURTH EDITION

Kenneth D. Crews

ALA
Editions

CHICAGO | 2020

Extensive effort has gone into ensuring the reliability of the information in this book; however, the publisher makes no warranty, express or implied, with respect to the material contained herein.

ISBNs
978-0-8389-1629-2 (paper)
978-0-8389-4690-9 (PDF)
978-0-8389-4691-6 (ePub)
978-0-8389-4692-3 (Kindle)

Library of Congress Cataloging-in-Publication Data
Names: Crews, Kenneth D., author.
Title: Copyright law for librarians and educators : creative strategies and practical solutions / Kenneth D.
    Crews.
Description: Fourth edition. | Chicago : ALA Editions, 2020. | Includes bibliographical references and index.
    | Summary: "This newly revised and updated edition by respected copyright authority Crews offers timely
    insights and succinct guidance for LIS students, librarians, and educators alike"—Provided by publisher.
Identifiers: LCCN 2019051377 (print) | LCCN 2019051378 (ebook) | ISBN 9780838916292 (paperback) |
    ISBN 9780838946909 (pdf) | ISBN 9780838946916 (epub) | ISBN 9780838946923 (kindle edition)
Subjects: LCSH: Copyright—United States. | Fair use (Copyright)—United States. | Librarians—United
    States—Handbooks, manuals, etc. | Teachers—United States—Handbooks, manuals, etc.
Classification: LCC KF2995 .C74 2020 (print) | LCC KF2995 (ebook) | DDC 346.7304/82—dc23
LC record available at https://lccn.loc.gov/2019051377
LC ebook record available at https://lccn.loc.gov/2019051378

Cover design by Monica Alejo.
Book design by Casey Bayer and Karen Sheets de Gracia in the Liberation Serif and Din typefaces.

⊗ This paper meets the requirements of ANSI/NISO Z39.48-1992 (Permanence of Paper).

Printed in the United States of America
24 23 22 21 20   5 4 3 2 1

To the many librarians, educators, attorneys, students, and creative thinkers
who have been in the audience
as I shared copyright around the world.
You honored me with your presence and insights,
and you have made me wiser.

CONTENTS

APPENDIXES

INTRODUCTION

This Book and the Importance of Copyright

COPYRIGHT AND CHANGE

Copyright is a creation of law, but even its legally defined strictures can be unsettled and the object of continuous adjustment, interpretation, and change. Congress revises the Copyright Act with new legislation; courts reinterpret statutes; owners set terms for use of their works; institutional policies give meaning to fair use and more. Copyright may well start with today's law, but that law is but a foundation for the many decisions and pursuits we necessarily build upon it. This book attempts to offer an insightful and practical foundation for readers who are working with copyright in the context of teaching, librarianship, research, publishing, and related cultural and social endeavors.

Copyright is integral to the advancement of innovative education, librarianship, and scholarship. Creative uses of protected works, and new applications of digital technologies, have stirred complex questions about the appropriate uses of copyrighted works, as well as the ownership and management of legal rights. Our interface with copyright can compel us to transform our efforts, whether to avoid certain activities or to discover new possibilities.

We also make our decisions from a foundation that is shifting and in steady need of reinforcement and reconstruction. Since the previous edition of this book, Congress has crafted new legal rights associated with early sound recordings and has implemented the Marrakesh Treaty, a multinational agreement with copyright standards to serve the needs of the visually impaired. International agreements have become a more prominent means for shaping much of copyright law in the United States and abroad. Almost as significant are the failures of Congress to act. Congress continues to avoid the orphan works problem and has taken little action on various proposals affecting a wide range of services by libraries and archives.

Courts have had a more elevated role in developing copyright through recent years. Judges have handed down major new rulings on vital issues, including fair use, ownership, and mass digitization. New interpretations of fair use that apply to collections of millions of scanned books have opened expansive possibilities. The case involving electronic reserves and fair use at Georgia State University was filed in 2008, and as of this writing it still cycles through appeals and reconsiderations by the courts.

Meanwhile, research and education are reinvented with the creation of new software, technologies, and understandings of how we remix and transmit information—and absorb the learning experience. The creation and use of information are in a nonstop revolution. This blend of dynamic change and slow development of the law has motivated private parties to take the lead in shaping some implications of copyright. Creative Commons is now an established feature of innovative publishing, and it is simultaneously a point of rebellion against broadened legal rights. The open access movement calls for sharing rights of use, and its widespread acceptance has transformed much of the scholarly publishing trade.

Educators and librarians grapple in other ways with the need to define the law where courts have not ruled. Institutional policies and agreements sometimes clarify or even supersede legal rights of ownership and can offer interpretations of fair use and other statutory exceptions. Institutions are motivated to draft detailed policies and contracts about works made for hire and the ownership of teaching materials, online courses, and academic publications. Libraries regularly acquire materials under license agreements that define terms of use of journals, books, software, motion pictures, and many other works. Archival collections are sometimes subjected to contractual restrictions on access and use. On the other hand, many textbooks and other educational resources are now freely offered online and openly available to download. Such private agreements and pursuits have become a dominant force on the shape of legal rights and responsibilities for many works.

SOLID GROUND

None of these private arrangements would be wise or possible without a solid grounding in copyright law. Parties would be remiss to make policy, negotiate agreements, or enter into licenses without knowing what the law already provides. In this manner, copyright becomes the launching platform for licenses and other bargains. Copyright is the starting point for drafting and negotiating effective deals. Without knowing the law, you are at a disadvantage when determining whether your policy or contract is expanding your rights, giving you something you already have, or taking away opportunities that the law has handed you. Moreover, regardless of the trend toward contracts and licenses, rapid shifts in materials, demands, creativity, and distribution networks mean that we will always need to return to principles of copyright to determine fundamental rights, responsibilities, and opportunities. What works are protected? Who owns the rights? How does fair use apply? How does the law facilitate library services or apply to music and recordings or distance learning? This book addresses exactly these questions.

We also need to return to the fundamentals of copyright, because as educators, researchers, librarians, and students, we continue to engage in new ventures. We digitize and upload diverse materials. We launch websites for programs and projects. We secure federal grants to establish vast digital collections as open resources for any user on the Internet. We download materials from databases and manipulate and incorporate them into online instruction. An understanding of copyright and our ability and willingness to work with the law can help make these important endeavors successful.

TAKING CONTROL

As professionals in the world of education and librarianship, we can be successful with the law's benefits only if we take control. We need to understand the principles of copyright and comprehend our rights as owners and as users. We ultimately need to identify alternatives that the law allows and make decisions about copyright that best advance our objectives as teachers, learners, and information professionals. If we do not manage copyright to our advantage, we will lose valuable opportunities for achieving our teaching and research missions. If we do not manage our own needs, someone else will make the decisions for us.

This book demonstrates that much of copyright law is within the reach of professionals with diverse backgrounds. Admittedly, some aspects of the law will be bewildering and occasionally unworkable. But most issues about ownership, publication, library services, and fair use are within our grasp, and we can make practical sense of them. Copyright does not have to be an annoying or threatening nuisance that merely burdens your work. With a fresh understanding of the law, you will discover that it can actually support librarians, educators, and scholars who are striving to meet their goals each day.

ACKNOWLEDGMENTS

This book is a full reevaluation and update of the previous edition. In many places, the law has changed. In other places, the explanations are reconsidered and improved. In yet other instances, I have evaluated anew some of my own views and interpretations of the law. Each chapter is expanded appreciably, with several chapters that are entirely new. The previous one chapter on distance education is now two. International law and foreign law fill two new chapters, with one more chapter exploring the sources of U.S. copyright law. The complex series of court rulings about electronic reserves at Georgia State University has produced various principles and guideposts that merit their own chapter. Congress gave us entirely new law on pre-1972 sound recordings in late 2018; just the basics of it fill another dedicated chapter.

I am grateful to many colleagues for the questions and conversations that have allowed me to explore and learn and capture the ideas that comprise the insides of this fourth edition. I am especially grateful to several colleagues and research assistants who contributed importantly to this edition. Most important has been my colleague Elizabeth Townsend Gard, professor of law at Tulane University Law School and co-director of the Tulane Center for IP, Media & Culture. She was always available to trade ideas, and her expertise on copyright duration and on the latest fair use rulings was an invaluable check. Professor Townsend Gard generously made this book an intensive research project for two of her intellectual property interns. Thomas Lemler and Ricardo A. Gonzalez did outstanding work checking my updates, adding new cases, and scrutinizing every word of most chapters.

Many contributors to earlier editions continue to influence this latest version. Dwayne K. Buttler, who holds the scholarly communications chair at the University of Louisville has had a role in this project since the first edition, and I continue to value his judgment and crucial contributions. The influence of several excellent research assistants from my years at Columbia Law School and Indiana University show through in various parts of this book: Sarah Burghart, Michelle Choe, Mary Jane Frisby, Kreg Katoski, Megan M. Mulford, Jacque M. Ramos, Meghan Schubmehl, and David A. W. Wong. I continue to be grateful for our many long and entangled conversations about the meaning of the latest cases or the most convoluted statutes.

Special thanks are due to my colleagues at Gipson Hoffman & Pancione in Los Angeles. They patiently allowed me to hole up with the book manuscript and fly around the world sharing insights about copyright. Two attorneys and clerks associated with the firm were especially helpful as they studiously reviewed chapters, challenged points, and tested the clarity of my exposition: Addison Bennett (currently at the University of Chicago) and Mickaël Le Borloch (now practicing in Rouen, France). My wife and life partner, Elizabeth

St. Clair Crews, is a survivor of all editions and many other publications, not to mention my late hours in the office and long journeys to distant lands. My gratitude to Elizabeth is never enough.

This book is dedicated to the thousands of information professionals, educators, students, authors, and attorneys—and to everyone—who chose to be in the room or online as I planted copyright seeds in nearly every U.S. state and in more than thirty-five countries. In meetings and presentations from Nairobi to Barrow (now Utqiagvik) and from Ulaanbaatar to Santiago, I have been blessed by your courtesy and friendships, and you have taught me much about copyright and its significance for your local heritage. I applaud my audience wherever I go—you are making the investment of time and energy, and you are making the choice to spend time exploring copyright. Copyright has been a source of adventure in literature, art, music, and all creativity. It also has allowed a steady expedition through geography and culture. I look forward to the next intellectual property expedition.

KENNETH D. CREWS
Los Angeles, California

PART I

The Reach of Copyright

THIS SINGLE photograph tells much about the scope and reach of copyright. Architectural works are protected, but only since 1990. Text, art, and the photograph itself are more conventional stuff of copyright protection. Each copyrighted element has a different owner, enjoys a different duration, and is subject to different exceptions. Featured prominently is an exhibition of works by Jeff Koons, who has relied heavily on fair use and the American court system as he integrates existing features into his new and creative art.

CHAPTER 1

THE COPYRIGHT MAP

Changing Needs and Copyright Solutions

THE CHAPTERS OF this book offer a systematic walk through the principles and functioning of copyright law. Although the journey may be rough at times—thanks to a law that does not always follow the most graceful path—the expedition should be intellectually engaging as well as practical. Indeed, working with copyright law in the context of applied situations is less of a quest for "answers" than it is a path that takes you toward a resolution, or at least an informed decision, about individual aspects of copyright.

THE GPS OF COPYRIGHT

No journey is successful without a trail map, and you can easily make strides in the wrong direction. Thinking of this book as a map, you can see that it starts with the fundamental concepts of copyright—the scope of works protected and how you secure that legal protection. It has a few forks in the road, such as the exploration of works that are without protection and in the public domain. The book leads you through the thicket of exceptions, especially fair use. The closing chapters give an overview of special demands along the route when you are working with music, manuscripts, and other works that carry their own challenges.

Now study the map and path from a different perspective. Each step along the way is a copyright discussion—a chapter or more from this book. But as you become more familiar with copyright, you will move quickly to the specific place where you need to focus your energies. Fair use, for example, might in general be an alluring route, but it might not really be the copyright issue at the center of your concern or that really resolves your need. Spotting the right issue is crucial.

Maybe this book is more like GPS than a common map. The navigation system on your mobile phone or car's control panel can pinpoint your current location and indicate where you might be headed. It can also help you reconsider and get you back to the right road. When the rules of copyright duration draw you deep into the quandaries of foreign publications and presidential proclamations, you might hear that consoling digital voice telling you it is time to recalculate. When the convolutions of music law clash with the intransigence of the law for distance education programs, you might see yourself at something of a dead end. Just as you need a map to take you someplace, you need wise counsel to recalculate a different plan. Like GPS, too, you are always pinpointed right in the center of activity, and you can recalculate when you miss a turn.

THE MOST COMMON QUESTION

Consider one of the most common copyright questions. You, or a colleague, are working on a project that involves the reproduction or other use of a book, film, song, or other work created by someone else. Too often the first copyright question is often simply phrased, *Is this fair use?* If you take the question at face value and go straight to analyzing fair use, you might quickly find yourself on a steep and rutted road, edged with the briars and thorns of a strangely haunting and alluring law.

On the other hand, by reflecting on the entire copyright trail and planning the trip more systematically from the beginning, you might find various stops along the way that give you a better, more direct, and even easier answer than you would find by starting with fair use. You might determine one of the following:

- *The work in question is not protected by copyright at all.* It may be a work of the federal government, or the copyright may have expired.
- *The use is not among the protected rights of the copyright owner.* You might, for example, be making a private performance of music, while the owner has rights only with respect to public performances.

Signs along the hiking trails of the Swiss Alps open a variety of options, each posing its own challenges and rewards.

■ *The intended use is within another statutory exception in the Copyright Act.* If you can fit your use within one of the detailed provisions for classroom use, library copying, or backing up software, you will probably find a more satisfactory answer than you will with fair use.

Any one of those possibilities is a clearer and more secure answer than you will likely find with fair use. This book should accordingly help you see the issues and possibilities of copyright unfold systematically as they apply to your real needs. You should also see how the issues change with the growing innovation and complexity of education, research, and technology.

THIS BOOK AS MAP

That foregoing list of possibilities reflects some of the construct of copyright itself, as well as the basic outline of this book. The book is often conceived as a practical map for applying the law to given situations. The examples in this chapter alone will make that point repeatedly. However, the full map is not always essential, and at times you will want to skip a thorough and systematic route and just get to the major obstacle between you and the end result. Consider this familiar question: *Does copyright allow the library to make digital copies of journal articles to give to users for their personal study?*

A full copyright map would start at the beginning and consider whether the works are still under copyright protection, whether you have identified the copyright owner, whether the uses potentially infringe, and more. Many libraries might for the sake of efficiency identify the major issue as an application of Section 108 of the Copyright Act on copies for personal study (see Chapter 17). Of all the copyright issues in this example, the Section 108 question possibly offers the greatest level of efficiency in clearing the use of textual materials, such as journal articles. If this library service fits within Section 108, then all other issues are moot. Resolving the Section 108 question can also get you to an end result, whereas resolving the question of copyright duration still leaves the Section 108 matter ahead on the trail.

SPOTTING COPYRIGHT ISSUES

This book is about law, but the real subject is teaching, research, innovation, and other spirited pursuits of educators and librarians. Because these pursuits regularly involve creating and using copyrighted works, the legal issues steadily arise. The issues change and grow with each new variation on each situation. Change the materials you might be using, or change the method or circumstances of their use, and you may well encounter a different set of issues and possibly different outcomes under the law.

Notice that this book is exploring *issues* and not necessarily *problems*. Not all copyright questions are problems. In fact, some copyright questions are relatively easy, and many lead to good news. For example, copyright law broadly permits some uses of works in the classroom, and it provides that all works eventually enter the public domain, where they may be freely used. Other questions are tougher, and not all will lead to a satisfactory conclusion. But as someone seeking to enjoy the benefits of the law, you will need to take a little time, learn a bit about the law, and make a determination about whether you are working within the terms and boundaries of the rules. Reading this book should be a great stride in that direction.

Let's start the journey. Throughout this book you will find a variety of cases, examples, and scenarios intended to reveal the practical application of copyright law in ways that are relevant to educators, librarians, researchers, and others. Before delving deeply into the chapters and details of the rest of the book, a familiar and evolving scenario can provide a meaningful introduction as well as a map through the upcoming chapters.

TAKE ME TO THE MOVIES

Begin the scenario with simple and familiar facts. With each additional fact will come new questions about copyright, and the Issues will highlight key points and lead you to chapters in this book for more information and guidance.

Scenario Installment A

You teach a college course on English literature, and you ask your students to buy and read the book *Pride and Prejudice.*

One of the curses of copyright is that you start to see issues everywhere. In even the simplest situation you have copyright questions—at this stage you have only *issues* or *questions*, not *problems*. You are proposing nothing that will violate the law, but to get to that conclusion systematically and accurately, you have to sort through a few copyright issues.

ISSUE A1: Is the book protected by copyright?

- Chapter 4 makes clear that *most such original works are protectable* under copyright.
- Chapter 6 surveys the law of *copyright duration*, and a book that was first published in 1813 is surely in the public domain.

ISSUE A2: Assuming the work were still protected, would buying or reading a copy be a violation of copyright?

- Chapter 8 surveys the *rights of copyright owners*, and simply reading a book is not on the list. On the other hand, the legal rights under copyright include the rights of distribution of copies, so the bookstore may be infringing with each sale.
- Chapter 9 is an overview of *exceptions to the rights of owners*, and the first sale doctrine is a major limit on the distribution rights, enabling bookstores to sell copies and libraries to check out books and more.

Scenario Installment B

To give your students a different understanding of the story, you would like to show the recent film version of *Pride and Prejudice* to the entire class.

ISSUE B1: Is the motion picture protected by copyright?

- Chapter 4 emphasizes that copyright *protects an extensive range of materials,* including text, sound recording, images, software, and movies.
- Multiple adaptations generally based on *Pride and Prejudice* have been turned into motion pictures through the decades. Chapter 6 explains that each

of these films, whether produced in 1940 or just recently, has *many years of copyright protection* and possibly not one of them is yet in the public domain.

- On the other hand, the 1940 version of the movie may likely still be protected, but it could be in the public domain if the copyright owner did not comply with the formalities required at that time. Chapter 6 will take you step-by-step through that possibility.
- Each new version and variation on the story, transposed into a new motion picture, can start the copyright duration clock running anew for the original elements. A fresh calculation started not long ago for *Pride and Prejudice and Zombies*.

ISSUE B2: Does showing the motion picture violate copyright?

- Chapter 8 itemizes the *rights of copyright owners*, and you may be making a "public performance" of the movie.
- Chapter 9 includes mention of Section 110(1) of the Copyright Act, a statute that broadly permits showing a film in the traditional face-to-face classroom. You may find that this *specific copyright exception* can be enormously important for your teaching.

Look at what is happening to our scenario. The simplest and highly familiar situation is rich with issues and subissues. Many of the issues outlined here raise two broad legal points. One point sets up the rights, and the next point establishes some relevant limits. For example, Issue A1 is first addressed by identifying that the book is protectable, but then acknowledging that the protection has a limited duration. *Issue A2* is first addressed by spotting the relevant right of the copyright owner, but next noting that the distribution right is subject to an exception.

By focusing on *issues*, and not *problems*, you can begin to work with the fundamental structure of copyright law as it grants rights and then curtails them. The limitations and exceptions are often more important than the rights themselves, and they can make many good pursuits of libraries and educational institutions perfectly legal. You are not going to jail and probably will not even get a nasty letter from a copyright owner's lawyer. But to know with confidence that you are acting within the law, you need to be astute about copyright. To get the best *answers*, you need to pause at the right issue. Spotting that issue should become easier as you get more familiar with copyright. Build in your memory a vision of a systematic path, starting at the beginning.

IT'S ALL DIGITAL

Networked technologies open new opportunities, allowing your students to view and study the film on their own, and not just during an assigned class session. However, storing the film on a server and making it available to students, even with password controls on access, can raise new copyright questions. Whenever you add or change the facts, you need to consider again the right path through copyright.

Scenario Installment C

You would like to show the film, not in the ordinary classroom, but through the course management system (such as Blackboard or Moodle). Students have to log on, and the video will be streamed to their computers at any location. Students have the advantage of setting their own schedule and being able to study the film in more depth by reviewing and selecting scenes for closer study.

ISSUE C1: Does copyright law permit you to digitize, clip, and post some or all of a motion picture for your students to study?

ACTUALLY, YOU may have multiple possibilities for lawfully delivering the video clips:

- Chapter 9 notes the importance of Section 110(1) of the Copyright Act. Although it broadly allows *performances of works in the classroom*, it probably will not apply to making copies, posting them to a server, and allowing access from different places at different times.
- Chapter 16 examines Section 110(2), also known as the TEACH (Technology, Education and Copyright Harmonization) Act. If you can meet all of its requirements, this statute permits *use of "reasonable and limited" portions* of audiovisual works.
- Fair use is a vital option. Chapters 10 through 14 explore fair use in detail and suggest how it may apply, particularly to portions of works in a limited context. Streaming video gets some focused attention in Chapter 12.
- You might supplement the film clips with historical works, such as photographs and manuscripts. If these materials are *unpublished archival materials*, Chapter 21 summarizes distinctive rules about protection, duration, and fair use.
- You might also focus on the film score and related musical works and recordings. Chapters 19 and 20 examine the copyright rules related to *musical compositions and sound recordings*.

ISSUE C2: You have studied the TEACH Act and fair use, and you conclude that you are simply not able to fit your use of the copyrighted film into any of these exceptions. Do you still have any choices?

- One obvious choice is to secure permission from the copyright owner. Chapter 24 offers pointers for *locating owners and securing permissions*. Sometimes permission is the most realistic or even necessary alternative.
- For many works, the permission may come in the form of a general license that the educational institution may have entered into for the acquisition of a film collection or other works. Advance permissions may also come in the form of a Creative Commons license, examined in Chapter 24.
- Chapter 24 also suggests as a strategy that you might need to *rethink your plans*. You might have an exact plan or project in mind, but in light of copyright considerations, you may need to reconsider the materials you are using and exactly how you are using them.

Scenario Installment D

Perhaps you have studied your needs and the applicable copyright law, and you confidently conclude that you are within the bounds of fair use or the TEACH Act for your use of the film. You put the DVD or other media into your computer in order to copy selected clips, only to discover that the source is embedded with a "copy protection code" that prevents making the clips.

ISSUE D1: You find on the Internet that you can download software that allows you to bypass the protection code and make the copies. If your use of the film is lawful and within fair use, are you also allowed to crack the protection code?

- Chapter 22 examines the complex and problematic law barring the *circumvention of technological protection measures.* You may be running afoul of that law.
- Chapter 22 also surveys *exceptions to the anticircumvention law.* Unfortunately, the exceptions are tightly limited, so you should study the details carefully. The various regulatory exceptions from the Library of Congress can open some important possibilities.

THE LIBRARY'S ROLE

The library at your college or university and the public library in your neighborhood provide essential support for your research and instructional planning. The film versions of *Pride and Prejudice* that you plan to use may be from the university library's collections. You are also finding journal articles, photographs, music, and many other works that you would like to make available to your students. For many of these materials, you need to revisit again the foregoing questions about copyright protection, the public domain, classroom performance, the TEACH Act, fair use, and permissions. The library is also willing to provide various services that often involve making copies and delivering content to you or to your students. When the library provides services, the librarians need to consider a few additional copyright issues.

Scenario Installment E

The librarians would like to make copies of some of the materials that you need for teaching, research, and other academic work.

ISSUE E1: Is the library allowed to make copies of various works and give them to you for your teaching and research?

- Chapter 17 details the conditions under which a *library may make copies* from the collection pursuant to Section 108 of the Copyright Act. The relevant provisions of Section 108, however, do not apply to all types of works, so the library may still need to rely on fair use or permissions when it copies some materials.
- Your local library may not have all materials you require, and you may need to request copies from another library. Chapter 17 details conditions under which the library may receive copies of some materials from another library as part of *interlibrary loan arrangements.*

ISSUE E2: Some of the materials in question are no longer on the market or are already damaged. One of the films is on a VHS tape; VHS players are scarce today, and the tape quality degrades with each use. Can the library make copies of these materials?

- Chapter 17 examines the provisions of Section 108 that allow a library to make copies of *unpublished works for purposes of preservation or security.*

This provision generally applies to manuscripts, photographs, and any other work that is not published.

- Section 108 allows a library to make copies of *published works that may be damaged, deteriorating, lost, or stolen*. These statutes have various conditions and requirements, but they offer important opportunities. If the VHS movie is no longer on the market, the library may be able to make up to three copies of it. Chapter 17 outlines the details.
- Section 108 further permits a library to make copies of works if the *format has become obsolete*. VHS and many other familiar formats either are obsolete today or will be someday soon. Again, Chapter 17 specifies exactly when a library may make replacement copies.

BECOMING AN AUTHOR AND A COPYRIGHT OWNER

Librarians, archivists, instructors, students, and nearly every member of the community create new works on a daily basis that may have copyright protection. They might be pithy e-mails, but they also might be scholarly publications and formal documents about institutional services and operations. In any event, we will sometimes need or want to know who might own the copyright.

Scenario Installment F

You have become fascinated by these copyright issues (who couldn't be?), and you decide to do some additional research and write a journal article on the quirks and challenges of copyright in the academic setting. You become known as something of a copyright expert around the campus and get appointed to chair the policymaking committee for the library and the university. You write a document outlining your institution's policy on fair use issues.

ISSUE F1: You are the sole author of the journal article, and it has been accepted for publication in your first choice of journals. Congratulations! But who owns the copyright in the article?

- Chapter 7 lays out the general rule that the author of the original work is the *owner of the copyright*.
- That chapter examines the doctrine of *work made for hire*, its application to academic work, and the importance of university policies.
- Chapter 7 also explores *publication agreements* and the possibility that they may include a transfer of the copyright. The copyright may have been yours initially, but be careful about what you sign. You might be inadvertently giving away your copyrights unless you read, understand, and negotiate carefully.
- That same chapter further raises the prospect of *open access* and alternatives for publication and copyright, such as *Creative Commons*.
- Regardless of who owns the copyright, the publication agreement can *clarify the specific rights of use* that you might retain. Negotiate and draft the agreement carefully.

ISSUE F2: You chaired the committee and drafted much of the policy on fair use, but several of your colleagues had a hand in writing portions of it. A member of the committee reflects on the finished policy and ponders aloud, "Who owns the copyright in our new institutional policy?"

- Chapter 4 examines the *broad scope of copyright.* Even a copyright policy issued by a library or college is most likely copyrightable.
- Under the general rule in Chapter 7, you and your colleagues may be the copyright owners. Together you may have a *joint copyright in the document.*
- Preparing the policy was likely one of your job assignments, and as such it is likely a *work made for hire* with the copyright owned by your employer. Chapter 7 explores the significance of that determination.
- Chapter 7 surveys *options for copyright management,* such as Creative Commons, which may be a good option for handling and sharing the copyright in an institutional policy or other document. Open access is a good option for clearing up the copyright questions surrounding institutional works.

STRATEGIES FOR COPYRIGHT DECISIONS

Finding the right trail through the law is clearly essential to any successful application of copyright. In addition to learning the law, however, you also need to develop an awareness of strategies and a process of decision making in an environment that is thoroughly affected by copyright. Copyright is, after all, the law. It comes with mandates and opportunities, rights and responsibilities. In the spirit of this book, most of your decisions should be centered on making a proper—and sometimes creative—application of copyright in furtherance of teaching, research, and library services. We cannot deny, however, that copyright decisions also raise risks and can lead to some (potentially) scary penalties.

Think back to some of the scenarios examined earlier. You want to clip excerpts from a motion picture and post them to your course management system for students. Consider just the question of whether you are acting within fair use. Chapters 10 through 14 provide considerable substance of the law and examples for thinking about the factors of fair use. But in addition to the substance of the law is the process of decision making. You are one person, holding your job and executing your duties, on the staff of a library, college, or university. Is copyright your responsibility? Are you the right person to make the decision about fair use?

One way to think about those questions stems from one basic legal principle about copyright: The person who makes the copies (or makes other uses) of a work is the first person responsible for any infringement that might result. In other words, if you are the one who operates the computer and does the clipping and uploading, you are on the front line of responsibility and liability. That would tend to place the decision squarely in your hands.

However, if you are making decisions and taking actions as part of your duties as a teacher, librarian, or another member of the institution, then in almost any typical situation, the liability will be shared upstream with the organization. The question then becomes this: Who is responsible for making legal decisions for the organization? Put that way, you might start looking at a corporate chart to find the senior administrative officer (could that officer be you?), or you might reach out to your organization's legal counsel. You could easily find yourself in one of these situations:

- *No lawyer in sight:* In many colleges, universities, libraries, and other organizations, no one is available to help with a lawyer's view of copyright. Either your organization has no attorney on hire, or the lawyer is not well versed in copyright or is not able to handle multitudes of recurring fair use dilemmas.

- *Legal help today, but not every day:* You may be among the fortunate few with direct access to an attorney, but the access is limited and infrequent. Often a good lawyer will in fact not be the person who will make every decision. A lawyer might shape the general principles and give guidance for different types of situations, but the daily decisions about individual situations often come back to you and your colleagues. The attorney's involvement may give you important reinforcement and protection, but you still need to make the final judgments. Chapter 18 of this book should give you some reassurance about your decisions, if you act responsibly and in good faith.

- *Building a support team:* You are hardly alone in your search for copyright advice. Rather than wait for legal support, you may meanwhile find colleagues who have dealt with similar questions. You may find good help from the insights and experiences of directors, department chairs, deans, or other colleagues who have authority to oversee business decisions or who have experience working with copyright. You might also simply want the support of colleagues and supervisors, but you might be the one person who knows and cares the most about copyright. Sometimes you need to take the lead, educating and building a team.

Regardless of which situation you confront, you cannot entirely avoid having a role in copyright decisions. Even complete deference to others is itself a decision. Moreover, if you are the one pushing the buttons on the machine and making the copies, you need to take good care of your own interests. You are, after all, responsible, even if your library or university shares the responsibility with you. Like the soldier on the front line, you might get orders, but in a calm moment, you have to decide if the orders are right.

What goes into your decision about copyright? This book provides a wide range of insights about that question. Naturally, you need to base decisions on an accurate and current understanding of the law. The best decisions about copyright also consider much more than just law. They take into account the risks, consequences, and alternatives. Is my project limited to my classroom, or will it be on the web for all to see? Am I using obscure photos from the 1930s or recent professional works with identified photographers? Multitudes of images are available from Flickr and other sources with generous Creative Commons licensing. A good decision contemplates alternatives. If you want the film clips because they are great scenes of London, then perhaps you should look for other clips that might be in the public domain or easily licensed. If you want all students to study the entire film and it is widely available to buy or rent, then maybe it is not unreasonable for each student to buy the Blu-ray disk or DVD.

You are not avoiding copyright. You probably cannot. But mix this fact of life into your strategy: You have only a finite number of hours in the day. You cannot make every decision, review every situation, and evaluate every risk. You need to save your "copyright energy" for the situations that demand attention. Copyright must be addressed to implement programs of library services, digitization of collections, innovative teaching, and the management of our scholarship and publication. These are the kinds of pursuits that merit attention. A careful, informed, and strategic approach to copyright can ultimately advance the needs of copyright owners as well as the objectives of researchers, teachers, students, and members of the public who will benefit from access to a wider range of information resources. The copyright map in this book is intended to give you a guide through copyright law, which can move you toward the goal of good stewardship and proper use of copyrighted works.

CHAPTER 2

SOURCES OF COPYRIGHT LAW

Constitution, Statutes, and Courts

KEY POINTS

- Copyright law comes from many different sources, including federal and state law as well as international and foreign law.
- Congress is the principal source of copyright law in the United States, enacting statutes that are then interpreted and applied in cases decided by federal courts.
- Some copyright law is made by state legislatures and decided by state courts.
- Occasionally the application of domestic law requires consideration of foreign copyright law.

A BRIEF LOOK at the footnotes in this book will reveal references to a diverse array of resources, led principally by citations to statutes and cases. Indeed, copyright law derives from those sources and many more. The artifacts of the law to which we often turn for principles and guidance are statutes and cases, for the most part, but also occasionally regulations and several international treaties that are of growing importance. As this book surveys copyright and its many dimensions, it will rely on a variety of materials to better understand the law, but copyright law in its legally binding quality comes from a few core sources.

Copyright in the United States is rooted in the Constitution and its original language adopted in 1787. The pragmatic rules and structures of copyright law are today laid out in the Copyright Act of 1976 and the many amendments to it. The Copyright Act is a set of statutes, enacted by Congress, defining the parameters and fundamentals of the law. Federal courts in turn interpret and apply the law, especially where the statutes are not highly specific and interested parties have divergent interests. The court rulings are essential for bringing any meaning to copyright. Copyright law is national law in the United States and in other countries of the world. Copyright as national law means that the same law applies in all parts of the country, although the judicial interpretations mix it up a bit—more about that later.

Despite the steady focus on copyright as national law, traces of copyright appear in the laws of some states. For example, federal copyright did not apply to sound recordings until 1972, and New York and several other states filled that gap with state statutory protection for these works.[1] State courts occasionally need to resolve questions about copyright that are collateral to interpreting a contract or resolving a divorce settlement.

THE CONSTITUTION

One of the foundational purposes of the U.S. Constitution is to outline the powers granted to the three branches of the federal government. Article I of the U.S. Constitution establishes Congress, offers some details about its structures and processes, and prescribes the composition of the Senate and House of Representatives. The Constitution then lays out, "The Congress shall have Power" to exercise authority on a reasonably specific list of various matters. The itemization includes the power to coin money, create a postal service, raise an army, and form a uniform system of bankruptcy law.[2]

In the case of copyright law, the provision is more than a mere listing. It is also a statement of purpose or aspiration. Standing out from all other items on the list is this power of Congress: "The Congress shall have Power . . . To promote the Progress of Science and useful Arts, by securing for limited Times to Authors and Inventors the exclusive Right to their respective Writings and Discoveries."

This constitutional language has been widely understood from the founding of the country to give Congress the power to make copyright and patent law. Unlike other recitals in this part of the Constitution, the Copyright Clause comes with rich prose and a statement of purpose. Congress has the authority to grant rights, but not merely for their own sake. Congress can grant those rights for a cause: "To promote the Progress" of what we would today call knowledge and learning. Indeed, the oft-repeated central purpose of copyright law is along these lines: Copyright law is a body of law that grants rights, initially to authors, to encourage the creation and sharing of new works—ultimately to foster learning and the growth of knowledge.

If the law can in fact encourage the creation, dissemination, and publication of new works, then everyone should benefit. The escalation of new works should, on the whole, breed an advancement of knowledge, insights, art, and other creativity. The bundle of legal rights should also give assurance for the investment in new works. That investment can be ethereal. It might be in the form of time, energy, wisdom, and creative talent.[3]

The investment can be tangible. It might be the financial expense of materials, rent, electricity, and assistance. It can also be the expense of producing an attractive book from a typed manuscript or promoting a multi-million-dollar film and getting it into theaters and advertised on television. Even the development of an open source platform for drafts of scholarly papers is not without cost. In varying ways, copyright plays a role in making all of these plans and ambitions possible. That function of copyright is enshrined in the language of the Constitution—that the granting of rights shall "promote the Progress."

Nevertheless, be cautious about reading too much into the constitutional details. Congress and various courts have used the grand language of the Copyright Clause as a guide and have cited it often. On the other hand, the Supreme Court has declined to give the prose much legal authority. Indeed, the Supreme Court ruled that the language of the Copyright Clause is not itself a delimiter on the power of Congress. Even the edict that Congress may grant rights for "limited Times" does not set any particular constraint on the length of

> **THE COPYRIGHT** Clause in the U.S. Constitution refers to "Authors and Inventors" and is widely regarded as defining the power of Congress to make copyright and patent law. Yet Congress clearly has exercised its power to make other forms of intellectual property law, most notably trademark law. That authority derives from the power of Congress to regulate commerce "among the several States," better known as the Interstate Commerce power. U.S. Const., art. I, § 8. As a result, federal copyright law can be comprehensive but federal trademark law can apply only to marks that are used in or connected to interstate commerce. States retain the right to make trademark law that applies to local activity.

copyright protection.[4] In practical effect, Congress has extraordinarily broad power to make (or not make) copyright law and to determine its shape and details.

FEDERAL STATUTES

The Constitution was ratified by the original thirteen states in 1787, and the first Congress of the United States convened in 1789. The next year, in 1790, Congress enacted the first Copyright Act.[5] It was a brief articulation by today's standards, but it was built on the model of the British law from 1710, known as the Statute of Anne.[6] The 1790 American act granted protection to maps, charts, and books.[7] It provided a legal right to control the reproduction of works, and it provided for registration and deposit of works with each local federal district court. The original term of protection was for fourteen years, renewable for another fourteen.

THROUGH AN ongoing sequence of legislation, Congress steadily extended the duration of copyright protection, from the earliest times through today. The Copyright Act of 1790 set a term of fourteen years, renewable for an additional fourteen years. In 1831, Congress changed the term to twenty-eight years, plus renewal for fourteen. In 1909, Congress changed the law to two terms of twenty-eight years each. Chapter 6 of this book surveys in detail the current law of copyright duration, which is an explicit culmination of growing copyright duration through the past several decades. The result is protection for most works for the life of the author plus 70 years. The era of fourteen-year terms is in the distant past.

The early law may seem narrow and quaint in retrospect, but the pressure for copyright reform arrived fairly soon. Amendments to the Copyright Act have occurred frequently throughout the nation's history, and the Copyright Act has been fully or substantially revised on a few widely scattered occasions: 1831, 1856, 1870, 1909, and 1976.[8] Among the changes that came with each new Copyright Act, Congress expanded the scope of protectable works, broadened the rights of copyright owners, and lengthened the term of copyright protection.

Early copyright law included little that explicitly referred to education or libraries. However, in 1870 the process of copyright registration was shifted from local courts to the Library of Congress. Previously authors had filed registration claims with their local federal district courts and those courts had received the statutory deposit copies. The entire process was consolidated with the Library of Congress, and for the first time the deposit copies were more reliably made the foundation of a stronger national collection in Washington, DC. In 1897 Congress formally established the new U.S. Copyright Office within the Library of Congress.

The most recent full revision of the U.S. Copyright Act was enacted in 1976.[9] President Gerald Ford signed it into law on October 19, 1976, but the process of debating, drafting, and contemplating the new law had begun in 1955. Copyright revision was a process of more than two decades of reports, studies, hearings, bills, and revisions, until finally Congress was ready to take a vote. The ordeal was long and complicated as new technologies of television, radio, speaker systems, local cable networks, photocopy machines, and even jukeboxes made the issues more complex than ever before.

ALTHOUGH CONGRESS heard from numerous interested parties through years of hearings leading to the 1976 revision, the general sense was that copyright remained the province of only an arcane group. *The New York Times* reported on the law's passage:

> No firecrackers went off when the compromise bill was cleared Oct. 1, the last day of the Congressional session, and no bells are likely to ring when President Ford signs the measure sometime this week. The matter is simply too technical, complicated and cumbersome for anyone but specialists to get very excited.

David E. Rosenbaum, "Ford Due to Approve New Copyrights Law," *New York Times*, October 11, 1976, at 11.

THE DMCA, legislation from 1998, may be best known for creating the new protection for technological protection measures. It was a lengthy bill that encompassed a roster of other copyright matters, including these:

- Limiting the potential liability of online service providers (see Chapter 18)
- Launching initiatives and studies leading to passage of the TEACH Act for distance learning (see Chapter 16)
- Amending Section 108 for libraries to explicitly allow digital preservation copies, but with restrictions (see Chapter 17)
- Granting new protection for designs of boat hulls (not within the scope of this book, thankfully)
- Creating limited protection for computer repair services (Section 117 of the Copyright Act)

To give authors, users, and everyone else time to prepare for the new set of rules in the 1976 Copyright Act, the new law did not take effect until January 1, 1978. The set of statutes known generally as the "1976 Act" is the basic copyright law in the United States today. It has been amended more than seventy times by various acts of Congress in the meantime.[10] Some amendments have been minor fixes, while others have represented major redirections. The year 1998 was a heyday for copyright revision in Congress. The Digital Millennium Copyright Act (DMCA) added the new concept of "circumvention of technological protection measures" and much more.[11] That same year, the Sonny Bono Copyright Term Extension Act added twenty years of copyright protection to most works.[12]

With these amendments, revisions, and much more, the basic cumulative copyright law in the United States today begins with the statutes that comprise the Copyright Act of 1976. These statutes give us the fundamental structure and outline of the law, laid out in discrete *chapters*. The first chapter of the Copyright Act addresses the scope of copyrightable works, the rights of owners, and the exceptions to those rights. The next is about ownership. The third chapter is about the duration of rights, and the fourth includes the formalities and procedures of copyright notice and registration. The fifth chapter details the penalties and consequences of copyright infringement. The Copyright Act continues through fourteen chapters, spanning various concepts from Copyright Office administration to the dedicated law for pre-1972 sound recordings. Obviously, not all details will have a prominent place in this book.

THE LATER chapters of the Copyright Act tell much about how the law has expanded to embrace the latest concerns to reach Congress. Consider these subjects of a growing body of what is broadly referred to as "copyright law":

- *Chapter 9:* Protection of semiconductor chips and mask works
- *Chapter 10:* Royalties and infringements of digital audio recording equipment and media
- *Chapter 11:* Prohibition on bootleg recordings of performances
- *Chapter 12:* Circumvention of technological protection measures and removal of copyright management information (see Chapter 22 of this book)
- *Chapter 13:* Protection of certain designs, specifically boat hulls
- *Chapter 14:* Protection of pre-1972 sound recordings (see Chapter 20 of this book)

A few of these chapters of the Copyright Act are of remarkably little consequence. They often missed their objectives and have produced law that few parties have exercised or litigated. They are often just a manifestation of a seemingly urgent matter that became lodged in the machinations of Congress.

COURT DECISIONS

Congress has the authority under the Copyright Clause to enact copyright statutes, and it has used its authority to require that all cases "arising under" the U.S. Copyright Act must be filed in the federal courts of the United States. In other words, lawsuits over infringement, claims of rights, interpretations of ownership, and much more are legal matters that are required to be heard in federal courts, not state courts or any of the variety of specialized courts. It is the *United States* Supreme Court that ruled on the scope of "employee" and "independent contractor" in the

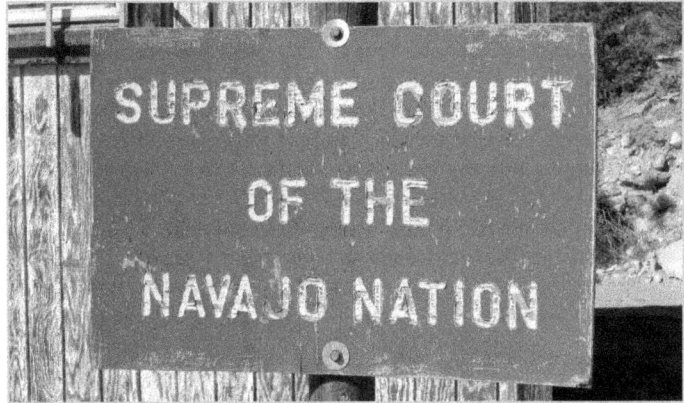

In addition to the many different federal courts, each state has its own system of various courts, and the United States is home to many other specialized courts. The Supreme Court of the Navajo Nation is based in Window Rock, Arizona.

law of works made for hire.[13] It is the *United States* Court of Appeals that ruled on the fair use of rock-and-roll posters in a book about music history.[14]

A basic explanation of the structure of the federal court system is in order. The overall system of federal courts does include various specialized courts, from military courts to the Court of Claims. However, the main three-level system will encompass almost all decisions related to copyright, especially the cases included in this book:

- *District courts:* Most cases begin in the district courts. This is the first, or the "lowest," level of the federal system. The United States has fifty states, but the country is also divided into ninety-four judicial districts. North Dakota has a relatively small population and has only one district for the entire state. California has a large population and is divided into four districts. Any of these district courts can hear copyright cases.
- *Courts of appeals:* A party who does not prevail to satisfaction (an occurrence better known as "losing") in a decision from a district court may appeal to one of the courts of appeals. The United States is divided into eleven geographic and numbered circuits. Some are large, and others are small. The Third Circuit includes only Delaware, New Jersey, and Pennsylvania. The Ninth Circuit covers nine western states, including California, Alaska, and Hawaii, plus Guam and the Northern Mariana Islands. The District of Columbia has its own court of appeals. A specialized court, called the United States Court of Appeals for the Federal Circuit, hears appeals on issues of patent law and a few other subjects.
- *Supreme Court:* The party not prevailing in the court of appeals has one more chance to be heard by petitioning to the U.S. Supreme Court. Parties seeking to bring their cases to the Supreme Court file a "petition for certiorari," which the Supreme Court may either grant or deny. With few exceptions, the Supreme Court has full discretion to hear cases brought to it. In a recent year, the Supreme Court received more than 8,000 petitions and heard and decided only about eighty cases.[15] Having a case heard by the Supreme Court is a statistically rare phenomenon.

Rulings handed down by the courts are binding on the parties, of course, and they are binding precedent in the geographic regions served. For example, decisions by the Supreme Court set the rule of law for the entire country. Decisions from a court of appeals are precedent in only the states within that circuit. Decisions from the district courts are generally

THE CONCEPT of deference to other decisions, even when not required, is known as *stare decisis*. It serves the purpose of creating fairness and continuity in the application of the law. Judges give great deference to stare decisis, even if it means upholding a ruling they might not like. Chapter 23 includes brief discussion of the Ninth Circuit decision regarding the copyright to the 1923 book *Bambi, a Life in the Woods. Twin Books Corp. v. Walt Disney Co.*, 83 F.3d 1162 (9th Cir. 1996). The court's ruling has been heavily criticized. Other judges serving on the Ninth Circuit seemed to share in that critique, yet they stood by the *Bambi* ruling when the legal issue came up again in a later case. The earlier case involved Bambi. The second case was about the sculpture of Renoir. Copyright is never boring and always a delight. *Societe Civile Succession Guino v. Renoir*, 549 F.3d 1182 (9th Cir. 2008).

precedent within only that one district. That is the technically correct explanation. As a practical matter, a well-reasoned opinion, or a decision on a specialized legal question courts rarely face, will be influential well beyond any particular boundaries.

As an example, a ruling from the Second Circuit Court of Appeals may be binding on the district courts in the states and territories of that circuit. It is precedent that will merit great deference should the Second Circuit later face the same or a related legal issue. That same decision may be only an influential guide for courts in other parts of the country. A ruling from any court offers at least lessons and insights to help all of us to better understand the law and perhaps influences the next court facing a similar legal challenge. The more persuasive the court's rationale, and the greater the judge's prominence and experience, the more a particular court ruling will have influence on the public's understanding of copyright and on the next court's legal analysis.[16]

STATE LAW

The Constitution gives Congress the power to make copyright law, which generally preempts the power of states to legislate on copyright matters. Copyright cases must also be heard in federal courts, similarly barring state courts from tackling copyright issues. But these are only general rules. There is a modest array of legislation related to copyright enacted by state legislatures. Further, state courts occasionally hand down rulings on copyright matters. For example, state courts regularly decide contract disputes, but if the contract is about the ownership or licensing of a copyrighted work, the state court may have to resolve the underlying copyright issue.

Here are some examples of state law related to copyright:

- The state of Indiana imposes by statute specific requirements for the agreements and licenses that collective societies may enter into with restaurants and other business establishments.[17]
- The state of Idaho provides by statute that it may hold copyrights in state statutes and that it will hold the copyrights in compilations of state statutes prepared by publishers.[18]
- The state of California has a statute on employment law providing that if any person commissions another party to create a work that is deemed by agreement to be "for hire" under copyright law, then the commissioned party is deemed to be an employee for some purposes under California law and may be entitled to certain employment benefits.[19]

- The state of New York offers common law copyright protection for sound recordings that were made before 1972, at a time when federal copyright law applied to only the more recent recordings.[20]
- State courts frequently decide cases related to contract disputes and other matters that are traditionally within state law but sometimes rule on copyright issues in the process.[21]

REGULATIONS

Many governmental agencies have the authority to issue regulations, and the Librarian of Congress does issue some regulations related to copyright. The U.S. Copyright Office is part of the Library of Congress, which has the authority to act. By comparison to some of the larger agencies with more diverse responsibilities, the Copyright Office operates with relatively few regulations. Section 108 of the Copyright Act, for example, provides that libraries may make copies of some works to provide to users, but the order forms must include a warning or advisory statement as prescribed by regulation. That statutory provision establishes the authority to issue the language of the notice in a regulation.[22]

The most significant regulations examined in this book are the triennial exemptions from the circumvention prohibition. The DMCA in 1998 enacted a general prohibition against circumvention, as mentioned earlier in this chapter. The DMCA also empowered the Librarian of Congress to adopt exemptions by regulations, to be issued every three years. The most recent were adopted in October 2018.[23]

INTERNATIONAL TREATIES

Steadily through the past few decades, international agreements have had growing influence on the shape of U.S. copyright law. While international agreements have a profound influence on the shape of American law, the copyright provisions of the agreements are not themselves binding on U.S. citizens; the treaty provisions become requirements that Congress must add into the copyright statutes. Once made a part of the Copyright Act, the international agreements complete their influence on domestic law. This dynamic is examined in the next chapter, with an overview of the Berne Convention and other treaties that have leading importance.

FOREIGN LAW

Foreign law is not to be confused with international law. The latter is the law of international treaties, agreements, and other affiliations. Foreign law, by contrast, is the law of a foreign country or other jurisdiction. As a general rule, when in Country X, apply the law of that country. Hence, when in the United States, apply the U.S. copyright law to the situation and the work. Even if the book, film, or other copyrighted work originated in France, Brazil, Japan, or elsewhere, most questions about rights or the proper use of the work inside the borders of the United States will be determined by U.S. law. Conversely, if a work originates in the United States, but the use of it is carried out in another country, the copyright questions will generally be determined by that other country's law.

Of course, general rules have exceptions. Sometimes the application of American copyright law can depend on applying foreign law. For example, in a ruling from the Second

Circuit Court of Appeals in 1998 regarding the infringement of a Russian newspaper in the United States, the court concluded that the ownership rights in the newspaper would depend on the application of Russian law.[24] Sometimes the statutes themselves require analysis of foreign law. Section 104A of the U.S. Copyright Act provides for the "restoration" of copyright in certain foreign works.[25] Under that detailed statute, a copyright may be restored only if the foreign work was still under copyright protection in its country of origin at the time of restoration under U.S. law. Thus, in order to know whether the work regained its American copyright, one must learn and apply foreign law—the law of the country where the work in question originated.

RICHES AND RESOURCES

An understanding and application of copyright law in any one country—the United States of America or otherwise—demand that we undertake research in a robust and diverse set of materials. The primary sources reflect the nature of lawmaking in our common law system. We depend on statutes and regulations, but we must understand the court decisions that expound on principles and interpret the statutory language. We need to grasp the terms of international instruments to see the critical role they play in shaping national law. Occasionally, albeit rarely, we need to dip into the law of individual U.S. states or the law of distant foreign countries. With luck, this book synthesizes some of the essential sources and brings them together for a comprehensible overview of copyright, even if one book of moderate length cannot tell the whole story.

NOTES

1. The complexities of copyright for sound recordings are examined in some detail in Chapters 19 and 20. Congress in late 2018 created a new species of legal protection for pre-1972 recordings.

2. U.S. Const. art. I, § 8.

3. Copyright law can encourage that investment, but it does not protect it. Copyright law protects original expression and works of authorship. The Supreme Court explicitly rejected the argument that copyright law protects money, hard work, or the "sweat of the brow." *Feist Publications, Inc. v. Rural Telephone Service Co., Inc.*, 499 U.S. 340 (1991).

4. *Eldred v. Ashcroft*, 537 U.S. 186 (2003).

5. Act of May 31, 1790, ch. 15, § 1, 1 Stat. 124.

6. Statute of Anne, 8 Anne c. 19 (1710).

7. Act of May 31, 1790, ch. 15, § 1, 1 Stat. 124.

8. A compiled collection of copyright enactments between 1783 and 1973 was assembled by the U.S. Copyright Office and is now available on the office's website at https://www.copyright.gov/history/Copyright_Enactments_1783-1973.pdf.

9. Copyright Act of 1976, Pub. L. No. 94-553, 90 Stat. 2541 (codified at 17 U.S.C. § 107).

10. The many copyright bills enacted since 1976 are listed at https://www.copyright.gov/title17/92preface.html.

11. Digital Millennium Copyright Act, Pub. L. No. 105-304, 112 Stat. 2860 (1998).

12. Sonny Bono Copyright Term Extension Act, Pub. L. No. 105-298, 112 Stat. 2827 (1998).

13. *Community for Creative Non-Violence v. Reid*, 490 U.S. 730 (1989).

14. *Bill Graham Archives v. Dorling Kindersley, Ltd.*, 448 F.3d 605 (2d Cir. 2006).

15. The numbers vary each year, but the number of cases brought before the court has escalated in recent decades. See https://www.supremecourt.gov/about/justicecaseload.aspx.

16. A court does have the power to overturn its own precedent, although courts generally do so reluctantly. The U.S. Supreme Court recently overturned a previous ruling from 1977 (unrelated to copyright), stirring a vigorous rebuke from dissenting justices. *Franchise Tax Board of California v. Hyatt*, 587 U.S. ___ , 139 S. Ct. 1485 (2019).

17. Indiana Code § 32-37-1-1 (2019), *et seq.* For example, if requested by the licensee, the collective society must provide information about the licensing rates and the musical works that are subject to the license.

18. Idaho Code § 73-210 (2019).

19. California Labor Code § 3351.5(c) (2019).

20. *Capital Records, Inc. v. Naxos of America, Inc.*, 4 N.Y.3d 540 (2005). The complications of pre-1972 sound recordings are examined in Chapter 20.

21. For example, a state court can decide a copyright issue that arises in a counterclaim or defense raised in what is originally a state case. *Green v. Hendrickson Publishers, Inc.*, 770 N.E.2d 784 (Ind. 2002).

22. Section 108 and the related regulations are examined in Chapter 17.

23. These regulatory exceptions are explored more fully in Chapter 22.

24. *Itar-Tass Russian News Agency v. Russian Kurier, Inc.*, 153 F.3d 82 (2d Cir. 1998).

25. Copyright restoration is examined more closely in Chapter 6 regarding the duration of copyright protection.

CHAPTER 3

SOURCES OF COPYRIGHT LAW

International Treaties, Trade, and Harmonization

KEY POINTS

- Libraries and educational institutions increasingly operate in an international context, and international legal developments have a profound influence on domestic U.S. law.
- Treaties are an enormously important source of U.S. copyright law and directly shape much of American legislation.
- The United States has engaged in international copyright protection since the first international copyright statute enacted by Congress in 1891.
- When the United States joined the Berne Convention in 1989, Congress had to revise American copyright law in many fundamental respects.
- The World Intellectual Property Organization is considering the development of copyright treaties that may become critical to librarianship and education.

ONE CANNOT COMPREHEND the source and basic structure of U.S. copyright law without grasping the international context. Indeed, although this book is centered on American domestic copyright law, references to international and foreign law necessarily appear throughout. American libraries and educational institutions regularly engage in international transactions as they purchase and use materials from throughout the world. Networked communication systems allow each of us to create and share copyrighted works with colleagues in every part of the world. A later chapter in this book will further examine how our domestic activities may be affected by foreign law. This chapter, by contrast, reveals the international treaties and other instruments that guide the substance of American copyright law and give domestic law a strong global context.

The United States is a signatory to numerous agreements that directly shape many substantive aspects of the law. By entering various treaty arrangements, the United States expanded the scope of protectable works, changed the duration of copyright protection, adopted the system of anticircumvention, and restored protection for many works that had been in the public domain. These legislative actions may or may not have been good policy decisions. Nevertheless, the law had to change if the United States were to

THE COPYRIGHT law regarding circumvention of technological protection measures and the law regarding the removal of copyright management information from a work are clear examples of the force of international agreements. Both concepts are rooted in the WIPO Copyright Treaty of 1996. That treaty moved relatively quickly through development and adoption by the World Intellectual Property Organization (WIPO). The United States was among the early signatories and adopters of the treaty, and it swiftly enacted the relevant statutory provisions as part of the Digital Millennium Copyright Act of 1998. The anticircumvention statutes are examined in Chapter 22 of this book.

be part of the multinational legal system. The United States was adapting to global norms. The international agreements hence have become a major source of American copyright law.

These international treaties are foremost a source that defines American law but are not themselves binding on individuals. Think of each treaty as an agreement among countries to form a copyright system generally along the same rules. If a country chooses to join that system, it signs on to the treaty and is obligated to adopt the rules. For most countries, that adoption comes in the form of enacted statutes. Treaties are thus a powerful force, setting substantive standards for the content of each country's statutes, but treaties are seldom the source you would cite as binding law on individual decisions and transactions. Despite the importance of international copyright, keep close track of this familiar tenet: The fundamental binding copyright law in the United States remains the domestic U.S. Copyright Act.

INTERNATIONAL AGREEMENTS AND TREATIES

The overall international dynamics that influence or drive domestic law can be diverse. Countries frequently look to their foreign neighbors, trade partners, and cultural compatriots for ideas and principles in lawmaking. In that spirit, American copyright law long has had an international heritage. The first American Copyright Act, from 1790,[1] was based in large measure on the British law of 1710.[2] American origins may be richly diverse, but many of the founders who devised the earliest laws and governmental institutions had careers and lives built on a British lineage.

Although American law gave nod to British origins, for a full century U.S. law protected only U.S. works. Foreign works that entered this country had no protection at all. Thus, the works of Charles Dickens, Oscar Wilde, and other foreign authors were in great demand in the United States, but they enjoyed no copyright protection. Anyone could carry copies of their works into the United States, and American publishers could freely copy and sell the latest foreign novels without permission and without paying royalties. The works of these best-selling British authors were especially popular, and naturally they were not happy to watch their works being exploited as part of the public domain in the growing American market. American authors were also not content, knowing that publishers could more cheaply print and sell books by competing foreign authors.

The economic realities of international copyrights and markets in the late nineteenth century were pressing for new legal developments. In 1891 Congress passed the International Copyright Act, better known as the Chace Act, which for the first time extended U.S. copyright protection to foreign works.[3] The protection was nonetheless highly restrictive. The new law added a "manufacturing clause" requiring that a book could be protectable only if the copies were actually printed or manufactured in the United States. The mutual protection was provided to only works from countries designated by the president. The initial protection in 1891 extended to only works from Great Britain, Belgium, France, and the Netherlands.

Various international copyright systems also began to emerge in the late nineteenth century, and they had proliferated by the end of the twentieth century. The Berne Convention of 1886 remains most important. This chapter summarizes a few treaties that include provisions especially relevant to libraries and education. In addition, copyright provisions play an important role in treaties on sound recordings, television broadcasts, rights of performers, and more. Copyright has a firm place in the text of an increasing number of free-trade agreements that the United States has negotiated with individual countries and groups of nations in a geographic region.

THE IMPORTANCE OF THE BERNE CONVENTION

The most significant of the many copyright treaties is the Berne Convention for the Protection of Literary and Artistic Works. A small group of countries, mostly in Western Europe, convened in Switzerland

> **IN ADDITION** to the Berne Convention and the Marrakesh Treaty, which are examined later in this chapter, examples of the many copyright treaties of potential interest to educators and librarians include the following:
>
> - Beijing Treaty on Audiovisual Performances (2012), addressing rights of performers
> - Rome Convention (1961), granting protection for performers and for producers of sound recordings and broadcasters
> - WIPO Copyright Treaty (1996), which includes anticircumvention provisions and more
> - WIPO Performances and Phonograms Treaty (1996), offering protection for performers and producers of sound recordings
> - The treaty of the World Trade Organization, with the Agreement on Trade-Related Aspects of Intellectual Property Rights (TRIPS) (1994), bringing many of the other treaty provisions into the requirements of international trade

to adopt the Berne Convention, initially in 1886. The most recent version dates to 1979. The Berne Convention today is largely a structured overview of the substance of copyright law that all member countries must follow, and as of this writing, 177 countries are members of Berne.[4]

The Berne Convention is the most expansive of all international agreements on copyright, and it applies to the most countries. Berne has two basic functions. First, it establishes the principle of "national treatment," providing mutual copyright protection for the works of other countries. Specifically, national treatment requires that each member country grant to foreign works at least the same protection that the country offers to its own works. Consider the simple example of a book from India that is in a library's collection in the United States. Both the United States and India are members of Berne. The book that originates in India receives at least the same protection that U.S. law would give to an American work.

Because U.S. law gives protection for original works that are fixed in a tangible medium and provides a roster of rights to the owner for life of the author plus 70 years, then U.S. law must offer at least the same protection to the work from India. Because 177 countries are signatories to Berne, American copyright law must also grant that protection to works from nearly every country of the world.[5]

The second function of the Berne Convention is to set standards for the substance of each country's copyright law. The Berne Convention details various statutory requirements for each member country, in the quest for harmonization of worldwide copyright laws. Perhaps the most consequential example is the prohibition in the Berne Convention of any "formalities" as a precondition to the enjoyment of the rights of the copyright owner. As a result, in preparation for joining the Berne Convention, the United States dropped formalities that had once been required, particularly the use of a copyright notice or the filing of a registration or renewal with the U.S. Copyright Office. Notice and registration are still available and often advisable, but failure to comply with these formalities cannot result in the loss of copyright ownership rights.[6]

THE UNITED STATES JOINS BERNE IN 1989

The many substantive requirements of the Berne Convention discouraged the United States from joining. The United States did not adhere to Berne until 1989, more than a century after it was first drafted. A leading reason for the hesitation was the requirement to conform American copyright law to Berne standards that were often far afield from American copyright norms. It became clear in the lead-up to passage of the Copyright Act of 1976 that the United States would eventually join Berne, and Congress began revising American law accordingly.

> **TECHNICALLY, BERNE** is about setting standards for the copyright protection of only foreign works. The substantive provisions are the minimal protection required for works originating from other member states. A Berne country is allowed to have different protection—or no protection at all—for works created by its own domestic authors. However, whatever rights a country gives to its own authors it must also give to foreign authors under the principle of national treatment. Realistically, good political and economic sense and the requirements of the World Trade Organization mean that every Berne member generally offers similar protection for domestic and foreign works.

For example, consider again the core requirement of Berne that copyright protection could not be dependent on any formalities, such as registration or a copyright notice on copies of the work. U.S. law had long included the requirement of a formal copyright notice on published works. The law was draconian, and even a minor defect in the form or content of the notice could cause a work to enter the public domain. Starting in 1978, a new provision of U.S. law allowed a copyright owner to remedy a defective notice and thereby rescue the copyright, albeit subject to multiple conditions and requirements.

The following are some of the many and critical changes that the United States needed to accept in order to fully implement Berne:

- *Protecting all types of original works and not just specific works:* Previously, the U.S. statutes included a list of protectable works, and any new work had to fit a prescribed category. Today, the rights vest in diverse original works of authorship.[7]
- *Eliminating the requirement of a copyright notice:* American law strictly required a precise form of a copyright notice on published works, or the copyright was lost. Today, the notice is optional, and mistakes and errors are of little consequence.[8]
- *Eliminating registration as a condition to protection:* Registration of a work with the U.S. Copyright Office is still available, but it is not a precondition of legal protection. Indeed, American law had dropped registration long before, but various incentives for registration made it function like a requirement.[9]
- *Adopting a unitary term of protection:* Previously copyright in the United States had an initial term that could be renewed by the author or owner. Failure to renew placed the work in the public domain. Today, once a work is protected, it is vested with rights for the full term without any need to anticipate renewal.[10]
- *Basing the term of protection on the life of the author:* The previous system set a term of years, but the Berne Convention mandates a basic term of life of the author plus 50 years. The United States converted to that measure,

starting in 1978. It has since exceeded the Berne requirements by adopting a longer term of life plus 70 years.[11]

- *Expanding federal copyright to include unpublished works:* Previously, the federal copyright law protected works only upon publication; unpublished works had been afforded uneven protection under state statutes and the common law.
- *Broadening the scope of protection to include architectural works:* Plans and drawings could previously be protected as graphic or artistic works; the buildings themselves as constructed were not protected at all until a revision in 1990.
- *Adopting moral rights:* The United States had no statutory recognition of moral rights until the limited rights examined in Chapter 8 were enacted. Congress hesitated on even this narrow gesture, waiting until the following year, 1990, to enact this statute.[12]

> **THE RULES** of copyright duration are surprisingly complex, even after the "harmonization" of laws under the Berne Convention. The basic rule is "life plus 50 years." Yet even the Berne Convention offers a few alternative rules for photography, motion pictures, architecture, and some other works. The WIPO Copyright Treaty of 1996 modified the rule for photography. On this issue, Berne is not setting strict rules but is setting minimums. The United States and many other countries have enacted even longer terms of protection. The United States and the European Union—and some other countries—have a basic term of life plus 70 years. A few countries have at times offered even longer duration. On this score, the law is not exactly harmonized.

The Berne Convention includes numerous other requirements related to the rights of owners, exceptions and limitations, and works without protection. Not all provisions required new revisions to the U.S. Copyright Act, but the foregoing list shows that the U.S. Congress indeed faced a formidable challenge in accepting fundamental changes to long-standing copyright principles.

Countries accept the challenge and the changes on the premise that countries and individuals benefit if laws are harmonized. The standards and requirements of the Berne Convention may or may not be good copyright policy. That is not necessarily the point. The greater objective is in the belief that a coordination or harmonization of copyright law among countries serves to make the law more predictable, to assure that certain levels of protection are available in each country, and to ease the process of engaging in international trade and enforcement of rights. Harmonization of the laws of all countries is a high expectation, but the treaties take major steps in that direction.

> **THE UNITED STATES** has entered into many trade agreements that include copyright provisions. The North American Free Trade Agreement (NAFTA) from 1994 includes a requirement to restore the copyrights in motion pictures that had entered the public domain. The World Trade Organization agreement in 1994 greatly expanded the application of the restoration principle. More recently, the Trans-Pacific Partnership (TPP) would have required each signatory country to coordinate the term of copyright to life plus 70 years and enact other copyright provisions. The United States withdrew from the TPP agreement in 2017, but the remaining eleven countries have continued the effort to develop a similar trade agreement under a new name. NAFTA is also in transition, but the proposed new incarnation also includes significant copyright provisions.

WIPO AND THE FUTURE OF COPYRIGHT TREATIES

The World Intellectual Property Organization (WIPO) has for several years engaged in a long-term process for the possible development of multiple treaties for copyright exceptions. WIPO is an agency of the United Nations, with headquarters in Geneva, Switzerland, and 192 member countries. One of its most important functions is to develop, manage, and implement many different intellectual property treaties. The treaties for which WIPO has responsibility govern copyright, trademark, patent, and many other areas of intellectual property law. Developing new treaties is a prolonged process of negotiation, mediation, and ultimately consensus. Reaching agreement among nearly all countries of the world is necessarily a laborious and lengthy challenge, with a long negotiation dance and subtle cues of demands and resistance.

WIPO has since 2005 pursued the possible development of treaties on copyright exceptions and limitations. Based on a proposal initiated mainly by a group of Latin American countries, WIPO made a decision to begin exploring the possibility of developing treaties on copyright exceptions for these purposes: making and delivering formats of works for persons who are blind or visually impaired, supporting the services of libraries and archives, and providing and using copies of works for education.

Headquarters of the World Intellectual Property Organization, located in Geneva, Switzerland, is within sight of the main entrance to the Geneva offices of the United Nations.

BEFORE WIPO began a focused effort to address copyright exceptions, the existing treaties gave only occasional reference to exceptions. Most of the instruments are about extending protections. Article 9(2) of the Berne Convention, however, permits countries to enact exceptions consistent with the "three-step test." As an example, a country may enact a library exception that could allow reproduction of works for preservation only if the statute conforms to three requirements in the treaty: The statutory exception may apply only "in certain special cases, provided that such reproduction does not conflict with a normal exploitation of the work and does not unreasonably prejudice the legitimate interests of the author." The three "steps" are the component parts of that quoted clause. The meaning of the three-step test is unexplained in the source documents and is thus much debated, but it remains the leading international guidance on the crafting of copyright exceptions.

THE MARRAKESH TREATY

In 2013, WIPO completed the development of a treaty on the first issue: serving the needs of the blind and visually impaired. The diplomatic conference that led to the final draft and adoption of the treaty was held in Morocco, giving the document the appellation "Marrakesh Treaty."[13] As of this writing, the Marrakesh Treaty has been submitted to the WIPO member countries for ratification and implementation in domestic law. Full implementation by any country generally means enacting or revising domestic copyright statutes to provide

> **PERHAPS THE** most innovative provision of the Marrakesh Treaty is Article 5 on cross-border exchange of copies. It authorizes the transfer of copies of works, adapted for persons with disabilities, across national borders, if the receiving country is also a member of the treaty and has adopted certain measures in its statutes. Article 5 is a breakthrough provision, foreshadowing issues that will arise in connection with library services and education, as institutions need to share copies of works across national boundaries for preservation, study, and many more purposes. Provisions for transnational transfers of copyrighted works might be the most important part of the current round of international pursuits.

for all the requirements of the treaty, specifically provisions that allow libraries and other institutions to make specialized formats of works for the needs of persons with certain disabilities.[14]

The Marrakesh Treaty is a landmark development for many reasons. It is the first worldwide copyright instrument dedicated to setting standards for exceptions with specific application. The Berne Convention, TRIPS, and other agreements include variations on the three-step test (examined in an earlier text box), but they offer nothing more about its meaning in application.[15] The Berne Convention has exclusions for "news of the day" and for educational uses, but they are nearly devoid of elaboration.[16] The Marrakesh Treaty, by contrast, specifies almost exactly how a country might choose to implement the law.

Marrakesh, as an instrument of copyright exceptions, puts to rest as well the question of whether WIPO even has authority to formally approve exceptions. The leading objective of WIPO after all is "to promote the protection of intellectual property throughout the world."[17] If WIPO has the purpose of protecting copyrights and other intellectual property, that guiding principle begs the question of whether WIPO has the power to adopt a standard that ostensibly curtails legal protections. The existence and implementation of Marrakesh refute that contention.

The Marrakesh Treaty is also extraordinary in substantive terms. Like most legal standards, it is a compromise of competing views. In the days leading to its endorsement by WIPO, the language of the treaty was in steady revision, tightening provisions in order to gain support from more countries. One significant adjustment that was probably essential in the prevailing political climate was the removal of motion pictures from the scope of works that may be modified or reformatted to serve the visually impaired. Countries could still allow uses of motion pictures under domestic legislation, but motion pictures are outside the scope of the Marrakesh Treaty itself.

WIPO AND EXCEPTIONS FOR LIBRARIES AND ARCHIVES

WIPO is next taking up the library issues, and as of this writing it has taken the opening steps with respect to the education issues. Meaningful conjecture or reliable predictions about the future of these discussions would be impossible at this stage. Treaty development can become contentious,

> **ONE OF** the first steps was the commissioning by WIPO of a series of studies on the state of the law in various countries. The present author was commissioned to prepare the studies on exceptions for libraries and archives. The first study was submitted to WIPO in 2008, and it analyzed the statutes from 149 of the countries. The most recent study was submitted in November 2017, and it encompassed the law from all countries that were members at that time. The studies are available on the WIPO website, and the 2017 study is available here: https://www.wipo.int/meetings/en/doc_details.jsp?doc_id=389654.

time-consuming, and politically charged. Success requires patience and persuasion. WIPO members could also choose to take a possible middle ground, not adopting a formal treaty but instead offering guidance and direction that can be integrated into the content of domestic legislation. All possibilities are open right now. Of course, finding any common ground among delegates representing 192 WIPO member countries, with their many differences in priorities and histories, can be a monumental challenge.

Whatever direction WIPO may proceed in, it has identified multiple issues for discussion and possible inclusion in a treaty or other instrument. Among the topics for consideration are these:

- Preservation and replacement of works
- Copies for research or personal study
- Cross-border transfers of copies
- Identification and use of orphan works
- Circumventing technological measures for library uses
- Relationship of exceptions to contracts and licenses
- Limits on infringement liability

The WIPO actions are not in isolation. They come at a time when many countries are moving forward with considering and enacting new statutory copyright exceptions on many subjects. The United Kingdom has expanded the range of materials that are subject to digital preservation. Kuwait has embraced the importance of digital technologies in its statutes. Chile was among the countries with no exceptions for libraries, but in recent years it enacted a series of relevant provisions. Major legislation on libraries and many other copyright issues is progressing in South Africa and is a part of the European Union directives of 2019.

Copyright exceptions in support of libraries, teaching, learning, and research are of growing importance in the United States and around the world. Some or all of these concepts are part of the copyright exceptions of nearly every country. The movement to elevate them into the terms of a treaty or other international instrument is further confirmation that countries are relying heavily on the international dynamic to help motivate and shape the enactment of copyright exceptions to support the interests of citizens, institutions, and businesses alike.

> **IN ADDITION** to reexamination of the library exceptions, a modest number of countries are considering adoption of a fair use statute, similar or identical to the U.S. statute. Among the countries with fair use law are Israel, Philippines, South Korea, Sri Lanka, and Taiwan. Some of the countries giving serious consideration to enactment of fair use statutes include Australia and Canada. Fair use is a centerpiece of legislation that was introduced in South Africa in late 2018. Where countries do not have some statutory flexibility to meet new and changing needs, courts have been confronted with cases that either demand a creative flexibility or face a stymied law.

NOTES

1. Copyright Act of 1790, ch. 15, 1 Stat. 124.

2. Statute of Anne, 8 Anne c. 19 (1710).

3. International Copyright Act of 1891, ch. 565, 26 Stat. 1106.

4. The WIPO website includes the full text of the Berne Convention and a current list of countries that are contracting parties to Berne and each of the related acts. *See* https://www.wipo.int/treaties/en/.

5. Notice the key phrase of "at least" the same protection. A country is allowed to grant greater protection for foreign works than it gives to its own works. Sound like folly? Well, U.S. law does give a few advantages to foreign works. Perhaps most salient, Congress enacted the restoration of copyright described in Chapter 6. That principle moved a great many works from the public domain back under copyright protection. But only certain foreign works could have the benefit.

6. Another formality is legal deposit, or delivering copies of published works, usually with the national library. The United States has a legal deposit requirement, calling for deposit of many new works, including two copies of the "best edition" of each newly published book, so that they are then available for possible addition to the collections of the Library of Congress. Failure to make the deposit can result in fines, but not the loss of copyright. For the legal deposit statute, *see* U.S. Copyright Act, 17 U.S.C. § 407.

7. U.S. Copyright Act, 17 U.S.C. § 102(a).

8. U.S. Copyright Act, 17 U.S.C. §§ 401–406.

9. U.S. Copyright Act, 17 U.S.C. §§ 408–412.

10. U.S. Copyright Act, 17 U.S.C. § 302(a).

11. U.S. Copyright Act, 17 U.S.C. § 302(a).

12. The moral rights statute is codified at Section 106A of the Copyright Act. It was part of a bill known as the Visual Artists Rights Act of 1990. That same bill included the copyright protection for architectural works.

13. The full text of the Marrakesh Treaty is available on the WIPO website at https://www.wipo.int/treaties/en/ip/marrakesh/. The full name of the instrument is Marrakesh Treaty to Facilitate Access to Published Works for Persons Who Are Blind, Visually Impaired or Otherwise Print Disabled.

14. The U.S. Senate approved the treaty in 2018, and it was fully ratified in February 2019. In October 2018, Congress enacted legislation implementing Marrakesh by revising Section 121 of the Copyright Act and adding the new Section 121A.

15. TRIPS, shorthand for the Agreement on Trade-Related Aspects of Intellectual Property Rights, is one of the agreements of the World Trade Organization, and consequently it has been signed by 164 countries, and its terms can be enforced through WTO proceedings and penalties. The text is at Annex 1C, https://www.wto.org/english/docs_e/legal_e/legal_e.htm.

16. *See* Articles 2(8) and 10(2) of the Berne Convention. The full text of the Berne Convention is available on the WIPO website at https://wipolex.wipo.int/en/text/283698.

17. Convention Establishing the World Intellectual Property Organization, art. 3 (1967), https://www.wipo.int/treaties/en/text.jsp?file_id=283854.

CHAPTER 4

THE SCOPE OF PROTECTABLE WORKS

KEY POINTS

- Copyright applies automatically to "original" works that are "fixed in a tangible medium of expression."
- Originality requires a minimum amount of creativity, and that the work originated with the author.
- A work is fixed if it is embodied in some stable form for more than a brief duration.
- A tangible medium allows a work to be perceived or communicated.

ONE OF THE most sweeping concepts of modern copyright law is the easiest and clearest to apply. The breadth and scope of the provision, however, also extend the reach of the law far beyond where copyright protection may be warranted or even desired. Consider the profundity of this principle: Copyright protection vests immediately and automatically upon the creation of "original works of authorship" that are "fixed in any tangible medium of expression."[1]

Under that provision, copyright protection applies instantly to nearly every e-mail, vacation photo, scribbled missive, and rant on Twitter. These works can easily meet the test of originality, and they are fixed in a tangible medium when penned to paper or saved to a computer drive or photographed with a smart phone. The result is an abundance of copyrighted works, without any further requirement of a copyright notice, registration, or any other step. That is good news if you want protection for your new works. Yet this law poses a steady challenge for librarians, educators, publishers, artists, and database developers who need to address the practical reality that many works are copyrighted, and finding the current rightful owner is often nearly impossible.

Despite the generous expanse of copyrightable works, we now know that the law applies to only human creations. The law begins and ends with the human race. In the notorious *Monkey Selfie Case*, the court ruled that only humans have recognized legal standing to bring an infringement action under the U.S. Copyright Act. An Indonesian macaque may pick up a camera and snap his grinning visage, but the court has ruled that nonhumans cannot assert copyright claims.[2]

ORIGINALITY

The notion of *originality* in copyright law has two components. Fundamentally, originality means that the work came from your inspiration and that you did not copy it from another source. Second, originality implies some degree of creativity. Originality is easily found in new writings, musical works, artwork, photography, and computer programming. Originality can also exist in a new organization or presentation of existing facts or information. Scientific findings or facts may not themselves be copyrightable, but their arrangement in a table or their presentation in text may be sufficiently original to be copyrightable expressions.

In all of these examples, the work is original if you did not copy it from another source, even if your photograph happens to look much like someone else's view of the Grand Canyon. You can stand at the same lookout point and snap a beautiful picture. The similarity is coincidence and circumstance, but not copying. Based upon this principle, much of what we create is copyrightable, from mundane paragraphs to elaborate artistic designs. The typical content and layout of a website are easily copyrightable. So would be everyone's Facebook page. Facebook is an amalgamation of text, images, advertisements, and more. Each piece—from the snarkiest comments to the most elaborate program applications—is someone's creative work and plausibly copyrightable.

Copyright protection can also apply to a new work that is built on an existing work, but any new copyright protection will apply to only the added creativity. For example, Homer's epic poems may never have had any legal protection under the laws of ancient Greece, and Homer's actual words are in the public domain under modern copyright law. Yet a new translation or graphic book version is an original work that is subject to new copyright protection as a derivative work. A derivative work uses the original work, for example, *The Iliad*, and recasts, transforms, or adapts the original to create a new work.

In addition to translations, other familiar derivatives include a motion picture made from a novel, a stage play based on a movie, songs based on poetry, and a sound recording of an existing composition. The possibilities are legion, and the derivative can also qualify for copyright protection. When a motion picture studio produces a film based on a Jane Austen book, the original book remains in the public domain, but the studio holds the copyright in its new dialogue, visuals, musical score, and other contributions to the movie. As will be examined more fully in Chapter 19, a sound recording of music can often embody at least two copyrights: one in the original composition and one in the original recording of a performance, which is a derivative of the score.

> **SORTING OUT** the copyrights on your Facebook page can be a challenge. It may be filled with photos, text, GIFs, linked content, and much more. Most of these pieces are within the expansive boundaries of copyright protection, and each element has its own separate legal status. You likely own the text you posted, but you might have received the photograph from a relative. The link might be to a new article, and that copyright might be held by the publisher, reporter, or others. Facts, such as names and birth dates are not copyrightable, and Facebook, Inc. surely holds rights in the layout, standard elements, and underlying computer code. Your friends have their own rights in the greetings and wisecracks they contribute to your wall. The limits of protection and the various ownership possibilities are explored in Chapters 5 and 7.

CREATIVITY AND ORIGINALITY

How much originality is required? A work must embody only some *minimum amount of creativity* to be considered original. Courts have held that almost any spark of creativity beyond the trivial will constitute sufficient originality. The U.S. Supreme Court ruled in 1991 that a "garden variety," alphabetical, white pages telephone book lacks the requisite minimum creativity for copyright protection. In a simple but pointed assertion of a standard for copyrightability, the Supreme Court declared that "there is nothing remotely creative about arranging names alphabetically in a white pages directory."[3] Cases since then

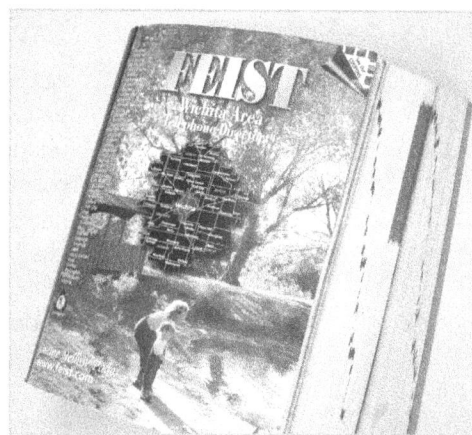

This genuine Feist telephone book includes white pages, yellow pages, and more. Some elements are outside the reach of copyright, but other parts of the book are surely protectable.

have affirmed this ruling but tested its limits. For example, a yellow pages listing may have sufficient originality resulting from its categorization of information into subject headings.[4]

Technology and innovation routinely test the applicability of copyright law. Courts in recent decades have addressed the copyrightability of computer software, bootleg recordings, and computer-generated content. Long ago, the U.S. Supreme Court faced similar questions about a photograph of the author Oscar Wilde from 1882. The Supreme Court in 1884 held that the picture met the standard of creativity because the photographer chose the camera, equipment, lighting, angles, and placement of the camera when shooting the picture. The Supreme Court noted that the image of Wilde was from the photographer's "own original mental conception" as demonstrated "by posing the said Oscar Wilde in front of the camera, selecting and arranging the costume, draperies, and other various accessories in said photograph, arranging the subject so as to present graceful outlines, arranging and disposing the light and shade, suggesting and evoking the desired expression. . . ."[5]

What if the photograph encompasses little choice about the content and elements? A federal court handed down an influential decision that a direct and accurate photographic reproduction of a two-dimensional artwork lacks sufficient creativity to be original.[6] The work of art may still be creative and protected by copyright, but not the simple and direct photographic reproduction. Unlike the Oscar Wilde case, the photograph of artwork was meant to be a reproduction and did not necessarily include creative lighting, coloring, or angles, nor did the art photo capture more than just the work of art itself. Similarly, another court held that digital models of automobiles that were meant to be exact reproductions were also not copyrightable.[7] These recent cases also stand for the general proposition that copyright law protects originality, not hard work. Copyright does not grant protection for the investment of labor, equipment,

THE PHOTOGRAPH of Oscar Wilde that was the subject of the Supreme Court ruling is reproduced here from the online collections of the Metropolitan Museum of Art. See https://metmuseum.org/art/collection/search/283247.

The use of the image here in this book is a handy opportunity to take a simple quiz about the layers of implicated copyright issues: Is a photograph within the scope of copyright? Does this photograph have sufficient originality? In what forms was it originally fixed? Was the original published or unpublished? What formalities were required under the law at that time? When would the original copyright expire? Does a new digital scan have a new copyright? If yes, when would it expire? Could reprinting it in this book be a fair use? What does the Creative Commons license on the Met's website permit? Keep reading this book for guidance through these concepts and more.

and know-how—unless the result is an original work with at least a minimum amount of creativity.

FIXED IN A TANGIBLE MEDIUM

For an original work of authorship to be eligible for copyright protection, it must also be fixed in some physical form capable of identification that exists for more than a "transitory duration."[8] Examples of fixed works might include scribbles on paper, recordings of music, paintings on canvas, and documents on web servers. A snapshot on film or in a digital camera is fixed. Sandcastles, ice sculptures, and spray-painted graffiti all can qualify as fixed in tangible media. The graffiti art on the 5Pointz building in Brooklyn, New York, was found to be protectable and was the subject of successful copyright litigation.[9]

The fixed form does not have to be readable by the human eye as long as the work can be perceived either directly or by a machine or device, such as a computer or projector.[10] Therefore, programming and substantive content stored on CDs, microforms, server drives, and other media are fixed as long as the works can be read with the use of a machine. The same is true about content stored on your computer, mobile phone, or camera. A work is fixed when you save it to your shared server, including that networked system of storage devices euphemistically and metaphorically called "the cloud."

EXPANSION OF COPYRIGHTABILITY

The tangible medium requirement expands copyright protection from traditional writings and pictures into the realm of video, sound recordings, computer disks, and Internet communications—any format now known or to be later developed.[11] If you can see it, read it, watch it, or hear it—with or without the use of a computer, projector, or other device—the work is likely eligible for copyright protection.

Harder questions surround works that exist in a particular form for a seemingly transitory duration. For example, are materials stored only on the random-access memory (RAM) of a computer sufficiently fixed? A court has determined that a work which is perceptible for slightly more than one second is not fixed.[12] By contrast, if that same work were saved, stored, or printed, it easily would fall within the purview of copyright. The necessary functioning of computer technology also gives rise to new works that may not be sufficiently stable to allow for copyright protection. Video games often involve scenes that arise from the particular play. The elements and characters might clearly be the copyright of the game developers, but the exact construct of a scene requires the actions of the consumer user. More fundamentally, the transitory scene might not even be fixed.

> **AN IMPORTANT** court case held that software programming loaded onto RAM could be sufficiently stable to qualify as a "copy" for purposes of establishing an infringement. *MAI Systems Corporation v. Peak Computer, Inc.*, 991 F.2d 511 (9th Cir. 1993). The concept of a work in a stable medium for purposes of copying is similar to the standard used to determine if the work is fixed in the first place to establish copyright protection. In this case, the work remained on the RAM until the system was shut down and was not merely fleeting.

CATEGORIES OF PROTECTED WORKS

Given the wide range of media and nearly boundless scope of originality, a vast array of works is brought under copyright protection. In addition, the statutes list various works that are generally protectable. Section 102(a) of the Copyright Act specifies that copyrightable materials can include the following:

- Literary works
- Musical works, including any accompanying words
- Dramatic works, including any accompanying music
- Pantomimes and choreographic works
- Pictorial, graphic, and sculptural works
- Motion pictures and other audiovisual works
- Sound recordings
- Architectural works[13]

These categories are illustrative and not exhaustive of all possibilities. Because the categories are construed liberally, "literary works" can range from novels to computer programs. Pictorial or graphic works can include maps, charts, and other visual imagery.[14] On the other hand, not all works that are copyrightable under today's law received protection in former years. Architectural works were not brought under copyright until 1990. As is examined in some detail later in this book, sound recordings of even the more important musical and literary works did not enjoy federal copyright protection until 1972.

Nevertheless, the reach of copyright is flexible and extensive. The law extends to new types of works and is not inhibited by new formats and media. Because of the law's vast reach, the important question may not be what *is copyrightable*, but what *is not copyrightable*. The next chapter identifies various types of works that are outside the reach of copyright protection.

THE GROWING range of copyrightable works is a reflection of the many forces that define copyright law. Some copyrightable works manifest technological change, such as the invention of photography, motion pictures, and computer programs. Some works tell us about the growth of certain economies and policy, such as commercial art and musical compositions. Other works are brought under the purview of copyright because of international norms, such as the extension of copyright to architectural designs in 1990. Sound recordings have followed a rugged path toward protection. Congress brought them under federal copyright protection starting only as of February 15, 1972. However, in October 2018, economic and legal pressures led Congress to enact the Music Modernization Act, which created an entirely new "neighboring rights" system of protection for pre-1972 recordings. That new law is examined in some detail in Chapter 20 of this book.

NOTES

1. U.S. Copyright Act, 17 U.S.C. § 102(a).
2. *Naruto v. Slater*, 888 F.3d 418 (9th Cir. 2018).
3. *Feist Publications, Inc. v. Rural Telephone Service Co., Inc.*, 499 U.S. 340, 363 (1991).
4. *BellSouth Advertising & Publishing Corporation v. Donnelley Information Publishing, Inc.*, 999 F.2d 1436 (11th Cir. 1993). Another court upheld the validity of using contracts to license directory content and to create legal restrictions on the use of data. *ProCD, Inc. v. Zeidenberg*, 86 F.3d 1447 (7th Cir. 1996).
5. *Burrow-Giles Lithographic Co. v. Sarony*, 111 U.S. 53, 60 (1884).
6. *Bridgeman Art Library, Ltd. v. Corel Corporation*, 36 F. Supp. 2d 191 (S.D.N.Y. 1999).
7. *Meshwerks, Inc. v. Toyota Motor Sales USA*, 528 F.3d 1258 (10th Cir. 2008), *cert. denied*, 555 U.S. 1138 (2009).
8. The word *fixed*, as well as many other terms, is defined in the copyright statutes. U.S. Copyright Act, 17 U.S.C. § 101.
9. *Cohen v. G&M Realty L.P.*, 320 F. Supp. 3d 421 (E.D.N.Y. 2018) (currently on appeal to the Second Circuit).

10. U.S. Copyright Act, 17 U.S.C. § 102(a).

11. U.S. Copyright Act, 17 U.S.C. § 102(a).

12. *Cartoon Network LP v. CSC Holdings, Inc.,* 536 F.3d 121, 130 (2d Cir. 2008), *cert. denied,* 557 U.S. 946 (2009).

13. U.S. Copyright Act, 17 U.S.C. § 102(a).

14. U.S. Copyright Act, 17 U.S.C. § 101.

CHAPTER 5

WORKS WITHOUT COPYRIGHT PROTECTION

KEY POINTS

- The lack of legal protection for some works can further the objectives of copyright.
- Works without copyright protection are said to be in the public domain.
- Works of the U.S. government are not copyrightable, but works created by state or local governments may be protected.
- Ideas and facts are not protected by copyright.
- Other specific types of works may be outside of copyright protection, but they may have limited protection under other laws.
- The public domain is also enriched when copyrights expire, and the duration of copyright is detailed in the next chapter.

THE PREVIOUS CHAPTER emphasized that copyright protection today extends automatically to a broad array of works that are original and fixed in a tangible medium. Despite that sweeping scope, copyright law also places several categories of works explicitly and completely outside the boundaries of legal protection. By limiting copyright's reach, the law places many works in the public domain, meaning they are wholly without copyright protection and are freely available for use without copyright restrictions. The next chapter of this book examines copyright duration and the expiration of copyrights. This current chapter is altogether different. It is about works that never had any protection at all.[1]

Some works are exempt from copyright for different reasons. For example, some U.S. government works are exempt on the principle that citizens supported with their taxes the creation of those resources and thus should be entitled to access and use them. Sometimes copyright does not apply for practical reasons. For example, a lecture or speech that is not written, recorded, or otherwise "fixed" may be difficult to protect. Imagine trying to prove the details in court without any written or recorded copy.

Some works have no copyright protection because no one should own the building blocks of human knowledge and communication. For example, ideas and theories are not protectable because they are the foundation of new knowledge and learning.[2] Ideas and other concepts can evolve, earn Nobel Prizes, and change the world, but they are also meant to be shared, nurtured, challenged, and revised. Locking up ideas with legal protection can be harmful to the public interest and the expansion of knowledge.

On the other hand, legal boundaries of the public domain can get blurry. If you tell a friend about your great ideas for a book or scientific breakthrough, she might use the ideas in her own work and you might have no copyright claim. By contrast, if you show that same shady friend your written manuscript, with detailed explanations and original analysis of the ideas, and she uses the same words in her own study, she might have tread on your copyrighted expression. Copyright does not protect ideas, but it does protect your words or your expression of those ideas. Your friend really ought to write her own book, with her own original expression.[3] Although ideas and such may be outside the bounds of copyright, they may be subject to other legal restrictions on use, from trade secrecy to national security.

Ultimately, many works are without copyright protection for good and important reasons. A leading objective of copyright protection is to encourage creativity and the dissemination of new works. Sometimes limiting or denying rights also serves that same purpose. If ideas were protectable, we might be left with only one version of a story, only one software package for each need, or only one work of art that expresses beauty or angst. Sometimes denying rights can better foster creativity and render the greatest benefit for individuals and for society in general.

> THIS IS good place to reflect on the difference between copyright and plagiarism. Copyright is a legal concept, while plagiarism is an ethical consideration about intellectual honesty and appropriate credit. Plagiarism is failing to give attribution for the sources you use as a foundation or inspiration for your new work and insights. You can ordinarily avoid plagiarism through careful use of quotation marks and citations. The honest use can still conceivably be a copyright infringement if, for example, your use is beyond the limits of fair use. Conversely, if you use only public domain materials, you will not have to worry about infringing copyright. However, even though your actions might be perfectly legal, they may still breach the ethical standard of plagiarism if done without proper attribution.

FACTS AND DISCOVERIES

Facts and discoveries are not protectable by copyright.[4] Facts cannot, by definition, be "original" as the law requires. You may conduct years of creative scientific study to discover a *fact* about the universe, but the fact itself is not *your* creative work. Denying legal protection for facts also assures that everyone can build on existing knowledge and share information.

On the other hand, you may have copyright protection for your original *compilations of facts* or your *writings about the facts and discoveries*.[5] For example, after years of research to find facts, you write a journal article about your research findings. The sentences and paragraphs are most surely creative, original, and protectable. Suppose your article also includes several tables that organize the facts in a manner that is meaningful to your readers. You might chart the boiling point of water, the rate of urban crime, or the election of presidents. If the chart is merely a presentation of facts, likely no protection is available. However, if the chart is a creative display of information, with original organization, depiction, and explanation, at least those creative elements are likely within the scope of copyright protection.

What exactly is a fact? A book about rare coins is surely protectable, but the stated value of each coin could be a fact about market prices—or not. If the price

> THE U.S. SUPREME COURT made clear that copyright protection depends on creativity, but the measure of creativity is modest at best: "[T]he requisite level of creativity is extremely low; even a slight amount will suffice. The vast majority of works make the grade quite easily, as they possess some creative spark, 'no matter how crude, humble or obvious' it might be." *Feist Publications, Inc. v. Rural Telephone Service Co., Inc.*, 499 U.S. 340, 345 (1991). One more category of works without protection encompasses those without even that slight creative spark.

is simply a recent actual selling price, it is a fact. On the other hand, one court has ruled that wholesale prices for collectible coins based on multivariable judgment calls and the appraiser's best guess are creative works protectable under copyright.[6] Similarly, historical interpretations may be creative fiction, or they may be presented as fact. The manner in which they are conveyed by the author will likely determine whether the court will treat them as unprotected fact or not.[7]

COMPILATIONS AND DATABASES

Although facts themselves are not protected, a collection of facts may be. To the extent that you have selected, arranged, or coordinated the facts in some original manner, you can claim a compilation copyright in the work. Still, the facts are not your intellectual property.

Another writer can extract the facts and include them in a new study, but if he copies your original expression of those facts, he is stepping into the realm of copyright.

Real examples of compilation copyrights are common, and the pressure for legal protection is profound. For example, many companies create, publish, and market bibliographies and other compilations of information. Individual author names, article titles, and the like are not protected under copyright,[8] but if the data are arranged in some original manner, the resulting database can have copyright protection. A single issue of a standard academic journal can illustrate the point. An editor may select your article for publication and arrange it with other writings into a new journal issue. You may still hold the copyright for your individual work, but the editor can hold a copyright in the compilation of the overall journal issue.[9]

The journal—like any other compilation or database—has copyright protection only if it is original in its selection, arrangement, or coordination of data elements. Selecting and organizing articles in a journal may entail some originality; an editor selects articles from multiple submissions and organizes them into a logical sequence within the journal issue. By contrast, gathering data and listing them alphabetically or chronologically, or just uploading the data in no order onto a computer, often involves no creativity; the editor is not making an original arrangement or necessarily selecting certain information for the compilation.

Without creativity, no copyright protection applies. The lack of protection for many databases is a great concern for companies that invest significantly to develop and market such works. In the 1990s, Congress considered legislation that would establish a new form of legal protection for data compilations, but none of the bills was enacted.[10] Many educators and librarians have cautioned against these bills, arguing that such a law would further restrain access to information. Meanwhile, many developers of databases have relied on licenses and contracts in an effort to impose some level of protection for or control over their products.

> **YOU MIGHT** write poetry in your spare time. You can have copyright protection for each poem. After some years of writing, you gather the poems, arrange them into a logical or interesting order, and publish the collection as a book. You can have an additional copyright in the original compilation. You can also have a compilation copyright if you gather the poems of other authors—with their permission or as otherwise allowed—and assemble them into one original collection.

> **WHILE DEDICATED** law on database protection has not taken hold in the United States, it has become well established in the European Union (EU). Pursuant to a 1996 directive, all twenty-eight countries of the EU must enact legal protection for databases that result from a "substantial investment" in their development. Council Directive No. 96/9/EC, O.J. L 77/20 (1996). The protection is generally limited to EU nationals, and it lasts for fifteen years. If the database is substantially changed, the term of protection can begin anew.

THE CONCEPT of *public domain* applies to a work that has no copyright protection. The label is often mistakenly applied to works that are publicly available, such as on websites, without any apparent conditions on access or use. Most materials that are freely available on the Internet are in fact protected by copyright, but the owners have simply permitted them to be openly available. Even open access works are usually copyrighted, but the owners again have chosen to make them within the public's reach. They are not necessarily in the public domain.

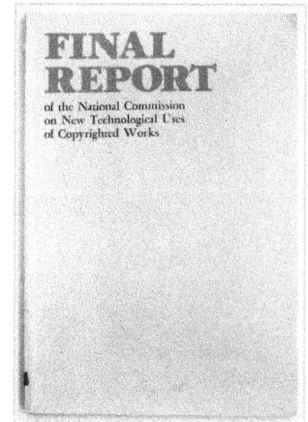

A report by an official commission of the U.S. government, the National Commission on New Technological Uses of Copyrighted Works (CONTU), is in the public domain under Section 105. The CONTU Report is visited again in **Chapters 13** and **17**.

All of these examples underscore the need to distinguish between various elements of a total work and to establish carefully whether each element is copyrightable. Some pieces may be in the public domain. Some components of a work may be separately copyrighted and held by different owners. Sometimes the distinction is fairly easy to determine, such as the difference between the article and the journal. In other instances, the legal protection for each element is less clear, such as the difference between facts and the compilation of data.

WORKS OF THE U.S. GOVERNMENT

The U.S. government produces numerous works that may be original and fixed but still not copyrightable. Section 105 of the U.S. Copyright Act specifically prohibits copyright protection for works of the federal government, such as the CONTU Report.[11] Therefore, reports written by members of Congress and employees of federal agencies as part of their official duties are not copyrightable. Decisions from federal courts and statutes from Congress are not protected. The same holds true for presidential speeches, pamphlets from the National Park Service, and websites developed by federal agencies.[12]

Even this broad rule of copyright is not as simple as it seems. Works written by nongovernment officials based on projects supported by federal funding are eligible for copyright. For example, your research may be funded by government grants, but that fact does not by itself put your work in the public domain. A work derived from a government-funded project that is not prepared by an officer or employee of the U.S. government is not a "work of the United States government" and is not in the public domain under this rule.

Similarly, just because a work is published by the federal government does not mean that it is a government work and in the public domain. A publication from the Smithsonian Institution, for example, may well have been prepared by nongovernment authors and is therefore protectable by copyright. A brochure from the National Park Service may include copyrighted photographs licensed from an independent photographer. You need to examine each item closely and inquire with the author or the issuing agency if you are in doubt.

As with so much of the law, keep digging and you will find more surprises.

BECAUSE OF the strong public interest in government works, even if a particular work is not in the public domain, the courts may be more willing to apply fair use. Federal statutes may be in the public domain, but statutes sometimes incorporate by reference numerous and diverse technical standards that are developed and sold as publications by private organizations. A nonprofit organization dedicated to making legal information readily available to the public purchased a set of standards from the professional society that developed them, scanned the materials in full, and uploaded them for public access. The court declined to rule that the standards became a work of the U.S. government and therefore in the public domain; the court determined instead that the scanning and uploading in the context of providing legal information could be within fair use. *American Society for Testing and Materials v. Public.Resource.Org, Inc.*, 896 F.3d 437 (D.C. Cir. 2018).

Only YOU can prevent forest fires

Seriously. We've been defunded. It's just you now.

THE NOTICE prescribed for materials with Smokey Bear's image states, in part, "Reproduction or resale is prohibited under 16 USC 580." Guidelines from the U.S. Forest Service remind readers that Smokey is protected by trademark law. One recurring theme of this book is that just as soon as you think you have figured out the rule, the law will almost always throw your way a surprising exception or variation. In this case Smokey may have no copyright protection, but he gets his own dedicated law, and he may be subject to trademark rights.

Smokey Bear's legal rights seem to be frequently violated, in this case to draw attention to the cut in funding for Smokey's causes. Source: https://www.teepublic.com.

Smokey Bear is a tremendously popular figure, playing a critical role in the U.S. Forest Service campaign against wildfires. Posters and brochures from the service are seemingly obvious examples of U.S. governmental works that are in the public domain. Yet elsewhere in the U.S. statutes, away from and with no explicit connection to the Copyright Act, federal law gives Smokey his own special legal shield from unauthorized uses.[13]

According to guidelines from the Forest Service, Smokey was attracting sufficient commercial interest by 1952 that Congress acted to "take Smokey out of public domain and place him under the control of the Secretary of Agriculture." In 1974, Congress authorized the department to engage in commercial licensing of Smokey.[14] Some of the brochures, posters, and other materials with his image that come from the U.S. government also include a statement prohibiting further reproduction. Bottom line, according to federal statutes, the "name and character 'Smokey Bear'" are "declared the property of the United States."[15]

WORKS OF STATE AND LOCAL GOVERNMENTS

The statutory exclusion in Section 105 of the Copyright Act applies to only works of the U.S. federal government. As a result, works created by state and local governments are protected by copyright unless those governments have expressly waived their claims of copyright by statute. For example, a California statute requires that a long list of official materials be made available to the public online, including the full set of state statutes, the constitution, and a host of legislative documents. The law further specifies that all such information is "within the public domain and the State of California retains no copyright or other proprietary interest in that information."[16]

Some states have gone the opposite direction. The Idaho legislature has provided a blunt and direct declaration about copyright for its statutes:

> The Idaho Code is the property of the state of Idaho, and the state of Idaho and the taxpayers shall be deemed to have a copyright on the Idaho Code. If a person reproduces or distributes the Idaho Code for the purpose of direct or indirect commercial advantage, the person shall owe to

the Idaho code commission, as the agent of the state of Idaho, a royalty fee in addition to the fee charged for copying the Idaho Code. Any person who reproduces or distributes the Idaho Code in violation of the provisions of this section, shall be deemed to be an infringer of the state of Idaho's copyright.[17]

Some claims of copyright in governmental works have not been sanguine. A resident of Inglewood, California, was a steady and nettlesome critic of the city government. The city council videotaped its proceedings, and those videos were handy fodder for clipping and assembling into an unflattering look at the local government. The city sued its own resident, asserting copyright infringement.[18]

COPYRIGHT PROTECTION for state statutes and court decisions has been disputed for many years. An initiative to post Oregon legal materials online at Public.Resource.Org led to an exchange of frank and confrontational letters with state officials. In June 2008, a committee of the state legislature adopted a resolution that the state would not assert copyright protection in the Oregon statutes. Various materials about this important development are posted at http://public.resource.org/oregon.gov/. By contrast, the state of Georgia sued the same organization and initially won a decision securing copyright protection for the annotations accompanying its published statutes. On appeal, the Eleventh Circuit reversed and ruled that the statutes and the accompanying annotations are in the public domain. *Code Revision Commission v. Public.Resource.Org, Inc.,* 906 F.3d 1229 (11th Cir. 2018). As of this writing, the Supreme Court is scheduled to hear the case and will probably rule on the copyright issue during 2020.

The main ruling of the court was not directly about the substance of copyright, but rather that the city lacked authority under California state law to hold and enforce copyrights. The videos may well be protected by copyright, but cities and other local governments exist with authorization of the state, and they may hold and enforce copyrights only if empowered to do so under state law.[19] Unless you are the rightful owner with the legal right to bring litigation, your case may be dismissed. Nevertheless, the court ruled that this particular use would have been within fair use had the city been able to proceed with its infringement claims. The *Inglewood* decision is rich with language emphasizing the importance of public access to governmental information.

When you need to use a work produced by a state or local agency, your approach can otherwise be in many respects like the strategy for using any other work: Look for a provision in state law or elsewhere that might indicate whether the work is public domain or other terms of use. If the works are protected, they are still subject to fair use and the other exceptions in federal copyright law.

The practical reality is that attitudes about copyright are as diverse as there are government officials who might have an interest or duty. Exactly whether or how an agency might assert rights in its works can be unpredictable. After checking whether the exceptions might apply, sometimes the most meaningful recourse is to inquire with the appropriate state agency and check its attitude.

WORKS OF FOREIGN AND INTERNATIONAL GOVERNMENTS

Notice again that the copyright exclusion in the U.S. Copyright Act applies to only works of the U.S. federal government. Where does that leave works from foreign or international governmental entities? The Copyright Act is explicit in some respects. It outright provides that U.S. copyright applies to works "first published by the United Nations or any of its specialized agencies, or by the Organization of American States."[20] Beyond that short provision, we need to turn to general concepts of the law.

Chapters 3 and 23 of this book take a close look at several copyright concepts related to foreign and international copyright. One of those general principles applicable here is

CONSIDER, FOR EXAMPLE, the study of copyright exceptions for libraries, commissioned by the World Intellectual Property Organization, and mentioned in Chapter 17. WIPO is an agency of the United Nations, meaning that it is eligible for copyright protection under U.S. law. Under the general rule of copyright ownership, the author would be the copyright owner. However, the author did indeed enter into an agreement that granted certain rights to WIPO, and WIPO in turn has adopted a general policy on open access. WIPO has made the study easily available on its website, with a generous public license. Further, much of the content of the study is factual summaries of copyright statutes and may not be copyrightable at all. Finally, this legal analysis presented here is a reflection of U.S. law, and the legal principles applied to government works and the outcome may be different in other countries. The open access license has the added virtue of leveling the terms of use around the world, despite differences in national legislation.

that, in general, foreign works that are located and used in the United States are governed by U.S. law. Thus, because U.S. law does not set a distinct rule for works by foreign governments, those works are evidently protectable as if they were any other original and fixed work.

Of course, many governmental works are not entirely original. Some statutes are the result of original drafting, but countries often rely on treaties and model laws, and they borrow statutory language from neighboring nations. Many governmental documents of all types are the stuff of great public interest, affecting millions of citizens. Access to the documents, data, and videos produced by governments offer insights into official actions and can inform citizens as they prepare to cast votes or just live by the law. In that spirit, many works of any government may be imbued with a strong public interest and may well find favor with fair use.

OUTSIDE THE SCOPE OF COPYRIGHT

Several additional categories of materials are generally not eligible for statutory copyright protection:

- Works that have not been fixed in a tangible form of expression, including choreographic works that have not been noted or recorded or improvisational speeches or performances that have not been written or recorded
- Titles, names, short phrases, and slogans, as well as familiar symbols or designs—although the law of trademark may offer some protection[21]
- Mere variations of typographical design, lettering, or coloring; mere listings of ingredients, as in recipes, or listings of contents[22]
- Ideas, procedures, methods, systems, processes, concepts, principles, discoveries, or devices,[23] although patent or trade secret law may offer protection for some of these works

ADDITIONAL WORKS may be in the public domain for a variety of reasons. An author may voluntarily choose to dedicate a work to the public domain. In other cases, Congress has simply chosen not to extend copyright protection to all works. For example, sound recordings are protectable today, but U.S. recordings made before Congress changed the law, effective February 15, 1972, are without federal copyright protection. The Music Modernization Act, enacted in October 2018, created an entirely new system of legal protection akin to copyright for pre-1972 sound recordings. That system of "neighboring rights" is examined in Chapter 20 of this book.

- Functional works or "useful articles," where any decorative or other copyrightable elements cannot be separated from the functional features
- Works consisting entirely of information that is common property and containing no original authorship, including standard calendars, height and weight charts, tape measures and rulers, and lists or tables taken from public documents or other common sources

EXPIRED COPYRIGHTS

Another important source of the public domain is the expiration of copyright for any work. Copyrights may last a long time, but they do eventually expire. Works that were protected in the past may have lost their copyright due to the age of the work. The copyright to works from before 1989 may also have expired due to failure to comply with formalities that copyright law once required. The process of identifying works in the public domain can demand a thorough investigation of historical documents and publication records.

THE U.S. SUPREME COURT handed down an important decision in 2017 on the copyrightability of decorative works that are integrated with functional works. It has long been a staple of copyright law that protection does not extend to clothing design. The clothes themselves are fundamentally functional works—they cover and protect. However, the design features on clothing, such as color patterns and pictures, can be separated. They are therefore protectable. The Supreme Court ruled that protection also extends to the designs on the front of cheerleader outfits, which are separable only in concept, even if they are integrated into the clothing design and cannot necessarily be physically removed. *Star Athletica, L.L.C. v. Varsity Brands, Inc.*, 580 U.S. ___ , 137 S. Ct. 1002 (2017).

The quest can be daunting, but the results can be tremendously important. Based on a review of historical records, courts have recently concluded that the songs "We Shall Overcome" and "Happy Birthday to You" are in the public domain.[24] Research into historical documents and publication records can be exhilarating as well as confounding. Yet if successful, the songs, books, movies, and other works can enter the public domain and become widely available without copyright permission or fees. The next chapter of this book takes a close look at the duration of copyright protection and the process of identifying works in the public domain.

NOTES

1. This book is of course about copyright law. A work may well have no copyright protection, but it may still be subject to other legal restrictions. For example, a government document might be without copyright, but uses of it may be subject to espionage or national security law.

2. U.S. Copyright Act, 17 U.S.C. § 102(b).

3. She also might not be much of a friend, but that is for yet a different book.

4. U.S. Copyright Act, 17 U.S.C. § 102(b).

5. *Feist Publications, Inc. v. Rural Telephone Service Co., Inc.*, 499 U.S. 340 (1991); *Silverstein v. Penguin Putnam, Inc.*, 368 F.3d 77 (2d Cir. 2004), *cert. denied*, 543 U.S. 1039 (2004).

6. *CDN Inc. v. Kapes*, 197 F.3d 1256 (9th Cir. 1999).

7. *Hoehling v. Universal City Studios, Inc.*, 618 F.2d 972 (2d Cir. 1980).

8. 37 C.F.R. § 202.1.

9. Section 201(c) of the U.S. Copyright Act states, "Copyright in each separate contribution to a collective work is distinct from copyright in the collective work as a whole. . . ."

10. For a good overview of the various approaches to database legislation in the United States and internationally, *see* Michael Freno, "Database Protection: Resolving the U.S. Database Dilemma with an Eye Toward International Protection," *Cornell International Law Journal* 34 (2001): 165–225.

11. U.S. Copyright Act, 17 U.S.C. § 105(a). A few days before this book went to press, new legislation amended Section 105, adding subsections 105(b) and 105(c) to specify that civilian faculty members at the various military academies own the copyrights in literary works that they produce "in the course of employment . . . for publication by a scholarly press or journal." The Secretary of Defense may direct the author to grant the government a broad license to use the work. Pub. L. No. 116-92 (2020). This language has narrow application, but it may fuel larger debates about whether such scholarly works might have been "work made for hire" without this statute.

12. The U.S. Copyright Act defines a "work of the United States Government" as "a work prepared by an officer or employee of the United States Government as part of that person's official duties." U.S. Copyright Act, 17 U.S.C. § 101. For an example of the application of this rule to court opinions, *see Matthew Bender & Company, Inc. v. West Publishing Co.,* 158 F.3d 693 (2d Cir. 1998), *cert. denied,* 526 U.S. 1154 (1999).

13. 16 U.S.C. § 580p-4(a) ("Whoever, except as provided by rules and regulations issued by the Secretary, manufactures, uses, or reproduces the character 'Smokey Bear', or the name 'Smokey Bear', or a facsimile or simulation of such character or name in such a manner as suggests 'Smokey Bear' may be enjoined from such manufacture, use, or reproduction at the suit of the Attorney General upon complaint by the Secretary."). Subsection 580p-4(b) applies a similar rule for the character Woodsy Owl.

14. *Smokey Bear Guidelines* (October 2016), https://smokeybear.com/guidelines/Smokey_Bear _Guidelines-9-30-16.pdf.

15. 16 U.S.C. § 580p-1 (2018). Likewise for Woodsy Owl.

16. California Government Code §§ 10248–10248.5.

17. Idaho Code § 74-123(1). The Idaho Code was revised substantially in 2015, but this language was retained from the previous statutes.

18. *City of Inglewood v. Teixeira,* 2015 WL 5025839 (C.D. Cal. 2015).

19. Chapter 7 of this book examines the issues of copyright ownership. Cases do arise regularly where the rightful ownership of the copyright is drawn into question, including the case brought against Georgia State University (see Chapter 14). When the publishers could not introduce evidence that authors had transferred their copyrights to the publishers, some of the copyright claims were dismissed. Be sure you can prove your own ownership before filing suit or even granting permissions; be sure you are working with the right party before you rely on permissions.

20. U.S. Copyright Act, 17 U.S.C. § 104(b)(5).

21. 37 C.F.R. § 202.1.

22. *Id.*

23. U.S. Copyright Act, 17 U.S.C. § 102(b).

24. *We Shall Overcome Foundation v. The Richmond Organization, Inc.,* 2017 WL 3981311 (S.D.N.Y. 2017); and *Marya v. Warner/Chappell Music, Inc.,* 131 F. Supp. 3d 975 (C.D. Cal. 2015). In January 2018, the parties agreed to end the litigation regarding "We Shall Overcome," with the copyright claimants dedicating the verse in question to the public domain.

PART II

Rights of Ownership

THE "**SCHOOL** of Writing," based in Hamburg, Germany, is encouraging aspiring authors—and turning them into copyright owners, with rights and opportunities in Germany and in almost every country of the world.

CHAPTER 6

DURATION AND FORMALITIES

How Long Do Copyrights Last?

KEY POINTS

- Copyrights last for a period of years; once the copyright expires the work enters the public domain.
- Most new works are protected for the life of the author plus 70 years.
- Works published before 1978 were required to have a copyright notice in order to gain protection.
- Works published between 1923 and 1978 could have protection for up to 95 years.
- Many foreign works that were in the public domain have had their copyrights restored.
- Current law no longer requires such formalities as a copyright notice, registration, or renewal.

COPYRIGHTS DO NOT last forever. They may last a long time, or they may expire in relatively short order. Either way, the question of copyright duration can be both enormously controversial and unduly complicated. The duration of copyright is important because it signals when a work will enter the public domain and become available for use, free of the limits and restrictions of copyright law. The number of years of protection a work receives under the law can depend on many facts and variables.

Under today's law, copyright duration for current works is relatively uncomplicated. Copyright in most new works lasts throughout the author's life plus 70 more years.[1] These rights today automatically vest for the full term without the need to undertake any processes or procedures.[2] For works created before 1978, however, copyright duration is inextricably dependent on the formalities of copyright notice, registration, and renewal. Without full compliance with these procedures, the copyright in early works may have lapsed and caused the work to enter the public domain. This chapter summarizes and attempts to make practical sense of the law of copyright duration.

ELIMINATION OF FORMALITIES

American copyright law has changed in many respects through recent decades, but one of the most important changes has been the elimination of formalities.

The requirement, and later elimination, of formalities has direct implications for duration. Under current law, the formalities of notice and registration are not prerequisites to receiving the full duration of legal protection. Copyright vests automatically as soon as you create an original work that is fixed in a tangible medium.[3] You receive the protection whether you want it or not. You need not do anything—other than create an eligible work—to get copyright for a new work. This state of the law imposes instant copyright protection on the vast range of materials in libraries, on the Internet, in file drawers, and in museums. Consequently, nearly every person in the country today is a copyright owner.

Before 1989 Congress required authors to follow certain formalities as a prerequisite to protection. In incremental steps, Congress changed and ultimately dropped those requirements. The earliest law, in 1790, required registration of new works with the federal government.[4] That provision disappeared early in the next century.[5] Surviving through much of American history was the requirement that publications bear a formal copyright notice. With the 1976 Copyright Act, however, Congress began to loosen that requirement. Although the notice was still required, authors could fix or remedy a missing or defective notice.[6] As of March 1, 1989, Congress finally dropped the notice requirement altogether. Today, omitting the notice or using an incorrect notice no longer places the work in the public domain. Rather, a newly created work—whether published or not—enjoys instant protection.

> **WHY DID** Congress systematically remove the requirement of all formalities? The answer lies in international law. In March 1989, the United States officially joined the Berne Convention, a multinational agreement on copyright law. Berne Convention for the Protection of Library and Artistic Works Implementation Act, Pub. L. No. 100-568, 102 Stat. 2853, 2858 (1988). The Berne Convention, which was already more than a century old, prohibits formalities as a condition to copyright protection. To join Berne, U.S. law had to drop formalities for new works—as most countries already had done. The significance of Berne and America's entry into it are covered in some detail in Chapter 3.

> **WHAT EXACTLY** is a copyright notice? Here are some familiar forms:
>
> - © 2019, Jane Smith
> - Copyright 1890, Mark Twain
> - Copyr. 1928, Walt Disney Co.

Although the rules for new works have become simpler, the rules for early works remain cumbersome. Whenever you are investigating the copyright in an early work, you will need to apply the law that applied at that time. In addition to the notice requirement applicable to works published before 1989, works that were published before 1964 were also subject to a required copyright renewal registration. If the copyright claim was not renewed twenty-eight years after first publication, the copyright expired and entered the public domain. However, for works published in and after 1964, Congress eliminated the need for renewal altogether.[7] These historical developments have ongoing implications today for evaluating whether an early work is protected by copyright—and determining the years of copyright duration each work receives.

This chapter organizes the discussion of formalities and duration in a chronological and pragmatic context, centered especially on the momentous change in the law that took effect in 1978. This chapter also focuses on published works. Special rules apply to unpublished works, and they are addressed more fully in Chapter 21.

> **EVEN THOUGH** the notice is not required, the Digital Millennium Copyright Act of 1998 created a new federal offense for the removal, under some circumstances, of "copyright management information," which is defined to include the copyright notice as well as a wide variety of other identifying information. U.S. Copyright Act, 17 U.S.C. § 1202. The DMCA and copyright management information are addressed in Chapter 22.

COPYRIGHT DURATION FOR WORKS CREATED IN OR AFTER 1978

The modern rule of copyright protection is relatively simple, at least for most common needs: Copyright protection applies automatically when the author fixes his or her original work in a tangible medium; the copyright protection for most works lasts for the life of the author plus 70 more years.[8] Registering the work and placing a copyright notice on it are no longer required to receive copyright protection for the full term. Registration and notice can confer a variety of legal and practical benefits for a copyright owner, but they are not a required condition to having a valid copyright in a new work.[9]

Works that are made for hire also receive automatic protection, but the duration of copyright is sharply different. A work made for hire has protection for the *shorter* of either 120 years from creation of the work or 95 years from its publication.[10] As examined in Chapter 7, the legal author of these works is the employer. That employer might be an individual person, but typically it is a corporation or other legal entity. A corporate author might never die, so duration based on a lifetime makes little sense. Hence, the duration is instead a determinate number of years.

For creators of new works, these rules are fairly easy to apply, and the benefits of formalities are extraordinarily generous. Formalities are not required, but they can confer a variety of legal and practical benefits. Registration and a copyright notice are also good ways to inform the public that you know and care about your copyrights and to provide the public with your contact information for questions about permissions or anything else. Among the legal benefits, registration is required as a condition to filing an infringement lawsuit, at least with respect to works first published in the United States or created by American authors.[11] Registration is also required for any work as a condition to receiving an award of statutory damages and attorneys' fees in litigation.[12] Because registration with the U.S. Copyright Office is a simple form with a fee as low as only $35, this benefit alone can often make registration worthwhile. You cannot register everything, but registration is a good idea for any work you seriously want to protect.

REGISTRATION MIGHT not be a prerequisite to having copyright protection, but it is a precondition to actually filing a lawsuit in many cases. Section 411(a) of the Copyright Act provides the general rule that before filing a civil case for the infringement of a "United States work," the work must be registered with the U.S. Copyright Office. The concept of *United States work* is broadly defined but generally includes any work created by a U.S. national or resident or that was first published in the United States. Therefore, most of what we might call foreign works are not subject to this requirement. See Chapter 23 for further examples of American copyright law granting some greater advantages to foreign works. In 2019, the Supreme Court also clarified that the statute requires that the registration process must be completed before filing the infringement lawsuit; mere submission of the application and related materials is not enough. *Fourth Estate Public Benefit Corp. v. Wall-Street.com*, 586 U.S. ___ , 139 S. Ct. 881 (2019). The practical lesson for copyright owners is to register soon after creation, if they might want to be in the strongest position to enforce legal rights in the future.

For users of works, however, the absence of required formalities and the bestowal of automatic protection mean that you often need to assume a work is protected until you learn otherwise. Users often need to investigate the background, origin, and publication history of each work of interest. Without full and accurate information about the origin of a work, a user may not be able to resolve the question of copyright duration with certainty. When exactly was it created? Was it made by someone acting as an employee and thus was made for hire?

The facts needed to confirm copyright duration are often elusive. The facts about people, employers, places, and agreements may be in private files or lost to history. The databases of registration and renewal records are publicly accessible and searchable online, but they are notoriously incomplete and not error-free. A duration search usually involves application of convoluted law, a quest for uncertain facts, and in the end a judgment call about risks and progress. More information about the practical implications of formalities is included later in this chapter and in Chapter 18.

COPYRIGHT DURATION FOR WORKS PUBLISHED BEFORE 1978

Before 1978, the rigorous rules demanding a precise notice on all publications had the result of placing many works instantly in the public domain. Copyright owners also sometimes overlooked—whether intentionally or accidentally—the need to renew their copyrights after twenty-eight years. This failure to renew meant the copyright could lapse.

> **LOOKING FOR** more information about registration or searching registration records? The best place to start is the website of the U.S. Copyright Office: https://www.copyright.gov. Searches of early registrations and renewals are becoming easier as more information goes online. Google has recently digitized the *Catalog of Copyright Entries*, easing the search of records from 1923 to 1978. See http://books.google.com/googlebooks/copyrightsearch.html.

These rules can be nettlesome when investigating the copyright status of early works. Consider a researcher wanting to know if a publication from, say, 1940 is in the public domain. The researcher needs to locate and inspect original, published versions of the work for a proper notice. Absent the notice, the work entered into the public domain upon publication. On the other hand, if the work had been published with the proper notice, then the clock started ticking on the duration of copyright protection.[13]

> **CONGRESS DID** not entirely drop the notice requirement until 1989. Between 1978 and 1989, Congress continued the old rule but allowed a copyright owner to remedy an omitted or defective notice. Consequently, the absence of a notice on a 1980s' book does not reliably put it in the public domain. U.S. Copyright Act, 17 U.S.C. §§ 405–406. The lack of notice may raise the likelihood of no copyright protection, but a missing notice on a "small number" of copies does not jeopardize the copyright. Further, the lack of a notice might have been remedied. For example, the owner could have rescued the copyright by adding a notice to existing copies and registering the work with the Copyright Office within five years of publication. A check of the registration records is in order.

How long did the clock tick? The law before 1978 granted two sequential terms of copyright protection for publications. Proper use of a copyright notice gave an initial term of twenty-eight years. At the end of that term, the copyright owner was required to file a renewal application with the Copyright Office in order to receive the second and continuous term of protection.[14] Failure to file meant the copyright lapsed at the end of the first term. In the case of that 1940 publication, it could have entered the public domain on at least two occasions: in 1940 if published without notice and in 1968 if not renewed.

RENEWAL OF COPYRIGHTS

How long is the renewal term? This question does not have a single answer. The renewal term was, under the 1909 Act, another twenty-eight years. In the early 1960s the renewal term was stretched to forty-seven years, for a total of 75 years of protection. In 1998, Congress added twenty more years to the protection for early works.[15] Today, a work published before 1978 can generally have a maximum term of protection of 95 years.[16] Gaining initial protection still depended on satisfying the notice requirement.

In 1992 Congress jiggled the rules again and eliminated the renewal requirement for all existing copyrights.[17] Consider the simple example of a book published in 1965. The

The Copyright Term Extension Act of 1998 was named for Sonny Bono, congressman, singer, composer, and copyright owner, who had died in a skiing accident early that year. This plaque in his honor is in Sonny Bono Memorial Park, located close to the offices of many major library and education associations in Washington, DC.

published copies needed to include a copyright notice to secure the initial twenty-eight years of protection. By the time the copyright was slated for renewal in 1993, Congress had dropped the renewal requirement. The 1965 book received an automatic continuation of protection to the full 95 years available under today's law. By contrast, a book published in 1940 was scheduled for renewal in 1968, and because the law still required renewals at that time, if not renewed, the copyright expired.

Amidst this jumble of rules and legislation, you might come across a broad statement that works published before 1923 are in the public domain. That benchmark has been a pretty good rule to follow, although it oversimplifies the rule and needs a bit of important explanation and adjustment. Recall that Congress extended the duration of these early works by twenty years in 1998, stretching their protection to a basic term of 95 years. When Congress made that change, works published in 1922 and before were already in the public domain. Congress chose to leave them there. The result was that works published in and after 1923 received protection for 95 years.

Time passed. Congress made that change in 1998, and at least as of this writing has made no further revision of this part of copyright law. As a result, the basic rule of 95 years remains in force. Works that were published in 1923 accordingly ran their full 95 years and entered the public domain at the end of the day on December 31, 2018. The corollary "1923 rule" was that works published before 1923 were in the public domain. With advent of the new year in 2019, the standard became the "1924 rule"—works published before 1924 are in the public domain. In 2020 it has become a "1925 rule," and the following year it will be a "1926 rule." Each year, a new wealth of material will enter the public domain and become available for all to use and enjoy. Also keep in mind that this rule of 95 years applies to only published works and only as a matter of U.S. law.[18]

IDENTIFYING WORKS that are in the public domain due to lack of notice or renewal can be enormously beneficial for readers and researchers, but it can also be a tedious process and fraught with uncertainties. A major project based at the University of Michigan, the Copyright Review Management System (CRMS), had as of 2018 conducted the research and review of 425,544 U.S. works that are included in the HathiTrust Digital Library. The analysis determined that 56.6 percent of those works are in the public domain. Those findings have the potential to open a wealth of materials for public use and enrichment. With further grant funding, the project has now extended to works from several other countries. For more information about the CRMS project, see https://www.hathitrust.org/copyright-review. To access a useful toolkit issued by the CRMS project, visit https://quod.lib.umich.edu/c/crmstoolkit/14616082.0001.001/.

FOREIGN WORKS AND RESTORATION

In general, the fundamental rules of American copyright law apply to domestic as well as to most foreign works that enter the jurisdictional boundaries of the United States. Recall that essential rule: When in the United States, apply U.S. law. Pre-1978 law in the United States, with its formalities and fixed duration, was an international anomaly. For more than a century, many countries had a system of automatic protection lasting for the life of the author plus at least 50 years. The United States went its own direction for most of its history.

The American system was especially troublesome for foreign authors who had the benefit of automatic protection in their home countries but often did not know the distinctive compliance procedures of American law. Many works gained full protection in a foreign country but went into the public domain within U.S. boundaries. The United States faced diplomatic pressures to conform its law to international standards and to remedy the perceived inequitable treatment foreign works received under American law.

The result was a complex twist of international law that restored copyright protection for many foreign works that had entered the public domain inside the United States for lack of compliance with copyright formalities.[19] This outcome produced yet another dose of confusion and unevenness in the law: Many foreign and domestic publications from before 1978 had entered the public domain for failure to comply with formalities of notice and renewal. Domestic works remained in the public domain, while many foreign works were brought back under copyright protection.

THE RESTORATION requirement was initially a limited provision adopted by Congress as part of the North American Free Trade Agreement Act. North American Free Trade Agreement, Pub. L. No. 103-182, 107 Stat. 2057 (1993). Restoration later became more comprehensive under the agreement of the World Trade Organization (WTO). Uruguay Round Agreements Act, Pub. L. No. 103-465, 108 Stat. 4809, 4976 (1994). Which foreign countries have their works restored under U.S. law? Almost all of them, starting with the 164 countries that are members of the WTO. For the latest listing, see http://www.wto.org.

RESTORATION CAN apply to works that have entered the public domain for other reasons too. For example, U.S. copyright did not apply to sound recordings until February 15, 1972. In 1996, many foreign sound recordings from before 1972 were for the first time given federal copyright protection. Recordings from Abbey Road Studios may now have protection, while early recordings from Sun Records in Memphis may not. Keep in mind that this rule applies to only the recordings; the underlying compositions can have a separate copyright. Because pre-1972 recordings have found new markets and have been the subject of expanding litigation, Congress enacted the Music Modernization Act in October 2018, establishing a new form of legal protection akin to copyright for these early recordings. The complex issues of state and federal protection for pre-1972 sound recordings are examined in **Chapter 20** of this book.

The restoration requirement became effective at the beginning of 1996. Copyrights gaining new life at that time continued through the end of the term they otherwise would have received had the copyright owners complied with all formalities.[20] For example, a Swiss publication from 1940 that was not renewed entered the public domain in the United States in 1968. In 1996 it once again—through restoration—became protected by copyright. Had the law not required formalities, American copyright law would have given 95 years of protection to the Swiss publication—until the year 2035. Assuming the work qualified for restoration in 1996, the copyright would resume at that time and continue to that same expiration in 2035.

PRACTICAL LESSONS FOR USERS

What do these rules mean for the user of a pre-1978 work? An early work may well be in the public domain for failure to comply with formalities. To reach that conclusion, however, you may need to investigate the original publication of the work and whether a renewal appears in the records of the Copyright Office. Registration records are public, and the Copyright Office will conduct searches for a fee. Online searches are also available through some database providers.

ANYTIME YOU are tracking an owner or tracing a copyright, keep detailed records of your pursuit and findings. The most immediate source is the registration records of the U.S Copyright Office, searchable from its website. Only records since 1978 are currently available, but the Copyright Office has launched a major project to digitize earlier records. Meanwhile, Stanford University has developed a searchable database that includes some earlier registrations; see https://exhibits.stanford.edu/copyrightrenewals. A highly innovative and ambitious project, initiated at Tulane University and known as the Durationator, allows for determining whether a work is in the public domain under the law of nearly any country in the world; see http://www.limitedtimes.com.

Even works that lacked the formality of renewal or notice may still be protected, if the work originated from one of the many foreign countries enjoying the benefits of the restoration provision. This twist applies to most, but not all, countries, and as usual the law includes many detailed nuances. A user of an early work clearly has a significant research project to complete before determining whether some publications really are in the public domain.

With respect to works created in or after 1978, users need to face the reality that the lack of a copyright notice or registration is not necessarily conclusive. Moreover, given the unusually long period of copyright protection for such newer works, the simple reality is that a user often needs to assume that nearly all recent works are fully protected until learning otherwise from the copyright holder.

IMPORTANT LESSONS FOR OWNERS

It is worth repeating that owners should not overlook the advantages of formalities for new works, even if not required. Placing the copyright notice on your work offers valuable information to readers who might need to locate you for permission or further information. The simple copyright notice can streamline searches for copyright owners and help assure that your interests will be respected. A proper copyright notice also has the legal effect of barring an infringer from claiming to be an "innocent infringer." This limited defense could apply if the user believed the activities were not infringing.[21]

Registering your work with the U.S. Copyright Office offers the practical consequence of creating a public pronouncement of your claim to the copyright as well as providing an address for contacting you. As mentioned earlier, registration additionally grants important legal benefits in the unlikely event of a lawsuit.[22] Those aspects of the law are revisited in Chapter 18, and they will in turn have some surprising and critical implications for librarians and educators who are struggling with fair use and thorny questions of infringement liability.

TO SECURE the full benefits of registration, it usually must be completed before the alleged infringement occurred. *The simple lesson: Register early.* The website of the U.S. Copyright Office includes extensive information, forms, and instructions about registration; see https://www.copyright.gov/registration/. As mentioned in an earlier text box, the U.S. Supreme Court in 2019 decided the case of *Fourth Estate Public Benefit Corp. v. Wall-Street.com*, holding that in fact the registration must be completed in the typical case before filing the lawsuit. Merely submitting the claim form and all other required materials and payment is not enough.

IMPORTANT BENEFITS FOR ALL

Copyright protection exists to encourage creativity, and so does the public domain. When copyrights expire or if owners do not act to claim their rights, that is all part of the copyright equation. Works enter the public domain as part of the tradeoff for legal protection in the first place. The public domain is also a reservoir of materials available to fuel the next generation of creativity. The practical problem for many users of copyrighted works—including librarians, educators, and researchers—is confirming that the work is in fact in the public domain.

> **SOMETIMES A CHART** can help clarify the rules of copyright duration. A fairly simple chart that will likely answer most common situations is included in a guide to copyright issues for graduate students. Kenneth D. Crews, *Copyright and Your Dissertation or Thesis* (ProQuest, 2013), https://media2.proquest.com/documents/copyright_dissthesis_ownership.pdf. A highly detailed chart that delves into the specifics of duration law and even the various interpretations from courts around the country has been prepared and maintained by Peter Hirtle and others at Cornell University. The Cornell chart is available here: https://copyright.cornell.edu/publicdomain.

In principle, the task should be easy, and it sometimes is. For example, select one of the multitudes of early books that you might find in your local library stacks. If all indications are that the book was clearly published in the United States in, say, the year 1900, then you might safely surmise that it is public domain. The maximum protection for such a work under U.S. law is 95 years. On the other hand, look again at the examples earlier in this chapter about books published in 1940 or 1965. In those cases, the copyright duration depends on additional variables and requires more information to resolve. The investigation can be formidable, and the needed information elusive.

One court recently delved into some of these issues in exploring whether copyright protection still applied to the song "Happy Birthday to You." The music and lyrics were created at different times, and the evidence introduced in the litigation enabled the court to trace the music and lyrics to published versions predating 1923. At the time of the litigation, the "1923 rule" applied. As published works from before 1923, the copyrights had run their course. The court ruled that the company asserting a copyright claim and collecting licensing fees could not prove it held any legitimate rights.[23] With no party able to convince the court of a valid copyright, the music and the lyrics have become part of the public domain and available for public use.

Similarly, a company that had been issuing lucrative licenses to use the song "We Shall Overcome" was determined to hold no valid copyright.[24] The court reviewed decades of evidence documenting different versions of the song, its elusive origins in folk and spiritual music, and the revision of lyrics through the years. A version of the song was published and copyrighted in 1948. The claimant failed to renew that copyright after twenty-eight years, placing that version in the public domain in 1976.

The defendant in the litigation was licensing rights in versions of the songs, with some changes in lyrics, that were registered with the U.S. Copyright Office and published in the 1960s. The court

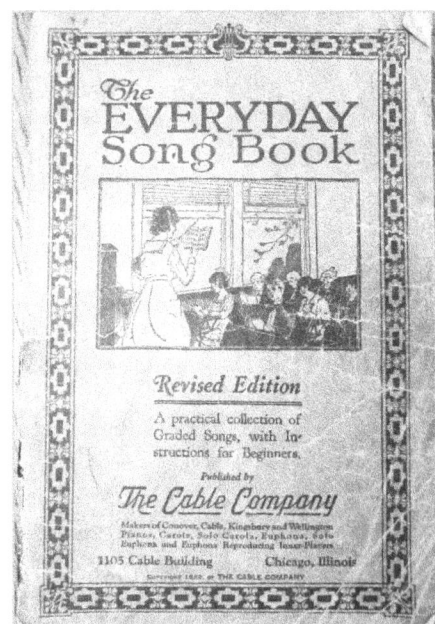

The copyright notice on *The Everyday Song Book* is from 1922, and as a result the content entered the public domain at the end of 1997. Included in the book are the lyrics and music to "Happy Birthday to You."

meticulously compared these versions of the songs from the 1960s with the lyrics that had entered the public domain in 1976. The court concluded that the changes were minor and did not constitute new copyrightable derivatives. As a result, the 1960s versions were also in the public domain, and the current claimant did not have any rights. The familiar opening verse of "We Shall Overcome" was determined to be in the public domain.[25]

These two recent cases are important on many levels. They show vividly that improper rights are often asserted, and that users should look critically at claims of rights and licensing fees for works that have been in existence for many decades and more. The cases demonstrate that proving—and disproving—a copyright claim to early works can be extraordinarily difficult. The needed evidence may be notes and drafts showing the original authorship, the records of ownership and transfers to other parties, and the different versions of a work that may have been created over time. The evidence is seldom available and often lost with aggressive emptying of files and clearing of offices.

Most important, these cases remind us of the importance of the public domain, and that sometimes it is worth the effort to identify new works in the public benefit. At the same time, we need to recognize that not everyone sees the public domain in the same way. The organization that had claimed a copyright in "We Shall Overcome" lamented that by placing it in the public domain, the song would be vulnerable to undesirable and offensive uses, and the stream of royalties would no longer be available to support charitable causes. In the end, the litigation costs began to outstrip the licensing value of the copyright claim.

> **THESE CASES** offer a variety of object lessons. They tell us much about the practical application of the law, and they remind us that protection really does come to an end. Copyright expiration is a good thing, and works in the public domain can be available for public use and become a foundation for future creativity. Determining whether a work is public domain can depend on diligent research into the work's full history of creation and publication. Sometimes the needed facts are long gone, or they surface after rigorous research or just luck. The cases also bring home the reality that some copyrights can be enormously valuable, and litigation can be frightfully demanding and expensive. The parties could litigate "Happy Birthday" because the licensing revenue and the cash value of the song were monumental. However, the loss by Warner/Chappell resulted in its paying tremendous fees and judgments. The party claiming ownership of "We Shall Overcome" was not so flush and ultimately could not justify further litigation; it voluntarily folded its cards. The law can hurt.

NOTES

1. U.S. Copyright Act, 17 U.S.C. § 302. For works that are anonymous or "made for hire," the term is the shorter of 95 years from publication or 120 years from creation.

2. For works created on or after January 1, 1978, copyright vests automatically at the time the work is fixed. U.S. Copyright Act, 17 U.S.C. § 102.

3. U.S. Copyright Act, 17 U.S.C. § 102.

4. Act of May 31, 1790, ch. 15, § 1, 1 Stat. 124 (repealed 1802).

5. The history of American copyright law is recounted in many articles and books, among them are these: Tyler T. Ochoa, "Patent and Copyright Term Extension and the Constitution: A Historical Perspective," *Journal of the Copyright Society of the U.S.A.* 49 (Fall 2001): 19–125; Robert L. Bard and Lewis Kurlantzick, *Copyright Duration: Duration, Term Extension, the European Union and the Making of Copyright Policy* (San Francisco: Austin & Winfield Publishers, 1998).

6. U.S. Copyright Act, 17 U.S.C. §§ 405–406.

7. U.S. Copyright Act, 17 U.S.C. § 304.

8. U.S. Copyright Act, 17 U.S.C. § 302(a).

9. The legal and practical implications of notice and registration are examined in this chapter and in Chapter 18.

10. The same term applies to anonymous and pseudonymous works. U.S. Copyright Act, 17 U.S.C. § 302(c).

11. The concept here is whether the work is a *United States work,* and the definition is fairly elaborate, with diverse rules for unpublished works, audiovisual works, and more. U.S. Copyright Act, 17 U.S.C. § 101.

12. For specific legal benefits afforded by the law, see U.S. Copyright Act, 17 U.S.C. §§ 411–412.

13. At least one court has held that the publication must have occurred in the United States to trigger copyright protection. If the publication occurred only in a foreign country, the absence of a copyright notice did not, according to these controversial rulings, place the work in the public domain under U.S. law. Moreover, the work may be published in the United States at a later date and then secure the benefit of U.S. copyright. *Societe Civile Succession Guino v. Renoir,* 549 F.3d 1182 (9th Cir. 2008).

14. Act of March 4, 1909, ch. 320, §§ 23–24, 35 Stat. 1075, 1080.

15. Sonny Bono Copyright Term Extension Act, Pub. L. No. 105-298, 112 Stat. 2827 (1998), (codified in scattered sections of the U.S. Copyright Act). *See also Eldred v. Ashcroft,* 537 U.S. 186 (2003).

16. U.S. Copyright Act, 17 U.S.C. § 304.

17. Copyright Amendments Act of 1992, Pub. L. No. 102-307, 106 Stat. 264, 266 (1992) (codified at 17 U.S.C. § 304).

18. Of course, all of this is subject to the will of Congress to change the law. I am making no bets.

19. U.S. Copyright Act, 17 U.S.C. § 104A. A court had to address the maze of laws about restoration in order to determine who, if anyone, held a valid U.S. copyright in the ubiquitous troll dolls with rubbery bodies and frenzied hair. *Troll Co. v. Uneeda Doll Co.,* 483 F.3d 150 (2d Cir. 2007).

20. U.S. Copyright Act, 17 U.S.C. § 104A.

21. U.S. Copyright Act, 17 U.S.C. § 401(d).

22. U.S. Copyright Act, 17 U.S.C. §§ 411–412.

23. *Marya v. Warner/Chappell Music, Inc.,* 131 F. Supp. 3d 975 (C.D. Cal. 2015). In a later procedure to conclude the case, the court approved a settlement "that results in a judicial declaration that the song . . . is in the public domain." *Good Morning to You Productions Corp. v. Warner/Chappell Music, Inc.,* 2016 WL 6156076 (C.D. Cal. 2016).

24. *We Shall Overcome Foundation v. The Richmond Organization, Inc.,* 2017 WL 3981311 (S.D.N.Y. 2017).

25. The parties settled the case in January 2018. The litigation concluded with agreement by the copyright claimant to decline asserting any further rights in the music or lyrics and dedicating the song to the public domain. *We Shall Overcome Foundation v. The Richmond Organization, Inc.,* 330 F. Supp. 3d 960 (S.D.N.Y. 2018).

CHAPTER 7

WHO OWNS THE COPYRIGHT?

KEY POINTS

- The creator of a new work is the copyright owner.
- Two or more authors working together may be joint copyright owners.
- The copyright owner of a work made for hire is the employer or commissioning party.
- Copyrights may be transferred by means of a written instrument signed by the copyright owner.
- Institutional policies are important for clarifying or sharing rights to new works, but they may be limited by statutory requirements.

THE PREVIOUS CHAPTERS make the broad and general point that an enormous range of works receives automatic copyright protection. For each work that has copyright protection, the law vests a set of rights—at least initially—with a copyright owner. In many common situations we might easily determine who holds the copyright. Indeed, the general rule is that the person who does the creative work is the author and owns the copyright.[1] If you write the book, you own the copyright. If you take the photograph, you own the copyright. If you design the website, the copyright is yours. The list goes on.

As in much of the law, the answers are not always so easy. The law of copyright ownership has variations and exceptions to the general rule. Moreover, the law is determining only the *initial* copyright owner. You might be the author of a work, and the law might make you the copyright owner. However, you might enter into an agreement that transfers the copyright to a publisher or another party, or you might have chosen to keep ownership of the copyright but convey only certain rights. As a result, being "owner of the copyright" is not necessarily the same as being the "holder of all rights" in the work.

It can get more complicated. Authors and other rightsholders eventually die, and the legal rights are transferred to heirs and beneficiaries—who often have no idea that they now own copyrights. Companies that hold copyrights might be sold or dissolved voluntarily or through bankruptcy. There is also a human dimension to authorship. Minors can be authors and copyright owners. They may, however, need consent from a parent or guardian to enter into agreements and licenses of their copyrights.[2]

Making the news lately has been the nonhuman creator of a work. Computers can generate music. Artificial intelligence can generate many types of creative works. An elephant can hold a brush and make an artistic painting. Courts have had to rule on religious documents that were said to be drafted through divine intervention controlling the human hand. As noted in Chapter 4, we also now have a judicial answer about whether a nonhuman animal can create and own a protected work.[3] The court denied the right of an Indonesian macaque to enforce a copyright claim in a photograph made by the six-year-old animal.

TRACING VARIOUS transfers of the copyright, through contract, death, corporate restructuring, or otherwise is especially important when you need to locate the rightsholder(s) to secure permissions for specific uses. Permissions are explored in Chapter 24. The quest for the current copyright owner of some works can be a detective story and involve contacting various players to let them know that they have the legal rights you need. The quest can also lead to some dead ends—and hence the identification of orphan works—when no current copyright owner can be found.

Amidst all these possibilities, this chapter focuses principally on identifying the initial copyright owner. In that spirit, return to the general rule that the author of the new work is the copyright owner. Some variations on that basic rule are of critical importance and arise often. First, two or more authors can create a work together and own a single copyright jointly. Second, someone might create a new work, but if it is a work made for hire, the copyright belongs to the employer.

JOINT COPYRIGHT OWNERSHIP

Many copyrights are the result of two or more authors working together. Two scientists may write a journal article. Two composers pool their talents to combine music and lyrics into a new song. Three designers might work on a website over a period of months or years. An enterprising class of students might contribute to a mural in the school hall. These works may be owned jointly.

The Copyright Act defines a joint work as "a work prepared by two or more authors with the intention that their contributions be merged into inseparable or interdependent parts of a unitary whole."[4] For example, "inseparable" contributions might be blended into a coauthored textbook or article. "Interdependent" contributions might be the words and music for one song or the text, images, graphics, and software code that constitute a single website.

COPYRIGHT PROTECTION for a jointly owned work usually lasts throughout the life of the last of the authors to die plus 70 more years. U.S. Copyright Act, 17 U.S.C. § 302(b). Clever writers could involve youthful coauthors in order to boost the likelihood of prolonging legal rights. However, keep in mind that if you are one of the joint owners, you may well outlive your coauthor and find yourself sharing legal rights with his or her children, grandchildren, or other heirs who inherit the copyright share.

A joint work must meet two other requirements. First, each coauthor must contribute copyrightable expression to the joint project. If one party gives only an idea for the project, that person has not provided copyrightable expression and therefore is not a joint author under the law.[5] Second, each contributor must have had the intent to create a joint work at the time the work was created. This intent refers to the authors' expectation to be collaborative authors. It does not necessarily mandate that they thought about owner-ship of their work in strictly legal terms.[6] As one court summarized, "the focus is on the parties' intent to work together in the creation of a single product, not on the legal conse-quences of that collaboration."[7]

PROBLEMS WITH JOINT OWNERSHIP

Joint ownership is astonishingly common. It is also a serious management headache. Joint owners of a work each hold an undivided share in the copyright.[8] Each co-owner may use or license the entire work but must account for profits received from use of the work to the other joint owners. On the other hand, a co-owner acting alone cannot transfer the copyright to another party or grant an exclusive right to use the work without the consent of the other co-owners.

Consider this simple example: You and a colleague jointly own the copyright to a research article. Each of you may individually post the paper to your websites. Each of you may permit other scholars and teachers to make and share copies of it. You may even collect a fee for giving nonexclusive permission, but you are liable to your co-owner for a share of the money. Acting alone, however, you cannot transfer the copyright to a publisher or anyone else, whether gratis or for payment, nor can you grant an exclusive license to use the work. For those transactions, all joint owners must participate together.[9]

Joint ownership easily gives rise to many management challenges. It may be lawful for one owner to grant nonexclusive rights, but if a co-owner objects, the relationship will quickly sour. Often the best solution is an agreement between authors, detailing a variety of concerns: Who is able to make decisions about use of the work? Who is responsible for finances? Who will be able to change or update the work? Who can enter into publication agreements? Because one author will almost always outlive the other, joint owners should look ahead. They should plan for the management of their works, anticipating the time when children, grandchildren, and others inherit a share of the copyright.

WORK MADE FOR HIRE

Another exception to the basic rule of copyright ownership is the doctrine of "work made for hire" (WMFH). For these works, the employer of the person who does the creative work is considered the author and the copyright owner.[10] The employer may be a firm, an organi-zation, or an individual. It bears emphasizing that once a work is deemed to be a WMFH, the person who really did the cre-ative work can lose all rights and recognition under the law. The employer steps in as not only the holder of legal rights but also the legally recognized author.

Under the U.S. Copyright Act, the law provides for two basic situations that can give rise to WMFH. The most com-mon situation occurs when an

DETERMINING THAT a work was made for hire has yet other profound legal consequences. These differences drive home the point that all parties should be informed and cautious when deciding whether a work will be created as WMFH.

- Ordinarily copyright lasts for the life of the author plus 70 years. By contrast, a WMFH is protected for the shorter of either 95 years from first publication or 120 years from creation. Chapter 6 provides a detailed look at copyright duration.
- Moral rights explicitly do not apply to a WMFH (see Chapter 8).
- A transfer of the copyright in a WMFH cannot be terminated. The termination of transfers is a technical and powerful device examined later in this chapter.

employee prepares a work within the scope of his or her employment.[11] If the copyrighted work is created under those conditions, the work is deemed to be for hire, and the copyright belongs from the outset to the employer.[12] No further agreement is required.

Examples of possible WMFH created in an employment relationship include the following:[13]

- Guides and manuals prepared by librarians or IT staff as part of their duties for an employer
- Reports and studies written by staff members employed by an independent research organization
- Software programs created by a staff programmer for Creative Computer Corporation
- Newspaper articles written by a staff journalist for publication in a daily newspaper
- Musical arrangements written for XYZ Music Company by a salaried arranger on its staff

A second WMFH situation involves independent contractors (as opposed to employees). Here the statute becomes more exacting. Such a work is for hire only if it is "specially ordered or commissioned" and is among the types of works itemized in the statute.[14] The statute specifies that this version of WMFH can apply only to works made

- for use as a contribution to a collective work;
- as a part of a motion picture or other audiovisual works;
- as a translation;
- as a supplementary work;
- as a compilation;
- as an instructional text;
- as a test;
- as answer material for a test; or
- as an atlas.

> **THE DEFINITIONS** of these labels make all the difference in the meaning and application of the law. The same statute that includes the list provides only two definitions:
>
> > For the purpose of the foregoing sentence, a "supplementary work" is a work prepared for publication as a secondary adjunct to a work by another author for the purpose of introducing, concluding, illustrating, explaining, revising, commenting upon, or assisting in the use of the other work, such as forewords, afterwords, pictorial illustrations, maps, charts, tables, editorial notes, musical arrangements, answer material for tests, bibliographies, appendixes, and indexes, and an "instructional text" is a literary, pictorial, or graphic work prepared for publication and with the purpose of use in systematic instructional activities. U.S. Copyright Act, 17 U.S.C. § 101.
>
> Look at that last definition. If I write a book to inform readers about copyright, the copyright in that book might be mine. If I write a book with the objective that it might be adopted for use in teaching, it could be a work made for hire, depending on the terms of my signed agreement. The most fundamental lesson merits repeating: Be careful about what you sign.

Even meeting those requirements is not enough for this version of WMFH; the parties must also expressly agree in a written instrument—signed by *both* parties—that the work shall be considered a WMFH. Only then will the new work be deemed "for hire," with all rights belonging to the hiring party.[15] Imagine you are the person who creates the new work under the right conditions and you are being asked to sign an agreement with the person who commissioned you. If that agreement has the right WMFH language, you could be losing your copyright. Be careful about what you sign. On the other hand, if you are enlisting talented collaborators for an expensive motion picture or other costly work, you might have good reason to structure the arrangement as for hire.

WHO IS AN EMPLOYEE?

One of the most important and sometimes difficult issues surrounding the WMFH doctrine centers on whether an "employee" or an "independent contractor" created the work. The law sometimes applies technical definitions of these terms that may not match common perceptions. The result can have profound implications for copyright ownership. For example, simply because you have paid money for a work does not make it for hire. You might pay a computer programmer a vast fortune to rework your business systems or give a photographer a tidy sum for shots of your kids, but payment alone does not make the programmer or photographer an employee. The freelance programmer and the photography studio are most likely independent contractors, and they hold the copyrights unless you agree otherwise. They also get to keep the money you paid them.

An independent contractor and an employee may work side-by-side on similar projects, only to have radically diverging ownership results. A newspaper may have full-time staff reporters. If they are employees, their articles are WMFH. A reporter at the next desk, however, may be an independent contractor. That reporter's articles are WMFH only if they qualify under the statute and the reporter and the employer have entered into a written agreement that the articles will be regarded as for hire. Remember, too, that a work of an independent contractor can be a WMFH only if it is on the list in the statute. News articles are not on the list, but the statute does encompass a "contribution to a collective work." That could be an article in a newspaper.

Educational institutions and libraries often retain independent contractors without necessarily attending to the question of WMFH copyright ownership. The organization may pay substantial amounts for the services of photographers, video producers, or public relations firms to prepare publications, websites, and glossy brochures, only later to discover that the hired contractors retain the copyrights and can control the use of the materials. A photographer can therefore ask for more money with each use of the pictures; the public relations firm can object when the images and words of a brochure are later restructured for the university website.

Leaving rights with the contractor may be perfectly acceptable in many situations, but the parties involved in each situation should always reach decisions carefully and deliberately. The parties have several choices. For example, they could agree to make the work for hire. They could leave the copyright with the contractor but agree to a license of rights to the hiring party. They could also choose *not* to make the work for hire and instead enter into a transfer of the copyright from the contractor. Each option is best undertaken with attention to details, and each option has distinct advantages and disadvantages.

TRANSFERS OF COPYRIGHT AND OPEN ACCESS

Transfers of copyrights are common in industry practice and in much academic work as well. Copyrights can be bought, sold, or simply given away. A transfer of a copyright—or an exclusive grant or license to use the work—is a transaction that must be in writing and must be signed by the copyright owner making the transfer.[16] Assume you write a song or create a painting and hold the copyright. You could give away or sell the copyright to those works, but the transfer is legally valid *only* if the terms of the transfer are in writing and the document is signed by you as the transferor.

Transferring the object itself is distinct from transferring the copyright. Consider the simple example of buying a book. You can enter the store and pay a price, but you walk out with only the book, not the copyright. The same is true in larger and pricier transactions.

You may be a successful artist and sell a painting to an appreciative collector for a hefty price. Selling the painting does not include a sale of the copyright, unless you specifically document the copyright transfer in a signed instrument. Neither a high price nor an oral statement of transfer will substitute for the statutory requirements.

In the academic world, many authors routinely transfer copyrights, but standard practices are changing. A professor writes an article and, barring application of WMFH, owns the copyright. Some journal publishers, however, upon accepting an article

AUTHORS WHO are faced with a publication contract that seeks transfer of the copyright should not hesitate to negotiate new terms or at least reserve rights to use their own works in future teaching and writing. If the negotiation is not satisfactory, authors should find a different publisher altogether. Academic authors should be especially watchful for any contract language that would make their works for hire. As emphasized in this chapter, the implications of the WMFH status can be profound. The SHERPA/RoMEO Project offers numerous examples of the terms of publication agreements; see http://www.sherpa.ac.uk/romeo/.

for publication, require that the author transfer the copyright to the publisher through the terms of the written and signed publication agreement. Not all journal publishers require assignment of the copyright. Publishers are increasingly employing a license, which usually leaves more rights with authors than does a full assignment of the copyright.

Many universities, libraries, research foundations, and other organizations have sought to push back against allowing faculty members and other authors to transfer all rights to publishers. Academic authors regularly need to hold some rights to build on their own scholarship and share research output with students, colleagues, and the wider community. The open access movement has proven to be a powerful and important initiative for organizations seeking to manage the rights of their authors. They implement it through formal policy that requires authors to grant the institution at least a license to deposit a version of each published journal article and some other works for online and cost-free public access through a digital repository. Harvard University was a prominent leader in shaping the movement and policy terms.

IN LITTLE more than a decade, literally hundreds of colleges, universities, and other organizations in numerous countries have adopted open access policies. They are listed and searchable in the Registry of Open Access Repository Mandates and Policies, also known as ROARMAP; see http://roarmap.eprints.org. At that website, you can browse long lists of institutions that have joined the effort, and links will take you to their specific policy language. The website also permits browsing by geography, revealing the strong influence of the policies in Europe, North America, and other parts of the world.

The policies vary widely in their terms and application. Some policies apply to only published journal articles; some apply only after an embargo of a year or other term following publication; some allow faculty authors to request a waiver. Nevertheless, researchers and other authors are giving greater attention to their publication agreements and policy requirements, and publishers have begun accepting that interests and expectations surrounding scholarly publishing have changed dramatically in recent years. The expectations of the publication infrastructure are changing steadily as authors, readers, and publishers take advantage of the flexibilities in law and technology.

Whether or not a publication might be subject to an open access policy, authors and publishers need to bear in mind that they have choices. A sweeping transfer of the copyright is seldom essential. Many publishers will negotiate terms of their agreements, and some

MANY GROUPS that fund research, such as the Wellcome Trust, also have adopted policies requiring open access of studies that result from their financial support. These initiatives have been strongly influential, especially when researchers know that their ability to secure future funding might depend on following through with the obligation to make previous studies publicly accessible. Similarly, many government agencies from numerous countries support new research and have adopted open access policies. In the United States, the National Institutes of Health was a leader, requiring deposit of articles in the PubMed Central database. More recently, dozens of U.S. federal agencies have followed the example pursuant to a policy implemented during the administration of President Barack Obama. The policies from funders and government agencies are also listed in the ROARMAP database.

even have alternative versions that offer greater rights to authors—but you need to raise questions and open a conversation in order to successfully negotiate for a better agreement.

In addition, deep in the Copyright Act is the concept of *termination of transfers*.[17] If you have transferred your copyright, or even granted a license to it, you have the right under law to reclaim your copyright. A window of opportunity to make that claim opens in most instances thirty-five years after making the transfer. Many authors, and their heirs, are discovering the value of recovering ownership of their copyrights in early books, music, art, and other works. An academic author who published a chemistry article in 1988, for example, may want to consider starting the process of terminating the copyright transfer and regaining ownership for the future.

THE STATUTORY provision and process for terminating a transfer is thick with details that must be followed with care. The window generally opens after thirty-five years, but a few alternative calculations might apply. The process begins with a notice to the current copyright holder, and the contents of the notice are elaborated in the law. The timing of the notice is critical. It must be made at least two years, but not more than ten years, before the designated termination date. Finally, the claim must be recorded with the U.S. Copyright Office before the termination date. Slip up, and the termination could fail. Adding to the mystique, the right to terminate generally belongs to the original author, with the statute detailing how rights are shared among spouse and descendants in the event of the author's demise. Don't be discouraged. But do get good advice and guidance.

INSTITUTIONAL COPYRIGHT POLICIES

These rules of copyright ownership, notably the rules of the WMFH doctrine, do not always apply clearly and neatly. Sometimes, to resolve doubts and lingering questions, an author and an employer may need a contract to specify the allocation of rights to use the work and the distribution of royalties or income. Many academic institutions develop formal policies in an effort to clarify whether new works belong to the institution or to the author.

The custom at most colleges and universities is for faculty authors to retain the copyrights in their scholarly works, or at least for the institutions not to assert rights of ownership in such works. That standard practice has served a variety of goals, both managerial and philosophical, and it is usually articulated in institutional policies and sometimes employment agreements.[18] The need for innovative and nuanced policies has escalated as technology and law have become more versatile.

Some rethinking of the convention of policymaking is taking place around the country as the nature of academic work changes, along with the expansion of possibilities for creating and using new works. For example, the growth of distance education and the considerable financial consequences of creating and marketing some new works have led to reexamination of conventional concepts of intellectual property at educational institutions. Online courses in particular are sometimes best managed through a sharing of rights between the instructor and the institution.[19] An agreement can allow the interested parties to allocate to each other specific and separate sets of rights, rather than one party owning the copyright and all rights. The open access movement is another departure from publishing conventions and a promotion of sharing rights of access and use.

Adding to the growing need to rethink copyright management, recent court rulings have drawn into question the effectiveness of institutional policies.[20] Some courts also have concluded that general policy statements may not be sufficient to effect a transfer of the copyright to the employee. The Copyright Act specifies that a WMFH belongs to the employer who holds the rights, "unless the parties have expressly agreed otherwise in a written instrument signed by them."[21] A general policy, however, is not ordinarily signed by the parties to each individual transfer of rights.

Thus, many works created at colleges and universities may in fact be recognized under the law as "for hire," even though customary policy and practice seek to place the copyright with the author of a scholarly book or article.

Thoughtful policies and agreements also offer the opportunity to share or unbundle the rights that would normally vest with a single copyright owner. Placing all rights with either the individual author or the employer can give rise to conflicts between the parties. Instead, agreements that detail allocation of rights among the parties may allow a work to be used by the author and the institution simultaneously, effectively, and equitably. Policymakers now often look beyond simple formulas to find creative and desirable solutions to the challenges of copyright ownership.

> **AT LEAST** one court has been critical of the ability of a general copyright policy at a university to reverse the legal conclusion that a work created by a staff employee was made for hire: "The Policy is patently inadequate to overcome the presumption of Brown's ownership under the work made for hire doctrine." *Forasté v. Brown University*, 248 F. Supp. 2d 71, 81 (D.R.I. 2003). A policy is important, and a policy can articulate the decisions and the values of the individuals and the institution. Sometimes, a policy also needs to be backed up with a written and signed agreement.

> **THE CONCEPT** of "unbundling" the rights of copyright ownership has roots in a project that started at California State University. The author of this book contributed substantially to that initiative. One outcome was a pamphlet titled *Ownership of New Works at the University: Unbundling of Rights and the Pursuit of Higher Learning* (CETUS, 1997) that presents the unbundling perspective. The pamphlet is archived here: https://doi.org/10.7916/D8FT8VS1.

CHANGING NEEDS AND INNOVATIVE POSSIBILITIES

This chapter is a general overview of principles of copyright ownership, but it reveals many underlying complications in the law. Sometimes the law's reach is unclear. Is the author an employee or independent contractor? Have the authors properly complied with all steps and procedures to effectively convey ownership or control of rights in the work to another person? Even if we can clearly identify the copyright owner (or owners) under the law, is that the result that makes most sense and seems most fair? Should the owner or other parties share rights with others or even relinquish rights?

Faced with such questions, diligent management of copyrights has become increasingly important. Put more bluntly, the rules of law about copyright ownership are often unsatisfactory for the changing needs of education, research, librarianship, and even publishing. If you are expecting the law to deliver the best results, you are sure to be disappointed.

Consequently, many innovations in copyright ownership and management are becoming widely accepted as an alternative to relying on just the law. Consider again the following developments that are today actively realigning the relationship between copyright and the many authors, libraries, educators, researchers, students, and organizations that are directly affected by the law.

Institutional Policymaking

In spite of—and maybe because of—legal principles about WMFH and copyright transfers, an innovative institutional policy is a vital part of determining copyright ownership and the possible sharing of rights. A policy can go far to clarify the expectations of the college, university, library, or other organization regarding the ownership of copyrights for works created by faculty, staff, students, and anyone else.

Creative Commons

Authors are now choosing to make many of their works available to the public under a Creative Commons (CC) license. This voluntary system is essentially a grant of permission to the public to use the work for certain purposes. One of the most common options permits any "noncommercial" uses of the work with attribution to the author or source. A work marked with that CC license may be used by anyone for, say, nonprofit education, provided the copies include the author's name or other identification.[22]

Publication Agreements

The terms of agreements for the publication of articles, books, and other works are becoming more nuanced. Publication agreements have existed for centuries, but they have become more often a platform for reallocating ownership and use of works. More publishers are accepting only a license of rights and allowing authors to explicitly retain certain rights for use of the publication. Many publishers are willing to negotiate terms, and authors should choose publishers who demonstrate flexibility.[23]

Open Access Publishers

Internet technologies have facilitated and expanded the alternatives for publishing, and they make a wealth of content available to readers worldwide. Many journals, books, and other publications are now by choice published online, making the content available in full on the Internet, without restriction. Readers may now find a growing roster of publications, openly available for reading and study. Open access is a choice made by the copyright owner—not to relinquish rights, but to use the legal rights in order to make the work easily accessible. Choosing open access may be a decision to give up some subscription revenue, but it is also a decision to boost readership and to promote the availability of scholarship and information resources.[24]

Open Access Policies and Mandates

A growing list of universities, funding agencies, and other organizations now requires that many publications be made open access. These initiatives have drawn wide attention to the possibilities of open access and have given the notion an important boost in credibility.[25]

These examples are only an indication of the transformation of copyright ownership and management in the academic and library communities. Yet each of these possibilities is an innovation built on the foundation of the law. The law becomes a default, and from that starting point copyright owners can determine how they may share or assert rights or creatively grant rights for the further use of their works. All of these initiatives require care and attention. If copyright owners do not take deliberate steps, the default principles of copyright ownership will apply to their works, and the benefits of creative stewardship will be lost. Investment of time evaluating the right options for managing copyright ownership is time wisely spent.

NOTES

1. "Copyright in a work protected under this title vests initially in the author or authors of the work." U.S. Copyright Act, 17 U.S.C. § 201.

2. *I.C. ex rel. Solovsky v. Delta Galil USA*, 135 F. Supp. 3d 196 (S.D.N.Y. 2015) (a second-grade student won the competition for a T-shirt design and could hold the copyright).

3. *Naruto v. Slater*, 888 F.3d 418 (9th Cir. 2018).

4. U.S. Copyright Act, 17 U.S.C. § 101.

5. *Gaiman v. McFarlane*, 360 F.3d 644, 658 (7th Cir. 2004).

6. *Erickson v. Trinity Theatre, Inc.*, 13 F.3d 1061 (7th Cir. 1994).

7. *Janky v. Lake County Convention & Visitors Bureau*, 576 F.3d 356, 362 (7th Cir. 2009), *cert. denied*, 559 U.S. 992 (2010).

8. U.S. Copyright Act, 17 U.S.C. § 201(a).

9. U.S. Copyright Act, 17 U.S.C. § 204(a).

10. U.S. Copyright Act, 17 U.S.C. § 201(b).

11. In *Community for Creative Non-Violence v. Reid*, 490 U.S. 730 (1989), the Supreme Court adopted a set of factors established in the common law as the definition of "employee" for purposes of determining WMFH.

12. U.S. Copyright Act, 17 U.S.C. § 201(b).

13. Some of the examples listed here were in an early version of one of the helpful publications from the U.S. Copyright Office. The Copyright Office issues a long list of Circulars addressing many issues in the law in clear language. For the full list, *see* https://www.copyright.gov/circs/.

14. See the definition of "work made for hire" at U.S. Copyright Act, 17 U.S.C. § 101.

15. For an example of a court working through the detailed requirements of employment and work made for hire, *see Myers v. Harold*, 279 F. Supp. 3d 778 (N.D. Ill. 2017). The court held that instructional materials prepared by a part-time dance teacher were not WMFH.

16. U.S. Copyright Act, 17 U.S.C. § 204.

17. For transfers or licenses executed on or after January 1, 1978, the window of opportunity generally opens after thirty-five years. U.S. Copyright Act, 17 U.S.C. § 203. For grants made before that date, the opportunity first opens after fifty-six years. U.S. Copyright Act, 17 U.S.C. § 304(c). In either situation, the law can be enormously important to authors, but the details of the law may require expert counsel.

18. Because many works created by faculty members, including teaching materials and scholarly works, could be WMFH, an agreement may be necessary in order to move the copyright ownership to the individual. *See*, for example, *Vanderhurst v. Colorado Mountain College Dist.*, 16 F. Supp. 2d 1297 (D. Colo. 1998). The same Colorado court, in an unrelated case, ruled that a professor's research article could also be WMFH. *The University of Colorado Foundation, Inc. v. American Cyanamid Co.*, 880 F. Supp. 1387 (D. Colo. 1995), *aff'd in part*, 196 F.3d 1366 (Fed. Cir. 1999).

19. Management of the right of ownership in online courses is examined in Chapter 15.

20. *Forasté v. Brown University*, 248 F. Supp. 2d 71 (D.R.I. 2003) (finding that the university policy did not alter ownership of photographs made by a university employee); and *Manning v. Parkland College*, 109 F. Supp. 2d 976 (C.D. Ill. 2000) (finding that the university policy did not alter ownership of instructional materials).

21. U.S. Copyright Act, 17 U.S.C. § 201(b).

22. The several different CC licenses are summarized here: https://creativecommons.org/licenses/. Multitudes of works are now available with CC licenses, whether online or in print. The CC website hosts a portal that allows easy searching of some of the largest collections of CC-licensed works. *See* https://search.creativecommons.org.

23. Mentioned earlier in this chapter is the SHERPA/RoMEO collection of publication agreements, allowing authors to review a publisher's standard agreement before sending a manuscript. *See* http://www.sherpa.ac.uk/romeo/index.php.

24. The Directory of Open Access Journals, a searchable database of open access publications, is available here: https://doaj.org.

25. Policies from throughout the world are collected and searchable here: http://roarmap.eprints.org.

CHAPTER 8

THE RIGHTS OF COPYRIGHT OWNERS

KEY POINTS

- For most works, copyright owners have exclusive rights to
  - reproduce the work;
  - distribute the work;
  - prepare derivative works;
  - publicly display the work; and
  - publicly perform the work.
- Some "works of visual art" also have moral rights, including the right to attribution and to prevent destruction of the works.
- Congress has responded to technological change by granting additional rights with respect to some works, particularly digital audio transmissions and the protection of digital rights management.

THE OWNER OF the copyright to a specific work has certain exclusive rights with respect to the work. In this context, "exclusive" means that only the copyright owner may exercise those rights and other individuals may not—unless authorized by the owner. For example, the owner of the copyright holds rights to make copies. Because the rights are exclusive to the owner, copies made by someone else without authorization are infringements. On the other hand, a copyright owner does not have all possible rights; Congress has provided only certain legal rights, and they are subject to the various limitations and exceptions detailed in other chapters of this book.

Section 106 of the Copyright Act itemizes the central rights,[1] often called the economic rights, that apply to most copyrighted works:

- The right to reproduce the work in copies
- The right to distribute the work in copies to the public
- The right to make derivative works
- The right to display the work publicly
- The right to perform the work publicly

These rights of owners, combined with the exceptions examined in later chapters, are fundamental to the concept of copyright law. By defining the rights, the law defines the range of possible infringements. You can violate the law only by infringing rights held by the owner. For example, a copyright owner has rights of public performance. The ability to control *private* performances of a work is not within the owner's rights, and therefore you may play music at a home party or act out a play for a small gathering.

This chapter demonstrates that these rights are hardly static. Congress has revised the statutes through the years, progressively expanding the legal rights. In the meantime, courts have regularly redefined and applied the law for new situations and needs. While this chapter also demonstrates that conflicts with the rights of copyright owners can occur easily and frequently, not all of these encounters are legal infringements. Many of the common uses of works that appear to be copyright violations may prove to be within fair use or other exceptions to the rights of owners. Those possibilities are addressed in Chapters 9 through 17.

Chapter 6 highlighted the growing duration of copyright protection through the past two centuries. Rights of copyright owners similarly have expanded steadily. The first U.S. copyright statute, in 1790, granted only rights to make copies of works. Congress added performance rights in 1831, permitting musicians and playwrights to control live performances and not merely sales of copies. The Act of 1909 expanded the list of owners' rights to something generally similar to the current law. The scope of rights, and thus the scope of lawful and unlawful uses, has been shifting for far more than 200 years, clearly in the direction of boosting owners' rights.

REPRODUCTION AND DISTRIBUTION RIGHTS

The right of reproduction of a work is fundamental and perhaps the easiest to grasp. Reproducing a work occurs in many circumstances and by means of a vast range of technological tools. You reproduce works when photocopying pages from a text, when quoting a sentence in a new article, and even when taking verbatim notes from research materials. You

The reproduction and display rights might rear up when a musical composition is painted on the exterior of a building. This example is a now-shuttered location of 101 Music in San Francisco.

reproduce works when scanning a cartoon into your computer to show in class and when digitizing images for a website or downloading works from the Internet.

You even reproduce works when you make a video of an urban street scene. The buildings, billboards, public art, and even music blaring in the background may be copyrighted works, now captured as copies by your pocket digital camera or mobile phone. As courts struggled to apply the law to new computer technology, an early ruling concluded that loading software onto a computer's random-access memory, or RAM, is a form of reproduction.[2]

Distributions are also surprisingly common. The possibilities are numerous: materials handed out in the classroom, pictures transmitted with a click on a website, documents attached to e-mails, and books sold in stores and even checked out of the library. A distribution involves the transfer of possession of a copy of a work. Many distributions could simultaneously be reproductions. Posting a document to a website may be a single reproduction. Each time a user accesses and downloads the work can be a further act of reproduction. It may also be an electronic distribution of the copy from the server to the user's computer. By contrast, simply linking to materials found at another site is ordinarily not a violation of either reproduction or distribution rights. Linking is merely a technological instruction for finding materials and therefore the linking alone does not produce a copy.[3]

The copyright owner has rights with respect to only distributions of copies made "to the public." Privately lending a book to a friend is not made to the public, but a library open for general use, or a store looking for maximum sales, is most certainly distributing to the public, regardless of costs and conditions. Of course, these transactions occur uncountable times each day without legal threat. Why? Because they are explicitly encompassed by an important exception in the law called the *first sale doctrine* (a principle that is explored further in Chapter 9).

DERIVATIVE WORKS

Of all rights of the copyright owner, the right to make derivative works has the most manifestations and may therefore defy pithy definition. Yet examples are common and familiar. A derivative work, as defined in the statutes, is "a work based upon one or more preexisting works, such as a translation, musical arrangement, dramatization, fictionalization, motion picture version, sound recording, art reproduction, abridgment, condensation, or any other form in which a work may be recast, transformed, or adapted."[4]

Movies are familiar examples of derivatives. An author writes the novel and owns the copyright to it. Another writer creates a derivative screenplay, and the motion picture studio makes a derivative of the novel and screenplay when producing the film. If the authors and studios are lucky, the movie is a hit, and more derivatives are forthcoming: toys, games, books, soundtrack albums, sequels, and much more. Writers, artists, composers, publishers, studios, and many others are lining up lawyers and money to cut the deals. Disney movies are often platforms for creative derivatives, including theme parks, Happy Meals, Halloween costumes, and ice shows.

The legal rights and financial investments in these deals regularly lead to elaborate licensing agreements, which in part grant either extensive or limited rights to use the copyrighted work. Academic works are seldom so complex, but the same concepts still arise. A professor writes a great algebra textbook, and agreements with publishers often contemplate derivatives, such as teacher's manuals, quiz banks and answer guides, website updates, translations, and even future revised editions of the book. All of these are derivatives, and a good publication agreement will address the right to create them and who receives payment. A good agreement will also specify who owns the copyright in any new derivative.

Derivative works come in many forms, and a painting might form the inspiration for toys, novels, movies, clothing designs, and much more. Johannes Vermeer could have a host of legal claims to pursue, but his seventeenth-century paintings are now safely in the public domain and available for public use without copyright restrictions. The reproduction of the painting is courtesy of Wikipedia.

When a copyright owner authorizes someone to make a derivative, it is not unusual for the copyright owner to assert some level of control over the resulting work. Photographers often control how an image might be shaded or cropped. Composers might require approval of any changes to a musical work. The estate of Harper Lee authorized a Broadway stage version of *To Kill a Mockingbird*, but it reserved the right to approve the production before its opening on Broadway. The estate challenged the depiction of characters in the play but settled the case without the changes it had demanded. Even though no court ruled in this dispute, the fact that the parties struggled over their rights will likely drive attorneys in future deals to draft even more rigorous language, asserting clearer and tighter control.

The list of possible derivative works is extensive: an index to a book, a sound recording of a musical composition, an abridgement of a novel, or a translation of an existing work. On the other hand, a work is not likely to be a derivative if it merely reproduces the original or changes the medium. Simple digitization of works is probably not derivative, nor would be a ceramic cast or 3-D print version of a bronze statue.[5] Those examples might violate a copyright owner's reproduction right, but not the right to create derivatives.

Derivative works sometimes create conundrums. Consider a simple example: The original version of an ancient Greek poem may have no legal protection, but a new translation of the poem is a derivative. The translation, however, is itself a new original work entitled to independent copyright protection. Thus, a movie based on the original poem may be a derivative, but no permission is

A DIGITAL version of a photograph showing a cityscape, significantly altered, is a derivative work. *Tiffany Design, Inc. v. Reno-Tahoe Specialty, Inc.*, 55 F. Supp. 2d 1113 (D. Nev. 1999). A court has ruled that an answer manual to accompany a textbook is an infringing derivative work. *Pearson Education, Inc. v. Nugroho*, 2009 WL3429610. A performance and a recording can be derivatives of a musical composition. A dance routine choreography can be a derivative of a ballet. A play can be made into a movie. The movie can become the basis of a stage musical. That musical production can lead to another movie. Perhaps at the root of it all is a novel or biography, and maybe the latest incarnation is built around a series of ABBA songs with altered lyrics. Layers and layers of derivatives.

THE MOTION PICTURE *300* is clearly a copyrighted work, released in 2007, but it retells the story of the Battle of Thermopylae in the year 480 BC. The movie is explicitly a derivative of a graphic novel with the same title from 1998. The novel in turn is apparently derivative of ancient stories that are public domain. However, if the novelist and filmmakers used copyrighted expression from modern translations, they may have infringed copyrights. More complicated, the novelist was reportedly inspired by another movie from 1962. Did he recast, transform, or adapt anything from the 1962 film? Tracing rights and uses can be complicated and intriguing.

needed to make a derivative of a public domain work. However, if the movie is based on a copyrighted translation, permission from the translator is in order. The public domain is actually a rich resource for the movie industry. The novels of Jane Austen and the plays of Shakespeare continue to yield fresh movie versions. Even *The 9/11 Commission Report*, a U.S. government work—and thus in the public domain—was turned into a film version for ABC Television and a graphic book.[6]

Whether the movie is a derivative of the original or a derivative of a derivative (e.g., of a translation), the filmmaker can have copyright protection for the new movie. But be careful. A derivative work that is made without authorization from the copyright owner of the original work, if not within fair use or another exception, can be an infringement and may not be eligible for legal protection.[7] The lesson is fairly simple: Be sure to check with the copyright owner or the applicable exceptions and limitations before investing time and energy to make or use a derivative work.

PUBLIC PERFORMANCE AND DISPLAY

Performances and displays are common occurrences in higher education and libraries. A display can be the simple showing of a page of text, a picture, or other static work. A work can be performed in many ways: when text is read aloud, when lines of a play are recited or acted, when a videotape or a film is shown on a screen or monitor, or when a song is played or sung aloud. The performance or display becomes a possible infringement only when it is public.[8] A public performance or display occurs, among other circumstances, when it is offered to a substantial number of persons beyond the usual circle of friends, family, and social acquaintances.[9]

We frequently make public displays and performances of copyrighted works. Up and down the halls of libraries, schools, and museums one can find scores of pictures, essays, and books out for public viewing. Why are schools not liable for pinning student essays on the bulletin boards or for hanging pictures on the walls? Why are libraries not liable for placing their collections in public view? Why are museums still in business?

The legal answers to these questions lie in the exceptions to the rights of owners. The rights of owners are tempered by exceptions or limitations that are further detailed in

PART OF the definition of public performance in the Copyright Act is based on the concept of transmitting the copyrighted content to the public or others. The Supreme Court ruled in 2014 on a case involving the ability to capture free, public television signals and resend them from a "farm" of individual antennas to individual subscribers at home. *American Broadcasting Companies, Inc. v. Aereo, Inc.*, 573 U.S. 431 (2014). For users in big cities, where tall buildings and other structures can block signals, this service was widely appreciated. The Supreme Court resolved, however, that the act of resending signals from a rooftop farm of antennas to home users scattered throughout the city is a transmission and hence a public performance. The service needed to secure a license, but the broadcasters sending the free TV signals were not willing to reach an agreement. The service has been shut down.

Chapter 9 and elsewhere in this book. The U.S. Copyright Act includes several important exceptions to the performance and display rights of the copyright owner. A specific exception to the copyright owner's display right allows the owner of an original work or a lawfully made copy of the work, such as a painting, a poster, or a photograph, to display that work where it is physically located. Thus, the museum can hang art on the walls, a teacher can put posters in the classroom, the library can put books in display cases, and you can project slides onto a screen.[10]

THE GENEROUS provision for performances and displays of copyrighted works in the classroom serves many daily needs of teachers. U.S. Copyright Act, 17 U.S.C. § 110(1). However, it does not explicitly allow the making of copies; it references only displays and performances. It also does not apply to distance learning. The TEACH Act restructured the law for distance education in 2002 and is examined in detail in Chapter 16. A roster of various other exceptions is surveyed in Chapter 9.

However, no similarly broad exception applies to performances. Consequently, no statutory exception covers the prospect of showing a movie in an auditorium or acting out a play on a school stage. On the other hand, a statutory exception permits *displays and performances* in the context of face-to-face classroom instruction.[11] Therefore, teachers and students in the traditional classroom setting may read text, recite poetry, play videos, sing songs, show art slides, project websites on a screen, and show an entire feature film. This particular statute is written in such a way that it might also permit displays and performances at library events that have an educational purpose.[12]

MORAL RIGHTS

As an obligation of joining the Berne Convention, Congress supplemented the rights of authors with the concept of moral rights.[13] Under the laws of many other countries, moral rights apply to many different types of works and grant extensive rights against alterations or revisions of works and the right to have the author's name on copies of the work. Moral rights under American law are extraordinarily limited by comparison. Moral rights in the United States grant to an artist the right to have his or her name kept on the work or to have the artist's name removed from it if the work has been altered in a way objectionable to the artist. Moral rights also give artists limited abilities to prevent their works from being defaced or destroyed.[14]

Perhaps most constraining, moral rights in American copyright apply to only a narrow class of "works of visual art."[15] Moral rights generally apply to only original works of art, sculpture, and other works of visual art that are produced in 200 or fewer copies.[16] For example, moral rights may apply to a limited series lithograph but likely do not apply to a photograph used in a mass-market magazine. Any work made for hire is also excluded from the scope of works that can enjoy moral rights.[17]

BECAUSE MORAL RIGHTS under the U.S. Copyright Act apply to only certain artworks, that limited scope leaves authors of books, articles, and other works without benefit of those rights. One court further denied an author's claim of common law moral rights when his scholarly article was published with numerous typographical and factual errors. *Choe v. Fordham University School of Law*, 920 F. Supp. 44 (S.D.N.Y. 1995), aff'd, 81 F.3d 319 (2d Cir. 1996).

A leading case on the issue of moral rights awarded monetary damages to an artist whose work was intentionally destroyed. The federal district court ruled that the city of Indianapolis violated the moral rights of a sculptor when

Destroying or defacing a work of art might violate copyright law as well as various local ordinances. This warning is posted at the Beach Boys Historic Landmark in Hawthorne, California. It was evidently not a violation of rights to have demolished their childhood house at that location in order to build a freeway.

the city demolished his large metalwork that had been installed on city property.[18] More recently, a court awarded $6.75 million in damages to graffiti artists when the owner of the 5Pointz building in Brooklyn, New York, whitewashed it in preparation for demolition of the structure.[19]

DIGITAL AUDIO TRANSMISSIONS

Not all rights apply to all types of works. Music especially receives peculiar treatment in this regard under the U.S. Copyright Act in many respects—including oddly different rights of public performance. For example, Congress began applying the performance right to musical compositions as early as 1856. However, sound recordings first gained federal copyright protection only as of February 15, 1972.[20]

Even when Congress granted rights to sound recordings, it allowed rights of reproduction and distribution—and some derivative rights—but it did not grant public performance rights. Therefore, when a radio station played a new song on the air, the composer had a performance right and could receive a royalty. By contrast, the owner of the separate copyright to the recording had no performance rights and was not entitled to any payment. When copies of the recording were sold, in physical format or as downloads, each sale implicated the reproduction and distribution rights. Thus, the copyright owners of both the composition and the recording had rights and could be paid.

The development of the Internet as a medium for delivering music has almost eliminated sales of CDs and other copies of recordings. If a user can receive transmitted performances of selected recordings on demand, the user has little need to buy CDs or even downloads.[21] To protect the interests of copyright owners of the recordings, in 1995 Congress granted performance rights, but only in the context of "digital audio performances."[22]

The sound recordings statute is relentlessly complex and runs for pages of convoluted conditions and exceptions.[23] In general, an "interactive" digital system—including a website—that delivers recordings on demand may now implicate the performance rights of both the composer and the performer. The result is an awkward patchwork of rights. When the latest hits from Post Malone or Lizzo are broadcast on conventional terrestrial radio, the rightsholder of the composition has performance rights and is surely paid, but the rightsholder of the sound recording has no performance right and no entitlement to a royalty. By contrast, the owner of rights in both the composition and the recording is entitled to a royalty for many digital broadcasts and for reproductions and distributions in the form of the sale of CDs or downloads.

Rightsholders are often in the news for lodging complaints about the size of their royalty checks, but thanks to this 1995 revision in the law, the holders of rights in the recordings are at least entitled to some payment for their digital transmissions on Spotify, Pandora, and other Internet-based broadcasters. To further complicate the law of music and sound recordings, Congress enacted in 2018 an entirely new body of law governing pre-1972 recordings. That new law is surveyed in Chapter 20 of this book.

DIGITAL MILLENNIUM COPYRIGHT ACT

The Digital Millennium Copyright Act of 1998 added two rights to the arsenal for copyright owners. Under the DMCA, copyright law prohibits "circumvention of technological protection systems." That is, if you crack the protective code on a disk or bypass the password interface to access data, you may have violated this new right. This right effectively allows authors to use technological measures that control access to copyrighted works. This relatively new right has led to the addition of digital rights management (DRM) as a means of controlling access to and uses of many copyrighted works.

THE DMCA was a lengthy bill that encompassed a long roster of changes to the Copyright Act. The provisions summarized here are among the most important, and they are codified in the U.S. Copyright Act, 17 U.S.C. §§ 1201–1202. The legal issues related to circumvention of technological protection measures are examined more closely in **Chapter 22**.

The DMCA also added a prohibition against the removal of copyright management information (CMI) from a copyrighted work. Under some conditions, removing the author's name or stripping away technological conditions for using materials may amount to a new form of copyright violation. These new DMCA rights are in addition to the traditional rights of copyright owners under Section 106. The rights of copyright owners continue to grow in variety and complexity. The exceptions to those rights, summarized in the next chapter, are essential for copyright to serve private as well as public interests simultaneously.

NOTES

1. U.S. Copyright Act, 17 U.S.C. § 106.
2. *MAI Systems Corporation v. Peak Computer, Inc.*, 991 F.2d 511 (9th Cir. 1993).
3. *Perfect 10, Inc. v. Amazon.com, Inc.*, 508 F.3d 1146 (9th Cir. 2007).
4. U.S. Copyright Act, 17 U.S.C. § 101.
5. *Alva Studios, Inc. v. Winninger*, 177 F. Supp. 265 (S.D.N.Y. 1959).
6. Sid Jacobson and Ernie Colón, *The 9/11 Report: A Graphic Adaptation* (New York: Hill and Wang, 2006).
7. *Anderson v. Stallone*, 1989 WL 206431 (C.D. Cal. 1989).
8. U.S. Copyright Act, 17 U.S.C. §§ 106(4), 106(5).
9. U.S. Copyright Act, 17 U.S.C. § 101.
10. U.S. Copyright Act, 17 U.S.C. § 109(c).
11. U.S. Copyright Act, 17 U.S.C. § 110(1).
12. More about this provision is addressed in Chapter 9.

13. For additional information on moral rights, *see* Melville B. Nimmer & David Nimmer, 3 *Nimmer on Copyright*, ch. 8D, § 8D.01, *et seq.* (New York: Matthew Bender & Co., 2018).

14. U.S. Copyright Act, 17 U.S.C. § 106A.

15. Moral rights apply to only a "work of visual art." A work of visual art is narrowly defined under the statute. *See* U.S. Copyright Act, 17 U.S.C. §§ 101, 106A.

16. U.S. Copyright Act, 17 U.S.C. § 101.

17. For much more information about works made for hire, see Chapter 7.

18. *Martin v. City of Indianapolis*, 982 F. Supp. 625 (S.D. Ind. 1997), *aff'd*, 192 F.3d 608 (7th Cir. 1999).

19. *Cohen v. G&M Realty L.P.*, 320 F. Supp. 3d 421 (E.D.N.Y. 2018) (currently on appeal to the Second Circuit).

20. Act of October 15, 1971, Pub. L. No. 92-140, 85 Stat. 391.

21. *See A&M Records, Inc. v. Napster, Inc.*, 239 F.3d 1004 (9th Cir. 2001), *aff'd*, 284 F.3d 1091 (9th Cir. 2002).

22. Digital Performance Right in Sound Recordings Act of 1995, Pub. L. No. 104-39, 109 Stat. 336.

23. U.S. Copyright Act, 17 U.S.C. § 114(d).

CHAPTER 9

EXCEPTIONS TO THE RIGHTS OF OWNERS

KEY POINTS

- One way that the public interest is addressed in copyright law is through the many exceptions to the rights of copyright owners.
- Fair use is the best known of the exceptions to the rights of owners, and it may be the most important.
- The U.S. Copyright Act includes numerous statutory exceptions, and many of them are vital to education and librarianship.
- The specific exceptions generally apply narrowly to only certain works for certain purposes, but fair use allows an added possibility for lawful uses of copyrighted works.
- This chapter provides an overview of exceptions, but Chapters 10 through 17 examine some exceptions in depth.

ONE OF THE most important aspects of copyright ownership is that the rights of owners are not comprehensive. The law grants a broad set of rights for an enormous range of materials, then proceeds to carve out exceptions to those rights. The best known of these exceptions is fair use.[1] The U.S. Copyright Act, however, includes not fewer than sixteen numbered statutory sections that establish exceptions to the rights of copyright owners. Unlike fair use, most statutory exceptions are relevant to only certain industries and specific activities, and they often require careful legal guidance to comprehend and apply.

Some exceptions apply to only the needs of the music, cable television, and other commercial industries. These statutes can stretch over many pages of obtuse and technical text, such as the meticulous rules for rebroadcast of cable television programs.[2] Others are brief, such as the provision allowing horticultural organizations to perform musical works.[3] A few of the statutory exceptions apply especially to the needs of educators and librarians. We are fortunate. Whether you like the law or not, the language of those provisions is sometimes relatively clear and direct—at least in comparison to other acts of Congress. Various statutory exceptions are the subject of several chapters in this book.

Seldom are the statutory exceptions as generous as one might hope. The statutes may allow uses that would otherwise be infringements, but most of the exceptions apply to only specifically identified types of works, only under

FAIR USE is the subject of more detailed examination in **Chapters 10 through 14**. Fair use is much debated, praised, and maligned, but it is crucial for the daily success of our teaching, learning, and research. The potential of fair use for commercial applications is also not to be downplayed. As this book points out elsewhere, fair use has allowed Google to digitize and make certain uses of millions of books, and it has allowed publishers and news organizations to reproduce and use many types of copyrighted works.

detailed circumstances, and only for the prescribed purposes. The key word is *some*. A typical copyright exception allows *some* uses of *some* materials under *some* circumstances. The exact wording of the statute will define when and how the statute may apply.

By contrast, fair use is unusual in its versatile breadth and flexibility. Not all uses are allowed as fair, but fair use can to some extent apply to all types of works and the full range of unpredicted future needs. For example, a statute applicable to library preservation activities applies to only unpublished works.[4] The preservationist should start with the application of that provision. But if the statute does not cover the specific needs at hand, fair use can be an important backup for preservation of published works or other needs. Similarly, the statute on classroom use of motion pictures applies to only performances; fair use could allow making some limited reproductions to facilitate the classroom performances.[5]

Most of the specific statutory exceptions may also be viewed as a baseline for rights of use. The law is essentially a starting point for understanding your rights. In general, private agreements can alter the rule from the baseline. If you want to make uses beyond the limits of a specific exception, you can always seek a license or permission from the copyright owner. On the other hand, licenses may be used to curtail allowed uses. In other words, rights of use under the exceptions are vulnerable to waiver and redefinition by contract. Read carefully before signing.

As a common example, a library may have clear rights under the Copyright Act to make some copies of works for research or preservation purposes. However, if the works were acquired under a license agreement—as is often the case—the agreement may include terms that purport to further define or even retract the library's baseline legal rights. Similarly, the library exceptions allow copies of unpublished works for preservation or research purposes, but often an archive or special collection will waive rights of reproduction in order to acquire a manuscript collection. Understanding the starting point of rights established under the law is critical for negotiating, drafting, and accepting better license terms.

THE ABILITY to exercise fair use or other rights of use under any of these exceptions may also be hampered by technological protection measures that control access to or use of the work. For example, DRM coding on a DVD may limit the ability to view a movie to certain types of players, or it may prevent making copies, even of short clips, a use that might otherwise clearly be lawful. When a library or other buyer accepts the film with the DRM restrictions, the library has in effect waived some of the rights of use that are part of the baseline of rights in the Copyright Act. The law against circumvention of the DRM also includes statutory exceptions, but they are more tightly confined than the exceptions surveyed here. The anticircumvention law is examined more fully in **Chapter 22**.

The following is a summary of exceptions that are of the greatest importance to educators and librarians. The section numbers indicate where they are codified in the U.S. Copyright Act. Later chapters in this book offer a closer look at many of these provisions.

SECTION 107: FAIR USE

This provision may be thought of as the umbrella exception. Fair use as it appears in the Copyright Act is not confined to any specific activity, nor does it apply to only certain works. It is a relatively unspecific provision that includes at its core four general factors for determining its meaning; those factors get close scrutiny in the coming chapters. It is broad and flexible in its scope, and it can apply to a potentially unlimited variety of unpredictable situations, ranging from simple quotations to complex cutting and pasting of pieces of works into a new collage, multimedia project, wiki, or website.[6]

Fair use is an umbrella in another sense. It is the exception that the user of a copyrighted work looks to for protection when the other statutes do not apply. For example, if your library is seeking to make copies of a copyrighted work but the plans do not fit the required conditions of the specific exception for libraries, Section 108, the library may look to fair use for one more possible right of use.

SECTION 108: **LIBRARY SERVICES**

Unlike the flexible and general nature of fair use, this statute is more detailed in its application. Section 108 provides that most academic and public libraries, as well as many other libraries, may make copies of certain types of works for specific purposes. Section 108 permits preservation copying, copying of individual works for research and study, and copying for interlibrary loans.[7] Chapter 17 examines this statute in detail. The statute works extraordinarily well to a certain extent, but its benefits do not always apply to all copies of all types of works.

> **THE DIGITAL** Millennium Copyright Act of 1998 amended Section 108 to clarify when libraries may use digital technology to preserve works in the collection and to reproduce works when the technological format has become obsolete. The amendments may have added some clarity to the law, but they also added some unwelcome restrictions. Section 108 and the use of digital technologies are examined in detail in **Chapter 17.**

SECTION 109(A): **THE FIRST SALE DOCTRINE**

This important exception limits the distribution rights of the copyright holder by providing that once the owner authorizes the release of lawfully made copies of a work, those copies may in turn be passed along to others by sale, rental, loan, gift, or other transfer.[8] The concept is that once a particular copy of the work has been released to others with authority of the copyright owner, the ability to control further distribution has been exhausted.[9]

Without this important copyright exception, a bookstore could not sell you a book and the library could not let you check out a book. Similarly, a video store could not rent movies, you could not sell your used DVDs on eBay, and you could not give books and CDs to your friends as birthday presents. You can begin to see that the exceptions may be necessary to make daily activity feasible.[10]

Without this statutory provision, many common and desirable transactions might be copyright infringements. They could be unlawful distributions of someone else's copyrighted works. The first sale doctrine is also under technological stress today. If you lend a paper book to someone, only one person holds the copy at any one time. But if you lend an e-book, the original digital file typically remains on your computer or device. The act of digital lending often involves the making of a copy. The essential nature of digital transfer, combined with licensing and contracts, seems to be a formidable barrier to sustaining the first sale doctrine in the digital world.[11]

Many rightsholders, such as publishers and music producers, have expressed concern about the application of the first sale doctrine to digital materials. Lending analog copies poses little or no serious threat to the market. Lending of print works does not generate

MANY PUBLISHERS and retailers of books have experimented with the quest for some alternative to the first sale doctrine for digital works. Under the terms of use for Amazon Kindle, customers may make limited sharing of a purchased e-book. The rules are not always consistent; you can share more generously with family members, and you might not be able to share at all if the publisher sets tighter restrictions. One publisher began floating several years ago the idea of allowing libraries to make exactly twenty-six loans of an e-book before the file would expire and need to be repurchased. These marketing structures represent the struggle between controlling copyrights and meeting the expectation of the market to make common and expected uses of books and other copyrighted materials. Continued experimentation with licenses, library practices, author interests, and the law might lead to good results. For example, a coalition of libraries is advancing the Controlled Digital Lending initiative, with a new understanding of fair use and first sale that could support e-lending of library books; see https://controlleddigitallending.org.

reproductions; simultaneous users are not likely; and the process of lending a paper book or other physical work can often lead to the loss or damage of the book. Frequent lending often leads to multiple sales. The market implications of digital lending can sometimes be completely contrary. Digital files can also be controlled and traced through DRM systems.

SECTION 109(C):
EXCEPTION FOR PUBLIC DISPLAYS

This provision greatly limits the copyright owner's public display right by allowing the owner of a lawfully made copy of a work to display it to the public at the place where the work is located.[12] Thus, the university museum that owns a painting may hang it on the wall and let the public enter the front door to view it. The bookstore can place books on display in its front windows, and the library may put its rare and valuable manuscripts in display cases for all to see. Without this exception, those activities could be infringements. This exception is so extraordinarily broad that it effectively limits the owner's display right to situations where the image is transmitted by television, Internet signal, or other system to a location beyond where the copyrighted work itself is physically located.

SECTION 110(1):
DISPLAYS AND PERFORMANCES IN FACE-TO-FACE TEACHING

This exception is crucial for the functioning and survival of basic teaching. It sweepingly allows performances and displays of all types of works in the setting of a classroom or similar place at most educational institutions, from preschool to graduate school. It allows instructors and students to recite poetry, read plays, show videos, play music, project slides, and engage in many other performances and displays of protected works in the classroom setting. This exception benefits multitudes of educators and students every day. Its rather simple language includes few limitations or burdensome conditions.

SECTION 110 is actually a series of separate statutes, creating different specialized exceptions that apply in diverse circumstances. In 2005, Congress added a new Section 110(11), the Family Movie Act, that permits members of a household, while viewing a motion picture, to make certain parts of the content (usually objectionable parts) imperceptible or to use a computer program that can block the content during private home viewing. In effect, we are free to set our own standards for bleeping words and deleting scenes. However, the statute is about modifying the showing (the performance) of the film at home, and it explicitly bars the making of a reproduction of the movie or an altered version (a derivative) of it. A court has ruled that this new Section 110(11) does not permit VidAngel, a private company, to copy and modify motion pictures and then stream them to customers. The court also determined that VidAngel's actions were not within fair use. *Disney Enterprises, Inc. v. VidAngel, Inc.*, 869 F.3d 848, 857–860 (9th Cir. 2017).

SECTION 110(2):
DISPLAYS AND PERFORMANCES IN DISTANCE LEARNING

Once we turn on the cameras or transmit instructional programs online—and engage in distance education—the law makes an abrupt shift. Section 110(2) was fully revised in 2002 with the passage of the TEACH Act.[13] While the new law offers many new opportunities, it is also replete with restrictions and conditions. The ability to make displays and performances in distance education is remarkably more constrained than the allowed uses in the classroom. For more detailed information about the TEACH Act, see Chapter 16.[14]

SECTION 110(4):
NONCOMMERCIAL PERFORMANCES

Although not specifically about educational activities, this statute is sufficiently broad to cover school bands or choirs, street musicians, poetry readings, and political soapbox speeches. It permits the performances so long as they are undertaken without commercial purpose and without payment of fees or compensation to any of the "performers, promoters, or organizers" for the performance.[15] Notice that the payment cannot be for the performance. If a teacher is directing the choir, for example, as part of his or her regular salary for educational services, that would not be a payment for the performance. The statute also allows performances of only nondramatic literary or musical works; not within its scope are performances of motion pictures and dramatic works such as plays, musical theater, and opera.

This section generally prohibits any admission charge for the performance, but not entirely. An admission fee may be collected so long as the proceeds, after reasonable expenses, are "used exclusively for educational, religious, or charitable purposes and not for private financial gain."[16] The statute is not much more elaborate than this summary, and you can probably see how it would allow anyone to perform music or other specified works in many familiar settings, from children's readings at the local library to musical programs of many different types, even performances by professionals, as long as they are not compensated.

SECTION 117: **COMPUTER SOFTWARE**

This provision generally allows the owner of a copy of a computer program to modify the program to work on his or her computer or computer platform and to make a backup copy of the software to use in the event of damage to or destruction of the original copy.[17] For most computer users, however, the ability to load copies of software is usually addressed in the license accompanying the program, minimizing the need to rely on the statute for that right.

SECTION 120: **ARCHITECTURAL WORKS**

THE DMCA of 1998 amended Section 117 to clarify that computer software may be reproduced in order to repair the computer on which the program is originally loaded. The statutory amendment was a response to a court ruling that had adopted a narrow construction of the statute. For the early software ruling, see *MAI Systems Corp. v. Peak Computer, Inc.,* 991 F.2d 511 (9th Cir. 1993)

Architectural designs are protected by copyright, giving architects the right to protect their designs from copying and from construction without permission. But Section 120 makes clear that once a building is constructed at a place visible to the public, anyone may make and use a picture of that building without infringing the copyright in the architectural design.[18] Architectural historians and structural engineers can be spared from infringement when they take pictures of existing structures and use them in teaching and research or for almost any other purpose. Not only is a picture of a building not an infringement, but a photograph, drawing, or other depiction of the building may well be a new copyrightable work.

Many countries have a similar copyright provision, sometimes referred to as the panorama right. The common application is the ability to take a photographic panorama of a city skyline without infringing multiple copyrights in the architectural works. Without this limit on the rights of owners, it could be an infringement to sell postcards of the New York City skyline or include photographs of the latest work by Frank Gehry in a book of modern architecture.

Occasionally some form of legal protection other than copyright might apply. For example, features of a building with a distinctive design, such as the Guggenheim Museum in New York City, can be protected as a trademark.[19] Some countries have claimed rights to control images of major historical and cultural sites, such as the Great Pyramids of Egypt or the Colosseum of Rome. In the United States, however, copyright principles of ownership and exceptions will likely serve most needs related to education, research, and library services.

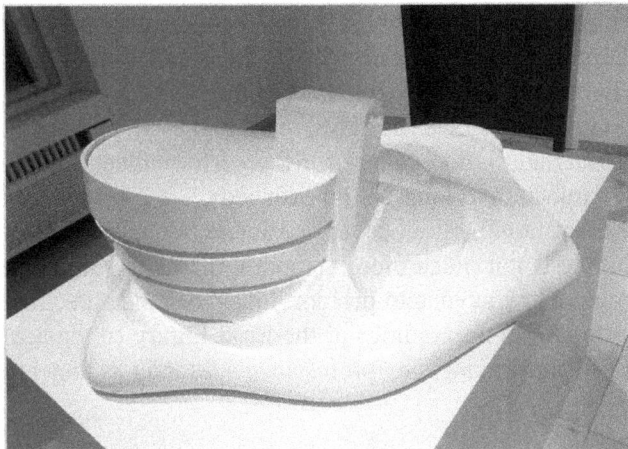

The Solomon R. Guggenheim Museum in New York was built before American copyright law extended to architectural works, so at least in the U.S. the design is available for creative pursuits, such as this artwork titled *Guggenheim–Melting* by Erwin Wurm. This artistic version can be protected as a new copyrightable work, and images of the Guggenheim have been registered as trademarks with the U.S. Patent and Trademark Office.

SECTION 121: **SPECIAL FORMATS FOR THE BLIND**

Congress first added this provision in 1996, and modified it in 2018, to allow organizations that serve the needs of the disabled to make accessible versions of published literary works or musical compositions so that they may be useful to persons who are blind, are visually impaired, or have other print disabilities. Under this provision, some educational institutions and libraries may be able to make large-print or Braille versions of some works in their collections. However, like so many statutory exceptions in the Copyright Act, this law grants rights to only certain qualified organizations and applies to only a defined class of works and activities.[20] Nevertheless it goes far to meet the needs of persons with disabilities and to fill the growing book famine.

A ROBUST and effective law for the benefit of persons with disabilities would cover all types of works and allow diverse and new technologies for accessibility. The copyright challenges arise not only because new formats and versions often involve making copies, but also because such copying can lead to the creation of derivatives. Some derivatives that can be most helpful may also have potentially lucrative markets for the rightsholders. The familiar closed captioning on a movie is important for anyone with a hearing disability, but captions and subtitles can also be product enhancements. As an example of the growing range of derivatives for community needs, consider this system for standardized descriptions of photographs: https://describingvisualresources.org. Another system promotes descriptions of diverse forms of artworks: http://www.artbeyondsight.org/handbook/acs-guidelines.shtml.

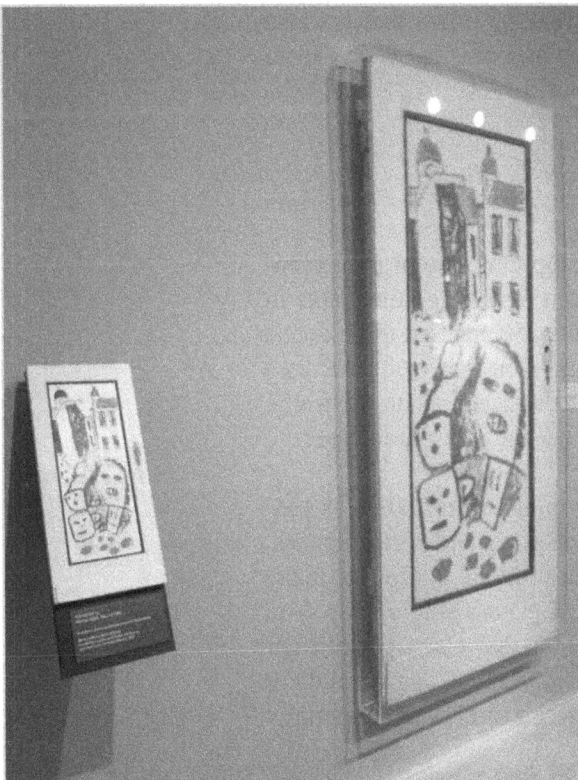

The Berlinische Galerie in Germany displays with some objects a small three-dimensional version, with Braille descriptions, allowing blind visitors to comprehend the artwork. This work is a spectacularly colorful door by Werner Heldt, and the smaller object has added dimension and tactile features, allowing it to be understood by touch.

SECTION 121A: **IMPLEMENTATION OF THE MARRAKESH TREATY**

In 2013 the World Intellectual Property Organization adopted the Marrakesh Treaty, which calls for member countries to enact a statutory exception permitting uses of copyrighted works for the benefit of persons who are blind or have other disabilities preventing their ability to read or handle printed works. As of this writing, nearly sixty countries have brought the new treaty into force. In 2018 the U.S. Senate gave its consent for the United States to enter into the Marrakesh Treaty, and a bill was introduced in Congress to amend the relevant copyright statutes.[21] The United States implemented the treaty in October 2018 by revising the existing Section 121 and adding a new Section 121A, largely on cross-border transfers of copies.[22]

Section 121 is generally about making and delivering works in accessible formats inside the United States. Section 121A implements the innovations in the Marrakesh Treaty that permit cross-border delivery of works to authorized recipients in some other countries. The new statute allows authorized entities in the United States to send copies of works in specialized formats to authorized entities or "eligible persons" in any of the other countries that are parties to the Marrakesh Treaty. Conversely, the

IN ADDITION to the two provisions for the benefit of the blind that are summarized here, Section 110(8) of the Copyright Act is an exception permitting the performance of *nondramatic literary works*, via transmission, directed to persons who are blind or who have other disabilities that make them unable to read print works. The transmission must be made through a governmental body, a noncommercial educational broadcast station, or an authorized radio subcarrier. The exception also allows transmissions of the works for the benefit of the hearing impaired who cannot hear the audio signals that accompany a visual transmission. Section 110(9) is an even narrower provision to help meet the needs of blind persons, by allowing a single one-time transmission of *dramatic literary works* that had been published at least ten years before. These statutes are not long, but they are sharply confined by many detailed conditions.

statute also permits an authorized entity or eligible person to import such copies. Like Section 121, this new provision applies only in cases of a "previously published literary work or of a previously published musical work that has been fixed in the form of text or notation."[23]

This new Section 121A is a big deal. Despite its limits, it does open new possibilities to meet real and growing needs. The Marrakesh Treaty also introduced the notion that a copy, made under an exception, could be delivered to a user in another country. The international coordination is possible largely because, among the countries that have implemented the treaty, the statutory exception as enacted in signatory countries is roughly the same.[24] However, easing the way for cross-border transfers means that the expense of creating a special format copy can be spared if it has been created elsewhere. Breaking down barriers also means that readers will have access to books and other literary and musical works from libraries and other authorized entities from many parts of the world.

RETURNING TO FAIR USE

What happens if you simply cannot meet all requirements for applying one of the exceptions? You still have choices. You can seek permission. You can rearrange your plans in order to fit within the relevant statute. You can find alternative materials that may not be protected by copyright or that have a Creative Commons license. You may also turn once again to fair use. At the beginning of this chapter, fair use was described as an umbrella. Fair use can apply broadly to many uses and many activities that the other more specific statutes may never have contemplated.

Fair use can also complement the other exceptions. For example, Section 110(1) is generous in its application for classroom uses, but it permits only displays and performances, not reproductions. Sometimes a teacher needs to copy a music or film clip in order to make an effective performance of it, yet the statute does not authorize even a single copy. You can then look to fair use to possibly allow these ancillary copies that Congress did not include in the specific exception. The flexibility of fair use to fill gaps that Congress did not anticipate is one of its greatest virtues. The following chapters offer a careful and pragmatic understanding of the law of fair use.

NOTES

1. The fair use statute is codified at U.S. Copyright Act, 17 U.S.C. § 107.
2. U.S. Copyright Act, 17 U.S.C. § 111.
3. U.S. Copyright Act, 17 U.S.C. § 110(6).

4. U.S. Copyright Act, 17 U.S.C. § 108(b).

5. U.S. Copyright Act, 17 U.S.C. § 110(1).

6. *See NXIVM Corporation v. The Ross Institute*, 364 F.3d 471 (2d Cir. 2004).

7. U.S. Copyright Act, 17 U.S.C. § 108.

8. U.S. Copyright Act, 17 U.S.C. § 109(a).

9. The doctrine of exhaustion of rights also exists in patent law, and it allows the practical ability of consumers and businesses to buy and sell patented inventions. Imagine the numerous patented inventions embedded in cars and kitchen appliances. If the patent owners could control all distributions, sales of common creations would be impossible. The Supreme Court has confirmed and expanded the doctrine. *Impression Products, Inc. v. Lexmark International, Inc.*, 581 U.S. ___ , 137 S. Ct. 1523 (2017).

10. The U.S. Supreme Court in 2013 confirmed an international scope of first sale under American law, holding that a sale of lawfully made copies of books conducted outside of the United States would trigger application of the doctrine and permit further resales inside the United States. *Kirtsaeng v. John Wiley & Sons, Inc.*, 568 U.S. 519 (2013).

11. The Second Circuit in 2018 rejected the application of first sale and fair use to an innovative system that would allow individuals to transfer music files, even though the original file was deleted after the work was delivered to a user, leaving only one usable copy at any time. *Capitol Records, LLC v. ReDigi Inc.*, 910 F.3d 649 (2d Cir. 2018), *cert. denied*, 139 S. Ct. 2760 (2019).

12. U.S. Copyright Act, 17 U.S.C. § 109(c).

13. Technology, Education, and Copyright Harmonization Act of 2002, Pub. L. No. 107-273, 116 Stat. 1910 (codified at 17 U.S.C. § 110(2)).

14. In addition, Chapter 15 examines the application of fair use and other copyright principles to distance education.

15. U.S. Copyright Act, 17 U.S.C. § 110(4).

16. After allowing admission fees under these various constraints, the statute then bars the fees if the copyright owner has delivered a formal notice of objection seven days in advance of the performance. Such a notice under those requirements seems highly unlikely. U.S. Copyright Act, 17 U.S.C. § 110(4)(B).

17. U.S. Copyright Act, 17 U.S.C. § 117.

18. Also heartening is that copyright protection for architectural works in general applies to only works created after December 1, 1990, and some unpublished and unconstructed works created before that date.

19. A museum in Cleveland, Ohio, with a distinctive design, was unsuccessful in asserting trademark claims against the use and sale of photographs of the building. *Rock and Roll Hall of Fame and Museum, Inc. v. Gentile Productions*, 134 F.3d 749 (6th Cir. 1998).

20. A regulatory exception to the anticircumvention law, reviewed in more detail in Chapter 22, includes an exception allowing circumvention of technological protection measures by persons with disabilities and for uses consistent with Section 121.

21. The U.S. participation in Marrakesh occurred in multiple steps. The United States signed the document in 2013, indicating its general endorsement. In June 2018 the U.S. Senate acted in accordance with the Constitution to give its advice and consent to the treaty by at least a two-thirds vote. The full Congress enacted the statutory revision in October 2018 to implement the terms. Finally, in February 2019 officials of the U.S. Department of State ratified the Marrakesh Treaty by depositing proper instruments with WIPO in Geneva, Switzerland.

22. U.S. Copyright Act, 17 U.S.C. § 121A.

23. *Id.*

24. The United States became the fiftieth country to ratify Marrakesh, and Section 121A allows for cross-border transfers of the copies with entities and persons in the other forty-nine countries and in any countries that join later.

PART III

Fair Use

· 1 8 9 3 ·

THE SCREAM, a famous painting by Edvard Munch, dates to 1893 and is likely in the public domain under U.S. law and in most other countries. If it were still protected, would this Minion version be fair use? Is the photograph and its inclusion here also within fair use?

CHAPTER 10

FAIR USE

Getting Started

KEY POINTS

- Fair use is an exception to the rights of copyright owners, and it is vital to the growth of knowledge and industry.
- Fair use is based on a balancing of four factors set forth in the statute.
- Fair use can apply to a wide range of materials and activities.
- Fair use does not have defined boundaries, but it is flexible to meet changing needs.
- Fair use ensures that copyrights do not become too restrictive and that the law can enable new creativity based on existing works.

FAIR USE HAS many descriptions and definitions. Functionally, fair use is an exception to the rights of copyright owners, allowing the public to make limited uses of a protected work. It can be defined as a limited right to use a copyrighted work without the copyright owner's consent—often under confined circumstances—for purposes such as education, research, news reporting, criticism, and commentary. By specifically supporting these pursuits, the law of fair use is important for the advancement of knowledge and the communication of ideas. Fair use is also at the foundation of creative business, publishing, and Internet services. Yet fair use does not allow everything. This chapter offers insight into the meaning and the limits of fair use.

WHAT IS FAIR USE?

Fair use is an essential counterbalance to the widening range of rights that copyright law grants to owners. At various times, fair use has been called a *right*, a *privilege*, and a *defense*. Whatever the label, the doctrine is a legally sanctioned opportunity. It allows the public to make limited uses of copyrighted works—uses that might otherwise constitute infringement—especially for advancing knowledge or serving other important social objectives. Applying fair use may be challenging at times, but understanding the law is vital for the growth of knowledge.

Fair use can rescue many would-be infringements and turn them into lawful uses, but only within limits. Consider some of the most common uses of copyrighted works and how they might theoretically get you into legal trouble. A short quotation from an existing paper added into a new report could conceivably be an unlawful reproduction of the quoted portions of the work. Hitting the print key for a paper copy of a web page can also be a reproduction. When a TV news crew broadcasts a downtown festival, the program may include images of outdoor art and clips of music in the background. Streaming a video or sound clip from a website could be a public performance.

The right of fair use may well rescue many of these activities from legal perdition. Many fair uses are common and familiar in education: a picture or song lyrics posted to a blog, a newspaper article posted to a class website, or a brief video clip on YouTube. Recent cases have taken fair use much further—by allowing the inclusion of art images in historical studies[1] and maintaining a trove of millions of scanned books in full text for indexing and research purposes.[2]

THE FLEXIBILITY OF THE LAW

Fair use is both an extraordinary opportunity and a source of recurring confusion.[3] Fair use has been the target of steady challenge, and it is the object of enormous praise. For education and research, fair use is the most important exception to the rights of copyright owners because it is flexible and adaptable to the many unpredictable situations and needs that occur as we pursue diverse projects and apply innovative technologies in academia. Fair use can apply to all types of media and all types of works. On the other hand, fair use can take on a new scope and meaning for each set of circumstances. The flexibility of the law may demand patience and attention, but that flexibility is one of the prized virtues of fair use.

Consider the short quotations that routinely appear in scholarly works. They are often easily within fair use.[4] On the other hand, the longer the quotation, the less likely it will be fair. The flexibility of the law means that some quotations are allowed while others are not. Similarly, using the quotations in one context might be fair, but the same quotations in a different project with different purposes may not be within the law. That same flexibility enables the law to encompass creative uses of distinctive materials, such as standardized survey instruments, motion pictures, or computer software. In recent years, courts have ruled on fair use as applied to rap versions of pop songs,[5] thumbnail images of photographs in search engines,[6] and contorted Barbie dolls in modern art.[7]

While the flexibility of fair use is one of its greatest strengths, it is also the source of uncertainty. Reasonable people disagree on what is "fair," and until a court rules on a particular case, the law does not offer exact and legally binding answers to most fair use questions. The law does, however, give many powerful indicators. Congress deliberately created a flexible fair use statute that gives no exact parameters, allowing courts to take into account the circumstances of each case.[8]

Don't be discouraged. Fair use decisions are no more baffling than many other legal or business judgment calls. You also have four factors to frame the analysis and a plethora of court rulings to guide your understanding and application of the principles. As addressed in Chapter 18, the Copyright Act includes protections for employees of educational institutions, libraries, and archives who make good faith decisions about fair use, even if those decisions turn out to be wrong.

> IN *HIGGINS V. DETROIT EDUCATIONAL TELEVISION FOUNDATION*, 4 F. Supp. 2d 701 (E.D. Mich. 1998), the court allowed the incorporation of short excerpts of a musical work into the background of a production that was broadcast on a local PBS affiliate and sold in limited copies to educational institutions through the application of fair use. This is one of those small exercises of fair use. At the end of this chapter is a brief look at the litigation arising from the Google Books project, no doubt the largest example of fair use, with some twenty million books digitized in full.

THE FOUR FACTORS

The fair use statute does not attempt to define exact parameters but instead sets guideposts. Section 107 of the U.S. Copyright Act sets forth the four factors to evaluate and balance in the analysis of fair use:

- The purpose and character of the use, including whether such use is of a commercial nature or is for nonprofit educational purposes
- The nature of the copyrighted work being used
- The amount and substantiality of the portion used in relation to the copyrighted work as a whole
- The effect of the use upon the potential market for or value of the copyrighted work[9]

These concepts are rooted in a series of judicial rulings stretching back to 1841.[10] Courts examined and refined the doctrine for more than a century until, in 1976, Congress for the first time enacted a statute securing an explicit place for fair use in the larger equation of American copyright law.[11]

Possible fair use examples are innumerable, but not all uses will be fair. Each new situation requires fresh application of the four factors, and short of an authoritative court ruling, the analysis may never produce easy or absolute answers. To date, courts have provided comparatively little direct guidance about fair use in the library or education setting. Yet courts are highly supportive of academic needs, and the fair use statute acknowledges explicitly the importance of an educational purpose. The next two chapters of this book will examine the court rules of particular importance to education and librarianship.

> **THE CASE** of *Folsom v. Marsh* is commonly cited as the wellspring of American fair use. In his elaborate opinion from 1841, Justice Joseph Story isolated variables that impinge on the determination of fair use, and those variables are remarkably similar to the four factors of current law. *Folsom v. Marsh*, 9 F.Cas. 342 (C.C.D. Mass. 1841). Story was at that time a justice on the U.S. Supreme Court, but he was sitting as a judge in this case at the circuit court level. In a delightful parallel, this earliest fair use decision involved the publication of works by and about a past president, George Washington. More than 140 years later, the Supreme Court decided a fair use case involving the writings of another past president, Gerald R. Ford. *Harper & Row Publishers, Inc. v. Nation Enterprises*, 471 U.S. 539 (1985).

> **MANY FAIR USE** cases are relevant to nonprofit education and librarianship, but few decisions bear directly on the question of infringement or fair use in the context of familiar teaching and research. The case most directly on point is familiarly known as the *Georgia State Case*. It raised the question about the fair use of scans of selected pages from nonfiction books for classroom reading through the library's electronic reserve system. *Cambridge University Press v. Becker*, 863 F. Supp. 2d 1190 (2012). That district court ruling from 2012 was vacated and remanded by the Eleventh Circuit, but the case continues to work through the court system, as yet not completely resolved. *Cambridge University Press v. Albert*, 906 F.3d 1290 (11th Cir. 2018); *Cambridge University Press v. Patton*, 769 F.3d 1232 (11th Cir. 2014). The court decisions in the case are examined in detail in Chapter 14.

THE FAIR USE STATUTE

Fair use is the subject of numerous misconceptions and myths. The best place to begin a clear understanding of fair use is the statute itself—the real source of fair use law in the United States.[12] The fair use statute takes hardly a minute to read and is remarkably simple and clear compared to many other federal statutes:

Notwithstanding the provisions of sections 106 and 106A, the fair use of a copyrighted work, including such use by reproduction in copies or phonorecords or by any other means specified by that section, for purposes such as criticism, comment, news reporting, teaching (including multiple copies for classroom use), scholarship, or research, is not an infringement of copyright. In determining whether the use made of a work in any particular case is a fair use the factors to be considered shall include—

> THE FULL text of the entire U.S. Copyright Act is available from many sources. The U.S. Copyright Office seeks to keep the full text, updated with amendments, available on its website at https://www.copyright.gov/title17.

(1) the purpose and character of the use, including whether such use is of a commercial nature or is for nonprofit educational purposes;

(2) the nature of the copyrighted work;

(3) the amount and substantiality of the portion used in relation to the copyrighted work as a whole; and

(4) the effect of the use upon the potential market for or value of the copyrighted work.

The fact that a work is unpublished shall not itself bar a finding of fair use if such finding is made upon consideration of all the above factors.

The statute establishes the framework for answering the extensive variety of questions you might have about clipping materials for websites, quoting from articles, making handouts for teaching, or sampling and remixing a sound recording.[13] Numerous court cases apply that framework to the facts at issue in order to determine whether an activity is fair use or infringement.

A CLOSER LOOK AT THE STATUTE

Of course, the law is never so simple. Fair use is the subject of numerous books, thousands of articles, and a growing cascade of court opinions. The following chapters in this book offer detailed insights, but for now the graphic included here provides a closer look at the language of the statute itself. Understanding fair use in any particular setting best begins with an overview of the language from Congress. The words of the statute may be relatively simple, but they are rich with meaning.

PRINCIPLES FOR WORKING WITH FAIR USE

The following chapters explore more fully the meaning and application of fair use, but always keep in mind these practical principles for working with this important copyright doctrine:

- *Fair use is a balancing test.* You need to evaluate and apply the four factors, but you do not need to satisfy all of them for a use to be fair.[14] The pivotal question is whether the factors overall lean in favor of or against fair use.
- *Fair use is highly fact sensitive.* The meaning and application of the factors will depend on the specific facts of each situation. Each time you face a new or changed situation, you need to evaluate the factors anew.
- *Don't reach hasty conclusions.* The question of fair use requires evaluation of all four factors. Do not conclude that you are within fair use merely because your use is for nonprofit education or has important scholarly objectives.[15] You have three more factors to evaluate. Similarly, a commercial use can be within fair use after examining all factors.[16]

THE TEXT AND MEANING OF FAIR USE

U.S. Copyright Act, Section 107

Sections 106 and 106A of the Copyright Act grant the basic rights of copyright owners.

The phrase **such as** means fair use can apply for many purposes in many situations, beyond those mentioned here.

If it is fair use, it is explicitly **not an infringement!**

Shall include suggests that other factors are possible, but realistically, courts almost always rely on the four stated factors.

The statute only directs that we **consider** the factors, but courts in fact weigh the strength of arguments about each factor and evaluate whether each factor tips in favor of or against fair use. Some patterns have emerged about the four factors that tend to be most persuasive in the analysis.

These **four factors** in the statute will be examined in detail in the following two chapters of this book.

Congress added this last sentence in 1992 in response to a series of court rulings that appeared to severely constrain fair use as applied to **unpublished** works.

The Fair Use Statute

Notwithstanding the provisions of **sections 106 and 106A**, the fair use of a copyrighted work, including such use by reproduction in copies or phonorecords or by any other means specified by that section, for purposes **such as** criticism, comment, news reporting, teaching (including multiple copies for classroom use), scholarship, or research, **is not an infringement of copyright**. In determining whether the use made of a work in any particular case is a fair use **the factors to be considered shall include**—

(1) the **purpose** and character of the use, including whether such use is of a commercial nature or is for nonprofit educational purposes;

(2) the **nature** of the copyrighted work;

(3) the **amount** and substantiality of the portion used in relation to the copyrighted work as a whole; and

(4) the **effect** of the use upon the potential market for or value of the copyrighted work.

The fact that a work is **unpublished** shall not itself bar a finding of fair use if such finding is made upon consideration of all the above factors.

Kenneth D. Crews, *Copyright Law for Librarians and Educators, 4th ed.*, Chicago: American Library Association, 2020.

- *If your use is not "fair," don't forget the other statutory exceptions to the rights of owners.* Fair use and the other exceptions apply independently of one another. You need to comply with only one of them to make your use lawful. Several of the other statutory exceptions are summarized in Chapter 9.
- *If your use is not within any of the exceptions, including fair use, permission from the copyright owner is an important option.* Indeed, unless you change your planned use of the copyrighted work, your more realistic choice might be to seek permission. Chapter 24 of this book offers guidance about seeking permissions.
- *Fair use is relevant only if the work is protected by copyright.* Do not overlook the possibility that the work you want to use may be in the public domain; if it is not protected by copyright, you do not have to worry about fair use. Similarly, if your use is not within the legal rights of the copyright owner, you are not an infringer, and you do not have to consider fair use.

> **A WORK** may be in the public domain for many reasons. Two common reasons are that the copyright has expired or the work was produced by the U.S. government. Much more about the public domain appears in **Chapters 5** and **6**.

BIG AND SMALL USES

Most fair uses are relatively modest. In fact, most examples of fair use usually do involve small excerpts or discrete activities of little concern to a typical copyright owner. Fair use applies to the customary quotations that appear in most nonfiction books. Fair use allows for photocopying pages from publications for later reading or preparing a lecture. Fair use allows a newspaper to capture an image or a clip of music related to current affairs. Frequently cited as a typical fair use is the reprinting of clips and quotations in a book or movie review.

These examples might be the most common fair uses, but they are hardly challenging. Under almost any variation on the facts, analysis of the four factors will most likely point away from infringement. Chapters 11 through 14 of this book explore fair use in greater depth and offer examples that involve more extensive uses of copyrighted works. The copying or other activity may be greater; the use may test technological capability; multiple copies may be widely disseminated to many individuals.

Recent years have brought court decisions on uses that might have seemed unimaginably big not many years before. The grandest exercise of fair use among all cases to date is surely the Google Books project. Started in 2004, the project was an initiative to scan the full text of more than twenty million books, many of them still under copyright protection. Google retained the full text in a secure storage system. The public could search the full collection but at most would receive only selected "snippets" of a few lines, showing the context of where the searched terms appear in the particular book.[17]

The court found the service to be akin to an index system, and it held that the use of the books for search purposes was a transformative use. Although Google is a commercial enterprise, it uses the books for a new and transformative purpose—tipping the first factor in favor of fair use. The court found the second factor to be of little significance in the analysis, and on the third factor, the court determined that a scan of the entire book was essential to make the indexing system possible.

The fourth factor completed the analysis. The copyright owners objected that Google Books was usurping their market to license the books for search purposes and to make digital derivatives. The court rejected those arguments, holding instead that when the uses serve a strong transformative purpose, particularly a new purpose that does not conflict with the original purpose of the books (i.e., Google Books was a search and index service, while the original books were intended to embody and convey information), then the uses are fair. Overall, the factors reinforced one another and pointed clearly toward a finding of fair use.

Only months before the final ruling in the *Google Books Case*, the same court (although a different panel of judges) ruled that the HathiTrust Digital Library, based at the University of Michigan, was also acting within fair use when it built a collection of millions of book scans.[18] Many of the scans at issue in the *HathiTrust Case* had been made by Google and provided to the libraries that held the original books. Those libraries in turn contributed the digital files to HathiTrust. The HathiTrust collection is searchable by the public, but a search retrieves only references to where the keywords appear in the books, without even showing a snippet. The court held that the HathiTrust initiative was within fair use. Despite the vastness of this exercise of fair use, the litigation ended with a simple and extraordinarily short statement to the court that the parties agreed not to pursue the case any further.

> **ANOTHER EXTENSIVE** claim of fair use did not turn out so well for the user. TVEyes operated a service of continuous recording of television news broadcasts to build a searchable database of news video. Clients of TVEyes could search and view selected clips up to ten minutes in length. Fox did not challenge the original recording and creation of the searchable database. Instead, the legal analysis centered on whether simply viewing the video clips could be fair use. Upon determining that viewing was not fair use, the court further resolved that downloading and sharing clips would also be infringements. *Fox News Network, LLC v. TVEyes, Inc.*, 883 F.3d 169, 180 (2d Cir. 2018). In weighing the factors of fair use, the court especially found the commercial purpose of the service and the potential interference with the copyright owner's market to weigh against a finding of fair use.

Few of us will embark on major projects that involve extensive scanning or other uses remotely comparable to millions of books. Yet these two cases are dramatic reminders that fair use can apply to extensive use of enormous quantities of copyrighted materials. It can involve reproduction of entire works. It can be pursued by commercial users, especially when the uses are transformative. Fair use is more than flexible. It has adapted and evolved to serve the public interest in copyright as well as the interests of all innovative players of all types. Fair use proves repeatedly that it is fundamental to copyright's purpose of nurturing the next round of learning and creativity.

NOTES

1. *Bill Graham Archives, LLC v. Dorling Kindersley Ltd.*, 448 F.3d 605 (2d Cir. 2006).

2. *Authors Guild, Inc. v. HathiTrust*, 755 F.3d 87 (2d Cir. 2014).

3. Even recent cases continue to repeat an unduly frightful assessment from 1939 that fair use is the "most troublesome" doctrine in all of copyright. *Monge v. Maya Magazines, Inc.*, 688 F.3d 1164, 1170 (9th Cir. 2012). Nevertheless, the same case provides, "Fair use is a central component of American copyright law." The 1939 appraisal of fair use is from *Dellar v. Samuel Goldwyn, Inc.*, 104 F.2d 661, 662 (2d Cir. 1939) (per curiam).

4. *Faulkner Literary Rights, LLC v. Sony Pictures Classics, Inc.*, 953 F. Supp. 2d 701 (N.D. Miss. 2013) (holding that short quotations from a literary work written into the screenplay of a commercial feature film is fair use and perhaps even de minimis use).

5. *Campbell v. Acuff-Rose Music, Inc.*, 510 U.S. 569 (1994).

6. *Kelly v. Arriba Soft Corporation*, 336 F.3d 811 (9th Cir. 2003).

7. *Mattel Inc. v. Walking Mountain Productions*, 353 F.3d 792 (9th Cir. 2003).

8. Copyright Law Revision, 94th Cong., 2d Sess., H. Doc 1476 (1976). The U.S. Supreme Court has stated clearly that fair use is a case-by-case determination. *Harper & Row Publishers, Inc. v. Nation Enterprises*, 471 U.S. 539, 549 (1985).

9. U.S. Copyright Act, 17 U.S.C. § 107.

10. *Folsom v. Marsh*, 9 F.Cas. 342 (C.C.D. Mass. 1841).

11. Copyright Act of 1976, Pub. L. No. 94-553, 90 Stat. 2541 (codified at 17 U.S.C. § 107).

12. U.S. Copyright Act, 17 U.S.C. § 107.

13. As detailed in Chapter 20, sound recordings were not subject to copyright protection, and thus no need to apply fair use, until 1972. However, in 2018 Congress created a new legal protection for pre-1972 recordings and included fair use in the overall legal structure.

14. "Because this is not a mechanical determination, a party need not 'shut-out' her opponent on the four factor tally to prevail." *Wright v. Warner Books, Inc.*, 953 F.2d 731, 740 (2d Cir. 1991).

15. *Encyclopaedia Britannica Educational Corporation v. Crooks*, 542 F. Supp. 1156 (W.D.N.Y. 1982).

16. *Campbell v. Acuff-Rose Music, Inc.*, 510 U.S. 569 (1994). A recent case held that the use of an entire work by a commercial party could be fair use. *Swatch Group Management Services Ltd. v. Bloomberg L.P.*, 756 F.3d 73 (2d Cir. 2014).

17. *Authors Guild v. Google, Inc.*, 804 F.3d 202 (2d Cir. 2015), *cert. denied*, 136 S. Ct. 1658 (2016).

18. *Authors Guild, Inc. v. HathiTrust*, 755 F.3d 87 (2d Cir. 2014). HathiTrust is pursuing other uses of the collection, particularly the development of formats for readers with disabilities. *See* https://www.hathitrust.org/accessibility.

CHAPTER 11

FAIR USE

Understanding the Four Factors

KEY POINTS

- The determination of whether a use is a fair use is based on an application of four factors set forth in the statute, and in the following points.
- *Purpose of the use:* A nonprofit educational purpose can support a claim of fair use. A transformative use can also be highly influential.
- *Nature of the work:* Uses of factual, nonfiction works are more likely to be within fair use, while fair use often applies more narrowly to creative works.
- *Amount of the work used:* The less the amount of a work used, the more likely it is fair use, but this factor can be much more nuanced.
- *Effect on the market or value:* Uses that do not compete with the market for the original copyrighted work are more likely fair use.

DETERMINING WHETHER A use is fair depends on an application of the four factors in the statute; before making that application, however, a thoughtful definition of each factor is critical. Especially in the years since Congress adopted the first fair use statute in 1976,[1] courts have handed down hundreds of decisions that give some meaning to the factors. The statute anticipates that other factors may enter into the decision about fair use.[2] In reality, however, courts rarely stray beyond the four factors set forth in the statute: *purpose, nature, amount,* and *effect.*

This chapter offers a general overview of the meaning and significance of the factors, with a focus on issues of special importance to educators and librarians. This overview demonstrates that educational uses may be more favored than commercial uses and that transformative uses may have even greater influence on the outcome. The overview also emphasizes that "less is more," but not always. The less of a work that you use, the more likely it will be a fair use, but sometimes using a limited amount may still be an infringement. On the other hand, sometimes using 100 percent of a work can still be permitted as a fair use.[3]

FACTOR 1: The Purpose and Character of the Use

The first factor examines whether the use of a copyrighted work "is of a commercial nature or is for nonprofit educational purposes."[4] With that crucial

> **SOMETIMES A** single fact can be important to more than one factor. For example, a typical electronic reserve system might use password logins or other restrictions limiting access to enrolled students. The simple act of password restriction will likely be important for the first factor and for the fourth factor. Limiting access can strengthen the argument that the materials are specifically for education, which reinforces the first factor. Limiting access can also control the number of readers and the risks of further duplication and dissemination of the copyrighted materials. Those possibilities can help minimize potential market harm, tipping the fourth factor toward fair use.

language, Congress signaled that nonprofit, educational uses generally would be favored whereas commercial uses would be less favored. Photocopying for classroom handouts is more likely to be fair use than would be making copies for a professional business meeting. Posting artwork on a website in connection with a research study is more likely to be fair use than would be reprinting the same copies for a commercial art catalog.

Fair use is common in education and librarianship and is of growing importance. With the expansion of electronic reserves and course management systems such as Blackboard, Moodle, and the dozens of competing products hitting the market, instructors are creating files of readings and easily posting the full text of articles, chapters, and other materials for students enrolled in various courses. For many of these situations, the most important copyright question is whether the activity is within fair use.

> **CONSIDER THE** landmark case of *Random House, Inc. v. Salinger*, 811 F.2d 90 (2d Cir.), *cert. denied*, 484 U.S. 890 (1987). Even though the user was Random House, a commercial entity, the court concluded that the first factor weighed in favor of fair use. The use was, in one respect, for the commercial purpose of selling books for profit. At the same time, the quotations from J. D. Salinger's correspondence were for the research purpose of writing a biographical study. Overall, the first factor tipped in favor of fair use. Yet after evaluating all four factors, the court concluded that the use was not fair. **Chapter 21** gives a closer look at *Salinger* and other cases involving fair use of unpublished, historical materials.

Certainly on this first factor, educators should be able to make a strong argument for fair use. If the materials are directly related to the course, if they are posted only at the direction of the instructor, and if passwords and other restrictions limit access to only students enrolled in that one course, then the claim of an educational purpose should be powerful and convincing. Indeed, the rulings so far in the *Georgia State Case*, involving nonprofit educational uses and examined in Chapter 14, tip this factor strongly in favor of fair use.[5]

Avoid jumping to conclusions. Your well-intentioned education or research activity may still not be within fair use. You may have an irrefutable argument on the first factor, but it might be outweighed by the application of the remaining three factors. Similarly, commercial needs are certainly not barred from the benefits of fair use.[6] Many for-profit entities have argued successfully for fair use. Although the first factor may not weigh in favor of fair use, the remaining three factors could yet tip the balance.

A single factor may also not weigh entirely for or against a finding of fair use. Some situations can create a mixed result on the first factor or any other. For example, when the U.S. Supreme Court considered whether a rap parody version of a pop song could be fair use, the court noted that the recording was a commercial product with considerable economic potential but emphasized that the use was also criticism or commentary for purposes of fair use.[7]

Transformative Uses

In addition to considering specific purposes, courts also favor uses that are transformative. Indeed, a finding that a use is transformative can weigh heavily not only in the evaluation of this factor but also in the overall balancing of the factors.[8] A transformative use may occur when the work is altered or transformed into a new work, such as a parody of a song or art image.[9] Courts have recognized the appropriation art of Richard Prince as a transformative use of copyrighted photographs, much to the chagrin of the photographer.[10]

Transformative uses also occur when the work is used in a new manner or context, distinct from the intended uses of the original. For example, art images in a scholarly study transform the use of the works from aesthetic creations to objects of academic analysis. This was the situation when a book about the Grateful Dead included reprints of small images of psychedelic concert posters from the early years of rock and roll. The author compiled extensive materials and placed the posters in the context of other images and text exploring music and the era.[11] Similarly, the use of a publicity photograph of a celebrity in an article about news events or public commentary can be transformative, even if the photograph itself is unaltered.[12]

> **IN A 1994 DECISION**, *Campbell v. Acuff-Rose Music, Inc.*, 510 U.S. 569 (1994), the U.S. Supreme Court emphasized the importance of transformative uses. The case was about a rap parody of a popular song, yet the Supreme Court pointedly addressed a different context for fair use: "The obvious statutory exception to this focus on transformative uses is the straight reproduction of multiple copies for classroom distribution." This statement is a reminder that a transformative use is not required for a fair use. This statement proved crucial to the district court deciding the *Georgia State Case*, examined in **Chapter 14**.

The notion of a transformative use is increasingly important to education and librarianship as diverse works become the subject of study and analysis and as technologies allow clipping, altering, and reworking of materials for research and teaching. Examples of transformative uses can include quotations incorporated into a paper or perhaps pieces of a work mixed into a multimedia project for teaching purposes.

The deployment of multimedia tools and innovative online courses will give rise to cutting and pasting, adding commentary, and exploring possibilities with images, text, and sound. Many of these uses may well be transformative. If the use is transformative, the first factor may lean strongly in favor of fair use, whether the use is for nonprofit or commercial purposes. Taking that point even further, one court stated clearly that when a use is transformative, "it is of little significance that the use is also of a commercial nature."[13] Remember, however, that a transformative use is not required. A solid case for nonprofit educational or research use can probably be enough to prevail on the first factor.

Multiple Copies

A teaching purpose gets one more important benefit in the law of fair use. Teaching is one of the favored purposes explicitly stated in the statute. The statute also specifically permits "multiple copies for classroom use," subject to the four factors.[14] According to the Supreme Court, multiple copies may therefore be allowed, even if not transformative.[15] But be careful. This language does not mean that all copies for classroom distribution are fair use. You still need to evaluate and balance all factors. The court in the *Georgia State Case* did exactly that, concluding that digital scans of selected pages from books for education could be within fair use—depending on the analysis of all four of the statutory factors.

FACTOR 2: The Nature of the Copyrighted Work

This factor examines characteristics and qualities of the work being used. The underlying concept is that some types of works are more appropriate for fair use than are others.[16] This second factor requires an examination of the qualities and attributes of the copyrighted work, allowing assessment of whether the work is of a type that merits greater protection and less fair use or is the kind of work that fair use encourages us to build upon in order to expand the growth and dissemination of knowledge.

Unpublished Works

Courts have had the occasion to draw some lines demonstrating this point. For example, several court decisions have concluded that the unpublished nature of historical correspondence can weigh against fair use.[17] The courts have reasoned that copyright owners should have the right to their own choices about the circumstances of first publication and whether, when, and how to make the works publicly available. As a corollary, when courts find that a work has been published, they tend to be more lenient with fair use.

> **IN 1985,** the U.S. Supreme Court ruled in *Harper & Row Publishers, Inc. v. Nation Enterprises*, 471 U.S. 539 (1985), that fair use applied narrowly to an unpublished book manuscript in order to preserve the "right of first publication." Where did this right come from, and what does it mean? **Chapter 21** of this book offers some insights. That chapter also traces the series of rulings about historical manuscripts that the *Harper & Row* decision spawned. Confusion about the issue eventually led Congress to modify the fair use statute.

The court rulings in the past decade or so have moved away from strict determinations about fair use based on the unpublished nature of the work. In a case involving the stage musical *Jersey Boys*, the court allowed the fair use of small excerpts of an unpublished book manuscript. Most important, the court noted that the rationale about the right of first publication was not logical when the copyright owner had sought deliberately but unsuccessfully to find a publisher: "A work that is only unpublished because it is unpublishable despite great efforts, however, is an atypical situation. Such a work is not unavailable to the public because of a deliberate choice by the copyright owner, but because it is not commercially viable."[18]

Fiction and Nonfiction

Fair use perhaps applies most generously to published works of nonfiction. Articles, books, and other works of nonfiction—whether about mathematics, sociology, politics, or any other subject—are exactly the types of works for which fair use can have the most meaning. Why? Because the central purpose of copyright law, including fair use, is to allow for the growth of knowledge.[19] To accomplish that goal, we regularly need to use and build upon earlier works. Most often, the successful growth of knowledge depends on using the nonfiction works of earlier scholarship. Courts have recognized that reality.

By contrast, copyright law gives greater protection for—and allows less fair use of—works of fiction.[20] Fair use will be relatively constrained for clips of novels, poetry, and stage plays. You will likely find a similar outcome for uses of other more creative materials, such as art, photography, music, and motion pictures. Indeed, an additional purpose of copyright law is to protect and reward creativity. Limiting fair use for the most creative works advances that objective. This rule does not mean that fair use vaporizes. It only suggests that this factor may need to be outweighed by the other factors.

Some cases have concluded instead that this factor may be neutral in the fair use equation. The Supreme Court ruled that the second factor may have little consequence in a case about parody; any type of work (especially well-known creative works) may be equally subject to the criticism and commentary that is the essence of parody.[21] Similarly, the court of appeals in the *Google Books Case* ruled that the nature of the book was of little consequence when the main purpose of the use is to create a search tool and not to compete with the content of the book.[22]

Consumable and Out-of-Print Works

Other examples can help bring practical meaning to the nature factor. For example, this factor may weigh against fair use when applied to copies of workbook pages and excerpts from other "consumable" materials. Publishers often produce and sell workbooks with the expectation that they will be fully consumed and repurchased with each use. Copies can undermine the copyright owner's expected market by harming the demand for individual and repeated sales.[23]

A more complicated, but common, circumstance has split legal authorities. Many copyrighted works go out of print, even though the copyright may live on for decades longer. A Senate report from 1975, and one early judicial opinion, asserted that if a work is out of print, copying that work may not harm the market.[24] After all, the copyright owner of an out-of-print book is not actively claiming a market and seeking sales.

At least one court has ruled differently about out-of-print materials. In the early decision involving Kinko's and coursepacks, the court highlighted that owners of out-of-print materials may still offer a license to make copies. The *Kinko's* court reasoned that even though a work is out of print, photocopying could still interfere with the marketing of a license to make copies. The court further found that when licensing is the primary market for an out-of-print work, the copies are especially harmful to the licensing market.[25]

What can you conclude from these cases? You may often need to investigate the realistic and current marketing of the work you want to use. If the work is available for purchase or actively licensed, you might be affecting that market. If the copyright owner has not made reasonable arrangements for licensing, out of print may not mean "tough luck" for fair use. On the other hand, out of print may become an obsolete concept. It may be uneconomical to keep a book in stock as a printed volume, but it might be feasible to retain the book indefinitely as a digital download. Many publishers and retailers have migrated to digital books, and Google continues an ambition to digitize, retain, and deliver multitudes of book to anyone anywhere. These revolutions in publishing are certain to have important consequences for fair use.

FACTOR 3: The Amount and Substantiality of the Portion Used

On first impression, the amount factor perhaps sounds like it should be reasonably straightforward. However, amount is measured both quantitatively and qualitatively, and no exact measure of allowed quantity exists in the law.[26] Rules about word counts and percentages have no place in the law of fair use. At best, such measurements are interpretations intended

---

A GOOD number of cases have found fair use even when the entire work is used. Consider this sampling of court rulings: The Supreme Court ruled that recording entire television programs at home is within fair use. *Sony Corp. of America v. Universal City Studios, Inc.,* 464 U.S. 417 (1984). The influential Second Circuit ruled that commercial use of an entire transcript of a corporate conference call was within fair use. *Swatch Group Management Services Ltd. v. Bloomberg L.P.,* 742 F.3d 17 (2d Cir. 2014). By contrast, the Second Circuit also cautioned that mere fleeting images of artistic works in a television production might not be within fair use. *Ringgold v. Black Entertainment Television, Inc.,* 126 F.3d 70 (2d Cir. 1997).

to streamline the determinations of fair use; at worst, they distract from the flexibility that makes fair use meaningful and adaptable to new situations. Quantity is best evaluated relative to the length of the entire original work and the amount needed to serve a proper purpose.

The appropriate amount can also depend on the nature of the work. Courts have measured amount differently for different types of works. When evaluating the fair use of journal articles, for example, a court has ruled that each article is an independent work. Thus, photocopying an article constitutes copying of the entire work.[27] Pictures and other visual works pose challenges for determining the appropriate amount. A user nearly always wants the full image, and ordinarily copying all of a work will lean strongly against fair use. Courts have found some flexibility by reasoning that copies of full images that are thumbnail size or are of low resolution may still constitute fair use.[28] The copying may be quantitatively large but at the same time qualitatively limited; low-resolution or thumbnail images are unlikely to compete with the full-size originals.

Quantity, Quality, and the Heart of the Work

The tension between quantitative and qualitative measures is most vivid with the concept of the *heart of the work*. The Supreme Court in 1985 analyzed whether *The Nation* magazine had exceeded fair use when it quoted some 300 words from President Gerald Ford's then-unpublished memoir in a news article. The Court ruled that while the quotations may have been quantitatively small, they were the pieces of the book that a reader would likely find most interesting. Specifically, the Court was evaluating the reprinting of parts of Ford's account of his decision to pardon President Nixon. Thus, *The Nation* had impermissibly lifted the heart of the manuscript. The quotation was quantitatively small, but the amount factor nevertheless weighed strongly against fair use.[29]

Practical Sense

How do you make reliable and practical sense of the amount factor? One simple rule remains in most situations: Shorter excerpts are more likely than longer pieces to be within fair use. Yet sometimes the briefest slice may constitute the heart of the work and be outside fair use. Nevertheless, even if you need a relatively large portion of a copyrighted work, you can strengthen the claim of fair use by tying the amount you borrow to your educational or research purpose. If you can meet your favored objectives by only excerpting the article, movie, or other work, the amount may be appropriate. Perhaps the strongest case for fair use in this context would include an unequivocal educational purpose combined with a clear demonstration of the importance of the work for achieving the educational needs.

FACTOR 4: The Effect of the Use on the Market

The fourth factor, examining market effects, can also raise some subtle issues, and some courts have called it the most important factor.[30] The effect factor encompasses whether the

> **SOMETIMES COPYING** the full work can be within fair use. Some years ago, such cases were rarities, but today we have various examples of the application of fair use for entire works. A few are mentioned earlier in this chapter. The most extraordinary example, of course, is the *Google Books Case*. Google was sued for making digital scans of the full text of more than twenty million copyrighted books. Surely the officers and attorneys at Google suffered considerable anxiety about the scanning project, and the lawsuit arrived in short order. The district court and the Second Circuit Court of Appeals ruled that even the use of the entire work was fair—based on analysis of all four factors. The Second Circuit found that the use was highly transformative because Google was utilizing the scanned reproductions for indexing and search purposes. The search interface delivered only a small snippet of each book, preventing the use from interfering with the market for the original works. The court also upheld Google's delivery of digital scans to the libraries that supplied the originals. *Authors Guild v. Google, Inc.*, 804 F.3d 202 (2d Cir. 2015).

use harms the market for the work or its value. In many cases, the question is whether the use is one that replaces what should have been a sale of the work or a license to use it. If your use detrimentally affects the copyright owner's ability to realistically make a sale—regardless of your personal willingness or ability to pay for such a purchase—the court may tip this factor against fair use. Occasional quotations or photocopies may pose little significant market harm, but full reproductions of software and DVDs can make direct inroads on the owners' potential markets for those works.

> **THE U.S. SUPREME COURT**, in *Harper & Row*, called this factor "most important." *Harper & Row Publishers, Inc. v. Nation Enterprises*, 471 U.S. 539 (1985). Realistically, one can see that the court put at least comparable weight on the unpublished nature of the work. Many other cases have cited that language from the Supreme Court, but a close reading suggests that those courts are also just giving added weight to the factors that have greatest prominence under the given facts.

Sales and Licenses

The easy cases occur when the use directly replaces a potential sale of a work that is marketed at realistic prices. A few readers might remember Napster. It was breakthrough technology at the time and in direct confrontation with interests of the music industry. Napster was a networked system that facilitated uploading MP3 files of musical sound recordings for accessing, downloading, and sharing the music files. The court ruled that downloading free music from Napster displaced likely sales of CDs or other lawful copies. Access to free downloads demonstrably harmed the copyright owners' market.[31]

> Chapter 12 includes further examination of *American Geophysical Union v. Texaco Inc.*, 60 F.3d 913 (2d Cir. 1994), cert. dismissed, 516 U.S. 1005 (1995). The court ruled that the existence of the Copyright Clearance Center and the relatively easy licensing of rights to make copies of journal articles established a possible market that the user may have affected through its copying activities.

More difficult cases involve uses that do not interfere with simple sales but may undercut licensing of the work. Photocopying of isolated articles might not replace subscriptions to the entire journal, but the copying might interfere with the system of permissions and collection of fees put in place by the publisher or other rightsholders.[32] Courts also look to potential harm to derivatives and related markets. A court ruled on whether a dictionary book, written to accompany the Harry Potter stories, infringed those copyrights. The court concluded that the dictionary would not harm sales of the original books, but it would harm the ability of J. K. Rowling to authorize another dictionary or other accompanying project.[33]

Identifying the Market

Possible market effects can vary greatly. You may be surfing the Internet and find a document, blog, picture, or other copyrighted work properly posted by the rightful owner. The copyright owner clearly has imposed no restrictions or conditions on access and is asserting no claim to payment for use. You might liberally copy, download, or print the materials in full, and you probably have done little to harm any realistic market. In fact, if the work is made available with a generous Creative Commons or other public license, then that fact can be evidence that the rightsholder was not nurturing any potential market.[34]

In yet a different situation, you might be creating original instructional materials to post on a course website. You want to include in your document sizable quotations and excerpts of various charts, images, music, and film from other sources. While many such uses are customary and pose little market risk, some interference with markets and licensing is possible. Even if the use does affect the value or market for the copyrighted works, any weight given to the fourth factor could be counterbalanced by the small amount, the educational purpose, and the factual nature of the content.[35]

Moreover, the fourth factor—on market effect—may also support application of fair use because moving those pieces into a new context and embedding them in an analytical study for educational purposes is not likely to interfere with a realistic and significant market. The more you alter the context of use and surround the works with original criticism or comment and educational content, the less likely you are impeding a market that the copyright owner has the right to control. Some of these same factual circumstances may also demonstrate that the use is transformative—an important consideration when analyzing the first factor.

Occasionally a use of a work might actually increase its value or marketability. That was the court's conclusion in the case about Grateful Dead posters, mentioned earlier in this chapter. The court determined that the appearance of the images in the book might reasonably generate new sales for reproductions of the copyrighted posters.[36] In another ruling about popular music, a court ruled that the use of elements of an unpublished book about the Four Seasons in the stage musical *Jersey Boys* did not harm the market but might instead create more interest in the manuscript.[37]

> Chapter 16 examines the TEACH Act for distance learning. While that law is not at all the same as fair use, it does include some analogous concepts. For example, the TEACH Act explicitly does not allow uses of materials marketed for digital distance education. Fair use has no such bar. On the other hand, if the copyright owners are targeting the specialized educational market, such a use is more likely to harm the defined market—and hence more likely not to be within fair use.

Market issues are challenging for educators, librarians, researchers, and even courts. Courts have analyzed this fourth factor in close connection to the purpose of the use. If your purpose is research or scholarship, market harm may be difficult to prove, and courts will generally apply the fourth factor somewhat generously. If your purpose is commercial, however, some harm to the market may be presumed, but even then it can be rebutted by other evidence.[38] Still, one can imagine how the rules become blurred when you have an educational purpose but the copyrighted work is one that is created and marketed especially for the academic community. The hard reality is that even some educational uses have direct and adverse market consequences.

Market issues can get complicated, but in the context of fair use they ultimately drive this line of thinking: How is the work actually marketed? What are the realistic potential markets? Is the work realistically marketed for my needs and my uses? Am I harming or inhibiting that market potential? Am I replacing a sale? Are my market effects significant? Would the market effects be significant if uses like mine were widespread?

Like almost all matters of applying fair use, this fourth factor depends on an array of facts. Those facts may be the circumstances of your use, and they are most certainly about the active or likely marketing of the work you plan to use. You need to have a firm grasp of your situation and investigate the work in question. You might also find that markets change. A work may have no market today but find a new market tomorrow. A work may be a best seller this year but be out of print in the near future. Testing the market might also mean retesting it again for later uses.

> DO NOT OVERLOOK the possibility that your use might actually *help* the market for the work. References, clips, quotations, images, and other such uses invariably draw attention to the original works. Some uses might take away a market; others might lead someone to want more and to make a purchase. Quotations in a book review are a familiar example of a use that might most often help the market. In *Campbell*, the Supreme Court resolved that sometimes market harm simply has to be tolerated. *Campbell v. Acuff-Rose Music, Inc.*, 510 U.S. 569, 591–592 (1994). A biting parody or devastating review can destroy the market for a work, and that is simply a risk that copyright owners have to accept.

NEW DIRECTIONS FOR FAIR USE

Fair use has changed through the years. New media and new opportunities to use copyrighted works have opened new possibilities. Courts have ruled on the fair use of images, art, music, and more. They have unraveled the questions surrounding mass digitization and capturing content from the web. Fair use was meant to have exactly that flexibility of possible applications. In responding to new technologies and creative media, the law is also proving that fair use is fundamental to the adaptability of copyright for an innovative future.

Court rulings have actually made fair use more flexible. Presumptions about commercial uses, for example, are gone. Courts also have moved beyond early cases that suggested a hard-and-fast rule against fair use of unpublished works. The fourth factor about market harm is no longer the most important factor if the facts in a particular case point to other factors as more persuasive. Classroom copying is no longer dominated by consideration of guidelines and cases about commercial sales of physical coursepacks.[39]

So much of the previous debate about fair use and education can now seem antiquated. Photocopying has steadily given way to scanning and digital distribution. Libraries are building larger collections of digital works that can be delivered to students by linking rather than copying. The nature of education also has been transformed, with escalating demands for more innovative uses of copyrighted works and with online options coming to life as MOOCs (massive open online courses) and other incarnations. Fair use law has been reshaped by the concept of transformative use, and courts have tested its meaning for diverse media and needs. This virtuous flexibility of fair use keeps it alive and relevant through all these changes. Indeed, fair use remains critical to the success of educational innovation, as will be shown in many chapters of this book.

Finally, fair use is taking on an extraordinary international dimension. While fair use is a distinctly American concept in origin, it is also finding a place in the laws of several other countries, as surveyed in Chapter 23.[40] Fair use is ultimately the infusion of flexibility that copyright needs if it is to survive and serve a public interest. Fair use is a limited concept, of course, but it allows reasonable uses of copyrighted works. In the process, fair use clears the way for the public to build on earlier works, respect the interests of rightsholders, and respect the role of copyright law as a means for serving diverse interests simultaneously.

NOTES

1. Copyright Act of 1976, Pub. L. No. 94-553, 90 Stat. 2541 (codified at 17 U.S.C. § 107).

2. The use of the word *include* when listing factors of fair use in the statute denotes that the factors listed do not constitute an exclusive list. U.S. Copyright Act, 17 U.S.C. § 107.

3. Perhaps the most salient example of fair use of entire works is the *Google Books Case*, examined elsewhere in this book. A more modest example is *Swatch Group Management Services Ltd. v. Bloomberg L.P.*, 742 F.3d 17 (2d Cir. 2014), in which Bloomberg news service was allowed under fair use to publish a recorded conference call with investors in the Swatch company.

4. U.S. Copyright Act, 17 U.S.C. § 107.

5. *Cambridge University Press v. Albert*, 906 F.3d 1290 (11th Cir. 2018); *Cambridge University Press v. Patton*, 769 F.3d 1232 (11th Cir. 2014); and *Cambridge University Press v. Becker*, 863 F. Supp. 2d 1190, 1232 (N.D. Ga. 2012).

6. "A commercial use weighs against a finding of fair use but is not conclusive on the issue." *A & M Records, Inc. v. Napster Inc.*, 239 F.3d 1004, 1015 (9th Cir. 2001).

7. *Campbell v. Acuff-Rose Music, Inc.*, 510 U.S. 569, 593 (1994).

8. *Lombardo v. Dr. Seuss Enterprises, L.P.*, 279 F. Supp. 3d 497 (S.D.N.Y. 2017), *aff'd*, 729 Fed. Appx. 131 (2d Cir. 2018) (treating the first factor as the heart of the inquiry in the case of parody).

9. *Blanch v. Koons*, 467 F.3d 244, 253 (2d Cir. 2006). Under this factor courts often ask whether the new work merely replaces the object of the original creation "or instead adds something new, with a further purpose or different character, altering the first with new expression, meaning, or message; it asks, in other words, whether and to what extent the new work is 'transformative.'" *Campbell v. Acuff-Rose Music, Inc.*, 510 U.S. 569, 579 (1994).

10. *Cariou v. Prince*, 714 F.3d 694 (2d Cir. 2013).

11. *Bill Graham Archives v. Dorling Kindersley Ltd.*, 448 F.3d 605, 609 (2d Cir. 2006).

12. *Philpot v. Media Research Center Inc.*, 279 F. Supp. 3d 708, 714 (E.D. Va. 2018).

13. *Lombardo v. Dr. Seuss Enterprises, L.P.*, 279 F. Supp. 3d 497, 510 (S.D.N.Y. 2017), *aff'd*, 729 Fed. Appx. 131 (2d Cir. 2018).

14. U.S. Copyright Act, 17 U.S.C. § 107.

15. *Campbell v. Acuff-Rose Music, Inc.*, 510 U.S. 569, 579 n.11 (1994).

16. This factor calls for recognition that some works are closer to the "core of intended copyright protection" than are others, with the consequence that fair use is more difficult to establish when the former works are copied. *Campbell v. Acuff-Rose Music, Inc.*, 510 U.S. 569, 586 (1994).

17. *Harper & Row Publishers, Inc. v. Nation Enterprises*, 471 U.S. 539 (1985); *Peter Letterese & Associates, Inc. v. World Institute of Scientology Enterprises*, 533 F.3d 1287, 1313 (11th Cir. 2008); *Salinger v. Random House, Inc.*, 811 F.2d 90, 97 (2d Cir.), *cert. denied*, 484 U.S. 890 (1987).

18. *Corbello v. DeVito*, 262 F. Supp. 3d 1056, 1069 (D. Nev. 2017) (currently on appeal to the Ninth Circuit).

19. U.S. Const. art. I, § 8, cl. 8.

20. *Campbell v. Acuff-Rose Music, Inc.*, 510 U.S. 569, 586 (1994).

21. *Campbell v. Acuff-Rose Music, Inc.*, 510 U.S. 569, 586 (1994).

22. *Authors Guild v. Google, Inc.*, 804 F.3d 202, 220 (2nd Cir. 2015), *cert. denied*, 136 S. Ct. 1658 (2016).

23. Copyright Law Revision, 94th Cong., 2d Sess., H. Doc. 1476 (1976).

24. Copyright Law Revision, 94th Cong., 1st Sess., S. Doc. 473 (1975); *Maxtone-Graham v. Burtchaell*, 803 F.2d 1253 (2d Cir. 1986), *cert. denied*, 481 U.S. 1059 (1987).

25. *Basic Books, Inc. v. Kinko's Graphics Corporation*, 758 F. Supp. 1522 (S.D.N.Y. 1991). Notice again that one fact—in this case the fact that a work is out of print—can become important in the evaluation of two factors: the nature factor and the effect factor.

26. *Campbell v. Acuff-Rose Music, Inc.*, 510 U.S. 569, 587 (1994); *Elvis Presley Enterprises, Inc. v. Passport Video*, 349 F.3d 622, 630 (9th Cir. 2003).

27. *American Geophysical Union v. Texaco Inc.*, 60 F.3d 913 (2d Cir. 1994), *cert. dismissed*, 516 U.S. 1005 (1995).

28. *Kelly v. Arriba Soft Corporation*, 336 F.3d 811 (9th Cir. 2003).

29. *Harper & Row Publishers, Inc. v. Nation Enterprises*, 471 U.S. 539, 564–566 (1985). By contrast, in analyzing a book about the musical group the Four Seasons, a court ruled, "Because the Work is biographical in nature, its 'heart' consists of unprotected facts." *Corbello v. DeVito*, 262 F. Supp. 3d 1056, 1075 (D. Nev. 2017).

30. *Harper & Row Publishers, Inc. v. Nation Enterprises*, 471 U.S. 539, 566 (1985).

31. *A & M Records, Inc. v. Napster Inc.*, 239 F.3d 1004 (9th Cir. 2001).

32. *American Geophysical Union v. Texaco Inc.*, 60 F.3d 913 (2d Cir. 1994), *cert. dismissed*, 516 U.S. 1005 (1995).

33. After evaluating all factors, the court ruled that the Harry Potter dictionary was not a fair use. *Warner Brothers Entertainment Inc. v. RDR Books*, 575 F. Supp. 2d 513 (S.D.N.Y. 2008).

34. *Philpot v. Media Research Center Inc.*, 279 F. Supp. 3d 708 (E.D. Va. 2018).

35. In the *Georgia State Case*, examined in Chapter 14, the court often tied market harm to the amount used—the greater the amount, the more the potential harm.

36. *Bill Graham Archives v. Dorling Kindersley Ltd.*, 448 F.3d 605, 614 n.5 (2d Cir. 2006).

37. *Corbello v. DeVito*, 262 F. Supp. 3d 1056 (D. Nev. 2017).

38. *Harper & Row Publishers, Inc. v. Nation Enterprises*, 471 U.S. 539 (1985).

39. Chapter 13 provides an overview of the origin and current status of the various fair use guidelines.

40. Fair use is generally traced to an 1841 court decision in the United States, but it does have some earlier roots. Matthew Sag, "The Prehistory of Fair Use," *Brooklyn Law Review* 76 (2011), 23.

CHAPTER 12

GETTING COMFORTABLE WITH FAIR USE

Applying the Four Factors

KEY POINTS

- Few court rulings about fair use directly address education or libraries.
- Various other court rulings concerning fair use offer important guidance for teaching and research activities.
- Example scenarios can be instructive for applying fair use to common or familiar needs.
- Professionals need to work with the factors and principles of fair use to reach reasoned and responsible decisions.

AMERICAN COURTS HAVE analyzed and applied fair use in hundreds of cases, but only occasionally have they interpreted fair use for education or library activities. As teaching and research change—and as technology enables innovative uses of copyrighted works—schools, universities, libraries, and other organizations are encountering new questions about infringement and fair use. Although we seldom have a court ruling to resolve definitely whether some activity is fair use, we need to be ready to analyze and apply existing law to familiar and innovative projects.

Without court rulings that might exactly answer our specific fair use questions, educators and librarians are left to infer what they can from the few cases that have some relevance to the academic community. Increasingly, educators and administrators must preemptively consider the fair use implications of their projects as innovative activities continue to raise questions regarding the boundaries of fair use law. The situations rarely progress—or degenerate—into lawsuits for various reasons. The parties settle; the questionable activities stop; the project rarely stirs prolonged legal anxieties. Moreover, if you have done a diligent job with your application of fair use, you may well be within the law, defanging the threat.

A mere smattering of cases offers some insight into judicial interpretations of fair use law in situations that are closely analogous to those faced by educators and researchers. An early example involved Kinko's Graphics, a once well-known national chain of photocopy shops, which was sued some three decades ago for making photocopied coursepacks without permission.[1] The court rejected Kinko's fair use defense, in large part because Kinko's was a for-profit entity and was photocopying for a commercial purpose. The *Kinko's* decision left educators, authors, publishers, and others to wonder how a court might rule in a case involving a nonprofit educational institution.[2]

A few cases address educational uses. In *Higgins v. Detroit Educational Television Foundation*,[3] the court allowed as fair use the incorporation of short pieces of a musical work into the background of a video production broadcast on a local PBS affiliate and sold in limited copies to educational institutions. The court sympathized with the educational and public-service purpose of the production. The defendant used a brief amount—only about thirty-five seconds of a popular song—and only in the background of the opening scenes. A song is generally a creative work, so the "nature" factor tipped in favor of stronger protection and against fair use. The copyright owner did not actively license the song for such uses, so the use had no adverse market effect. Three of the four factors weighed in favor of fair use, and the court allowed this tightly limited use of music.

The more recent court decision of *Reiner v. Nishimori* held that the use of copyrighted photographs as part of a classroom exercise about the creation of advertising campaigns was within fair use. The first factor weighed in favor of fair use largely because of the nonprofit educational purpose. In analyzing the fourth factor, the court put the burden on the copyright owner to show evidence of market harm. "As a preliminary matter, Reiner [the plaintiff] has not proven even that there is a market for photographs to be used as part of educational design exercises." The court further admonished the copyright owner for failing to produce "evidence of a single instance in which he or anyone else was voluntarily paid for the right to use a photograph in a student-created mock advertisement or other student design project."[4]

The court's handling of just the fourth factor has a few meaningful lessons for educators using copyrighted works in the classroom. The court firmly placed the burden on the rightsholder to prove harm to the value of or the market for the works in question. More specifically, the owner had to show evidence of an actual market for the kinds of educational uses in question. Some authors and publishers do actively license for the educational market, but most copyright owners have not pursued licenses with schools, universities, and teachers. In this case of relatively small-scale uses, the court further concluded that even "widespread use of the photographs" would not harm the potential market.

These cases about seemingly modest uses of copyrighted works offer terrific guidance because they reflect familiar and common needs. Other chapters in this book examine recent cases involving Google Books, HathiTrust, and other parties that go far beyond these limited uses. Those cases affirm that a nonprofit educational purpose can tip the first factor strongly in favor of fair use. The fair use defense of HathiTrust, and the storage and search of millions of full-text books, turned on a nonprofit purpose. The court also recognized that utilizing the books for search and indexing was transformative—reminding us that transformative and innovative teaching and research uses of copyrighted works can well be within fair use.[5]

Other decisions revealed some parameters of fair use. Consider these conclusions from various courts:

- The full text of newspaper articles posted to a publicly accessible website—even to further a social cause—is not fair use.[6]
- Playing music in the background while phone callers are placed "on hold" is not fair use.[7]

A MAJOR case against officials of Georgia State University, involving questions of copyright infringement and fair use for educational copies, has been working its way through the court system for more than a decade. In a lawsuit filed in 2008, a group of publishers accused the university of exceeding the limits of fair use when copying excerpts from various books, particularly for posting to electronic reserves. **Chapter 14** of this book offers a detailed examination of the case, the court rulings to date, and the lessons for policymaking on fair use in libraries and educational institutions. Some of the scenarios in this chapter benefit from the judicial opinions handed down in that case. As of this writing, the case is still working its way through the process of appeals and remands.

THE CASE of *American Geophysical Union v. Texaco Inc.*, 60 F.3d 913 (2d Cir. 1994), *cert. dismissed*, 516 U.S. 1005 (1995), is a reminder that the limits of fair use can arise in the most seemingly innocuous circumstances. The case involved photocopying of individual journal articles by a Texaco scientist for his own research needs. The company circulated lists of new journals and articles, and employees were allowed to make copies for their individual reference. The court ruling that even single copies were not fair use appeared to have been influenced largely by the commercial objectives of Texaco and the availability of a license from the Copyright Clearance Center for exactly this type of use. Interestingly, months after making its ruling, the court amended its opinion to narrow its analysis to "systematic" copying, which does not necessarily include independent and isolated single copies.

- Recording and publishing the full content of telephone conferences with corporate investors, despite clear assertions that the calls were to remain confidential, is within fair use when the content is newsworthy and the user is a business news service.[8]
- File sharing of music—the uploading and downloading of commercially available recordings—through the original Napster and similar services is not within fair use.[9]
- Downloading and caching from the Internet the full text of content from multitudes of websites for the purpose of facilitating web searching and reliable access to websites is fair use.[10]
- Glimpses of photographs in the background of a movie or television production have left courts seemingly divided. One court ruled that if the images are fairly prominent in the set for a cable TV show, they may not be fair use.[11] Another court ruled that fuzzy and fleeting images in a motion picture scene are fair use.[12]

This chapter explores the meaning of fair use in the practical context of addressing a variety of scenarios.[13] The scenarios and the fair use analyses are intended to offer guidance for thinking about fair use, especially as applied to familiar activities that are often at the core of common practice among educators and librarians. The principal point of each scenario is not to declare that some activity is or is not fair use but instead to model the process of thinking through the four factors. That process should help you move toward a conclusion about fair use and take you to a point where you can be comfortable working with the factors and making decisions about fair use. The scenarios begin with the simplest and build to larger-scale projects and newer technologies.

QUOTING IN PUBLICATIONS

SCENARIO

Professor Tran is writing a lengthy historical study and wants to include various quotations and clips of other copyrighted materials. Is she protected by fair use?

Whether Professor Tran is staying within the boundaries of the law will depend on a multitude of variables, but the analysis starts with the most familiar situation and moves to the more complex. Begin with a simple quotation from one work included in her new historical study. She may be writing about aviation technology and quoting sentences from a biography of Amelia Earhart, or perhaps she is undertaking a study of historical epidemics and needs to comment critically on existing studies of plagues and social structure. Professor Tran needs to consider the four factors, and she should look to helpful and relevant cases, such as *Penelope v. Brown*.[14]

In that case, a professor, Penelope, wrote a book about English grammar and language usage. Brown, a writer of popular fiction, later wrote a manual for budding authors, with examples of proper writing. Amidst five pages of Brown's 218-page book, she apparently copied sentence examples from Penelope's work. The court ruled that Brown's use was fair. Here is how the court addressed the four factors:

> *Purpose:* The court found that the second book greatly expanded on pieces borrowed from the first, making the use "productive," and the new book was not merely superseding the original. The court today might call it a "transformative" use. Both books to some extent shared the purpose of educating readers about language and writing, but apparently in different contexts. The court also found little commercial character in the use of the small excerpts, and it found no improper conduct by Brown. This first factor favored fair use.[15]

> *Nature:* The court looked to the nonfiction nature of the work used and its limited availability to the public. This factor favored fair use.

> *Amount:* The defendant borrowed only selected sentences and examples from the first book, and the court found that the excerpts were a small amount. This factor favored fair use.

> *Effect:* The court found little adverse effect on the market for the original, noting that the two books might appear side-by-side in a store but a buyer is not likely to see one as a replacement for the other. This factor also favored fair use.

WHEN PROFESSOR TRAN prepares her book, assembles her materials for teaching, or makes other uses of existing works, she should almost always be sure to cite her sources. She should add footnotes or other references. Citing sources is crucial for academic honesty, but it is not a major variable in fair use. Fair use is about copyright and law. Citing sources goes to issues of ethics and plagiarism.

THE NOTION of a "productive" or "transformative" use is examined in Chapter 11. Courts are more generous with fair use when the new work transforms the original and gives it a new purpose or function—or if the use builds on the original in some productive manner. In either instance, the court is allowing greater fair use in order to promote the progress of knowledge and creativity, the policy of copyright rooted in the U.S. Constitution. The transformativeness of the use is analyzed as part of the first factor of fair use. The Supreme Court gave the concept an enormous boost in *Campbell v. Acuff-Rose Music, Inc.*, 510 U.S. 569 (1994), when the Court ruled that a rap parody was a transformative use of the original pop song.

The *Penelope* decision might give Professor Tran considerable peace of mind if she is using modest quotations from a published, nonfiction work. One court case, however, does not tell the limit of fair use. What about long quotations? What if she were copying not published text but instead pictures, poetry, unpublished manuscripts, or other types of works? These cases are slow to come to the courts, and only in recent years did one court rule on the fair use of photographs in a classroom setting. A few highlights of that case, *Reiner v. Nishimori*, are mentioned earlier in this chapter and may suit Professor Tran's needs.[16]

The case of *Maxtone-Graham v. Burt-chaell* suggests how Professor Tran might be able to reprint lengthy quotations and excerpts.[17] A book about pregnancy and abortion included interviews with women about their own experiences. Sometime later, another author prepared his own book on the same

EVEN THOUGH permission may be denied, fair use can still apply. Sometimes the denial of permission can mean that fair use is the only means for using the work, and courts seem to be especially sympathetic if the use has some social good, such as examining important issues of public interest. In the case of *Bill Graham Archives v. Dorling Kindersley Ltd.*, 448 F.3d 605 (2d Cir. 2006), efforts to obtain permission failed, yet the court eventually ruled that the unpermitted publication of artistic posters was fair use in the context of preparing and publishing a historical study of music and culture.

subject and sought permission to use lengthy outtakes from the first work. The author of the original work, the plaintiff in this case, refused permission, and the defendant proceeded to publish his work with the unpermitted excerpts. The borrowed material encompassed slightly more than 4 percent of the original work, including many insightful passages from the interviews. The court relied on the factors to conclude that the extensive quoting was fair use.

Purpose: The defendant's book was published by a commercial press with the possibility of monetary success, but the main purpose of the book was to educate the public about abortion and about the author's views. This factor favored fair use.

Nature: The interviews were largely factual, which also favored fair use.

Amount: Quoting 4.3 percent of the plaintiff's work was not excessive in light of the critical analysis. The verbatim passages were also not necessarily central to the plaintiff's book. Again, this factor supported fair use.

Effect: The court found no significant threat to the plaintiff's market. Indeed, the court noted that the plaintiff's work was out of print, and the two books were not likely to appeal to the same readers. This factor favored fair use.

This case affirms that quotations in a subsequent work are sometimes permissible even when they are extensive. This case also suggests much about using materials in the educational setting, where an instructor may be employing pieces and clips of various works to prepare teaching materials or an online course. Even large pieces could be within fair use, particularly for the favored purpose of education. Fair use is also stronger if the instructor is using the excerpts in the context of original teaching materials and with accompanying comments and criticism.

What if the user is doing more than merely copying pieces and embedding them in a new original publication? What if Professor Tran is looking to copy materials in full without original commentary? The next cases shed some light on straight copying.

IF LENGTHY quotations in a book can be within fair use, then should large portions of copyrighted works used in the context of teaching materials also be okay? Consider the early case of *Marcus v. Rowley*, 695 F.2d 1171 (9th Cir. 1983). A schoolteacher prepared a twenty-four-page pamphlet on cake decorating for her adult education classes. Eleven of those pages were taken directly from a copyrighted pamphlet prepared by another teacher. Even though both pamphlets were of limited circulation and were for teaching purposes only, the court held that the copying was not fair use. The defendant copied a substantial part of the original pamphlet, the copying embraced the original pamphlet's most significant portions, and the second pamphlet competed directly with the original pamphlet's educational purpose. Under the right circumstances, some uses of educational materials, such as the scanning of selected pages for electronic reserves, can still be fair use. The *Georgia State Case* centers on such uses and is examined in Chapter 14.

COPYING FOR CLASSROOM TEACHING

SCENARIO

Professor Tran teaches at a community college and wants to make photocopies or digital scans of articles and book excerpts as handouts or electronic reserves for her students. Is she within fair use?

Until recent years, any attempt to resolve this question would have leaned heavily on two court decisions decided during the 1990s. The first was *Basic Books, Inc. v. Kinko's Graphics Corporation*, decided in 1991.[18] Kinko's was found to be infringing copyrights when it photocopied book chapters and sold them for profit to students as coursepacks needed for their university classes. The second case, from 1996, was *Princeton University Press v. Michigan Document Services, Inc.*[19] The facts and outcome in *Michigan Document Services* were similar in many ways to those in *Kinko's*.

Michigan Document Services was most notable for having been decided on rehearing en banc by the court of appeals. All thirteen judges of the Sixth Circuit heard arguments and handed down their ruling that the copying was not fair. A majority of the court was especially persuaded by the availability of options for licensing the materials before making the copies. Like the *Kinko's* decision, this ruling was also shaped by the commercial uses that potentially competed with sales or licensing of the books. Nevertheless, five judges dissented, indicating at the least that even federal judges could differ greatly on their interpretations of fair use.

A court's analysis today about fair use for classroom copying could be considerably different. The cases from the 1990s would be part of the analysis, but they are explicitly about commercial copying services. They also involved substantial portions of textbooks that were aimed at the educational market. These early cases are also overshadowed by rulings involving electronic reserves and classroom readings at Georgia State University, examined in detail in Chapter 14. Moreover, since the 1990s, courts have expanded on the meaning of fair use for diverse materials and have reshaped some fundamental principles through the concept of transformative use.

In light of these developments, Professor Tran's thinking today about the fair use factors for nonprofit classroom copying might be something like this:

Purpose: If she is teaching at a nonprofit educational institution, this factor will likely weigh in favor of fair use. This factor will weigh even more decisively in favor by taking additional steps to emphasize that the use is for education: She selected materials tightly related to her teaching, and only students could access the materials, either as handouts in class or by password restriction on course management resources. If the use is transformative in any way, her case could be greatly strengthened.

Nature: If the works are factual or nonfiction—such as works of history, sociology, and other fields of study—this factor will likely tip in favor of fair use. However, a court might see this factor as neutral or of little weight, recognizing that any type of work may be suitable or important for education.

Amount: The *Kinko's* court analyzed the percentage used of each work, finding that copying 5 to 25 percent of the original full book was excessive, tipping this factor against fair use. By contrast, recent cases have been more flexible and have centered this factor on whether the amount used was appropriate or necessary for achieving the favored purpose.

Effect: This factor is related to the amount factor; the amount used should serve the educational purpose and at the same time not be so great as to have any appreciable adverse effect on the market for the original works. In *Kinko's*, the shop was photocopying from textbooks and therefore competing with potential sales of the original books to the

The publishers in *Kinko's* relied heavily on the *Classroom Guidelines* from 1976 and urged the court to rule that any anthology or coursepack could not be allowed under fair use. The court rejected that contention, concluding instead that one must analyze each article, chapter, or other work separately and determine whether each item in the coursepack is within the law. More recently, the court opinions in the *Georgia State Case* also rejected the *Classroom Guidelines* as an appropriate standard. The guidelines are summarized and referenced in full in Chapter 13.

students. The courts in the *Georgia State Case* also considered whether the use directly harmed not only the market for the books but also the market for licensing rights of use.

What do these cases tell us about Professor Tran's needs? She should plan her selection and use of materials to fit as comfortably as she can within fair use. She has a definite advantage over the commercial shops when she makes limited copies on the college's photocopiers and scanners. She can also help her cause by keeping the materials as brief as possible—that is, limiting her copying to only the amount needed for her educational purpose—and checking the market for the reasonable availability of permission or affordable purchase of the works from the publisher or other source.

THE USE of electronic delivery, whether through e-reserves or a course management system, can have major implications for fair use. Digital uses raise concerns about misuse and proliferating copies. Digital files may be easily copied, uploaded, and shared without the obvious constraints of hard copies. However, the technology can also offer some reassuring protections. To help her case for fair use, Professor Tran can use the technology to restrict access with password protections or other controls. Delivery through a secured system gives greater opportunity to reach students with messages about copyright implications and the hazards of misuse. Further, limited access can simultaneously reduce the risk of market harm and reinforce that the materials are made available for only educational purposes.

CLIPPING AND COPYING FOR AN ONLINE EDUCATIONAL PROJECT

SCENARIO

Professor Tran wants to create an innovative teaching tool, cutting and pasting a variety of works into a single cohesive set of materials for the students enrolled in her classes. She plans to gather and edit the materials as an evolving wiki, available to her students, and to be further revised and edited with newer materials all semester. Students access the entire project through a password-protected site.

If Professor Tran's project includes little more than copies of reading and other materials, then her analysis of fair use may be much like the scenarios involving coursepacks or selected quoting. One could argue that she is just producing a digital version of the familiar print materials and making them available to only the students in her class. Even so, she probably has more flexibility about fair use than Kinko's had for its commercial copying.

Similarly, if she is clipping pieces and excerpts of materials, arranging them to suit her innovative needs, and enveloping them with original commentary and instructional content, then she may be making a high-tech version of a book or other teaching materials. In many respects, her fair use questions and challenges are not unlike the approach she might have applied to more conventional or familiar situations. She may be safely within fair use when she uses brief portions that are incorporated in a transformative manner; she may need to reflect more carefully when using large portions of works as straight reproductions.

In any event, the question of fair use will turn on the circumstances surrounding each individual item. If she is using clips of nonfiction text, fair use should be reasonably flexible. If she is using music, art, poetry, and other more creative works, she should be more circumspect. If she is wrapping the use in commentary and criticism, her uses may be transformative, and she is on safer ground than she would be with straight copying. A few instructive court cases remind us that fair use can support Professor Tran's educational project, but with limits:

> **ONE OF** the advantages of an online resource, wiki, or other digital innovation is the ability to link to other sources and to embed video and other materials from places such as YouTube. Linking and embedding do not require copying and pasting of the content and as a result seldom stir serious copyright questions. To the extent that Professor Tran can avoid making her own copies, she also has likely avoided the need to evaluate fair use. Apart from fair use, Professor Tran may also be able to use the TEACH Act, a separate statute that offers an alternative set of rules for using copyrighted works in distance education or "transmissions." **Chapter 16** examines the TEACH Act in detail.

- In *Los Angeles Times v. Free Republic*, the court ruled that posting the full text of newspaper articles to a website open to the public, even for the purpose of allowing readers to comment on those articles through the website, is not fair use.[20] Professor Tran, by contrast, is proposing to use materials for nonprofit education and only with restricted access. She can strengthen the possibilities of fair use by using only excerpts of articles. She can avoid issues of fair use entirely by linking to databases that might be available from her library or to sources openly available on the Internet.
- In *Warren Publishing v. Spurlock*, the court allowed the fair use of reproductions of covers and other art images from monster fan magazines that were a pop culture phenomenon decades before.[21] The images were included in a book that was commercially sold, but they were reprinted as cultural artifacts and presented in the context of their historical and artistic significance. Similarly, in *Bill Graham Archives v. Dorling Kindersley Ltd.*, a court ruled that the reproduction of small-size images of artistic posters was fair use, particularly if they are used in the context of a historical study.[22] The reproductions were fair use even in a book produced for sale by a commercial publisher. Fair use in both cases depended in part on the selection of relevant images and their presentation in an analytical study.

ONLINE LIBRARY EXHIBITION

SCENARIO

Professor Tran is working with her university's library to curate a web-based exhibition that builds on Tran's research on the life of aviator Amelia Earhart. The topic will center on Earhart's visit to Tran's university campus in the 1930s. Professor Tran wants to include some of the same works that she was including in her online teaching resource along with many of the original documents, photographs, news clippings, letters, speeches, and other materials of importance. Can the exhibition be publicly accessible and still be within fair use?

In some respects, an online exhibition such as this one may be a bit like the online educational resource or electronic reserves. It involves the scanning and posting of (presumably) copyrighted materials built around a core theme. But unlike reserves and instructional resources, the exhibition is public and not behind a password control. In that regard it may be a bit more like a book or other publication, where fair use can allow quotations and other brief selections. Unlike a typical book, the exhibition is not created for sale or for any likely profit.

The library's online exhibition is, on the other hand, fundamentally different from the other projects. The exhibition has the distinctive trait of being specifically *about* the documents, photographs, and other items. The exhibition is not just telling a good or important story. It is a means for sharing with others the history of the university and the important materials in the library, archives, or special collections. Its primary purpose may in fact be to display images, in full, of the historic artifacts. Without the copyrighted objects, the exhibition has little meaning.

Professor Tran and her library colleagues might evaluate fair use along these lines:

Purpose: Although not necessarily connected with a particular course or educational program, the purpose of the exhibition is to inform and educate readers about Earhart, the university, and the library collections. This factor will be greatly strengthened if the materials are presented in a context that centers on their historical importance, with accompanying explanation of the library collections.

Nature: The copyrighted works are of a diverse nature, and many are unpublished.[23] However, they are also specifically selected to further the favored nonprofit and educational purpose of informing visitors. As long as they are selected principally because they are from the collections and not for their copyrighted content, this factor may not weigh strongly in either direction.

Amount: In some cases, short quotations and clips will suffice. For some documents, photographs, and other works, their entirety is needed to make the point.

Effect: If the library owns the materials, the market value for the artifacts probably belongs to the university. On the other hand, if the copyrights are held by third parties—such as professional photographers—the rightsholders may want to exploit the value of the copyright through licensing or sale. Librarians preparing the exhibit may need to check the realistic market for the materials and whether a known copyright owner is exploiting the rights.

> **THE FACT** that the exhibition is available online sends Professor Tran and the librarians down the path of fair use and other copyright issues. If the exhibition were of the more traditional ilk, with the various materials available for visitors to study on location, the copyright questions would be much simpler. Section 109(c) of the Copyright Act permits the display of copyrighted works at the place where they are located—such as in glass cases at the library. The exception does not apply if the same works are displayed online for viewers at remote locations. The process of putting the artifacts online also generally requires posting digital *reproductions* to the server—acts beyond the mere *display* allowed under Section 109(c). If the works are audiovisual or are sound recordings, their use may be a *performance* of the content and also not mere *display*. The exception of Section 109(c) is good and important, but it is also restrictive. U.S. Copyright Act, 17 U.S.C. § 109(c).

THE CONUNDRUM OF STREAMING VIDEO

In the context of education especially, the demand for streaming video stirs some of the most frequent questions about fair use. Practical access to and delivery of audiovisual (AV) works can be critical for many needs. Video is an important resource for teaching, and streaming can facilitate wider access from collections and allow for more reliable preservation of the works. By streaming the video works from a server, educators and other users are more likely to find the work, to be able to access it, and to include it in the classroom experience at a wide range of locations.

SCENARIO

Professor Tran is planning her courses for next year and is working with her campus library to be sure that all of the AV works she wants to use will be available. The library has the works that Professor Tran needs but in various formats, from VHS and film to DVD and Blu-ray. Some of the AV works are available online only under license from the developer of database collections. Professor Tran would like these works to be available to use in the classroom and for students to view on their own.

At least with respect to the works on physical media, whether analog or digital, the library could allow instructors and students to check them out consistent with the first sale doctrine in Section 109 without significant copyright complications. However, everyone involved can see immediately that streaming the works from a library server would be much more effective. The works would be more reliably available at any given time; the server could permit simultaneous use when multiple students are doing their late-night studies; and the risk of loss or damage to the originals could be kept in check.

Of course, this vision of streaming video raises a few additional copyright questions. First, streaming often requires one more action—reproduction of the works. Some systems can stream content from the original, but usually a library or an educational institution will need to digitize the work and copy it to the server. That process is necessarily one or more reproductions. Second, the technological process of transmitting the digital stream is a form of making yet additional copies. Third, if the system allows multiple simultaneous uses—so students can do their assignments on time—each stream may compound the number of copies. Fourth, the definition of *public performance* in the Copyright Act includes situations where the users may access the AV work and watch it from separate places at different times.

Despite these added copyright barriers, the law does offer considerable promise for streaming video under the right circumstances. Some uses might be helpful for Professor Tran:

- Section 110(1) of the Copyright Act allows performances of entire works in the face-to-face classroom or similar location. Some libraries do set up systems for streaming AV content in the classroom, and at least that limited access could well be within this important exception.
- Section 110(2) permits performances of video and other works in transmission for education. Chapter 16 surveys the many detailed restrictions and

THE DETAILS of the right of public performance are explored more fully in **Chapter 8**. The scope is in the definitions in Section 101 of the Copyright Act, and one possibility seems to have been targeted exactly at the nascent computer industry of 1976 and the emergence of networked communications. A public performance can occur when a work is transmitted "by means of any device or process, whether the members of the public capable of receiving the performance or display receive it in the same place or in separate places and at the same time or at different times." U.S. Copyright Act, 17 U.S.C. § 101. The copyright law never fully tells us the definition of *public*, but we do know that transmitting the AV work to facilitate individual views can add up to a public performance. The law was also seemingly foreshadowing online education and was not being especially supportive.

requirements of the law, but in the end, it does permit limited streaming of video to students, who may access the content at their locations and on their schedules.

- Section 108, the library exception in the Copyright Act, allows libraries to make digital copies of works for preservation purposes. Those digital copies may be accessed inside "the premises of the library or archives." Chapter 17 explores the complications of that language, but it at least allows Professor Tran to send her students to the library to view some streaming video.

The foregoing statutory possibilities are in addition to the digitization and transmission of works that are in the public domain. Further, some works may be used without elaborate legal analysis because of permission, whether an individual permission or a public license, such as Creative Commons. In fact, in the given scenario, some of the AV works are available through the library pursuant to a license from the rightsholder or a database aggregator. That license might be highly restrictive about the uses of videos, or it might instead open up possibilities for streaming to classrooms or for students to view in their own dorms and homes after hours. The librarians need to press for favorable terms, and Professor Tran needs to inquire about the rules and possibilities.

Each of these prospects may be enlisted as beneficial for Professor Tran's teaching. But each is limited in scope and application, and each is subject to a variety of requirements and preconditions. Consequently, fair use becomes a compelling alternative. Chapter 15 demonstrates how to apply fair use as an alternative to the cumbersome Section 110(2) (aka the TEACH Act) for distance education. Even when using the clearer and simpler Section 110(1) for classroom use, fair use can support making a digital copy of a video to facilitate the classroom performance and perhaps even allow the library to retain the copy on a server for streaming to the classroom. In navigating the many alternatives, fair use becomes not only a gap filler but also an equalizer in shaping educational experiences.

MOVING FORWARD WITH FAIR USE

As Professor Tran pursues a range of activities, from simple quoting to creating innovative teaching materials, she regularly encounters questions about fair use. The answers to her questions will depend not only on the factors and judicial interpretations but also on the wide-ranging facts. She may be within fair use when she uses articles but not motion pictures; she might be within fair use for the photographs but not for the unpublished letters. These are just a hint of the factual variations that lead lawyers to give the classic answer, "It depends."

The flexibility of fair use makes it highly dependent on the specific facts of each situation. Fair use can apply in all of these situations and more. It can apply to a full range of materials, from text and software to music and art. Fair use has enormous potential to support Professor Tran's work, even if it does not always allow everything. Exactly how it applies depends on the details.

The flexibility of fair use can also make it challenging and at times downright frustrating. The flexibility of fair use means that it often has no clear, firm, and established limits. It is variable in its scope, and its meaning is open to debate. The next chapter examines the guidelines that have attempted to bring some clarity to the law. In the process, however, those same guidelines also have done considerable harm to the greatest virtues of fair use: its flexibility and its adaptability to new situations and new demands.

ACTING IN GOOD FAITH

As she works through fair use, Professor Tran is likely to feel a burden of responsibility and an accompanying risk of legal liability. Indeed, Chapter 18 of this book will tell of severe consequences that may befall an infringer of someone's copyrighted work. Congress, however, recognized the dilemma that educators and librarians face when applying fair use. The law therefore includes an important provision that eliminates much of the financial liability Professor Tran might otherwise face, but she will have that advantage only if she applies the law of fair use in a reasonable and good faith manner.

WHEN CONGRESS enacted the fair use statute in 1976, it recognized that educators and librarians would need to make difficult judgments about fair use. The Copyright Act therefore includes some important protection for users who act in good faith as they strive to learn about and apply fair use. **Chapter 18** provides the details.

Chapter 18 of this book provides more details, but for now the message is clear: If Professor Tran takes the initiative to learn and apply the factors of fair use, she likely will have the benefit of greatly reduced liability. Do not overlook the better and more direct message: If Professor Tran learns and applies the factors of fair use, she also stands a good chance of actually being within the law and in full accord with fair use. In the process, Professor Tran should keep notes about her decision and possibly use the fair use checklist in Appendix B to help document her thinking and conclusion. Maintaining records and notes can go a long way to help confirm her informed and good faith decisions and protect her in the event of legal challenge.

NOTES

1. *Basic Books, Inc. v. Kinko's Graphics Corp.*, 758 F. Supp. 1522 (S.D.N.Y. 1991).

2. The author of this book examined the court's ruling shortly after it was handed down. *See* Kenneth D. Crews, "Federal Court's Ruling against Photocopying Chain Will Not Destroy 'Fair Use,'" *Chronicle of Higher Education*, April 17, 1991, A48. Kinko's was acquired by FedEx, and by 2008 the famous Kinko's name was almost entirely gone from the storefront shops.

3. *Higgins v. Detroit Educational Television Foundation*, 4 F. Supp. 2d 701 (E.D. Mich. 1998).

4. *Reiner v. Nishimori*, 2017 WL 1545589 (M.D. Tenn. 2017).

5. The cases involving HathiTrust and Google Books are examined in Chapter 10.

6. *Los Angeles Times v. Free Republic*, 54 U.S.P.Q.2d 1453 (C.D. Cal. 2000).

7. *Infinity Broadcasting Corporation v. Kirkwood*, 63 F. Supp. 2d 420 (S.D.N.Y. 1999).

8. *Swatch Group Management Services Ltd. v. Bloomberg*, 742 F.3d 17 (2nd Cir. 2014).

9. *A & M Records, Inc. v. Napster, Inc.*, 284 F.3d 1091 (9th Cir. 2002).

10. *Field v. Google Inc.*, 412 F. Supp. 2d 1106 (D. Nev. 2006).

11. *Ringgold v. Black Entertainment Television, Inc.*, 126 F.3d 70 (2d Cir. 1997).

12. *Sandoval v. New Line Cinema Corporation*, 147 F.3d 215 (2d Cir. 1998). The district court ruled that the activity was within fair use, but the court of appeals was even more generous and called the use de minimis.

13. A common assumption underlying all of the scenarios is that you already have explored the more fundamental copyright questions: Is the work even protectable under copyright? Has the copyright expired, placing the work in the public domain? If the work is not protected for any reason, there is no need to address fair use.

14. *Penelope v. Brown*, 792 F. Supp. 132 (D. Mass. 1992).

15. A commercial purpose can sometimes tip the first factor away from fair use even if the use is transformative. *Elvis Presley Enterprises, Inc. v. Passport Video*, 349 F.3d 622, 627 (9th Cir. 2003).

16. *Reiner v. Nishimori*, 2017 WL 1545589 (M.D. Tenn. 2017).

17. *Maxtone-Graham v. Burtchaell*, 803 F.2d 1253 (2d Cir. 1986), *cert. denied*, 481 U.S. 1059 (1987).

18. *Basic Books, Inc. v. Kinko's Graphics Corp.*, 758 F. Supp. 1522 (S.D.N.Y. 1991).

19. *Princeton University Press v. Michigan Document Services, Inc.*, 99 F.3d 1381 (6th Cir. 1996), *cert. denied*, 520 U.S. 1156 (1997).

20. *Los Angeles Times v. Free Republic*, 54 U.S.P.Q.2d 1453 (C.D. Cal. 2000).

21. *Warren Publishing v. Spurlock*, 645 F. Supp. 2d 402 (E.D. Pa. 2009).

22. *Bill Graham Archives v. Dorling Kindersley Ltd.*, 448 F.3d 605 (2d Cir. 2006).

23. *NXIVM Corp. v. The Ross Institute*, 364 F.3d 471 (2d Cir. 2004). Another important case allowed, in a scholarly study, the use of lengthy excerpts from an unpublished novel by Marjorie Kinnan Rawlings. *Sundeman v. The Seajay Society, Inc.*, 142 F.3d 194 (4th Cir. 1998).

CHAPTER 13

THE MEANING OF FAIR USE GUIDELINES

KEY POINTS

- Various groups have developed guidelines that apply fair use to diverse situations.
- The guidelines may be helpful for some needs, but users must remember that they are not the law, and courts have refused to adopt them as a legal standard.
- Many uses that are not within the range of these guidelines may still be fair use under the law.
- Only by returning to the four factors can you have the full benefit of fair use.

INTERPRETIVE GUIDELINES OF some form have been part of the discussion of fair use since Congress enacted the first fair use statute in 1976.[1] Many users of copyrighted works, including educators, researchers, and librarians, pressed for more explicit delineation of the law's scope and meaning for many common needs. In some respect, all of the guidelines have run counter to the essence of fair use. Congress made clear that the law of fair use was never intended to anticipate specific answers for individual situations. Indeed, Congress acted deliberately to assure that it would not "freeze" the doctrine of fair use by giving it a narrowly defined meaning.[2]

We can at least rest assured that the guidelines are not enforceable law. The lack of precision in fair use may be one of the doctrine's greatest strengths. The variability of the law can also lead reasonable people to disagree about the meaning of fair use in even the most familiar applications. Given that courts have not addressed many of the fair use needs of education, we are often left to learn, debate, and sometimes simply disagree about the reach of the law. The need for answers, however, continues to create pressure for guidelines.

EVOLUTION OF GUIDELINES

Educators, librarians, and others expressed great concern about the possible ambiguity of fair use even before Congress enacted the first fair use statute in 1976. Congress urged interested parties to meet privately and to negotiate shared understandings of fair use. The result was a series of guidelines that attempt to define fair use as applied to common situations. The first of such guidelines emerged in 1976 on the issues of photocopying for classroom handouts and the copying of music.[3]

Through the years, various groups have devised guidelines on other issues, from off-air videotaping to library copies. In the 1990s, guidelines gained renewed prominence with the formation of the Conference on Fair Use (CONFU). CONFU was a federal initiative with participation from a broad range of interested parties: teachers, librarians, industry and government officials, and many others. The final report from CONFU proposed three more guidelines for newer technological issues.[4] Despite great investment of effort, CONFU never got past the proposal stage.

These early guidelines had little influence over the law or actual practices. Where they might have achieved some intended outcomes, they also were greeted with sharp criticisms and rebukes. Nevertheless, some of them continued to draw attention. The attraction of alternative guidelines, or perhaps "guidance," has persisted. A few organizations have issued new guidelines on specific areas of interest. An initiative known as the *Codes of Best Practices in Fair Use* has emerged in recent years. While they are not without their problems and limitations, these *Best Practices* offer a fresh direction for understanding and applying fair use.

The guidelines examined in this chapter ordinarily share these characteristics:

1. From the perspective of their developers and proponents, the guidelines offer interpretations of fair use law.
2. The guidelines are offered to the public with the posture that they are from an authoritative and legally reliable source.
3. The developers intend for third parties to adopt the guidelines as standards of practice.
4. The developers anticipate that the guidelines may be adopted as is or incorporated into formal policy at a library, an educational institution, or another organization.

To facilitate their practical acceptance, most of the guidelines are relatively short—sometimes the equivalent of a few or several pages. However, as the issues have become more complex, so have the guidelines become lengthier, more elaborate, and infused with citations and legal references.

> **LIBRARIANS AND** educators are hardly the only professionals developing guidelines. The Association of Art Museum Directors (AAMD) in 2017 issued an updated set of guidelines for fair use. The document from AAMD is more of a narrative and legal analysis, supported by formal citations to legal authority. It does not have the appearance of a typical policy, but it is offered with a voice of experience and intended to help users through the law. See https://aamd.org/document/guidelines-for-the-use-of-copyrighted-materials-and-works-of-art-by-art-museums.

EARLY GUIDELINES, 1976–1998

Various groups have issued guidelines since 1976. The following list comprises the most significant of those guidelines, in chronological order.[5]

Agreement on Guidelines for Classroom Copying in Not-for-Profit Educational Institutions with Respect to Books and Periodicals, March 1976.

These *Classroom Guidelines* are the best known of all interpretive standards. They were developed at the behest of Congress and appeared in a congressional report accompanying passage of the Copyright Act of 1976. That appearance in a governmental report gave the *Classroom Guidelines* a strong authoritative appearance. When the guidelines get to the substance of fair use, they are excruciatingly narrow and rely not on the four factors but on concepts such as *brevity, cumulative effect,* and *spontaneity.* Later court decisions have deeply undercut any argument that the *Classroom Guidelines* are even close to an actual measure of fair use law. In the meantime, many institutions have folded these meticulous and even misleading standards into their formal policies.[6]

Guidelines for Educational Uses of Music, April 1976.

These standards appeared in the same congressional report in 1976. They address the ability of instructors to make limited copies of sheet music for instruction. They apply to only a few needs and offer a tight construction of fair use law. For these reasons and more, they are seldom part of the conversation about fair use today.

Guidelines for Off-Air Recording of Broadcast Programming for Educational Purposes, October 1981.

These guidelines set detailed rules for allowing educational institutions to record television programs off-air, retain copies for a short period, and permit viewing for educational purposes. Again, their appearance in a congressional report vested these standards with some semblance of authority. However, in 1984 the U.S. Supreme Court ruled that recording for home viewing was within fair use.[7] Soon, the technology of recording and viewing became ubiquitous, and the economic calculus shifted as more television went to cable and recording became a part of the market determination.

Model Policy Concerning College and University Photocopying for Classroom, Research and Library Reserve Use, American Library Association, March 1982.

The American Library Association (ALA) provided important leadership with this counterpoint to the 1976 *Classroom Guidelines.* Especially on issues of copies for classroom handouts or for library reserves, these standards deviate sharply from the rigid rules and strict limits on word counts from the *Classroom Guidelines.* This document also addresses important issues beyond fair use, such as the identification of the public domain, permissions and licensing, and the status of governmental works. ALA is of course a leading professional society, and these guidelines more clearly reflect actual needs of libraries and capture some of the flexibility of fair use. On the other hand, they are from 1982. Much has changed in the law and library services since then.

MARY HUTCHINGS REED has had a lively career as an attorney with major firms in Chicago and as a successful author. She is proof that you can survive the giant law firm and find excitement writing books and sailing in the open seas. She is the author of more than eleven novels and is active in the Chicago arts community. Debra Stanek was also with a major firm in Chicago, moved to solo practice, and today is in-house counsel at Wilton Brands in Chicago. Her career is at the intersection of intellectual property law and baking supplies. Copyright can take you in unexpected directions.

Library and Classroom Use of Copyrighted Videotapes and Computer Software, American Library Association, February 1986.

ALA went beyond fair use to identify other provisions of the Copyright Act permitting the performance of audiovisual works in libraries and classrooms and the lending of AV works and software. The document includes an extensive set of simple scenarios in question-and-answer (Q&A) format, clearly intending to give practical guidance to librarians and other users. The named authors of this work are Mary Hutchings Reed and Debra Stanek. Reed was an attorney in a major firm representing ALA, and Stanek was at that time a law student at a leading university. Their credentials gave the work solid authority.

Using Software: A Guide to the Ethical and Legal Use of Software for Members of the Academic Community, EDUCOM, January 1992.

Software was barely entering our libraries and classrooms when this document was released. The developer, EDUCOM, was later restructured into the group known today as EDUCAUSE. This work gives only a brief and perfunctory discussion of fair use, with little foresight about the growing importance of fair use for developing and decompiling code; depicting images on screens; incorporating text, images, and stories into programs;

and making intermediate copies for study, repair, compatibility, or reverse engineering. The guidelines do, however, include some helpful overviews of shareware, freeware, and the public domain.

The Conference on Fair Use: Final Report to the Commissioner on the Conclusion of the Conference on Fair Use, Information Infrastructure Task Force, Working Group on Intellectual Property Rights, November 1998.

The Conference on Fair Use, better known as CONFU, was conducted under the oversight of the U.S. Patent and Trademark Office as part of the National Information Infrastructure program. The Task Force was a far-reaching effort by the U.S. government to address the expansion and implications of the Internet.[8] The CONFU final report includes the original publication of the three proposed guidelines on issues of digital images, distance learning, and educational multimedia:

- *Proposal for Educational Fair Use Guidelines for Digital Images*
- *Proposal for Educational Fair Use Guidelines for Distance Learning*
- *Proposal for Fair Use Guidelines for Educational Multimedia*

In addition to having all the traits of other guidelines, the CONFU proposals have the distinction of finding little acceptance once offered to the public.[9] Like the *Classroom Guidelines*, the CONFU standards are detailed and rigorous. They leave little flexibility in the understanding and application of fair use. They seldom reflect on the actual law and the four factors.

The final version of the proposed guidelines from the Conference on Fair Use appeared in the final report, issued in November 1998.

The CONFU process also lacked any controlling, independent authority. It was hosted by the U.S. Patent and Trademark Office, with the U.S. Copyright Office participating at every stage. The process was ultimately open to any interested party, and a typical meeting had about forty participants representing a wide range of perspectives. The results were a committee project with political compromises. The effort gave little promise that the guidelines would be an objective application of fair use for institutional policy, or that they would be a legally sound interpretation that should withstand challenge in litigation.

Perhaps one more reason for the meager acceptance of the CONFU proposals is that they came exactly when fair use was beginning a fresh transformation. The changes in technology, publishing, communication, and teaching were giving rise to growing demand for guidance about fair use. But those same pressures may also have led to the conclusion that it was the wrong time to lock in any interpretations.

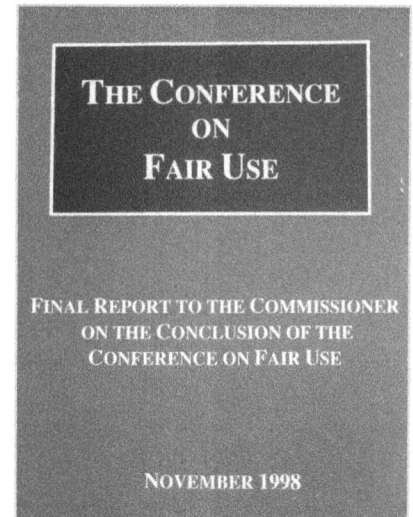

YET ANOTHER set of copyright guidelines from 1979 centers on making copies for interlibrary loans. Those guidelines are not about fair use but are instead an interpretation of a provision of Section 108 for libraries. They are the work of the National Commission on New Technological Uses of Copyrighted Works, a governmental commission with the confusingly similar acronym CONTU. These interlibrary loan issues are examined in Chapter 17 of this book.

THE CONFU participants in 1996 considered proposed guidelines on electronic reserves, but they were not included in the final report. As with so many interpretations, some critics saw them as too narrow while others challenged them as an overly broad view of fair use. These reserve guidelines were not included in the CONFU report. In any event, the issue of fair use and electronic reserves finally came before a court in the *Georgia State Case* (see Chapter 14), and the court's interpretation turned out to be a more flexible and perhaps broader understanding of fair use than had been debated by the CONFU participants. The 1996 proposal is available here: www1.mville.edu/Administration/staff/Jeff_Rosedale/guidelines.htm.

CODES OF BEST PRACTICES

Whatever the purpose or effect of the guidelines, their existence has been a mixed blessing. For many users, guidelines are a source of certainty when fair use seems unsettling. For many other users, guidelines are a constraint on the law's flexibility. The model of guidelines from 1976 through the CONFU proposals has in any event run its course. Offering a new approach to guidelines has been the development of *Codes of Best Practices* initiated by the Center for Media & Social Impact at American University.[10]

Although the *Best Practices* are different in many ways from the earlier guidelines, they still share the essential characteristics of the guidelines summarized in this chapter. For example, the *Best Practices* offer an interpretation of fair use. They carry an authoritative voice, with interpretations based on research carried out by highly experienced experts. They are developed and promoted as standards of fair use that individuals may adopt and apply in their work, and that institutions can incorporate into their policies and formal guidance.

Unlike the earlier guidelines, which were drafted by interested groups or negotiated by interested parties, the *Best Practices* are an outcome of interviews with practitioners and experts and focus groups comprising librarians, educators, authors, filmmakers, and other professionals who are expected to adhere to the relevant standards of fair use. The *Best Practices* are built on a premise that identifying community standards and accepted practices can be essential to a definition of the meaning and scope of fair use.[11]

Several *Best Practices* documents have been developed for application to diverse situations. Of greatest relevance to this book is the *Code of Best Practices in Fair Use for Academic and Research Libraries*, issued in January 2012 in partnership with the Association of Research Libraries.[12] Following interviews with numerous librarians, this code identifies a set of broad principles, stating that it "is fair" for libraries to engage in various uses of the collections, such as digitization of materials for teaching or for preservation, to make archival collections more accessible and to make materials more accessible for students with disabilities.

Each statement of principle is broad, but the code then adds "limitations" that condition and rein in the reach of principles that would otherwise be too sweeping. Those limitations implicitly reflect the concepts of the four factors in the fair use statute. The code further offers "enhancements" that a library might also adopt to strengthen the argument that the activities are within fair use.

As an example, one principle states generally that it "is fair use to make digital copies of collection items that are likely to deteriorate . . . for purposes of preservation" and to make those copies available. Among the limitations is the guidance that access to the digital copies offsite should be limited to "authenticated members of the library's patron community." If a library wants to add a measure of additional legal caution, a suggested enhancement would be the addition of "technological steps to limit further redistribution of digital surrogates."

In addition to the *Code of Best Practices* for libraries, the project has produced similar guidance for an extraordinary range of applications for which fair use has been essential and often challenging: scholarly research, online video production, documentary films, poetry, dance choreography, orphan works, images in teaching, open courseware, and more. Each published set of guidance is rooted in the methodology of interviews with members of the community, with the articulation of principles, limitations, and enhancements to shape the understanding and application of fair use.

Like earlier guidelines, the *Best Practices* have their critics. The first court ruling in the *Georgia State Case* on fair use and electronic reserves took an unsettling swat at the validity of community standards: "In the absence of judicial precedent concerning the limits of fair use for nonprofit educational uses, colleges and universities have been guessing about the permissible extent of fair use."[13] But with so few cases on the issues of importance to colleges and universities, policymakers have scant choice but to survey the law and environment and reach a reasoned conclusion.

Some scholarly analyses have raised other points of criticism, notably that the *Best Practices* are based on interviews with limited stakeholders.[14] That criticism may be valid. In the case of the *Code of Best Practices* for libraries, the developers acknowledge that rightsholders were not brought into the project. The entire initiative is based on a premise that practices within a community can discern proper fair use. However, the earlier guidelines show that when stakeholders with divergent views need to reach consensus, the result is a set of guidelines that bear little relationship to actual law and that are far too restrictive to have meaningful application.

WHAT TO DO WITH THE GUIDELINES?

The main motivation behind most of the guidelines has been to bring some degree of certainty to common fair use applications. Yet none of these guidelines has done so with any legal validity. None of the guidelines have been enacted into law by Congress, and none have been adopted as a binding standard of fair use in any court decision. Do the guidelines even present appropriate *answers* to any fair use problems?

This is one of those rare questions for which the answer is monumentally complex, but we might all be best served with a simple "no." That said, we next need to have a look at some of the nuances of guidelines. The present author has written at length about their shortcomings.[15] Deficiencies of the guidelines include the following:

- They often misinterpret fair use, infusing it with variables and conditions that are not part of the law.
- They create rigidity in the application of fair use, sacrificing the flexibility that allows fair use to have meaning for new needs, technologies, and materials.
- They tend to espouse the narrowest interpretations of the law in order to gain support from diverse interest groups.
- They are often the work product of parties who have an interest in an interpretation of fair use, and seldom does a truly independent voice have a leading role in developing or promoting the guidelines.

OUTSIDE THE scope of this chapter about guidelines is the Fair Use Checklist; it is referenced in **Chapter 14** in connection with the *Georgia State Case*. A version is included in this book as **Appendix B**. The checklist is offered as a means for understanding and applying fair use, and it can be adopted by an individual or an institution as part of a policy. Unlike the guidelines in this chapter, the checklist does not specify conclusions or answers to fair use questions. It does not prescribe answers or even offer an interpretation of the law. It can therefore be used apart from any other guidance or combined with guidelines and analysis as added means for understanding or applying fair use law.

The *Classroom Guidelines* from 1976 may have effectively suffered a fatal blow in the rulings from the district and appellate courts in the litigation involving electronic reserves at Georgia State University.[16] The case is not yet at its conclusion, but both courts declined to adopt the *Classroom Guidelines* as a legal standard for fair use. The plaintiff publishers had strongly advocated that the court should enforce the 1976 standards and compel the university to incorporate them into institutional policy.

The district court in the *Georgia State Case* was dismissive in its initial ruling in 2012: "[T]he Guidelines establish numerical caps on how many words a teacher may copy and still stay within the safe harbor. This brightline restriction stands in contrast to the statutory scheme described in § 107, which codified a multi-factorial analysis in which no factor is dispositive."[17]

The court of appeals handed down its first decision in 2014, with these words of caution about the *Classroom Guidelines*: "Whatever persuasive value the Classroom Guidelines may possess, we must keep in mind that they (1) were drafted by partisan groups, (2) 'state the minimum and not the maximum standards of educational fair use under Section 107,' and (3) adopt the type of 'hard evidentiary presumption[s]' regarding which types of use may be fair that the Supreme Court has since repeatedly warned against."[18]

Whatever the virtues or hazards of any guidelines, each individual or institution considering them should make an informed and independent decision about whether to adopt or follow them. Even the most enthusiastic supporter of the guidelines cannot avoid their weaknesses. The guidelines are not law, and they will never address all future needs. Rather, we must always be ready to turn to the factors in the law to understand fair use for each new situation.

The guidelines also demand diligent oversight and enforcement if they really are to become the policy standards for educators, librarians, and others. For example, if a library were to adopt a new set of guidelines on orphan works as the sole standard of fair use, then the library would need to educate the staff and establish systems of compliance with the full roster of detailed measures that the guidelines might embody. If the past is any predictor of the future, we can expect that new guidelines will often be more restrictive and more convoluted than the actual law of fair use.

Basing a decision on the four factors in the statute rather than on the guidelines can have many advantages. The law's flexibility is important for enabling fair use to meet future needs and to promote progress in the academic setting or elsewhere. Accepting that flexibility also allows some important protections for educators and librarians. The good faith application of fair use can lead a court to cut entirely some of the liabilities that educators or librarians might face in an infringement lawsuit. The only way to apply fair use in good faith is by learning the law and applying it; the only way to apply the law is by working with the four factors in the statute. In the final analysis, the law itself ultimately offers greater security than does the belabored or negotiated illusion of any fair use guidelines.

FULL TEXT OF THE GUIDELINES

The following citations can take the reader to the full text of the leading guidelines surveyed in this chapter.

Agreement on Guidelines for Classroom Copying in Not-for-Profit Educational Institutions with Respect to Books and Periodicals, March 1976.

   Source: U.S. Congress, House Comm. on the Judiciary, *Copyright Law Revision*, 94th Cong., 2d Sess., H. Rept. 94-1476, at 68–70 (1976).

Guidelines for Educational Uses of Music, April 1976.

   Source: U.S. Congress, House Comm. on the Judiciary, *Copyright Law Revision*, 94th Cong., 2d Sess., H. Rept. 94-1476, at 70–71 (1976).

Guidelines for Off-Air Recording of Broadcast Programming for Educational Purposes, October 1981.

   Source: U.S. Congress, 127 *Congressional Record*, no. 18, at 24,048–49 (1981).

   Source: U.S. Congress, House Comm. on the Judiciary, *Report on Piracy and Counterfeiting Amendments*, 97th Cong., 1st Sess., H. Doc. 495, at 8–9 (1982).

Model Policy Concerning College and University Photocopying for Classroom, Research and Library Reserve Use, American Library Association, March 1982.

> Source: Originally published as a freestanding pamphlet from ALA; a copy is available here: https://library.truman.edu/forms/Model_Policy.pdf.

Library and Classroom Use of Copyrighted Videotapes and Computer Software, American Library Association, February 1986.

> Source: Reed, Mary Hutchings, and Debra Stanek, "Library and Classroom Use of Copyrighted Videotapes and Computer Software," *American Libraries* 17, no. 2 (February 1986): supp., AD, https://www.jstor.org/stable/25629908.

Using Software: A Guide to the Ethical and Legal Use of Software for Members of the Academic Community, EDUCOM, January 1992.

> Source: Originally published as a freestanding pamphlet from EDUCOM, a predecessor organization to EDUCAUSE; the text is available here: https://www.educause.edu/ir/library/html/code.html.

Fair-Use Guidelines for Electronic Reserve Systems, March 1996.

> Source: Originally developed by participants in CONFU; a copy of the guidelines and a background document are available here: http://www1.mville.edu/Administration/staff/Jeff_Rosedale/guidelines.

Proposal for Educational Fair Use Guidelines for Digital Images, Conference on Fair Use, November 1998.

> Source: Working Group on Intellectual Property Rights of the Information Infrastructure Task Force, *The Conference on Fair Use: Final Report to the Commissioner on the Conclusion of the Conference on Fair Use* (Washington, DC: U.S. Patent and Trademark Office, 1998), 33–41, https://www.uspto.gov/sites/default/files/documents/confurep_0.pdf.

Proposal for Educational Fair Use Guidelines for Distance Learning, Conference on Fair Use, November 1998.

> Source: Working Group on Intellectual Property Rights of the Information Infrastructure Task Force, *The Conference on Fair Use: Final Report to the Commissioner on the Conclusion of the Conference on Fair Use* (Washington, DC: U.S. Patent and Trademark Office, 1998), 43–48, https://www.uspto.gov/sites/default/files/documents/confurep_0.pdf.

Proposal for Fair Use Guidelines for Educational Multimedia, Conference on Fair Use, November 1998.

> Source: Working Group on Intellectual Property Rights of the Information Infrastructure Task Force, *The Conference on Fair Use: Final Report to the Commissioner on the Conclusion of the Conference on Fair Use* (Washington, DC: U.S. Patent and Trademark Office, 1998), 49–59, https://www.uspto.gov/sites/default/files/documents/confurep_0.pdf.

NOTES

1. Copyright Act of 1976, Pub. L. No. 94-553, 90 Stat. 2546 (codified at 17 U.S.C. § 107).
2. A report from the House of Representatives accompanying passage of the 1976 act provided that "there is no disposition to freeze the doctrine in the statute, especially during a period of rapid technological change. . . ." U.S. Congress, House Comm. on the Judiciary, *Copyright Law Revision*, 94th Cong., 2d Sess., H. Rept. 94-1476, at 66 (1976).
3. The present author has written extensively on the development and influence of the early guidelines. Kenneth D. Crews, *Copyright, Fair Use, and the Challenge for Universities:*

Promoting the Progress of Higher Education (Chicago: University of Chicago Press, 1993). That book offers a look at the "Gentlemen's Agreement" of 1935, often viewed as a harbinger of later guidelines.

4. Working Group on Intellectual Property Rights of the Information Infrastructure Task Force, *The Conference on Fair Use: Final Report to the Commissioner on the Conclusion of the Conference on Fair Use* (Washington, DC: U.S. Patent and Trademark Office, 1998). The full report is available here: https://www.uspto.gov/sites/default/files/documents/confurep_0.pdf.

5. Citations to a full-text source for each of the guidelines are listed at the end of this chapter.

6. Although criticism of the *Classroom Guidelines* has grown, these standards continue to appear in a publication from the U.S. Copyright Office. They likely persist out of legal inertia and the continued visceral desire for relative certainty. For one critique, *see* Sara R. Benson, "Interpreting Fair Use for Academic Librarians: Thinking beyond the Scope of the Circular 21 Guidelines," *Journal of Academic Librarianship* 43 (2017): 105–7.

7. *Sony Corporation of America v. Universal City Studios, Inc.,* 464 U.S. 417 (1984).

8. The roots of the Conference on Fair Use are found in a 1995 report from the National Information Infrastructure program, available here: https://eric.ed.gov/?id=ED387135.

9. The drafting and promotion of the multimedia guidelines were led by the Consortium of College and University Media Centers. Even that organization chose to "retire" the multimedia guidelines in December 2012. See http://archive.cmsimpact.org/blog/fair-use/ccumc-adopts-librarians %E2%80%99-code-retires-previous-fair-use-guidelines.

10. For copies of the many different codes developed by the center, *see* https://cmsimpact.org/codes -of-best-practices/.

11. As stated in the *Code of Best Practices in Fair Use for Academic and Research Libraries,* "Ultimately, determining whether any use is likely to be considered 'fair' requires a thoughtful evaluation of the facts, the law, and the norms of the relevant community." *See* https://www.arl .org/resources/code-of-best-practices-in-fair-use-for-academic-libraries/.

12. For the full publication and background information, *see Id.*

13. *Cambridge University Press v. Becker,* 863 F. Supp. 2d 1190, 1232 (N.D. Ga. 2012), *rev'd in part, Cambridge University Press v. Patton,* 769 F.3d 1232 (11th Cir. 2014).

14. Perhaps the most thorough critique of the *Best Practices* is here: Jennifer E. Rothman, "Best Intentions: Reconsidering Best Practices Statements in the Context of Fair Use and Copyright Law," *Journal of the Copyright Society of the USA* 57 (2010): 371–87.

15. Kenneth D. Crews, "The Law of Fair Use and the Illusion of Fair-Use Guidelines," *Ohio State Law Journal* 62 (2001): 599–702.

16. Chapter 14 of this book provides a close examination of the substance of the court rulings as well as an overview of the route the case has taken through the federal court system.

17. *Cambridge University Press v. Becker,* 863 F. Supp. 2d 1190, 1229 (N.D. Ga. 2012), *rev'd in part, Cambridge University Press v. Patton,* 769 F.3d 1232 (11th Cir. 2014).

18. *Cambridge University Press v. Patton,* 769 F.3d 1232, 1246 n.12 (11th Cir. 2014).

CHAPTER 14

EDUCATION, FAIR USE, AND THE *GEORGIA STATE CASE*

KEY POINTS

- Few court cases had addressed fair use for nonprofit education until the rulings in the *Georgia State Case*.
- This district court and the court of appeals have issued elaborate decisions, shaping the meaning of fair use in education.
- The rulings offer many broad and general insights into the four factors, applicable beyond this one case.
- The decisions provide important guidance for developing library and university policies.
- An overriding practical lesson from this case is the importance of developing institutional policy on fair use.
- The case is still not final, and educators and librarians should be watching for new developments in this important case.

THE FAIR USE of copyrighted works in connection with teaching and classroom uses has been at the center of many debates—and some litigation—since the enactment of the fair use statute in 1976. It also has been a central topic of various parts of this book. Chapter 12 applies fair use to specific scenarios, with an examination of court rulings about photocopied handouts and coursepacks for education. Chapter 13 surveys the fair use "guidelines" that have attempted to interpret uses of copyrighted works for teaching. Many of these developments came to a head in the recent litigation involving electronic reserves at Georgia State University (GSU).

Despite the continued importance and expansion of fair use for teaching, research, and libraries, few cases have even considered fair use in the genuinely nonprofit educational context. We finally have a landmark case, although lessons from the court rulings are still not entirely clear. This chapter provides a close look at the case of *Cambridge University Press v. Becker* (the series of court rulings is known more familiarly as the *Georgia State Case* or the *GSU Case*), as federal judges have striven to give meaning to the four factors of fair use as applied to scanning select pages from copyrighted books as part of the electronic reserve system at Georgia State University. This chapter also makes the point that the litigation in this case continues, with more lessons to come.

THE ORIGINAL and related cases proceeded through the federal court system for more than a decade, yielding multiple rulings that reflect the judicial understanding and application of fair use. Four rulings are of particular interest, and this chapter follows this convention of citations:

Cambridge I: *Cambridge University Press v. Becker*, 863 F. Supp. 2d 1190 (N.D. Ga. 2012) (first decision from the district court).

Cambridge II: *Cambridge University Press v. Patton*, 769 F.3d 1232 (11th Cir. 2014) (ruling from the court of appeals, elaborating on fair use and remanding to the district court).

Cambridge III: *Cambridge University Press v. Becker*, 2016 WL 3098397 (N.D. Ga. 2016) (reapplication of fair use by the district court; appealed again to the court of appeals).

Cambridge IV: *Cambridge University Press v. Albert*, 906 F.3d 1290 (11th Cir. 2018) (vacating Cambridge III and remanding to the district court for reapplication of fair use).

The case was commenced nearly a decade before this writing, and we have elaborate and substantive rulings from the federal district court and from the court of appeals. The lengthy analyses of fair use from those courts offer a trove of guidance for librarians to mine and ponder as they seek to establish a reserve system. The opinions offer elaborate guidance for educators who are selecting course readings and making them available to students in a manner consistent with the law. This chapter seeks to identify points of insight from the *GSU Case* rulings that can help exactly those parties find the principles of fair use they need.

Before delving into the substance of the case, two points of caution are in order. First, a disclosure: The author of this book was retained by the defendants (the university officials) as an expert witness, filing two reports in the case and testifying at length during the trial.[1] Second, the litigation in this case is still open and active. Future court rulings could alter or even upend some lessons that we draw in the meantime. To put it simply, everything summarized in this chapter is subject to change, depending on whether the courts choose to reexamine and revise the principles of fair use. This book makes no predictions about how the courts might decide the case on further consideration or about which direction the litigation might take, but we have to learn what we can in the meantime.

BACKGROUND AND CONTEXT

Events in the *Georgia State Case* arose from a dispute between a major public university in Atlanta, Georgia, and various publishers, acting through the Association of American Publishers (AAP). The AAP had long been disputing the scope of fair use for electronic reserves and in the years prior to 2008 had submitted challenges to several universities about the prevailing interpretations of fair use that they were employing.

The AAP was successful in reaching resolutions with a few universities without resorting to litigation. In particular, Hofstra, Marquette, and Cornell Universities reached agreements with the AAP to adopt a revised fair use policy that allowed electronic reserve services to continue, with an interpretation of fair use that was built on the Fair Use Checklist (reprinted as Appendix B of this book) and without reference to the rigidity of the word counts and

THE LITIGATION was brought against various named individuals rather than against the university itself because of the complications of the Eleventh Amendment to the U.S. Constitution. The amendment severely constrains the ability to bring a lawsuit in federal court against a state or a state agency, such as GSU, particularly for a monetary remedy. The individual defendants are not the state, but they are leaders with authority to direct activities at GSU. The case could proceed against the individuals, especially because the plaintiff publishers mainly sought an injunction that would bar further scanning beyond a more rigorous standard of fair use. They were not necessarily looking for dollar damages. Peter J. Karol, "Fair Use, Meet *Ex parte Young*," *Patent, Trademark & Copyright Journal* (BNA) 89 (Jan. 16, 2015). 689.

other restrictions of the 1976 *Classroom Guidelines* (those guidelines and others are surveyed in Chapter 13).[2]

Despite those clashes and resolutions, no settlement was forthcoming when the AAP challenged the reserve system at Georgia State University. Instead, in 2008, a group of three publishers, with financial support from the AAP and the Copyright Clearance Center, filed a lawsuit against a long list of university officials, including all members of the trustees, the president, and the director of the university library. The case went to trial in May and June 2011, and many of the officials, librarians, and faculty members testified about their use of the books and their decision to assign and scan pages as part of the e-reserve service.

To get a clear vision of the litigation saga, a basic understanding of the structure of the federal court system, summarized in Chapter 2, becomes essential. The case was filed with the federal District Court for the Northern District of Georgia. The trial was held in that court before Judge Orinda Evans, without a jury, in 2011. Judge Evans handed down her ruling nearly a year later in May 2012. In a span of about 350 pages, she offered an overview of fair use and detailed its meaning in the context of education and e-reserves. She also analyzed fair use for each book excerpt in question.

Early in the litigation process, the case identified ninety-nine instances of alleged infringement, and the plaintiff publishers later reduced their claims to seventy-five infringing excerpts from sixty-four books. One book was not registered with the U.S. Copyright Office, as required before filing the lawsuit, reducing the claims to seventy-four.[3] After an elaborate analysis, the judge rejected twenty-six of those possible infringements for reasons other than fair use. Most significant, she found that in sixteen examples, the plaintiff publishers had failed to introduce evidence that they actually owned the copyrights.[4] Of the remaining forty-eight claims, the court found only five instances of infringement and concluded that forty-three of the contested examples were fair use.

Judge Evans's lengthy opinion from 2012 includes detailed applications of the four factors of fair use to each of the forty-eight instances. One by one, she meticulously determined whether each instance of scanning selected pages from a specific book constitutes fair use or is infringement. Because the defendants (the university parties) were successful with their defense against all but five allegations, she declined to enter the injunction sought by the publishers. Judge Evans also determined that the defendants were the prevailing parties and ordered the publishers to pay their attorneys' fees and costs.

This was a startling loss for the publishers, who were obviously expecting a different outcome. They appealed. An important concept of appeals is that appellate courts decide only issues

BASIC LESSONS about copyright ownership proved devastating for some of the publishers' claims. Recall from **Chapter 7** that authors can transfer their copyrights to publishers or anyone else. However, a copyright transfer must be in writing and signed by the copyright transferor. Often an agreement between author and publisher does just that. But if the agreement or any other documentation is lost and no other supporting evidence is introduced at trial, the court cannot assume that the copyright in fact belongs to the publisher. Without the needed evidence to show that the publishers were the right parties to enforce the copyrights for some of the books, the court rejected sixteen of the publishers' claimed infringements. Lesson of the story: Keep careful records of your copyrights, and keep copies of your publication agreements.

of law, not issues of fact. To put it another way, the court of appeals can hear and decide arguments that the district court erred in its understanding and application of the law, but the appeals court does not determine whether the facts are right. Reviewing evidence to determine facts is the domain of the district court.

The Eleventh Circuit Court of Appeals issued its ruling in 2014, affirming many of the points of law that the district court had applied, but reversing others. The appeals court adjusted and elaborated in various respects the district court's legal interpretation of fair use. The court firmly slammed the suggestion by Judge Evans in her decision that fair use could be determined in part by measuring the exact quantity (e.g., 10 percent of a book) of the work used.[5] Perhaps most significant, the Eleventh Circuit placed greater weight on the fourth factor (the effect on the market) and allowed greater consideration of any evidence of sales and potential market harm.

The court of appeals remanded the case back to the district court to apply the revised interpretation of fair use to the forty-eight instances of alleged infringement. From the same facts and using a somewhat redefined standard of fair use from the Eleventh Circuit, the same judge at the district court found four instances of infringement. It had found five instances in the 2012 ruling. The other forty-four alleged infringements remaining in consideration were all determined to be fair use. The court again found the defendants to be the prevailing parties and awarded attorneys' fees.

The publishers appealed one more time. Hearings were held again before the Eleventh Circuit in July 2017. That court issued a relatively short decision in October 2018. This latest decision was again a critique by the appeals court of Judge Evans's application of fair use. The court wholly rejected the effort by Judge Evans to weigh the four factors with a

The appeals of the *Georgia State Case* were argued and decided in this historic courthouse, with its deep and ornate architectural features. The trial was held in the nearby federal building, a high-rise structure of the international style of the 1970s.

> **WHERE COULD** the *Georgia State Case* go after the 2018 ruling from the Eleventh Circuit? The appellate court ordered a remand, and the case is in fact back with Judge Evans in the district court. She is asked to reevaluate one more time her determination about fair use; we can anticipate her next ruling during 2020. The case could have taken a different path. The parties might have asked for the full roster of Eleventh Circuit judges to rehear and rule again (called an en banc hearing). The parties might have petitioned the U.S. Supreme Court to grant certiorari and hear the case. In the face of continuing uncertainty and expenses, the parties might at any time be privately considering an agreement to settle their differences and end the litigation. Of course, they could have settled at any earlier time, but they obviously did not.

mathematical equation. The court seemed to admonish Judge Evans for even reevaluating the evidence on the fourth factor, instructing that the earlier ruling asked her only to give more weight to that factor and to revisit her previous determinations of whether it favors or disfavors fair use.

FAIR USE ACCORDING TO THE *GSU CASE* RULINGS

Although the 2018 ruling from the Eleventh Circuit may be perplexing in some respects, we nevertheless have the benefit of detailed insights from the district court and the Eleventh Circuit about their understanding of fair use for electronic reserves. These courts have given us elaborations about the law, with guidance to shape fair use standards for e-reserves and possibly more. We can learn much from these rulings as we consider the meaning of the law and develop reserve policies in support of education.

Delving into the *GSU Case* demands a cautious legal analysis. When a case goes up on appeal, the conventions of legal research generally mean that the appellate decision supersedes the lower court's ruling on any of the same issues. But that is not always true. Sometimes the appellate court addresses only certain of the issues and concepts, leaving the analysis of other matters in the lower court's ruling still open for consideration and application.

Such is the dynamic of the *GSU Case* rulings. While both courts examined the details of fair use, the district court gave greater attention to the crafting and evaluation of the university policy standards. The district court also addressed a few aspects of fair use that were not considered on appeal. To the extent that the district court's reasoning is not superseded or contradicted by the higher court, the guidance from the district court can remain at least influential as we seek to understand the law.

The nature of the *GSU Case* decisions is even more subtle. A dominant legal question before the courts was whether, based on the record of alleged infringements, the university was engaged in "ongoing and continuous conduct" that should be enjoined. The court's real need was to determine whether the university was acting properly in its application of fair use. The focus was on the results, rather than on the standards, policies, and procedures. Yet, the university had policy standards in place, and the courts found few instances of infringement. We might infer various policymaking lessons for the next library or university grappling with fair use. The decisions also remind us that fair use evolves with experience, and continuing developments in this case and any other future court rulings might shed further light on the full meaning of fair use.

FAIR USE IN GENERAL

The *Georgia State Case* can be mined for principles of fair use that could be broadly relevant to many situations where fair use applies. Most of all, it is the rare case about common teaching activities and library services. Many of the principles at the root of the *GSU Case* decisions are familiar from other contexts, but the courts have applied them in a way that affirms their value for educators and librarians. Consider the following:

- *Fair use is based on the four factors.* Fair use turns primarily on an application of the four factors. No one factor controls, and the outcome depends on a reasoned analysis and application of all factors. The four factors work together in the analysis, and they are to be weighed together in light of the purposes of copyright. Further, the relative weight each factor receives in the analysis depends on the facts and circumstances: "In keeping with this approach, a given factor may be more or less important in determining whether a particular use should be considered fair under the specific circumstances of the case."[6] The factors are not to be given a quantified weighting but are to be reviewed holistically in light of the given facts.[7]
- *Nonprofit education is favored.* The courts gave strong support for the nonprofit educational purpose. The appellate court put it most succinctly: "[A]llowing latitude for educational fair use promotes the goals of copyright."[8] The Eleventh Circuit reiterated the point with emphasis: "Thus, we are persuaded that, despite the recent focus on transformativeness under the first factor, use for teaching purposes by a nonprofit, educational institution such as Defendants' favors a finding of fair use under the first factor, despite the nontransformative nature of the use."[9]
- *Transformative uses are not required.* Both the district court and the Eleventh Circuit held that the scanning of pages for the electronic reserve system in this case does not constitute a "transformative use" of the copyrighted works. The court of appeals found that they "are verbatim copies of portions of the original books which have merely been converted into a digital format."[10] Ordinarily, the more transformative the use, the more expansive the potential of fair use. One could therefore argue that had the court determined that the use was transformative, instructors and libraries might be able to apply a broader scope of fair use and consequently reproduce longer excerpts from the books.

  - Although a transformative purpose can allow greater fair use, it may not be a reasonable assumption that any of the judges ruling in this case would have been inclined to allow significantly greater fair use for this use (perhaps a few more pages?), regardless of whether or not it is labeled *transformative.* More important, the fact that the court did not find a transformative use may be a blessing and an opportunity. Courts rule on cases, with the specific facts as presented. Because the courts concluded that this use was not transformative, the court was therefore leaving undecided the scope of fair use for transformative uses in education. That opens the possibility of future cases about more innovative teaching activities. It also leaves open the ability of each institution to set its own policy or standard for fair use when instructors are developing creative instructional tools that utilize copyrighted works in transformative ways.

- *The "nature of the work" is not a critical factor.* For decades, courts had generally applied a more rigorous standard of fair use for highly creative works, such as fiction, poetry, and art. In the *GSU Case*, the courts downplayed this second factor of fair use, and the appellate court declared it to be of "relatively little importance."[11] Reducing the significance of the second factor has at least two immediate and practical implications. First, when the influence of one factor is reduced, the other factors become more important. In the overall balancing of factors, the weight of evidence on the remaining three factors can become even more crucial.

  - Second, by reducing the role of the *nature of the work*, the courts are signaling that fair use can apply to all types of works, and education can accordingly benefit from all types of works. The diminished role for this factor makes good sense for education. Teaching and learning can be built on any type of work, and the *GSU Case* rulings help get past any idea that certain types of copyrighted works—especially creative music, art, and literature—are somehow less suited for education.[12]

    > **THE SECOND** factor has been downplayed in other court decisions related to education and research. Notably, in the Google Books and HathiTrust decisions, the Second Circuit Court of Appeals ruled that this factor had little significance in the context of digitizing books to create a system for searching and indexing. The Second Circuit wisely determined that when the works were not being used for their expressive content, fair use should not depend on whether that content is simple and factual or highly creative. These cases are examined in **Chapter 10**.

- *The "amount of the work" is not strictly defined.* The district court articulated some familiar precepts related to the third factor, such as this: "The portion used must be reasonable in relation to the work from which it was taken and the purpose for which it was used."[13] The appellate court shifted the focus, adding a connection between amount and the potential market harm: "The District Court should have performed this analysis on a work-by-work basis, taking into account whether the amount taken—qualitatively and quantitatively—was reasonable in light of the pedagogical purpose of the use and the threat of market substitution."[14] Both courts rejected entirely the application of strict quantified measures.[15] The concept of counting words, as in the 1976 *Classroom Guidelines*, is an anathema to the courts' analyses.[16]

- *Market effects may include potential harm to licensing.* Licensing is a cognizable market for evaluation of fair use; if the scanning and educational uses interfere or conflict with the available license for copying and distributing the work, that finding can tip this factor away from fair use.[17] On the other hand, the absence of an available realistic license can weigh in favor of fair use. According to the appellate court, when the copyright owner does not make a license available, the "inference is that the author or publisher did not think that there would be enough such use to bother making a license available."[18]

- *Copyright owners have the burden to show licensing harm.* The court placed the burden on the publishers to demonstrate that licensing was available and to present evidence of market harm. The district court, on remand, clarified and applied the test: "Plaintiffs bear the burden of showing that CCC provided in 2009 'reasonably efficient, reasonably priced, convenient access' to users who wanted to copy the excerpt in question."[19] The district court expanded on the reasoning and the practical procedures: "Where a license to make digital copies of an excerpt was not available in 2009, there is a presumption that Defendants' use of the excerpt did not harm the plaintiff-publisher. Plaintiffs can overcome the presumption of no market by going forward with evidence of license availability and also with evidence of a potential, future market."[20]

- *Market harm is potentially greater for nontransformative uses.* Both courts unquestionably did not require a finding of transformative purpose. However, nontransformative uses have a greater potential of conflicting with the market for the original. According to the Eleventh Circuit, "Because Defendants' use is nontransformative and fulfills the educational purposes that Plaintiffs, at least in part, market their works for, the threat of market substitution here is great and thus the fourth factor looms large in the overall fair use analysis."[21] The Eleventh Circuit emphasized that point in its 2018 ruling. The practical implication is the greater need to check the market for some nontransformative uses.

POLICYMAKING AT UNIVERSITIES

While the courts, parties, and lawyers struggle with this case, education must continue. Colleges and universities long have offered reserve services and have developed principles and policies for fair use. In light of the rulings in the *Georgia State Case*, we can find affirmation of some familiar policymaking and we can see places where some adjustment may be in order. If you are charged with drafting your fair use standards, the *GSU Case* offers the following pointers:

- *The* Classroom Guidelines *are not law.* The publishers tried repeatedly to have the *Classroom Guidelines* from 1976 adopted as the standard of fair use for classroom use, including electronic reserves. The Eleventh Circuit rejected them as a legal standard: "We note that the Classroom Guidelines, although part of the legislative history of the Copyright Act, do not carry force of law."[22] Given the Eleventh Circuit's vigorous rejection of quantified standards in its 2018 decision, educators and librarians might do well to drop the 1976 guidelines entirely.[23]
- *The* Classroom Guidelines *have limited persuasive value.* The Eleventh Circuit went further in its rejection of the *Classroom Guidelines* and would not even allow them to be an indicator or gauge of fair use: "Whatever persuasive value the Classroom Guidelines may possess, we must keep in mind that they (1) were drafted by partisan groups, (2) 'state the minimum and not the maximum standards of educational fair use under Section 107', and (3) adopt the type of 'hard evidentiary presumption[s]' regarding which types of use may be fair that the Supreme Court has since repeatedly warned against."[24]
- *The Fair Use Checklist is appropriate for policy determinations.* The GSU reserves policy included the adoption of the Fair Use Checklist as a tool to help instructors and librarians reach decisions about fair use.[25] Neither court specifically endorsed the checklist or any other particular resource; that was not the role of the courts. Instead, the courts reviewed the facts of the case,

including incorporation of the checklist into the university's policy, and noted that through appropriate application, the policy and checklist helped guide members of the university community to correct determinations in nearly all instances of alleged infringement.[26]

- *The case offers numerous suggestions for policies.* Each aspect of the courts' analyses of fair use can potentially be recrafted into a specific policy element. The district court in its 2012 ruling offered a roster of practical and helpful takeaways for libraries and educational institutions that are developing new policy standards for classroom copying and e-reserves. The policy conditions add up to "[c]arefully monitored circumstances"[27] that supported a finding of fair use:

  - The policy should not overlook fundamentals: "Access shall be limited only to the students who are enrolled in the course in question, and then only for the term of the course."[28]

  - Password or other restriction on access can help demonstrate that the materials are used only for the educational needs of a specific course. Limited access can also prevent wider access or other misuse that could harm the market.[29]

  - Works included in e-reserves should be closely related to the subject matter of the specific course: "[T]he selected excerpt must fill a demonstrated, legitimate purpose in the course curriculum. . . ."[30]

  - The amount of a work placed on reserve should be limited to the amount needed for the educational purpose. According to the district court, "the selected excerpt . . . must be narrowly tailored to accomplish that purpose."[31]

  - Students should be "prohibited by policy from distributing copies to others."[32] A policy against sharing materials beyond the needs of the course can be part of the effort to use the works solely for education and to minimize possible market harm.

  - Similarly, students "must be reminded of the limitations of the copyright laws," perhaps by policy or possibly on a log-in screen.[33] Reminders might reduce misuse and market harm. They might also provide a brief chance for students to learn that copyright applies to the readings and merits attention and respect.

> **A COMMON** question about e-reserves is whether students may have access to the online readings after the course is completed. Of course, the law does not set a strict rule, but it calls on you to be reasonable and to justify your decision. For example, relatively open accessibility during the first weeks of the semester can be useful as students make their final course selections. That temporary and expanded use could be a valid educational objective. On the other hand, allowing indefinite ongoing access so students can have the readings for future reference may strain the comfort zone of fair use.

WHAT'S NEXT?

This chapter includes a caution about the future. The *Georgia State Case* is still active litigation, and the courts may make yet further changes in the meaning of fair use and its practical application. Whatever the courts might do, the case is a clear call to action by policymakers.

Libraries and other institutions should act soon to develop policy reflecting the lessons of the *Georgia State Case* and other rulings on fair use. The policymaking will inevitably be in some respects defensive and protective. But the rulings in the *GSU Case* offer much more. The courts are giving numerous signals about the lawful scope of fair use, and the public should act to reap the benefit of the opportunity in support of teaching and learning.

NOTES

1. This chapter represents the views of the author and not necessarily the view of any party or attorney associated with the *Georgia State Case*. The author did not share this chapter with any such person prior to publication.

2. The early cases against photocopy shops and the threats of litigation that preceded the *Georgia State Case* are recounted in Brandon Butler, "Transformative Teaching and Educational Fair Use After Georgia State," *Connecticut Law Review* 48 (December 2015): 503–8.

3. As detailed in Chapter 6, registration is not a requirement for copyright protection, but for many works it is a required step before commencing an infringement lawsuit.

4. According to the court, the absence of a contract conveying the copyright from author to publisher was "fatal to Plaintiffs' prima facie case" of infringement. *Cambridge University Press v. Becker*, 863 F. Supp.2d 1190, 1223 (N.D. Ga. 2012) [hereinafter *Cambridge I*]. In ten other instances, the court called the use de minimis based on the fact that the reading was only supplemental and data showed that few students even accessed or read it.

5. One analysis argues that the Eleventh Circuit failed to understand that courts should be able to "use rules to elaborate the standard without forgoing the court's decisional freedom to deviate from such guidelines." Niva Elkin-Koren & Orit Fischman-Afori, "Rulifying Fair Use," *Arizona Law Review* 59, no. 1 (2017): 188.

6. *Cambridge University Press v. Patton*, 769 F.3d 1232, 1260 (11th Cir. 2014) [hereinafter *Cambridge II*].

7. *Cambridge University Press v. Albert*, 906 F.3d 1290, 1302 (11th Cir. 2018) [hereinafter *Cambridge IV*].

8. *Cambridge II* at 1267.

9. *Id.*

10. *Id.* at 1262.

11. *Id.* at 1270.

12. The court was following the example of the U.S. Supreme Court, which ruled that the second factor has little significance when applied to parody. *Campbell v. Acuff-Rose Music, Inc.*, 510 U.S. 569, 586 (1994).

13. *Cambridge I* at 1227.

14. *Cambridge II* at 1283.

15. The Eleventh Circuit also rejected the mathematical weighing of the four factors undertaken by Judge Evans: "The district court must eschew a quantitative approach to the weighing and balancing of the fair use factors and give each excerpt the holistic, qualitative, and individual analysis that the Act demands." *Cambridge IV* at 1302.

16. The district court did originally offer an interpretation based in part on copying single chapters and not more than 10 percent of the book. The Eleventh Circuit wholly rejected such quantified measures.

17. One analysis concluded that the Eleventh Circuit gave comparatively greater weight to the commercial and market implications of the uses. Laura Burtle & Mariann Burright, "Academic Libraries as Unlikely Defendants: A Comparative Fair Use Analysis of the Georgia State University E-Reserves and HathiTrust Cases," *Library Trends* 68 (Fall 2018): 376–93.

18. *Cambridge II* at 1277.

19. *Cambridge University Press v. Becker*, 2016 WL 3098397, slip op. at 5 (N.D. Ga. 2016) [sometimes referenced as *Cambridge III*].

20. *Id.* Leaning on this analysis from the district court comes with some risk. The Eleventh Circuit in 2018 reprimanded the district court for revisiting this factor. It does not mean that the analysis is necessarily wrong, but it evidently was not the route that the Eleventh Circuit wanted Judge Evans to take.

21. *Cambridge II* at 1275.

22. *Id.* at 1273.

23. According to one analysis, "The Eleventh Circuit's opinion in the GSU case is a half-measure in the right direction. It marks the end of the Guidelines-coursepack paradigm, but it does not offer a useful substitute." Brandon Butler, "Transformative Teaching and Educational Fair Use after Georgia State," *Connecticut Law Review* 48 (December 2015): 479.

24. *Cambridge II* at 1246 n.12. The Eleventh Circuit reiterated the caution against the "hard evidentiary presumption" later in the opinion. *Id.* at 1273.

25. The Fair Use Checklist and variations on it are available on numerous websites, including the copyright office website of Columbia University: https://copyright.columbia.edu/basics/fair-use/fair-use-checklist.html. A slightly updated version of the checklist is included as Appendix B of this book.

26. In addition to the checklist, many other resources exist to help the public understand and apply fair use. For example, the Authors Alliance has gathered links to several examples: https://www.authorsalliance.org/2017/03/08/resource-roundup-fair-use/.

27. *Cambridge I* at 1238.

28. *Id.* at 1243.

29. Password protection was mentioned in the facts of the case in the district court's decision. *Id.* at 1220.

30. *Id.* at 1233.

31. *Id.*

32. *Id.* at 1243.

33. *Id.*

PART IV

Focus on Education and Libraries

MOST COUNTRIES of the world, including Nepal, have copyright statutes that apply to libraries and allow limited uses of copyrighted works in support of library services.

CHAPTER 15

DISTANCE EDUCATION AND THE PRINCIPLES OF COPYRIGHT

KEY POINTS

- Distance education has changed over the years in form and technology, but it long has raised complex copyright questions.
- Familiar concepts of public domain, fair use, and licensing are perhaps the most important means for lawfully including copyrighted works in a distance education course.
- Distance education courses are often transmitted across borders, possibly raising the need to apply the copyright law of other countries.
- Claims of copyright ownership in distance education courses can be contentious, but they can be addressed through policy and contract.

THE CONCEPT AND construct of *distance education* has evolved steadily through the past several decades, and with each development, the relationship to copyright becomes more convoluted and more strained. Distance education has transitioned from filling the wee hours on public television to the delivery of online courses reaching multitudes of learners around the world. Whatever the format of the course or the technological means for delivery, distance education has consistently raised questions about the proper use of copyrighted works as well as diverse claims of ownership in the courses and instructional materials.

The copyright issues surrounding distance education also have escalated and thus are separated into two chapters. This chapter is built on fundamentals of copyright as they apply to distance education. It will survey principles of fair use and the public domain, closing with a few pointers about some alternatives for rethinking copyright ownership in the educational context. The next chapter explores the TEACH Act. Congress enacted the TEACH Act in 2002 in an effort to ease and clarify the ability to use copyrighted works in distance education. Unfortunately, the TEACH Act has proven awkward to apply, and it

WHATEVER THE label, distance education has existed in many forms for decades. It has been found on broadcast television and in correspondence courses offered by subscription. MOOCs may be one of the newer incarnations, but even MOOCs are not of one variety and are not the first to be free. A historical lineage of distance courses, especially no-fee programs, is summarized in a most helpful book by the copyright officer of Harvard University; see Kyle K. Courtney, *MOOCs and Libraries* (Lanham, MD: Rowman & Littlefield, 2015), 2–5.

has not been widely embraced by educators. As a result, the general copyright concepts in this chapter often remain most important for distance education.

WHAT IS DISTANCE EDUCATION?

Distance education has been an important pursuit of colleges, universities, and many other educational institutions for decades. In this chapter, and elsewhere throughout the book, the expression *distance education* will be used as a general label for all the many types of means for reaching students and other learners at their locations and not necessarily where the instructor is based. The students or other participants may receive the educational content in some place other than a conventional classroom or the place where the instructor might give a lecture or transmit the material.

Distance education may be synchronous, with all students tuning in at a designated time. It might also be asynchronous, perhaps uploaded to a server, enabling students to tap into the learning experience at times of individual choice. Sometimes an entire course is delivered via distance education. Sometimes a traditional course includes a distance component whereby students might learn online and not need to be in the classroom.

Although distance education exists in diverse forms and formats, any such undertaking inevitably stirs copyright questions. In decades long gone, distance education was largely limited to the low-demand hours of your local public television station, without even a VCR to capture it. Even then, debates began about the appropriate use of readings, maps, music, art, and other copyrighted works. Jumping forward to recent years and the advent of MOOCs (massive open online courses), we still ask many of the same copyright questions about the use of protected materials. Yet the new technologies often mean that the answers today differ greatly in nuance and complication.

> **MOOCS ARE** also the subject of one of the regulatory exceptions, issued most recently in 2018, to the prohibition against circumvention of technological protection measures. The provision is examined in detail in **Chapter 22**. In summary, it permits educational institutions to circumvent such measures in order to make lawful uses of short portions of motion pictures for inclusion in MOOCs. The exception has many other detailed conditions, including some technological restrictions that reflect terms of the TEACH Act and that might also help with the argument that the film clips are within fair use.

The copyright issues today also differ as a matter of degree and opportunity. The copyright quandaries surrounding MOOCs and other current forms of online education are different because we are able to develop much more creative and effective courses and deliver them to students in limitless numbers and locations. The transmissions are not confined to designated time slots, but rather students can access the content on their own schedules.

Students today may also receive vastly more content through Internet-based transmission than was ever imaginable with early morning television broadcasts. Online systems of today raise the possibility that the copyrighted content might be captured, reused, and disseminated in various ways by the students. Not only do these differences place a heightened responsibility on the developers of the course to address the copyright challenges, but they also have implications for the protective measures and the interpretation of fair use that are appropriate for developing and disseminating a robust online educational experience.

If you have reviewed the earlier chapters of this book, many of the copyright concepts in this chapter should be familiar. In the context of distance education, however, they sometimes take on a different meaning. The context becomes particularly significant when the course is delivered to a broad audience, across national borders, and perhaps even without any condition or restriction on access.

The context also raises challenging copyright questions when the course and the content may be downloaded by the students. The ability to retain and share copies of the materials can sometimes strain the reach of fair use and may even hamper the ability to secure permissions from the copyright owners. Thus, as we have seen with so many other copyright issues, the exact circumstances of how the work may be created and used will often drive the ability to apply the law in a meaningful manner.

THE PUBLIC DOMAIN

Perhaps the most definitive means for clearing a work for use in distance education is to rely on the public domain. Many works are in the public domain because the copyright has expired or the work was not eligible for copyright protection in the first place.[1] Other works are in the public domain because their term of copyright protection has run its course, and the copyrights are expired.[2] Consider these realistic examples:

> **AMONG THE** many useful and informative materials available on the U.S. Copyright Office website are these resources: the full text of the current U.S. Copyright Act; various circulars or brochures that succinctly explain many aspects of copyright; summaries of fair use decisions; forms and instructions for registrations; and detailed and insightful studies conducted by the office. Visit the website at https://www.copyright.gov.

- *Professor Tran is teaching an online course on U.S. copyright law.* She is in luck because Section 105 of the U.S. Copyright Act bars copyright protection for works of the U.S. government.[3] Professor Tran is off to a good start collecting materials she can use in her online course because the federal copyright statutes are in the public domain, as are decisions from the federal courts as well as regulations from different federal agencies. In fact, Professor Tran will find a wealth of useful materials on the website of the U.S. Copyright Office. If those materials were created by that federal government agency, they are in the public domain and freely available for her to use.[4]

- *Professor Suarez is teaching a course on American history from 1900 to 1941.* Given that works published in the United States more than 95 years ago are in the public domain, Professor Suarez can find a wealth of materials available for her to use, at least covering the early part of the course. She can draw upon books, newspapers, speeches, maps, and photographs that were published long ago. However, she has a more complex calculation for the works that were published less than 95 years ago. As for unpublished journals, letters, and other materials, she generally needs to determine if the author has been deceased for more than 70 years.

> **INSTRUCTORS AND** anyone developing an online course would do well to study closely **Chapter 6** of this book. The rules of copyright duration are not simple. Because they do open the possibility of extensive public domain resources, they are well worth studying. That chapter will demonstrate, for example, how each year a new crop of early publications will enter the public domain and how many works may have lost their copyrights due to failure to comply with formalities. On the other hand, the rules can be considerably different as applied to many foreign works and to works made for hire.

For certain subject matters, the public domain is a useful trove of resources. But if either Professor Tran or Suarez were teaching literature, journalism, or other courses that rely heavily on other types of materials and newer resources, the public domain is not likely to be as rich a resource. Although the public domain offers good news for some courses, it is obviously not enough. More recent materials and other types of works are still under protection. It would be a sparse course indeed that is built solely on the public domain.

A main point of this chapter is that copyright law offers multiple routes for the proper use of diverse works in distance education. In applying current law, we need to be ready to use all routes simultaneously. In the case of Professors Tran and Suarez, they have discovered that the public domain is a valuable resource, but they also know that it is not enough. They will find the public domain to be very useful for some materials, but they will also likely rely on fair use, permissions, and even the TEACH Act for different materials included in the same courses.

FAIR USE AND DISTANCE EDUCATION

Of all the alternatives, fair use is probably invoked most often to support including copyrighted works in a distance education program. Fair use is examined in detail in Chapters 10 through 14 of this book, and the determination of fair use is based on the application of four factors set forth in the statute.[5] The meaning of those factors will always depend on the specific facts of the situation. The following analysis reveals how the four factors can take on distinct meaning when using a work in distance education.

Factor 1: Purpose of the Use

In all different formats and media, the main goal of distance education is usually the advancement of learning and the sharing of knowledge, whether in the context of a degree program or general public education. This factor should in most such situations lean in favor of fair use, particularly when the course is delivered by a nonprofit educational institution. By contrast, if the course is delivered on behalf of a for-profit organization or is otherwise used as a vehicle for advertising or another commercial pursuit, this factor may not favor fair use so strongly.

Factor 2: Nature of the Work Used

As in many other cases, this factor may well be neutral. As long as the material selected is appropriate and relevant to the topic of the course, it may not matter whether it is scholarly text or artistic poetry. In any event, the instructor or other developer of the course should be careful to select material for its significance to the topic of the course and always with a view toward fulfilling the educational objectives.

Factor 3: Amount of the Work Used

As in other educational pursuits, the copyrighted material should be narrowly tailored to meet the educational objectives. In other words, the film clips, images, quotations, and other materials should be carefully edited to include no more than is necessary to serve the educational objectives of the course. Of course, all courses can likely benefit from having the full text or lengthy portions of any kind of work. However, the selection of materials should be generally limited to portions of works—whether minuscule or extensive—that can be clearly justified as necessary for the learning experience at hand.[6] The litigation involving electronic reserves at Georgia State University gives some guidance about the amount of published books that might be appropriate; another case has allowed uses of full artistic images, if they are small in scale and of low resolution.[7]

Factor 4: Effect of the Use on the Market

If the selection of materials is tightly connected to the educational purpose and if the portion is narrowly tailored to serve that educational purpose, the use may have little or no effect

IF PERMISSION is necessary, Chapter 24 of this book offers guidance and tips for seeking permission from the copyright owner. Many works are also licensed in advance for use in teaching, including distance education. In particular, the wealth of materials available under a Creative Commons license is surveyed in Chapter 7. Further, many of the databases and other collections that might be acquired by your library under a license agreement allow for the use of some works in online and distance education.

on the market for or the value of the original work. However, unlike traditional classroom uses, the inclusion of material in a distance educational program can, and often does, involve digitization, duplication, transmission, storage, downloading, and other uses of the copyrighted work. These uses can raise concerns about potential widespread dissemination that can undercut the market for the work, especially if it is available from an authorized source on reasonable terms.

Perhaps most significant, when the copyrighted materials are used in a way that becomes realistic competition for the potential sale of the same content to students, the use could jeopardize the market for or value of the original copyrighted work. Examples might include lengthy portions of a motion picture that is readily available for affordable purchase or streaming or the inclusion of multiple chapters from a standard textbook published for this type of course. Fair use applies, but at some point, the use will hit the legal limits. Instructors then need to evaluate their options, including securing a license or having the students purchase the materials.

INTERNATIONAL IMPLICATIONS

Distance education is often a multinational endeavor, especially when the courses are widely available online. A high priority in the development of a distance education program is to reach a range of students wherever they may be, often including students in many different countries. Colleges and universities also frequently have campuses or other facilities around the world, where they commonly deliver the same curriculum that is offered at the flagship location. As a result, the copyright issues raise some peculiar and important international implications. Examples include the following:

- *Identifying the public domain:* If the course is being developed in the United States but made available to students elsewhere, the rules of copyright in the other countries may apply. The determination of public domain is a matter of domestic national law. What is public domain in the United States may not be public domain in Canada, Japan, France, or other countries. For example, the basic rule in the United States is that copyrights expire after the life of the author plus 70 years; in Canada the duration is life plus 50 years. Government works are also subject to widely varying rules about protection and public domain.
- *Fair use and other exceptions:* Although international treaties have created some similarity or "harmonization" of copyright law among the many countries of the world, one place where the law is not well harmonized is in the context of copyright exceptions and limitations. For example, the TEACH Act exists only in the United States and no place else. Some other countries address distance education explicitly, but on their own distinctive terms. Fair use is principally an American copyright doctrine, although it has been adopted in similar terms in a modest number of other countries. Even so, one cannot assume that what is within fair use in the United States would also be allowed as fair use in, for example, South Korea or Sri Lanka.[8]
- *Permissions and licenses:* Fortunately, many copyright owners have moved away from the convention of limiting copyright permission to one country or to the continent of North America. Many of today's permissions for educational needs come with no geographic restrictions. Occasionally, however,

permissions are conditioned on these regional confines. As a result, you may well obtain permission to use some essential work in your online course only to discover that you may include it only when transmitting inside the United States. As this book has emphasized elsewhere, if permission either is not forthcoming or is subject to onerous conditions, you may need to consider your alternatives. In the meantime, ask for a *worldwide* license when you seek permissions.

COPYRIGHT OWNERSHIP AND DISTANCE EDUCATION COURSES

Faculty members and administrators leading the effort to develop an online course frequently ask this familiar question: Who owns the copyright in my online course? The question might seem simple, but the answer may be complex or uncertain. The fundamental principles of copyright ownership explored elsewhere in this book apply to educational materials and online courses as well.

High tension surrounds the ownership discussion as soon as someone suggests that the university or another employer might be the copyright owner under the doctrine of work made for hire.[9] The concept is often an affront to guiding principles of academia because it places all rights with the employer and undercuts the ability of the instructor to build on and use educational materials in furtherance of research, scholarship, and teaching. On the other hand, leaving all rights with the individual instructor may create risks for the continuation and growth of the university's degree programs.

Further complicating the ownership answer, an online course is almost inevitably the work of multiple contributors of creative content. One or more instructors may well develop the bulk of the substantive educational content. Other technical and artistic colleagues may be responsible for creating graphs, maps, and other creative depictions of works transmitted to the screen. Consequently, multiple individuals may make integrated or competing claims to the overall finished work.

> **CONSIDER THE** fundamentals of authorship and copyright ownership as examined in Chapter 7. For example, a basic rule is that the person who did the creative work is the copyright owner. If the instructor developed the online course, that person is presumably the copyright owner. But if the materials are developed as works made for hire, then the employer may be the copyright owner. Further, the initial owner may in turn transfer the copyright to another party. As with any other work, you have to investigate the background and origin of the work, and any later transfers, to determine who might be the proper rightsholder today.

If we decipher this situation in copyright terms, we may well conclude that the work is a jointly owned copyrighted work, with all contributors owning the copyright together. Also reasonably likely is that each author owns his or her own individual contribution separately. Either way, relying on common legal principles may easily lead to an *answer* about copyright ownership. However, that answer may leave the parties with a new set of challenges, frustrations, and conflicting claims as they seek to exercise their legal rights and make constructive uses of their creative work.

THE IMPORTANCE OF COPYRIGHT POLICIES

Advance planning can defuse much of the uncertainty and complication surrounding copyright ownership. Rather than debate ownership and struggle with tension and uncertainty, the parties could address the copyright issues in advance—or after the fact, if necessary—with a written agreement or institutional policy. A written and signed instrument can have the effect of placing the copyright with the intended party. A policy or agreement, if properly implemented, can establish whether the institution, the individual, or another party is the formal copyright owner.[10]

However, identifying a technical and legal owner of the course or materials is *not* the most important point. Instead, the most important matter to resolve is identifying specifically the rights of use that each interested party will have with respect to the new materials. For example, the educational institution may have invested heavily in staff, talent, and equipment. It has an interest in seeking a possible return on investment through registrations or licensing of the course. Most important, an educational institution has a strong interest in assuring that it has the right to continue offering the course as part of a degree program and to revise and update the course in the years ahead.

> **AN INSTITUTIONAL** policy on copyright ownership that delineates the rights of use of new works has the potential to set clear standards that may be applied evenly for all faculty members, librarians, and others. A separate signed contract may also be necessary. For example, if the policy has the effect of moving the copyright from one party to another, such a transfer must be made by a signed writing. Also, if the parties are seeking to agree that a new work will be deemed to be a work made for hire, that agreement must also be signed by both parties. **Chapter 7** offers details.

The instructors share some of these same interests, and they ordinarily need assurance that they can include the content in their future teaching and rework the materials as a textbook or other scholarly work. The instructors bring their knowledge and expertise to the project. The talents they contribute are often at the core of their scholarship and careers. A policy or agreement can grant rights of use to the institution while at the same time specifying that the contributing instructors may rework and reuse the course content in other pursuits.

In many situations, there may be yet other interested parties. The web designers and other technical contributors need to be able to use their elements in other courses that they prepare for the home institution. Foundations that underwrite course development may want to hold rights or require open access. The public may have an interest in assuring that course materials developed with public funding are made widely available and not managed for profit. Copyright law alone will not solve these needs or respond to these interests. Only a carefully crafted policy and agreement—developed with consideration of the specific priorities of key stakeholders—can go far toward preventing disputes and releasing tensions surrounding copyright ownership and distance education.

NOTES

1. As surveyed in Chapter 5, works may be in the public domain because they were never eligible for copyright protection (such as ideas and facts), while others are in the public domain because they are works of the U.S. government.

2. Chapter 6 provides a detailed examination of the duration of copyright protection, and thus the expiration of copyright and the beginning of the public domain.

3. U.S. Copyright Act, 17 U.S.C. § 105.

4. Chapter 5 of this book notes the generous scope of the public domain for government works, but it cautions users about the possible copyright or similar protection for state, local, and foreign materials, as well as for the image of Smokey Bear.

5. U.S. Copyright Act, 17 U.S.C. § 107.

6. Not to be overlooked is the fact that sometimes fair use permits the use of an entire work. Many of the cases examined in the fair use chapters of this book involve copying entire works, including the scanning of full books by Google and the recording of entire television programs for home viewing.

7. The *Georgia State Case* is scrutinized in Chapter 14. For a groundbreaking case about the fair use of images, *see Bill Graham Archives v. Dorling Kindersley, Ltd.*, 448 F.3d 605 (2d Cir. 2006).

8. Chapter 23 includes a brief survey of fair use and other exceptions in some foreign countries.

9. The two varieties of work made for hire—applicable to employees and to independent contractors—and their extensive implications are addressed in Chapter 7.

10. The author of this book has written elsewhere on the importance of policies for copyright ownership. Kenneth D. Crews, "Instructional Materials and 'Works Made for Hire' at Universities: Policies and the Strategic Management of Copyright Ownership," in *The Center for Intellectual Property Handbook*, ed. Kimberly M. Bonner (New York: Neal-Schuman, 2006), 15–38, https://ssrn.com/abstract=1540811.

CHAPTER 16

DISTANCE EDUCATION AND THE TEACH ACT

KEY POINTS

- The TEACH Act from 2002 is an exception permitting the use of copyrighted works in distance education.
- The statute poses complications and challenges for educators, and as a result it is not widely used.
- Implementation of the law requires adopting copyright policy, putting in place a variety of technological protections, and adhering to specific limits on the copyrighted works that may be used.
- The law permits some conversions of works from analog to digital formats.
- The TEACH Act is not a replacement for other opportunities but may be used in addition to the public domain, fair use, and other copyright principles.

THE PREVIOUS CHAPTER delved into an understanding of general copyright principles applied to distance education. This chapter gives a close examination of a specialized copyright exception known as the TEACH Act. Congress recognized the growing importance of distance education when it enacted the TEACH Act in late 2002.[1] The new law added a new exception to the rights of copyright owners by allowing educators to use protected works in distance education without the risk of infringement.[2] Some educational institutions have found the TEACH Act to be useful, but most have found it to be too cumbersome and of dubious virtue. This chapter is a guide through the details with a dose of optimism about the possibilities.

The TEACH Act did not replace the other possibilities, such as fair use. It was never a substitute for applying the more familiar principles of copyright to distance education. The new law is instead a supplement; it is one more path that an educator might use when creating a distance education program. As we have seen in other situations, we need to keep all paths open and use all of them simultaneously. For example, when developing a distance education course, an instructor might include copyrighted materials under the terms of the TEACH Act but might also include in the same course other materials that are in the public domain, that are within fair use, or that are licensed for use or are available with permission from the copyright owner. In other words, robust planning of distance learning should include simultaneously concepts from the TEACH Act and copyright concepts from the previous chapter.

GOOD NEWS AND BAD NEWS

The TEACH Act, or more formally the Technology, Education and Copyright Harmonization Act, offers benefits along with limits and responsibilities. As long as educators remain within the boundaries of the law, they can avoid infringements and need not seek permission from, or pay royalties to, the copyright owner. These benefits, however, are not easy to secure. Indeed, complying with the TEACH Act means satisfying a rather lengthy list of conditions detailed in the statute.

As is examined in this chapter, the TEACH Act requires development of institutional policy and adoption of technological controls on access to and use of the course content. Even after making these arrangements to comply with the statute, the TEACH Act places limitations on the types and quantity of individual copyrighted works allowed to be included in the educational program. If instructors and their educational institutions are to reap the law's benefits, they need to take careful steps to implement it.

Like most copyright exceptions, the TEACH Act attempts to establish a boundary between protecting the rights of copyright owners and allowing limited uses of works for education. In the process, the law exposes the tension between copyright owners and users within the educational setting. For example, authors and publishers of textbooks, producers of films, composers of music, and other copyright owners often want maximum protection for their works and the ability to generate any possible revenue from educators. For such works, educational uses are often the leading market and a principal source of revenue.

By contrast, instructors preparing new online courses might want broader and more flexible opportunities to use diverse works, especially if the objective is nonprofit education. The TEACH Act is a compromise between maximum protection and extensive rights of use. Like many copyright exceptions, the statute allows only some uses of certain works under specific circumstances in distance education. The first challenge is to understand the statute. The next challenge for educators is to decide if it crafts a formula that works well—or well enough—to support an effective distance education course.

While the TEACH Act attempts to address the changing landscape of modern education, the statute is largely built around a particular vision of distance education that generally involves performances and displays of works in a manner emulating a typical classroom experience. The vision of an online course under this law is seemingly very conventional. The TEACH Act permits uses of copyrighted works in the context of "mediated instructional activities" that are akin in many respects to the conduct of traditional instructional sessions.[3] For example, the law anticipates that students will sometimes access materials only within a roughly prescribed time period and may not necessarily store or review them later in the academic term.[4]

Similarly, instructors may use copyrighted materials but often only in portions or under conditions analogous to conventional teaching. Stated more bluntly, this law is generally not intended to permit scanning and uploading of lengthy works to a website for unlimited access. Again, these constraints reflect the struggle between the economic interests of copyright owners and the expectations of an educator who is seeking to deploy modern technology in support of teaching and learning.

> **THE TEACH ACT** is codified in Section 110(2) of the Copyright Act. It replaced the original Section 110(2) that had been part of the revised copyright law that took effect in 1978. The prior statute had limits and constraints that made it generally unworkable for online education and web-based courses. The earlier statute, drafted in the mid-1960s and built around the model of asynchronous television, allowed uses of only narrowly defined types of works. By comparison, the TEACH Act is an improvement.

The structure of the TEACH Act gives it another pervasive trait: No one person acting alone can realistically comply with it. The law requires the adoption of institutional copyright policies, distribution of information concerning copyright to the educational community, implementation of technological controls, and adherence to the "portion" limits of allowable materials.[5] Contrast that description with fair use. An individual professor can learn about fair use and make meaningful and accurate decisions about the scope of the law and its application to his or her course planning. Copyright compliance can be the instructor's responsibility.

Under the TEACH Act, however, compliance requires active participation from various players at the educational institution, including the technology team, policymakers, and course designers. That basic structure of the law can be discouraging for many educators. It can also be prohibitive, if the school or university is not equipped to offer policy planning and technological services anticipated by the TEACH Act.

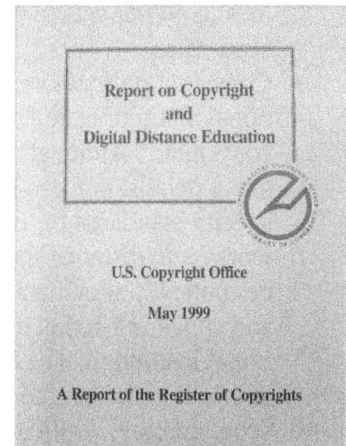

The groundwork for the TEACH Act was laid in the passage of the Digital Millennium Copyright Act of 1998, which directed the U.S. Copyright Office to prepare a study of copyright issues related to distance education. The report was issued in 1999, and the subsequent hearings and negotiations led to the new statute, enacted in 2002.

REQUIREMENTS OF THE TEACH ACT

Unlike the relatively broad and flexible terms of fair use, the limitations of allowed uses of copyrighted works under the TEACH Act are detailed and exacting. The statute itself is not always clear in its structure. This chapter accordingly breaks out the elements of legal language and organizes the detailed provisions into three categories: institutional and policy requirements, technology requirements, and instructional planning requirements. Keep in mind that you can take advantage of the TEACH Act's benefits only upon meeting all statutory requirements.

> **THE REQUIREMENTS** of the TEACH Act are organized into a checklist included as **Appendix C** of this book.

Institutional and Policy Requirements

As a first step toward implementing the TEACH Act, the educational institution needs to prepare a variety of formal copyright policies, information resources, and notifications for students.[6] Developing these materials can sometimes demand careful interpretation of the law, and the resulting policies and copyright guidance may have implications beyond online courses. To the extent that the law calls for formal policymaking, the proper officials with due authority also need to assume a role. These requirements may well become the responsibility of deans, directors, legal counsel, or other central administrators.

- *Accredited institutions:* The TEACH Act applies to only a "government body or an accredited nonprofit educational institution."[7] In general, colleges and universities accredited by a recognized agency or elementary and secondary schools recognized under state law will easily qualify. Programs offered by federal, state, or local government agencies, including public libraries, may also qualify. The application of the TEACH Act to government bodies can be broad, encompassing professional enrichment courses offered by local governments to the full curricula of military academies.

- *Copyright policy:* The new law requires educational institutions to "institute policies regarding copyright."[8] Although the statute does not offer many details, one can surmise that policies should specify standards for incorporating copyrighted works into distance education. Whatever the form or content, policymaking usually requires deliberate and concerted action by authorities within the educational institution. The law is not explicit about the level of required policy authority; one institution may adopt a guidance statement just for online programming, while the next institution may adopt a formal policy document approved at the highest levels.

- *Copyright information:* The institution must "provide informational materials" regarding copyright.[9] In this instance, the language specifies that the materials must "accurately describe, and promote compliance with, the laws of United States relating to copyright." These materials must be provided to "faculty, students, and relevant staff members." Institutions might consider developing websites, distributing printed materials, or providing information through the distance education program itself.

- *Notice to students:* The statute further specifies that the institution must provide "notice to students that materials used in connection with the course may be subject to copyright protection."[10] This notice may be a brief statement simply alerting students to copyright implications. The notice could be included on distribution materials in the class or perhaps on an opening frame of the distance education course or in a pop-up box on the course website.

> **POLICY DEVELOPMENT** can be a complicated process, involving lengthy deliberations and multiple levels of review and approval. Formal policymaking may be preferable, but informal procedural standards that effectively guide relevant activities may satisfy the TEACH Act requirement as well.

> **MANY EDUCATIONAL** institutions are developing copyright information resources to help instructors and others. The rich trove of information readily available online and in publications means that we can borrow and learn from one another. Creating a website with links to available materials can ease the way toward satisfying this requirement.

Technology Requirements

Networked technologies are obviously driving the growth of distance education. The transmission of digitized content is also raising concerns about possible copyright infringements; technological solutions may also ease some copyright consternation. The TEACH Act indeed requires the use of technological innovation to inhibit abuse of copyrighted materials. The law requires institutions to implement a variety of technological methods for controlling access to and dissemination of the copyrighted works.

- *Limited access to enrolled students:* The new law calls upon the institution to limit the transmission to students enrolled in the particular course "to the extent technologically feasible."[11] This requirement should not be difficult to satisfy. Most educational institutions have course management systems or other tools that implement passwords or other restrictions on access.

- *Technological controls on retention and further dissemination:* The TEACH Act applies to a wide variety of means for delivery of distance education, but a few provisions apply only in the case of *digital transmissions.* Where the course is delivered digitally, the institution must apply technical measures to prevent "retention of the work in accessible form by recipients of the

THIS NOTION of a *class session* is undefined in the law, and it is one of the most perplexing aspects of the TEACH Act. It is sometimes understood to mean that the work can be made available for only a limited span of time. Such a rule would defeat a key benefit of distance education—to enable students to work with materials at their own pace and return to earlier readings for reinforcement. A close reading of the statute does not necessarily lead to that conclusion. The language limits the duration of a *student's* retention of the work. The main concern appears to be the ability of students to download and keep the materials. Congress is not necessarily requiring that the materials be removed or blocked after the duration of a class session. However, Congress does seem to be controlling students' ability to keep copies.

transmission . . . for longer than the class session."[12] The statute offers no explicit definition of a *class session*, but language in congressional reports suggests that a student's ability to receive any digital transmissions of works in a retainable format would be somehow limited in duration.

- *Technological controls on dissemination:* Also in the case of digital transmissions, the institution must apply "technological measures" to prevent students from engaging in "unauthorized further dissemination of the work in accessible form."[13]

These technological requirements need not be airtight. The TEACH Act specifies that the technology must "reasonably prevent" the activity. The technology might not be perfect—and a hacker might find a way to defeat it—but at least the institution should use its best effort to stay informed about the latest possibilities. Good faith steps to implement these controls should satisfy the legal standard.

Technological Complications

These restrictions on accessing, copying, and further sharing of materials address serious concerns from copyright owners. On the other hand, many technology experts question whether the implementation of *effective* technological protections is even possible. Once content reaches the student's computer, blocking all means of downloading or copying the materials may be impossible. Once stored, little can restrict further duplication and distribution.[14] Educational institutions will need to continue to find reasonably available means—even if imperfect—for complying with the law. Revisiting copyright policies and technological tools on an ongoing basis can be an important aspect of compliance with the TEACH Act.

Various other technological requirements appear in the law. For example, the copyrighted content may be protected behind restrictive codes or other embedded "protection systems" to regulate access to or reproduction of the works. If so, the educational institution may not "engage in conduct that could reasonably be expected to interfere with [such] technological measures."[15] Interference with technological control measures may further expose the educational institution to violations of the anticircumvention provisions of the Digital Millennium Copyright Act.

The TEACH Act also exonerates educational institutions from liability that may result from most "transient or temporary storage of material."[16] Further, the TEACH Act amended Section 112 of the Copyright Act, addressing the issue of ephemeral recordings.[17] The revised Section 112(f)

Chapter 22 of this book provides an overview of the anticircumvention law and its meaning for access to and use of copyrighted works that may be locked behind technological controls. In general terms, this law creates a form of copyright violation based on the breaking or other circumvention of the controls. A common example would be the code embedded on a DVD or another medium that may restrict copying the content on the disk or even playing a motion picture or accessing the content on certain types of devices.

(1) explicitly allows educational institutions to make and retain copies of their digital transmissions that include copyrighted materials used pursuant to the TEACH Act. The provisions of the law create added responsibilities that will most likely become added duties for the local technology team.

Instructional Planning Requirements

So far, this chapter has laid out the many conditions about access, technology, and policy required for compliance with the TEACH Act. Only after building a compliant system can we turn attention to the substantive content that can be included in the course. The statute sets specific limits on the allowable content. While policymakers and technology experts might handle other aspects of the implementation, most decisions about course content are usually left to instructors. Instructors are expected to be masters of their subjects, and traditions of academic freedom are best upheld when faculty members make crucial decisions about the selection and quantity of materials to incorporate into distance education courses. As is noted later in this section, the instructor is sometimes required to be involved.

In complying with the TEACH Act, the instructor's decisions about course content will often be defined in detail by the rigors of copyright law. Certain works are allowed, and others are barred. Different works are subject to distinct quantity limits, and other works may only be performed or displayed under limited conditions.

Works Explicitly Permitted

The TEACH Act permits the following:

- Performances of nondramatic literary works
- Performances of nondramatic musical works
- Performances of any other work, including dramatic works and audiovisual works, but only in "reasonable and limited portions"
- Displays of any work "in an amount comparable to that which is typically displayed in the course of a live classroom session"[18]

One of the most troublesome questions about the TEACH Act is the concept of "portions" of audiovisual works. The law does not give any significant guidance, but a report from the Congressional Research Service suggests that sometimes an entire audiovisual work may be allowed:

> [T]he legislative history of the Act suggests that determining what amount is permissible should take into account the nature of the market for that type of work and the instructional purposes of the performance. For example, the exhibition of an entire film may possibly constitute a "reasonable and limited" demonstration if the film's entire viewing is exceedingly relevant toward achieving [an] educational goal; however, the likelihood of an entire film portrayal being "reasonable and limited" may be rare.[19]

No such report is binding on any court that might have to interpret and apply the law in a future case. However, a report from a congressional office, which might be the sole authoritative and accountable voice on the law's meaning, could be influential.

> **THE LIMITS** in the TEACH Act may be best understood by a comparison to an earlier statute that it replaced. The law enacted by Congress in 1976, and which took effect in 1978, drew even sharper distinctions between allowed and disallowed works. These distinctions were built upon the statutory concepts of *displays* and *performances*. Previous law allowed displays of any type of work in distance education, but it allowed performances of only nondramatic literary works and nondramatic musical works. Consequently, many dramatic works were, under previous law, excluded entirely from distance education, as were performances of audiovisual materials and sound recordings. Such narrowly crafted provisions were problematic at best. For all of its constraints, the TEACH Act grants somewhat greater latitude for the use of many copyrighted works.

> **Chapter 8** examines the rights of copyright owners and explains the concepts of *displays* and *performances*. Displays are generally static images, whether of artwork, text, photographs, or other works; performances generally occur with the playing of music or audiovisual works and the recital of text, poetry, or plays. Distance education, like classroom instruction, routinely includes many displays and performances.

LITIGATION SEVERAL years ago involving UCLA began to test the scope of the TEACH Act and fair use as applied to video streaming. The case did not result in any judicial rulings to cite as authority on these points, but various commentators did offer insights about the nature of copyright and online education. This statement is from a consortium of library associations: https://www.librarycopyrightalliance.org/documents/united-states -documents/other-matters/lca-releases-issue-brief-on-streaming-of-films-for-educational -purposes.

For a contrary view by one of the parties involved in the UCLA controversy, see the paper here: http://lutzker.com/wp-content/uploads/2018/06/AIME-Spring-2010-Educational -Video-Streaming.pdf.

Works Explicitly Excluded

The following categories of works are specifically left outside the range of permitted materials under the TEACH Act:

- Works that are marketed "primarily for performance or display as part of mediated instructional activities transmitted via digital networks": Possibilities might include materials available through online databases or marketed in a format delivered for educational uses through digital systems. The law generally steers users to those sources directly, rather than allowing educators to digitize and deliver their own copies.
- Performances or displays given by means of copies "not lawfully made and acquired" under the U.S. Copyright Act: These may be outside of the TEACH Act if the educational institution "knew or had reason to believe" that they were not lawfully made and acquired.[20]

WHAT ARE mediated instructional activities? This language means that the uses of materials in the program must be "analogous to the type of performance or display that would take place in a live classroom setting." The concept of *mediated instructional activities* also does not include uses of textbooks and other materials "which are typically purchased or acquired by the students." U.S. Copyright Act, 17 U.S.C. § 110(2). The statute again seems to be making a fundamental point: If students would ordinarily buy and keep the materials, that content should not be scanned and uploaded as part of distance education. It is yet another indication that the original vision of distance education under the TEACH Act was in large part traditional teaching, albeit in an online environment.

Instructor Oversight

The statute mandates the instructor's participation in the planning and conduct of the distance education program as transmitted. An instructor seeking to use materials within the scope of the TEACH Act must adhere to the following requirements:

- The performance or display must be "made by, at the direction of, or under the actual supervision of an instructor."
- The materials are transmitted "as an integral part of a class session offered as a regular part of the systematic, mediated instructional activities" of the educational institution.
- The copyrighted materials are "directly related and of material assistance to the teaching content of the transmission."[21]

These three requirements share some common objectives—ensuring that the instructor ultimately oversees uses of copyrighted works and that the materials serve educational pursuits and are not for entertainment or other purposes.[22]

CONVERTING ANALOG TO DIGITAL

Troublesome to many copyright owners was the prospect that their analog materials would be converted to digital formats and hence made susceptible to easy downloading and dissemination. The TEACH Act takes a cautious approach and allows conversions only in quantities allowed for performance and display in the course, and only if a digital version of the work is not already "available to the institution."[23]

The law also allows conversion of works from analog to digital if the digital version available to the educational institution "is subject to technological protection measures that prevent its use" in a manner consistent with the TEACH Act. This clause is harkening to the fact that some copyrighted materials are protected by technological measures and circumventing or breaking the technological locks may be a violation of the Copyright Act. This concept is covered in Chapter 22.

Notice carefully what is actually allowed. The TEACH Act is allowing digitization of works that may be behind these technological locks. You are not authorized to break the lock; you are instead allowed to copy from an analog version of the work. Imagine you are planning an online course. You have complied in full with the TEACH Act, and you are planning to include "reasonable and limited" clips from a motion picture. You have a digital version of the film on DVD, but a technological measure bars clipping and copying. Faced with this situation, Congress could have created an exception to the anticircumvention law. It did not. Instead, Congress granted permission to make a digital copy of the needed portions from an analog version of the film.

As you prepare your course, you are expected to set aside the digital copy, whether on DVD, Blu-ray, or another format, and then make a digital copy of the film clips from an alternative analog source, such as a VHS tape or 16 mm film. It may be clumsy, awkward, time-consuming, and expensive. It might result in lower quality film clips that could diminish the educational experience. This state of the law is hardly ideal. In fact, it is altogether absurd. If you did not already have reason to write to your member of Congress, you might have one now.[24]

MAKING PLANS AND LOOKING AHEAD

The TEACH Act holds out the prospect of allowing a considerable range of copyrighted works in distance education, but only after meeting the significant burden of compliance. Clearly no one person is likely able to meet these challenges alone. Multiple parties within the college or university will need to participate; central administrators and policymakers will have leading roles; technology experts will need to implement systems and controls; instructors must develop courses with attention to limits on the types and quantities of allowable materials.

Because the TEACH Act has limits, many uses of copyrighted works that may be desirable or essential for effective teaching may simply be outside the scope of the TEACH Act. In anticipation of those limits, educators should also be prepared to explore alternatives. Some possibilities include the following:

- Employ alternative methods for delivering materials to students, including the expansion of innovative library services and access to databases and retrieval systems.
- Apply the law of fair use, which may allow uses beyond those detailed in the TEACH Act and without the many mandated rigors of compliance.
- Secure permission from copyright owners for uses not sanctioned by the TEACH Act, fair use, or other provisions of the law. Permission comes in many forms, including Creative Commons licenses.

PERHAPS THE first step in implementing the TEACH Act is to assemble a team of leaders and experts at your educational institution. The first questions might be these: Are we willing and able to do the work expected of us under the law? Do we have a ready team of instructors, technologists, and policymakers? If the group is not motivated to make the law work, it simply may not be right for your institution. After all, the TEACH Act is not mandatory. You may instead rely on fair use, permissions, and other fundamentals.

The TEACH Act is approaching its twentieth year since enactment, but it has gained only modest acceptance. The principal reason may be simply that the law is too complicated for thorough compliance, and its conditions may appear confusing, foreboding, or perhaps impossible. The TEACH Act may find its greatest potential when applied to courses that are initiated and overseen by a centralized office. Someone with oversight authority may have the best opportunity to assure that all legal details are addressed and that the policymakers and technology specialists are enlisted to offer their skills and services.

By contrast, the individual instructor who is scanning and uploading materials to a website may not have the authority, resources, talents, or simply the time to address every provision of the TEACH Act. An individual instructor is typically not well positioned to evaluate the detailed law and to make all judgments about legal interpretations, choices, compliance, and policy implementation. Until some level of centralized authority at an educational institution takes the lead, the TEACH Act will probably be a little-used option, but instructors have the continuing opportunity of turning to fair use and other constructive alternatives.

NOTES

1. Technology, Education and Copyright Harmonization Act, Pub. L. No. 107–273, 166 Stat. 1758, 1910 (2002) (codified at 17 U.S.C. §§ 110(2) & 112(f)).

2. This chapter is based in part on the following article by the same author: Kenneth D. Crews, "Copyright and Distance Education: Making Sense of the TEACH Act," *Change* 35 (November–December 2003): 34–39. While the statute has not changed, the passage of time has allowed new insights and perspectives on the law.

3. U.S. Copyright Act, 17 U.S.C. § 110(2).

4. U.S. Copyright Act, 17 U.S.C. § 110(2).

5. U.S. Copyright Act, 17 U.S.C. § 110(2)(D).

6. U.S. Copyright Act, 17 U.S.C. § 110(2)(D).

7. U.S. Copyright Act, 17 U.S.C. § 110(2).

8. U.S. Copyright Act, 17 U.S.C. § 110(2)(D).

9. U.S. Copyright Act, 17 U.S.C. § 110(2)(D).

10. U.S. Copyright Act, 17 U.S.C. § 110(2)(D).

11. U.S. Copyright Act, 17 U.S.C. § 110(2)(C).

12. U.S. Copyright Act, 17 U.S.C. § 110(2)(D)(ii).

13. *Id.*

14. At the direction of Congress, in connection with passage of the TEACH Act, the U.S. Patent and Trademark Office collected information concerning effective technological controls in a 2003 report titled *Technological Protection Systems for Digitized Copyrighted Works: A Report to Congress,* https://www.uspto.gov/web/offices/dcom/olia/teachreport.pdf.

15. U.S. Copyright Act, 17 U.S.C. § 110(2)(D)(ii)(II).

16. U.S. Copyright Act, 17 U.S.C. § 110(2).

17. U.S. Copyright Act, 17 U.S.C. § 112(f). Section 112 is a series of detailed and narrow provisions allowing limited copies of broadcasts and other recordings in order to facilitate uses that are permitted under some of the specified statutory exceptions.

18. U.S. Copyright Act, 17 U.S.C. § 110(2).

19. Jared Huber et al., *Copyright Exemptions for Distance Education: 17 U.S.C. § 110(2), the Technology, Education, and Copyright Harmonization Act of 2002* (Washington, DC: Congressional Research Service, 2006), 4, http://www.ipmall.info/sites/default/files/hosted _resources/crs/RL33516_060706.pdf.

20. U.S. Copyright Act, 17 U.S.C. § 110(2).

21. U.S. Copyright Act, 17 U.S.C. § 110(2)(A)–(C).

22. Someone other than the instructor might actually have final oversight of these requirements, but as a practical matter the instructor will most assuredly be in the best position to know the course objectives and confirm that the requirements are met. This is not to be confused with determining liability under the statute. Any decision maker could be liable for infringement, but if the course is part of the educational curriculum, the educational institution will most likely have ultimate responsibility.

23. U.S. Copyright Act, 17 U.S.C. § 112(f)(2).

24. An alternative charge up the hill could be participation in the triennial rulemaking, whereby the Librarian of Congress may issue regulatory exceptions to the anticircumvention provision, as reviewed in Chapter 22. The current exceptions do contemplate that the quality of some copying may not be adequate, and better quality copies are permissible under rigorous provisions.

CHAPTER 17

LIBRARIES, ARCHIVES, AND THE SPECIAL PROVISIONS OF SECTION 108

KEY POINTS

- Section 108 allows many libraries and archives to make copies of materials for preservation, private study, and interlibrary loans.
- The opportunities under Section 108 do not extend equally to all types of works.
- Section 108 requires compliance with various requirements, but most libraries and archives should be able to meet them and enjoy the benefits of the law.
- The provision allowing many library uses of works in their last twenty years of copyright protection has newfound potential.
- Movements are afoot for a possible revision of Section 108, and many countries in all parts of the world are considering adding and revising their copyright statutes applicable to libraries and archives.

AMERICAN COPYRIGHT LAW includes numerous specific provisions limiting the rights of copyright owners. These provisions establish rights for the public to use protected works under specified circumstances. Section 108 is one such section. This statute allows libraries and archives to make and distribute copies of protected materials for specified purposes under specified conditions. Although meticulous, it can offer important support for certain library services.[1]

Section 108 allows libraries, within limits, to make copies of many works for the following three purposes: for preservation of library collections; for private study by users; and for participation in interlibrary loan arrangements. Section 108 was first enacted in 1976 as part of the overall revision of the U.S. Copyright Act. Although Congress has occasionally revised the statute, it still embraces only these few traditional library services. This chapter closes with an overview of efforts to open Section 108 for a more extensive restructuring and expansion.

Meanwhile, the existing Section 108 follows the pattern of other copyright exceptions; it allows limited uses of certain works under defined circumstances. A library that is seeking to apply Section 108 can work through the basic structure of the law by resolving the following questions:

- Is the library *eligible* to exercise the benefits of the law?
- Is the copyrighted work among the *types of works* that may be used pursuant to this statute?
- Has the library *adhered to the conditions* for making copies for each of the allowed purposes?

ELIGIBILITY REQUIREMENTS OF SECTION 108

Before a library can benefit from Section 108, it must comply with certain general requirements and limits. Most academic and public libraries will have little trouble meeting these requirements. The statute establishes the following ground rules for using Section 108:

- The library must be open to the public or to outside researchers.[2] Nearly every public and academic library will meet this standard.
- The copies must be made "without any purpose of direct or indirect commercial advantage."[3] This requirement may exclude copies that are made by a commercial document delivery service. On the other hand, it may also mean that a corporate library could be eligible to use this law, although copies that are made specifically for commercial purposes are not within Section 108.
- The library may make only single copies on "isolated and unrelated" occasions and may not, under most circumstances, make multiple copies or engage in "systematic reproduction or distribution of single or multiple copies."[4] The request for a single copy seldom raises a question. Multiple requests for the same item from several students in the same course may be "systematic."
- Each copy made must include a notice of copyright.[5] The notice on the copy should usually be the same copyright notice that appears on the original work. In fact, some libraries simply copy the page with the notice on it along with the pages of particular interest.

> **WHAT LIBRARIES** will not qualify to use Section 108? Private libraries, corporate libraries, and other libraries that are closed to outside users are often outside the scope of Section 108. But the exclusion is not sweeping. A library qualifies if it is open to outside users "doing research in a specialized field." U.S. Copyright Act, 17 U.S.C. § 108(a)(2). In other words, if a specialized corporate library admits outside researchers, even selectively, that library may qualify. The ability to qualify for Section 108 can open enormously important opportunities for preservation of archival collections and making individual copies for research.

Not all copyrighted materials have a formal copyright notice, and as explained in Chapter 6, a notice is no longer a requirement for copyright protection. If no notice appears on the original, Section 108 requires that the copy include "a legend stating that the work may be protected by copyright." Many libraries place the following statement on all copies when no formal copyright notice is available: *Notice: This material is subject to the copyright law of the United States.* That generic notice at least gives readers a nudge to think about possible copyright implications if they make further uses of the copy.

> **ALTHOUGH SECTION** 108 generally permits only single copies, the provisions that apply to preservation copies allow up to three copies of a single work. The law allows multiple copies in recognition of the reality of preservation services. However, the limit of three copies is generally a relic from the age of microfilm. Library preservation services today are largely digital, with multiple copies as an inevitable by-product. A more fluid quantity would be more realistic, with perhaps a cap on the number of copies that may be in use simultaneously. The details of the preservation requirements are outlined later in this chapter.

**A digital future
for the collections**

Take a look through the window.

In this space Museum staff are working hard to conserve, catalogue and take digital photographs of the Museum's collections.

With over 3.5 million items in the collections, we are constantly learning more about them and new ways to look after them.

The more we learn and make available digitally, the more we can share with you.

Did you know there are already over a million items for you to explore online?

aucklandmuseum.com/collections

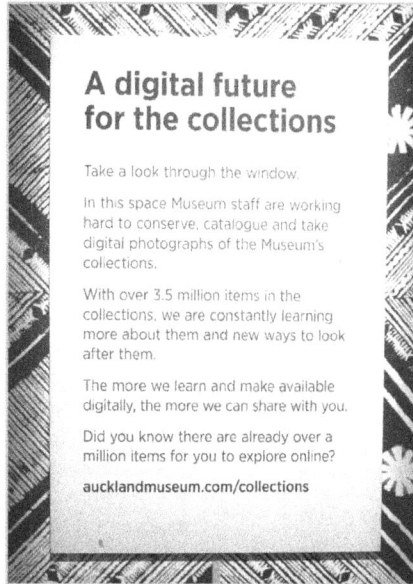

Throughout the world, photographs are among the works in greatest demand from libraries and archives. Fortunately, the copyright exception in American law allows libraries and archives to make preservation copies of photographs. However, the law often does not permit these institutions to make reproductions of photographs to give to users for research or private study. Fair use can fill some gaps in the other exceptions, but few countries have the benefits of fair use in their law.

TYPES OF WORKS THAT MAY BE COPIED

Section 108 sets specific limits on the types of materials that libraries or archives may copy. Exactly which works may be reproduced will vary greatly, depending on the purpose for making the reproductions. If the copies are for preservation or replacement of library materials, the scope of materials is unrestricted.[6] The institution may make preservation copies of manuscripts, photographs, artworks, and any other works. By contrast, if the copying is for a user's private study, Section 108 imposes tight constraints. Consider motion pictures, for example. If the purpose is preservation or replacement, a library may reproduce any type of audiovisual work. If the purpose is for a user's private study, audiovisual works may be reproduced only if they are about the "news."[7]

The scope of materials that may be reproduced and given to users for their private study is as follows:

- Journals, newspapers, books, and other textual works. The scope of allowed works could also extend to computer software, architectural works, dance notations, and a wide range of copyrightable materials.
- Pictures and graphics, but only if they are "published as illustrations, diagrams, or similar adjuncts" to works that may otherwise be copied.[8] In other words, if you can copy a journal article for the library user, you

REGARDLESS OF the type of work, however, the provisions of Section 108 allowing copies for private study are not themselves explicit about whether they extend to digital works or to making copies in digital formats. The statute is generally regarded as technologically neutral and can apply to all media. An alternative view is that Section 108 does indeed explicitly allow digital applications. The statute permits libraries to make copies, which are defined as material objects "in which a work is fixed by any method." That expansive phrasing definitely includes digital. A similar broad definition applies to *phonorecords*. Courtesy of the scope of the definitions, digital technologies fit squarely into the construct of Section 108. The definitions are in Section 101 of the U.S. Copyright Act.

can also copy the picture or chart that is in the article.

- Audiovisual works, but only if they are works "dealing with news."[9] A library may therefore make a copy of a video clip of the program *Meet the Press*, but not a clip from the movie *Broadcast News*.
- Sound recordings may also be copied, but only recordings of certain works. Because this part of Section 108 does not apply to musical compositions, the library may copy a recording of a public domain work or a recording of spoken words, such as a speech or a reading of an article, book, or other item that is on the list of allowed works.

Section 108 explicitly bars the large categories of works that may be copied for purposes of private study. Those forbidden categories include musical compositions, motion pictures and other audiovisual works, and pictorial, graphic, and sculptural works. This delineation of different types of works may be helpfully specific, but it is also a tremendous constraint on library and archival services. In particular, photographs are often in greatest demand from archival collections, but they are not within the scope of the allowed works for individual study. Where Section 108 does not apply, librarians might then consider the alternatives of fair use or permission.

> **A SOUND RECORDING** often encompasses two separate copyrights. First, the recording itself is often an original work, and the sounds of voices and instruments captured are copyrightable. Second, the underlying text or musical composition has its own copyright. The copying of a sound recording thus often implicates rights of two separate owners, and they need to be considered separately. As a result, if the recording is of a musical composition, Section 108 creates the awkward outcome of the law's permitting reproduction of the recording but not necessarily reproduction of the underlying work. You can still seek permission or explore fair use for the use of the composition. The distinctive rules of copyright and music are surveyed in Chapters 19 and 20 of this book.

COPIES FOR PRESERVATION OR REPLACEMENT

The analysis of Section 108 finally gets to the substance. So far, this chapter has been about the preliminaries of eligible libraries and permitted works. Once getting past the determination that the library is qualified to use Section 108 and the works to be copied are within scope, the statute then sets the substantive conditions for engaging in the allowed activity. Specifically, under what conditions may the library make copies for preservation or replacement?

This part of Section 108 generally bifurcates around whether the work is unpublished or published. If the work is *unpublished*, copies are permitted for the purpose of preservation upon meeting both of the following conditions:[10]

- The work is currently in the collection of the library making the copy.
- The copies are solely for preservation or security or for deposit at another library. The library can therefore make a copy of a manuscript for patron use and store the original for safekeeping. The library that owns the original may also make and contribute a copy to the collections of another library. The library receiving the copied work must also be eligible under the terms of Section 108.

If the work has been *published*, Section 108 permits the library to make copies to replace the item in the library's collection upon meeting both of these conditions:[11]

> **WHAT IS** an obsolete format? The statute defines the notion to mean that the machine or device necessary to read or perceive the work in that format "is no longer manufactured or is no longer reasonably available in the commercial marketplace." U.S. Copyright Act, 17 U.S.C. § 108(c). In other words, if you cannot find newly made or sold players, you may be able to make preservation copies of your collection of eight-track disco music. VCRs and slide projectors are evidently gone. The revived interest in vinyl has reinforced a market for stereo turntables, leading to the utterly unhelpful conclusion that, for now, hipsters and aficionados may have forestalled obsolescence of the equipment and perhaps slowed the ability to preserve some LP music collections.

- The copies are solely for replacement of an item that is damaged, deteriorating, lost, or stolen or if the format of the work has become obsolete.
- The library conducts a reasonable investigation to conclude that an *unused* replacement cannot be obtained at a fair price. The law does not offer guidance about what constitutes a *reasonable investigation* or *fair price*, but librarians should almost always check customary sources for acquisitions and maintain notes and records of findings.

The Digital Millennium Copyright Act of 1998 amended Section 108 to clarify the rights of a library to make digital copies for preservation and replacement.[12] Digital copies may be made of both published and unpublished works under the conditions already set forth, plus "any such copy or phonorecord that is reproduced in digital format" may not be "made available to the public in that format outside the premises of the library or archives."[13] The concept of *premises* is undefined in the law, but the statutory language raises concerns that preservation copies in digital format may have to be confined to the library building or buildings.

Some libraries contend with this restriction by making one digital copy for access online on the premises and one analog copy of the same work that may be circulated. Unfortunately, Congress did not contemplate many awkward consequences of this law, including the problem of works that are born digital. A library today will often need to make preservation copies of CDs, DVDs, data files, and other works that were created and acquired in digital form. The originals were freely available for circulation outside the premises. Digital preservation copies, however, are apparently confined to some indeterminate physical territory.

> **WHY WOULD** Congress apparently seek to confine the digital copies to some special scope of the premises of the library? One justification lies in the nature of digital media and networked systems. If a library could make a preservation copy and upload it to a server for wide accessibility, the library would be acting very much like a publisher of that work. From that perspective, the law is a device for protecting markets and business models. The problem with that rationale is that it aims to protect the domain of publishers, with respect to all works, including those with no realistic market. However, if the objective of the law is to encourage preservation and information access, confining works to the premises of the library could hamper those goals. Put more bluntly, this part of the statute may be simply an effort to prevent libraries from intruding on the conventional activities of publishers, whether they are ready to act on the rights or not.

COPIES FOR PRIVATE STUDY

The next major library activity within the bounds of Section 108 is the service of making copies for library users to receive and keep for their own personal reading and study. This statute is an exception that permits the library staff to make the copies on request. If the user chooses to make his or her own copies, that might be fair use, but it is definitely not covered by Section 108. The law here, too, is drafted as a bifurcation generally based on the length of the work in question. One standard applies to copies of articles or other short works. A slightly more demanding standard applies to copies of entire books and other longer works.

If the copy is of an *article, book chapter,* or *other portion of a larger work,* these conditions apply:[14]

- The copy becomes the property of the user.
- The library has had no notice that the copy is for any purpose other than private study, scholarship, or research.
- The library displays a warning notice where orders for copies are accepted and on order forms. This warning notice is not to be confused with the general requirement that the library place a copyright notice or general legend on the copy itself.

If the copy is of *an entire book or other work,* or of *a substantial part of such a work,* the following conditions apply:[15]

- The library conducts a reasonable investigation to conclude that a copy cannot be obtained at a fair price.
- The copy becomes the property of the user.
- The library has had no notice that the copy is for any purpose other than private study, scholarship, or research.
- The library displays a warning notice where orders for copies are accepted and on order forms.

IS THE LIBRARY actually required to *know* that the copy is for private study only and not for business or other purposes? No. The library must have only *no notice* that the copy is for another purpose. Knowing absolutely nothing about the user's purpose for the copy satisfies the law. However, once the librarian has reason to know that the copy is for some purpose other than private study, scholarship, or research, the library's ability to use Section 108 for that transaction could end. This nuanced condition in the statute is consistent with a fundamental ethical tenet that librarians should generally not ask the purpose of a patron's information need. It also sets up another dilemma when the user proudly announces his or her exciting intentions—as is so often the case.

THE NOTICE placed on order forms and displayed at the place where orders are received is detailed in regulations issued by the U.S. Copyright Office (37 C.F.R. § 201.14, https://www.copyright.gov/title37/201/37cfr201-14.html). The prescribed text is as follows:

NOTICE WARNING CONCERNING COPYRIGHT RESTRICTIONS

The copyright law of the United States (title 17, United States Code) governs the making of photocopies or other reproductions of copyrighted material.

Under certain conditions specified in the law, libraries and archives are authorized to furnish a photocopy or other reproduction. One of these specific conditions is that the photocopy or reproduction is not to be "used for any purpose other than private study, scholarship, or research." If a user makes a request for, or later uses, a photocopy or reproduction for purposes in excess of "fair use," that user may be liable for copyright infringement.

This institution reserves the right to refuse to accept a copying order if, in its judgment, fulfillment of the order would involve violation of copyright law.

COPIES FOR INTERLIBRARY LOAN

At least in the worldview of copyright and Section 108, the making copies for the purpose of interlibrary loan (ILL) is a species of copying for a patron's private study.[16] The fundamental difference is that the user is making the request at a library other than the one actually making the copy. In fact, the provisions of Section 108 that allow a library to make copies for users anticipate that the copies may be "made from the collection of a library or archives where the user makes his or her request or from that of another library or archives."[17] The user may be local or afar. Either way, the library making the copy should in general apply the same copyright rules about copies for private study.

The copyright concern, however, is that a library could rely inordinately on ILL requests, placing a burden on other libraries to fulfill orders and avoiding the need to purchase certain works or journal subscriptions. ILL could conceptually cut into the copyright owner's market. Section 108 provides an attempt to allow ILL, but within limits placed on both the *supplying* and *receiving* libraries. For the library *supplying* a copy, the same requirements outlined earlier about copies for private study would apply.

The rules for the library *receiving* the copy, however, are additional and different. That library must adhere to this standard: The interlibrary arrangements cannot have "as their purpose or effect" that the library receiving the copies on behalf of requesting patrons "does so in such aggregate quantities as to substitute for a subscription to or purchase of such work."[18] This is a market protection clause. The point of this language is to remind receiving libraries that when the demand for a journal or other work reaches a sufficient level, the library ought to consider buying its own copy of the work instead of relying on ILL. The challenge, of course, is that the law does not exactly define the limit.

> **THE CONTU GUIDELINES** are hardly comprehensive. They encompass only copies of recent journal articles. Libraries are left to their good judgment about the limits of the law as applied to older materials, book chapters, and other works. For the full text of the CONTU final report, see http://www.digital-law-online.info/CONTU/contu1.html.

To help clarify the limit on a library's ability to receive copies, Congress established the National Commission on New Technological Uses of Copyrighted Works, commonly known as CONTU, shortly after enacting Section 108. In its final report issued in 1979, CONTU proposed guidelines that bring specificity to the quantity limits of the law. The CONTU standards generally allow a library to receive during one calendar year up to five copies of articles from the most recent five years of a journal title.[19]

After reaching that quota, the general expectation is that the receiving library will evaluate its alternatives. The library may purchase its own subscription to the journal. Some libraries simply choose not to fulfill requests for additional articles from that journal, a strategy that leaves the next user completely unserved. Many libraries instead seek permission from the copyright owner, or they pay a fee to the Copyright Clearance Center for a license to make the additional copies. Other libraries might more directly reconsider the appropriateness of the CONTU guidelines. The specific standard of five copies is not the law, and libraries have the ability to evaluate whether some other interpretation of Section 108 may be appropriate.

COPY MACHINES IN THE LIBRARY

This statute has one more provision that is routinely important to libraries. Section 108(f)(1) gives libraries protection from infringements that a visitor may commit when using unsupervised copy machines in the library. As long as the library displays a notice informing users that making copies may be subject to copyright law, the statute can release the library and its staff from liability.[20]

> **HERE IS** one form of a notice commonly posted on reproducing equipment in libraries and archives: "Notice: The copyright law of the United States (Title 17, U.S. Code) governs the making of photocopies or other reproductions of copyrighted material. The person using this equipment is liable for any infringement." The law does not prescribe the exact wording of this notice, so a library could add references to fair use and permissions and provide other information about copyright that might be helpful.

The user of the machine is still responsible for any infringements.

The statute offers protection to libraries that post notices on unsupervised "reproducing equipment" at the library. The statute does not narrowly refer to photocopy machines. The benefit to libraries that post the notices could be considerable, and the cost of compliance is negligible. A library is well advised to post a notice on all unsupervised photocopy machines as well as on CD and DVD burners, VCRs (if you can find one), tape decks, microfilm readers, computers, printers, and any other equipment that is capable of making copies, whether a new device or a relic from the library's stash of decrepit hardware. While the provision applies to only equipment in the library and archives, many educational institutions post the notice on machines throughout the campus. It can't hurt, and it may do some good.

THE REJUVENATION OF SECTION 108(H)

The Sonny Bono Copyright Term Extension Act of 1998 added an entirely new subsection to Section 108.[21] Congress was at that time adding twenty years of protection to existing works, long delaying the date when millions of works in library collections would enter the public domain. The new law was effectively postponing the ability of many libraries to benefit from the public domain for building digital collec-

The Typewriter Repair Shop in Los Angeles so far has survived technological change and obsolescence. Typewriters are also devices that could be used to reproduce copyrighted works, albeit laboriously. Should a library post a warning notice on any typewriters available for public use?

tions and other activities. Congress added Section 108(h) as something of a balance against the bonus years of protection that the law was granting to copyright owners.

This relatively new provision is a broad authorization allowing libraries and archives to "reproduce, distribute, display, or perform in facsimile or digital form a copy or phonorecord of such [published] work, or portions thereof, for purposes of preservation, scholarship, or research."[22] It applies, however, only during the final twenty years of the work's copyright duration. Confining the statutory exception to just the final twenty years imposes on the library a calculation that is sometimes a monumental challenge.

Look again at Chapter 6 of this book, with its belaboring of the rules of copyright duration. Sometimes the calculation can be simple arithmetic. Often, however, the determination of copyright duration depends on elusive factual circumstances or legal determinations that can incorporate international agreements and foreign legal rulings. If the duration of copyright is uncertain for a particular work, then determining the last twenty years will also be elusive.

Even within that twenty-year span, the grant to libraries and archives does not apply if any *one or more* of the following three conditions is true with respect to the particular work:

- The work is subject to "normal commercial exploitation," which generally means that the work is currently in use or marketed by the rightsholder.
- A copy or phonorecord of the work can be obtained at a reasonable price.
- The copyright owner has provided a notice, consistent with regulations from the U.S. Copyright Office, asserting that either of the preceding two conditions applies.

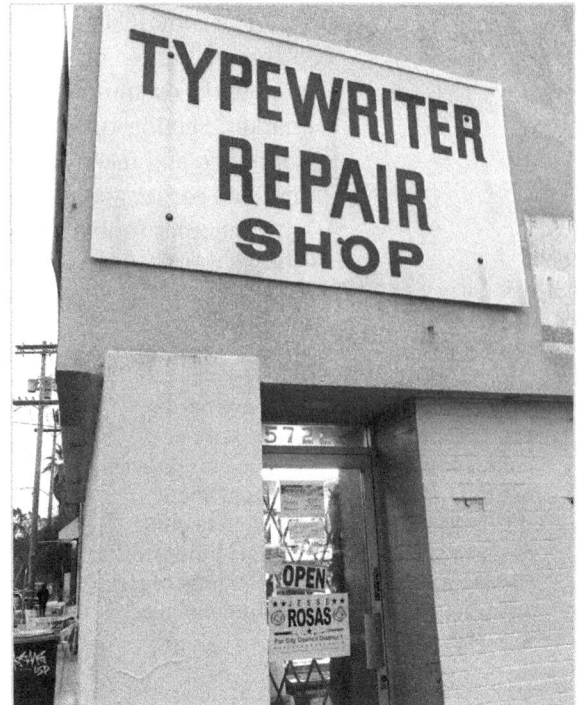

Despite the sometimes awkward structure and application of Section 108(h), some analysts and librarians have sought to find the statute's full potential. A research team at Tulane University has tested the application of the statute against a large collection of books that had been published between 1923 and 1941—books that would have been in their final twenty years of the maximum possible protection at the time of conducting the study.[23] The study found that many works that had been published in those early years were no longer commercially exploited and could be used by libraries consistent with the statute.

THE LISTING of the three conditions is linguistically odd. Apparently, the list of three conditions actually offers two conceptual means to defeat the ability of a library to use Section 108(h). First, if the facts related to a particular work are such that either of the first two conditions is true, then the exception does not apply. Second, the final condition anticipates that the copyright owner may record a notice declaring that the other factual conditions are true and apply to a specific work. That third condition functionally has overarching power. By making the assertion, the copyright owner in one gesture can render Section 108(h) inapplicable to the work.

Section 108(h) also has an important place in the Music Modernization Act of 2018. The act extends a form of legal protection akin to copyright for pre-1972 sound recordings, and it preserves the application of Section 108 and certain other exceptions to the use of the recordings. When applying Section 108(h), however, the act tells us how to understand the statute's language: "[W]ith respect to a sound recording fixed before February 15, 1972, the phrase 'during the last 20 years of any term of copyright of a published work' in such section 108(h) shall be construed to mean at any time after the date of enactment of this section."[24]

In other words, when applying the law to pre-1972 sound recordings, libraries are spared the task of calculating the actual duration of legal protection to find when the last twenty years might kick in. Instead, the library needs to know only whether the use complies with the other details of the law, and simply whether the use is occurring after October 11, 2018, the date of enactment.[25] For sound recordings, this extraordinary provision removes entirely the messy and sometimes elusive calculation of the "last 20 years" of copyright protection.

The Tulane study and the simplified calculation for pre-1972 sound recordings are harbingers of the good potential of Section 108(h). Indeed, the Internet Archive has put into practice the Tulane study and built a collection of digitized books that are in their final twenty years. In a spin on the name of the copyright extension statute, the Internet Archive affectionately calls the project the Sonny Bono Memorial Collection.[26] Section 108(h) is proving to become a usable grant for libraries and archives if they are willing to make the calculations and investigate the commercial availability of the early publications. Some libraries are taking up the challenge and opportunity.

THE FUTURE OF SECTION 108

Section 108 was an entirely new statute, largely drafted during the legislative process in the 1960s. That Section 108 is the subject of review and proposals for change should therefore come as no surprise. No statute will satisfy everyone, interests in copyright have shifted significantly, and libraries have revolutionized their services through the decades. The current Section 108 may be confined to limited library functions, although it continues to serve a vital purpose and function reasonably well. Nevertheless, much discussion continues to swirl around the possibility of revising this statutory exception for libraries and archives.

Yet one still has to wonder why the demand for change to Section 108 would be so imperative. After all, no litigation has tested the core meaning of the statute since its enactment in 1976, and numerous libraries and archives across the country have gone to great lengths to understand the law and give it a meaningful implementation. By that standard, Section 108 has been an enormous success. Perhaps the most important congressional action could be to expand the scope of activities covered by the law rather than revise the basics of the status quo.

It is easy to see ways that Section 108 could be improved, but revision has hazards. Frankly, some revisions Congress made to the law in 1998 made the statute less serviceable in some respects for the goals of libraries and archives. The 1998 changes hamstrung the access to works that were preserved with digital technologies by confining the digital copies to the premises of the library. In 1998 Congress also added Section 108(h), but its dicey calculations and procedures have slowed its adoption.

Perhaps the main criticism one could raise about Section 108 is that it is inherently limited in its scope of activities. Section 108 is about three main activities: preservation and replacement, research and study, and interlibrary lending. Utterly untouched is a broad sweep of functions that are becoming more and more desirable and important for libraries and archives: data and text mining; services for persons who are blind or have other learning disabilities; archiving of websites and other ephemeral or transitory materials; and the assurance that license agreements will not undercut the statutory rights of use, whether in Section 108 or under fair use.

A rigorous and high-level effort to revise Section 108 began in the early 2000s with the establishment of the Section 108 Study Group, a task force appointed by the Librarian of Congress and comprising representatives from libraries, publishers, and other interested parties. In March 2008 the group delivered its report after three years of investigation and negotiation.[27] The report recommended numerous revisions of Section 108, including these:

- Expanding Section 108 beyond libraries and archives by including museums within its scope
- Replacing the fixed limit on the number of preservation copies to allow for a "reasonable" number of such copies
- Permitting a library to circulate a digital preservation copy outside the library, if the original was in such a format and had been allowed to be circulated
- Enacting a new provision to permit robust programs for building preservation copies of published works, subject to detailed conditions for security and maintenance of the collection
- Adopting a new provision to permit preservation copying of websites and other online materials, subject to allowing copyright owners the ability to opt out of preservation programs

The Section 108 Study Group submitted its final report in 2008, but no legislation based on the report was ever introduced in Congress. Yet revision of Section 108 remains a priority of the U.S. Copyright Office. In 2016 the office began the process of jump-starting a fresh examination of Section 108 by soliciting comments from the public. The outcome was the issuance in 2017 of a Discussion Document with suggestions for possible revision of the statute.

The latest proposals track some of the recommendations of the earlier study group by adding museums to the scope of entities, bringing greater flexibility to the preservation sections, and facilitating more extensive access to preservation copies in the library. These proposals offered for discussion in 2017 would make Section 108 more versatile and effective in other ways, such as expanding it to permit displays and performances of some works and allowing copies of a broader range of materials for private study

> **THE DISCUSSION** Document issued by the U.S. Copyright Office in 2017, with numerous supporting documents, is available here: https://www.copyright.gov/policy/section108/.
>
> The final report of the Section 108 Study Group as issued in 2008, along with extensive background materials, may be found on the group's website: http://www.section108.gov.

by users. On a most critical point, the Copyright Office proposed that some rights under Section 108 would not be waivable by nonnegotiable contractual terms.

The effort to improve Section 108 is important and complex. The only sure expectation is that change will be slow and contentious. What is good from one perspective is a devastating threat from another view. The quest for any consensus on reform is certain to be a major and perhaps an insurmountable challenge. Legislative change usually comes slowly, and the politics in Congress can be on edge these days. As a result, any prediction about amending the text of Section 108 would be a hazardous endeavor indeed.

> **THE WIPO** research study of copyright exceptions was conducted by the author of this book. The 2017 version of the report collects and analyzes the relevant statutes from all 191 countries that were then members of WIPO, and it identifies some trends and patterns among the laws. For the full report, see Kenneth D. Crews, *Study on Copyright Limitations and Exceptions for Libraries and Archives: Updated and Revised, 2017 Edition* (Geneva, Switzerland: World Intellectual Property Organization, 2017), http://www.wipo.int/meetings/en/doc_details.jsp?doc_id=389654.

LIBRARIES AND COPYRIGHT AROUND THE WORLD

The United States is hardly alone in having a statutory exception for libraries and archives, and many other countries are exploring the possibility of expanding or revising their current laws. A treaty on these issues would most assuredly motivate major changes in domestic copyright law. Beginning in 2005, the World Intellectual Property Organization (WIPO), an agency of the United Nations based in Geneva, Switzerland, began the process of the possible development of treaties related to copyright exceptions and limitations. The role of WIPO and the significance of treaty developments are examined in Chapter 3.

A priority in the WIPO discussions has been the possibility of drafting agreeable language for a treaty or other instrument that can support and guide the development of statutory exceptions for libraries and archives. WIPO has commissioned a series of studies examining the statutes from all member countries. The WIPO studies demonstrate that Section 108 in the U.S. law is not radically unlike some other statutes around the world. In particular, the most common subject matter of the statutory exceptions is the same set of issues that are prominent in American law: copies for preservation and replacement and copies of works for private study and research.[28]

At this stage, discussions in WIPO are centering around some form of instrument that would encourage and support member countries and whether to embrace new issues such as data and text mining and waivers of rights under license terms. One can easily see that the process of achieving consensus for any action among the many diverse member countries is necessarily complex and slow. On the other hand, many countries around the world are not waiting for a WIPO treaty before considering possible statutory revisions.

A modest number of other countries have completed significant changes in their provisions for libraries in recent years. Some of those countries include Canada, Kuwait, Russia, and the United Kingdom. Various other countries are also giving their law serious examination that may well lead to revision of the library provisions and maybe even the addition of fair use and other exceptions. Those countries include Armenia, Australia, New Zealand, and Nigeria.

These developments remind us of a few fundamental truths about the law: Copyright law is made by our legislatures, and it can be changed by our legislatures. It is often in transition, and each of us needs to find a way to participate in order to make those transitions the best they can possibly be. The existence of these statutes around the world and the attention they are receiving right now also remind us that libraries and copyright have a critical and symbiotic connection. Libraries serve the objectives of copyright by fostering new works and building collections of diverse works for the advancement of knowledge. Libraries serve the needs of copyright owners by purchasing and licensing extensive collections, and at the same time, libraries foster the next generation of creativity through their ability to work with copyrighted materials to assure that they will be available to researchers in all parts of the world for all time.

NOTES

1. U.S. Copyright Act, 17 U.S.C. § 108. Although this statute regularly refers to "libraries and archives," this chapter will often use the term *libraries* as a general and inclusive concept for purposes of simplicity. My roots are in archival work, and I deeply appreciate the important and distinctive work of archives.

2. U.S. Copyright Act, 17 U.S.C. § 108(a)(2).

3. U.S. Copyright Act, 17 U.S.C. § 108(a)(1).

4. U.S. Copyright Act, 17 U.S.C. § 108(g).

5. U.S. Copyright Act, 17 U.S.C. § 108(a)(3).

6. As a reminder of the diverse materials that a library may need to preserve, a regulatory exception to the anticircumvention provisions of Section 1201 applies specifically to accessing video games for preservation by an eligible library, archives, or museum. *See* 37 C.F.R. § 201.40(b)(8)(i)(B). Anticircumvention and the statutory and regulatory exceptions are examined in Chapter 22.

7. U.S. Copyright Act, 17 U.S.C. § 108(i).

8. U.S. Copyright Act, 17 U.S.C. § 108(i).

9. U.S. Copyright Act, 17 U.S.C. § 108(i).

10. U.S. Copyright Act, 17 U.S.C. § 108(b).

11. U.S. Copyright Act, 17 U.S.C. § 108(c).

12. This chapter includes earlier mention that digital technologies can be used under Section 108 by virtue of the broad definitions of *copies* and *phonorecords*. If that is true (and I believe it is), then the pressure to clarify the statute was misplaced.

13. U.S. Copyright Act, 17 U.S.C. §§ 108(b) & (c).

14. U.S. Copyright Act, 17 U.S.C. § 108(d).

15. U.S. Copyright Act, 17 U.S.C. § 108(e).

16. Section 108 is principally about allowable reproduction of copyrighted works. The ILL issues in this chapter are accordingly limited. If a library is sending an original work to another library without making a copy, that is simply an exercise of the first sale right under Section 109(a), as summarized in Chapter 9.

17. U.S. Copyright Act, 17 U.S.C. § 108(c) and (d).

18. U.S. Copyright Act, 17 U.S.C. § 108(g)(2).

19. U.S. National Commission on New Technological Uses of Copyrighted Works, *Final Report of the National Commission on New Technological Uses of Copyrighted Works* (Washington, DC: Library of Congress, 1979): 54–55.

20. U.S. Copyright Act, 17 U.S.C. § 108(f)(1).

21. U.S. Copyright Act, 17 U.S.C. § 108(h).

22. *Id.*

23. Elizabeth Townsend Gard, *Creating a Last Twenty (L20) Collection: Implementing Section 108(h) in Libraries, Archives and Museums* (October 2, 2017), https://ssrn.com/abstract=3049158 or http://dx.doi.org/10.2139/ssrn.3049158.

24. U.S. Copyright Act, 17 U.S.C. §1401(f)(1)(B).

25. The act was signed into law and took effect on a memorable occasion at the White House attended by Kid Rock, Mike Love, Sam Moore, and other recording artists. Even more memorable was the appearance that afternoon by Kanye West in the Oval Office. The conversation was more about alternate universes than about music or copyright.

26. Brewster Kahle, "Books from 1923 to 1941 Now Liberated!," *Internet Archives Blogs*, posted October 10, 2017, https://blog.archive.org/2017/10/10/books-from-1923-to-1941-now-liberated/.

27. Section 108 Study Group, *The Section 108 Study Group Report* (Washington, DC, March 2008), http://www.section108.gov/docs/Sec108StudyGroupReport.pdf.

28. The latest study from WIPO, cited in a text box in this chapter, includes some basic statistics. However, the first study from 2008 includes an extensive introduction with a more detailed examination of trends in the statutes. Kenneth D. Crews, *Study on Copyright Limitations and Exceptions for Libraries and Archives* (Geneva, Switzerland: World Intellectual Property Organization, 2008), https://www.wipo.int/meetings/en/doc_details.jsp?doc_id=109192.

CHAPTER 18

RESPONSIBILITY, LIABILITY, AND DOING THE RIGHT THING

KEY POINTS

- An infringer of copyright can potentially face extensive liabilities, but some of the more significant liabilities are available only if the work is registered with the U.S. Copyright Office.
- Educators and librarians who exercise fair use in good faith may avoid some liability, especially statutory damages.
- The law offers a safe harbor from infringement for online service providers who institute a takedown system.
- State universities, schools, libraries, and other state agencies may be protected under the constitutional doctrine of sovereign immunity.

SO FAR, THIS book has avoided much mention of liability for copyright infringement. Steering clear of liability is no accident. This book does not have among its leading objectives to explore litigation and legal action. The fundamental objective of this book is instead to educate readers and prepare each of us to handle copyright situations in an informed and good faith manner, thus helping to avoid lawsuits and liability. This is a book about finding a meaningful path through copyright law.

Yet the time may come when you might need to add up the consequences of a possible copyright infringement. For example, you may have reproduced a protected work without permission and in a manner that is not within fair use or another exception. You might have more than passing curiosity of the consequences. You might also be in the early stages of planning an innovative project that may not be clearly within fair use. You are eager to get approval, but the dean or director will likely ask about the risks and costs if it turns into a lawsuit. In yet other circumstances you might be the copyright owner seeking to assert your rights. What legal ammunition do you have to stop an infringement? In each situation you want to know the remedies, expenses, and penalties that can come from legal action. You also want to know how to avoid them.

WHAT ARE THE LEGAL RISKS?

What is at stake in an infringement action? If a judge rules that you have committed an infringement, the consequences can be formidable. An injunction

ONE INDICATOR of the importance of determining the financial consequences of litigation has been the simple fact that the U.S. Supreme Court has handed down multiple major rulings on the matter in just the past few years. In 2016, the Court held that district courts have considerable flexibility, but as a leading consideration, courts should give "substantial weight to the objective reasonableness" of the position asserted by the nonprevailing party. *Kirtsaeng v. John Wiley & Sons, Inc.*, 579 U.S. ___, 136 S. Ct. 1979 (2016). In 2019, the court clarified the scope of the costs that a party might recover in litigation. See *Rimini Street v. Oracle* in the next text box.

can bar further unlawful uses; the court can impound the copies and your equipment; you can be ordered to reimburse losses that the copyright owner incurred or to pay the profits you gained from the wrongdoing.[1] This portion of the chapter will lay out a worst-case litany of liabilities. The remainder of the chapter will offer a more tempered vision of the possible consequences of an infringement allegation.

The copyright owner who successfully makes an infringement claim may also be entitled to receive two more remedies that involve significant dollars. First, the owner can seek statutory damages of up to $30,000 per work infringed, in lieu of actual damages or profits.[2] Second, the owner may also ask for reimbursement of attorneys' fees and the costs of litigation.[3] These amounts are not to be underestimated. Recall the case of *Basic Books, Inc. v. Kinko's Graphics Corporation* from Chapter 12.[4] The court ruled that Kinko's had infringed the copyrights and ordered the company to pay $510,000 in statutory damages.

Because that case involved registered copyrights, Kinko's was also ordered to pay the publishers' attorneys' fees and costs, in the total amount of $1,395,000.[5] Of course, Kinko's also had to pay for its own lawyers. That litigation occurred nearly three decades ago; the dollar amounts today would surely be much higher, assuming that the court would again find no fair use. On the other hand, the right to claim attorneys' fees works in the other direction. Had Kinko's prevailed on its fair use defense, the court could have ordered the publishers to pay Kinko's for the cost of its lawyers.[6] The lesson here for users of copyrighted works is critical. If you can demonstrate a strong case for fair use or another defense, not only might you win a lawsuit, but the prospect of paying enormous fees might even discourage the rightsholder from filing the lawsuit.[7]

IN ADDITION to awarding statutory damages and attorneys' fees, Section 505 of the Copyright Act allows that "the court in its discretion may allow the recovery of full costs by or against any party other than the United States or an officer thereof." U.S. Copyright Act, 17 U.S.C. § 505. The award of costs is not conditioned on being the prevailing party or on having registered the work. Congress took the occasion to protect itself and the entire federal government from this hit. Further, the Supreme Court ruled in 2019 that the concept of "full costs" is limited to costs listed in the general statutes about federal litigation. *Rimini Street, Inc. v. Oracle USA, Inc.*, 586 U.S. ___, 139 S. Ct. 873 (2019). Notably missing from the list are costs associated with most expert witnesses.

THE IMPORTANCE OF COPYRIGHT REGISTRATION

The financial consequences may be overwhelming, but statutory damages and attorneys' fees are generally available to the copyright owner only if the owner registered the work with the U.S. Copyright Office before the infringement occurred.[8] Chapter 4 of this book emphasizes that copyright vests automatically and that registration and other formalities are not required. Without early registration, you can still be the copyright owner, and you can still win your lawsuit and obtain damages and other remedies. But only after timely

TO BE ELIGIBLE for statutory damages and attorneys' fees, the work ordinarily must be registered before the infringement occurred. In the case of a published work, the Copyright Act allows a grace period of three months after first publication to make the registration. U.S. Copyright Act, 17 U.S.C. § 412(2). Registration can occur long after publication, but the owner will qualify for the added rights only with respect to infringements occurring after the registration date. With respect to pre-1972 sound recordings, the Music Modernization Act of 2018, examined in **Chapter 20** of this book, allows these remedies with the simpler requirement that the claimant add the titles to a schedule of protected works maintained by the U.S. Copyright Office. U.S. Copyright Act, 17 U.S.C. § 1401(f)(5).

registration are you entitled to what are often the most lucrative remedies in an infringement case—statutory damages and attorneys' fees.

The lesson to copyright owners is clear: If you are serious about protecting your copyrights, you ought to consider registering your claim of copyright with the U.S. Copyright Office.[9] You should also register early, before any infringement has occurred. A corollary to this rule is also true: If you are seeking to use a copyrighted work and your investigation reveals that the work is not registered, the risks of facing the largest dollar damages may drop sharply.[10]

The decision to move ahead with a use of a work based on research of registration records should be done with great care and professional advice. A lack of registration can mean only a reduction of penalties—not an elimination of them. You do not want to be an infringer, and you should still make the determination that you are reasonably within fair use or other legal authority. At the same time, your research should be thorough and careful to avoid overlooking relevant registration records. If you move ahead without due regard for the rights of owners, you may be accused of willful infringement. In that event, the statutory damages (for registered works) can jump to $150,000 per work infringed.[11] The legal provisions about damages and registration offer important rights and responsibilities, but mistakes can be costly.

> **IF YOU** have committed a willful infringement, you may also face criminal penalties—including monetary fines and time in the federal prison system. U.S. Copyright Act, 17 U.S.C. § 506(a). A willful infringement typically arises where you not only know your actions but also know that they are a violation of the law. This is one more reminder of the importance of acting in good faith, as explored elsewhere in this chapter.

GOOD FAITH AND GOOD NEWS

Confronted with a variety of potential legal liabilities, how can librarians, educators, and others reasonably live amidst the uncertainty that copyright sometimes brings? Fortunately, the Copyright Act offers some important protection in response to exactly this realistic need. The law calls on each of us to act in an informed and good faith manner.

That basic advice may seem trivial, but it is actually of central importance, particularly for educators and librarians working with fair use. Reasonable people can and will disagree about the meaning of fair use. Congress recognized that it was enacting a law open to significant differences of interpretation, so Congress provided an important safety valve for educators and librarians.

Recall that one of the possible remedies for infringement is statutory damages of up to $30,000 per work infringed. Imagine you are in front of a judge who has just ruled that you are an infringer and is preparing to assess damages. Large dollar figures may be looming.

The law of statutory damages, however, proceeds to give an important break for educators and librarians. In fact, the court may be required to cut the statutory damages all the way to zero. This protection applies if you are an employee or agent of a nonprofit educational institution, library, or archives, if you were acting within the scope of your employment, and if you "believed and had reasonable grounds for believing" that the copies you made were fair use. If you can meet those requirements when faced with infringement, the court must remit the statutory damages in full—cut them entirely.[12]

How can you demonstrate that you had reasonable grounds to believe that you were within fair use? The best bet may be to do your homework. You might not have to become an expert, but you might have to learn a bit about fair use. You will have to apply the four factors and weigh your evaluation. You need to make a reasoned and reasonable conclusion about whether you are acting within the law. As a result, the court may still disagree with you about fair use, but the court may see your good faith efforts and cut your liabilities accordingly.

> **EVEN IF** statutory damages are eliminated, you are not completely off the hook. You can still be an infringer subject to all other remedies, such as actual damages and injunctions. Further, the exception for librarians and educators does not cover all possible uses of copyrighted materials. It only explicitly addresses reproducing the work in copies or phonorecords. No court yet has had the need to test the meaning or extent of this law. This state of the law brings us back to a familiar objective: Learn about copyright and apply a reasoned and good faith understanding of the law.

WHO IS LIABLE FOR THE INFRINGEMENT?

Initially, the person who actually commits the infringement is liable. That person might be the librarian filling orders for copies, the research assistant duplicating materials for a professor, the webmaster creating a cut-and-paste website, or the teenager downloading music files. In general, liability begins with the person who pushes the button to make the copy or actually commits the infringing activity.

In reality, in the setting of a business, library, or educational institution, liability often flows upstream to the supervisors who oversee the project and to the company or organization itself. Chapter 12 of this book includes summaries of cases about fair use. The liable parties were often corporations—such as Kinko's and Texaco—and not the individual employees. The truth is that all implicated individuals and organizations may share in any liability exposure.

> **A COMPANY** or another party can be held liable for the actions of another person on the basis of at least two theories: Contributory infringement can occur when someone provides the equipment or other means for creating infringements and knows, or should have known, of the infringing actions. Vicarious liability can occur when someone has the right to supervise the activity and stands to benefit from it. Knowledge of the infringing activity is not necessary. Employers are often in exactly that situation, at least with respect to activities that are part of an employee's job.

As a practical matter, however, the supervisors and the organization are at greater risk. Not only are they more likely to have more assets to claim, sometimes called "deep pockets," but a successful lawsuit at the highest level is more likely to have the greatest influence on shaping future behavior. Suing the Kinko's company, for example, led to changes in photocopy practices at Kinko's shops around the country. In fact, holding that one company liable helped persuade competing photocopy shops to reassess their similar services and legal risks.

A SAFE HARBOR FOR SERVICE PROVIDERS

Sometimes contributory or vicarious liability can be imposed on an Internet service provider (ISP). Think of EarthLink, Google, Microsoft, or any other provider of e-mail and Internet services. Consider the online services provided by your own university or another organization. Can these entities be held liable if they provide an e-mail or web server account and you use it to commit a copyright infringement? Is Google liable if you download a music file and send it by e-mail to a thousand close friends? Is the university liable if you scan your favorite book chapters and post them to your website?

So far, the answer is *maybe*. The ISP can be liable, depending on the level of oversight and control and the knowledge that officials had of the infringing activities. The reach of the law is evolving and murky.[13] Congress confronted this dilemma with new law in 1998. Congress did not exactly settle the law but instead crafted an opportunity for ISPs to find a safe harbor—protection from possible liability for copyright infringements committed by the users of their systems.[14]

The statutory protection for service providers is complicated, but it is proving to have profound consequences. To enjoy protection, the ISP must meet a lengthy list of elaborate conditions. Moreover, the safe harbor protects only the educational institution or other ISP itself from liability. The individuals who actually commit the infringement may still be liable. Other legal claims—such as trademark, privacy, or libel—that may arise from the same situation remain unaffected.

GENERALLY SPEAKING, the safe harbor usually applies only in situations where the ISP is truly passive. The statute extends to situations where the infringing materials are merely in transit through the system, are cached as an automated technical requirement of the system, or are resident on the system at the user's discretion and without the ISP's knowledge. This statutory provision was part of the wide-ranging Digital Millennium Copyright Act of 1998. The ensuing litigation has allowed the courts to define many details of the law. For example, the safe harbor does not apply if the service provider knew of the infringement. The Second Circuit ruled that the standard is high, and the service provider must have actual knowledge of facts that "indicate specific and identifiable instances of infringement." *Viacom International, Inc. v. YouTube, Inc.*, 676 F.3d 19, 32 (2d Cir. 2012).

For educational institutions, fitting into the safe harbor may often prove problematic. In addition to the foregoing conditions, the safe harbor might apply to a faculty website only if the infringing materials on the site were not "required or recommended" course materials within the preceding three years and the institution has received no more than two notifications of claimed infringements committed by that faculty member. The institution also must provide all users of its system materials that "accurately describe, and promote compliance with" copyright law.[15]

This brief summary only hints at the layers of complication in the statute. The centerpiece of the law, however, is the procedure known as *notice and takedown*. For any ISP to enjoy the safe harbor, it must register an agent with the U.S. Copyright Office. The agent will then receive notices of claimed infringements. For example, suppose a professor has posted materials to his or her website, and the copyright owner discovers them and objects. Under this statute, the copyright owner can send a proper notice to the designated agent for that ISP.

In order for the ISP to have full protection, it must then "expeditiously" remove or "take down" the materials from the system. The ISP may later investigate and maybe even restore the materials if they are ultimately not a violation. But the ISP must remove them first and ask questions later. Educational institutions of all types and sizes have discovered the prevalence and power of these legal procedures. With the growth of peer-to-peer networks for posting and sharing files, copyright owners have sometimes inundated university agents with notices about the multitudes of music, movie, and other files posted by students and others on high-speed networks run by the educational institution. The administrative burden alone is leading many organizations to begin educational campaigns and sometimes restrict student use of Internet access. Congress also has joined the effort for stronger oversight by colleges and universities.

Despite these travails, years of experience now have shown that the notice-and-takedown mechanism has many benefits. The law's safe harbor has enabled online enterprises such as YouTube, Flickr, and Facebook to exist. Users post the content; the service is merely the host or conduit. A user can post a video clip to YouTube, and if the copyright owner objects, the owner can send a notice to YouTube's agent. Ordinarily, the ISP must expeditiously remove the item in order to have the benefit of the safe harbor. Without a notice, however, the clip remains on YouTube. Even with a notice from the owner, YouTube can repost the clip if the user makes representations about its lawfulness and consents to the court's jurisdiction.

> **DOES YOUR** college, university, library, or other organization have a registered agent? The full list is posted on the website of the U.S. Copyright Office: https://www.copyright.gov/onlinesp/. If your organization is an ISP, the occasion may well arise when you would want the benefit of the DMCA safe harbor. Registering an agent is a simple and inexpensive step in the process. If you registered an agent before 2018, you might want to check again to see if you are on the list. The Copyright Office restructured the registration system, and all previous registrations were deemed to have lapsed at the beginning of 2018 unless reregistered. Registrations now need to be renewed every three years.

In this context, an enormous amount of copyrighted content is now on YouTube and elsewhere because it has stirred no objection or is justified as fair use.[16] The ISP, if it meets the statutory requirements, is in a safe harbor, protected from liability. However, the protection does not apply with respect to materials posted by the ISP itself. Thus, a library digitizing and posting collections and a professor using third-party materials on an instructional website will likely not qualify for the benefits of this law. Nevertheless, some organizations that create and share materials online essentially imitate the notice system and respond appropriately to copyright claims. The true safe harbor protection may not apply to initiatives such as the Internet Archive or HathiTrust, yet each organization offers guidance to copyright claimants, and few copyright claims are likely to persist after the claimed materials are removed from public access.[17]

> **THE SYSTEM** of notice and takedown has been the subject of much litigation since its enactment in 1998. One important and delightful case involves the song "Let's Go Crazy" by Prince and a very happy and energetic child. Stephanie Lenz posted to YouTube a short video of her eighteen-month-old son dancing joyfully to the song, which was generally audible in the video. The rightsholder of the recording, Universal Music, sent a notice to YouTube for removal of the video. Under the statute, the person posting the work has the right to challenge the takedown notice, as Lenz did with support from the Electronic Frontier Foundation. In *Lenz v. Universal Music Corp.*, 815 F.3d 1145 (9th Cir. 2016), the Ninth Circuit Court of Appeals ruled that a copyright claimant must make a good faith assessment of whether the activity may be within fair use before sending the notice. This important decision places a responsibility on rightsholders to make claims that respect their rights as well as the interests of the public.

NOTE ON SOVEREIGN IMMUNITY

Some copyright infringers may escape liability altogether under a sweeping constitutional doctrine. The Eleventh Amendment to the U.S. Constitution provides one more means for possibly avoiding monetary risks from copyright infringement. The Eleventh Amendment stipulates that a state or state agency may not be sued in a federal court for dollar damages.[18] A series of recent cases from the U.S. Supreme Court has brought renewed meaning to the

CONGRESS HAS attempted to eliminate or at least reduce the application of sovereign immunity. In 1990, Congress added Section 511 to the Copyright Act, explicitly stating that states and state employees are not protected from liability. The question still remains whether Congress has the power to undercut a constitutional protection by enactment of a statute.

provision, which is intended to protect the sovereignty of the states from being held accountable by a federal judiciary.[19]

By an act of Congress, all copyright cases must be brought in federal court.[20] In recent years, a few federal courts accordingly have dismissed cases that were brought against states and state agencies. Of notable consequence, one court has ruled that a unit of the University of Houston (a public university) could not be sued for copyright infringement.[21] On the other hand, the copyright case against Georgia State University, examined in Chapter 14, could continue because the copyright owners sought an injunction against individual university officials. The Eleventh Amendment will not necessarily bar a case that is not making claims for monetary damages.[22]

While these developments may give some leeway to states and state institutions to consider the appropriateness of their activities—rather than acting out of fear of liability—these cases by no means give public institutions complete protection. They may still be liable for equitable remedies, such as injunctions. Even a successful defense can cost a fortune in attorneys' fees. More important, if a public university acted in willful disregard of the law, it could still face criminal action.

DO THE RIGHT THING

This chapter begins with a litany of legal risks and some disturbing dollar amounts that a copyright infringer might face. Much of this chapter, however, is about the limits of possible liability. Educators and librarians who exercise fair use in good faith may avoid statutory damages. Online service providers may find a safe harbor from infringements committed by individual users. The sovereign immunity provision of the U.S. Constitution may allow state agencies to avoid liability altogether. Just as important, the recent historical record shows that common activities of educators and librarians have not been the target of copyright lawsuits, although that pattern appears to be shifting as litigation proceeds at Georgia State University and elsewhere.[23]

If the chances of being sued appear slim, why should we bother paying attention to the complications of copyright at all? The answer is simple: Because we live (we hope) in a cooperative society, and the law is an intermediary for defining many cooperative relationships. The law may be quirky and sometimes a little baffling, but the law has an important role in shaping the terms through which we relate to one another in a civilized world. Often the law deserves to be challenged and changed. Yet, we need to give respect to the interests of others if we are to gain respect for our own claims of rights and fair use.

If we do not like the law, we should demand change, and we should press the law's meaning. Meanwhile, we must remind ourselves that the law we challenge today may be the law that protects us in the future. Educators and librarians live in two copyright worlds at the same time. We are users of copyrighted materials, questioning the limits of fair use and seeking new opportunities for distance learning and other pursuits. Simultaneously, members of the academic community are increasingly concerned about rights in intellectual property.

Yet that symmetry is shifting steadily. Fairness and good ethical practices still demand mutual respect for the diverse interests within our own communities, and academic authors are increasingly recognizing that the copyright legal system may not serve their objectives as users or as copyright owners. That shift in attitude has given rise to the open access movement, Creative Commons, and other innovations in copyright management.[24] These efforts are bringing fresh understandings and alternative rules to the marketplace where ideas and works are shared. In the meantime, the reality of the law, with its benefits and liabilities, is an inevitable part of the research and learning environment. The law also forms the framework of rights that empower us to reshape standards for our own works and for our communities.

NOTES

1. The statutes governing the remedies or liabilities under copyright law are U.S. Copyright Act, 17 U.S.C. §§ 502–513.

2. U.S. Copyright Act, 17 U.S.C. § 504(c)(1).

3. U.S. Copyright Act, 17 U.S.C. § 505.

4. *Basic Books, Inc. v. Kinko's Graphics Corp.,* 758 F. Supp. 1522 (S.D.N.Y. 1991). Readers today might not realize that Kinko's was the name of an extensive network of shops across the country that offered photocopying and other services.

5. *Basic Books, Inc. v. Kinko's Graphics Corp.,* 21 U.S.P.Q.2d 1639 (S.D.N.Y. 1991).

6. The Supreme Court clarified in 1994 that a party asserting a successful defense can also request that the court order recovery of its fees and costs. *Fogerty v. Fantasy, Inc.,* 510 U.S. 517 (1994).

7. At least in the 2012 ruling from the district court in the *Georgia State Case,* examined in Chapter 14, the court found that the university parties had prevailed on fair use and therefore were entitled to recovery of attorneys' fees.

8. U.S. Copyright Act, 17 U.S.C. § 412. Registration is not a prerequisite to awards of attorneys' fees and statutory damages in the case of violation of moral rights under Section 106A. Thus, the graffiti artists who painted the 5Pointz building in Brooklyn, examined in Chapters 4 and 8, did not face the same registration requirement. The artists prevailed on a violation of moral rights and in 2018 were awarded $6,750,000 in statutory damages. *Cohen v. G&M Realty L.P.,* 320 F. Supp. 3d 421 (E.D.N.Y. 2018) (currently on appeal to the Second Circuit).

9. As noted in Chapter 6, the Supreme Court clarified in 2019 that the registration process must be completed before filing the infringement lawsuit; mere submission of the application and related materials is not enough. *Fourth Estate Public Benefit Corp. v. Wall-Street.com,* 586 U.S. ___ , 139 S. Ct. 881 (2019). A court may well adhere to the same requirement on the question of registration as a prerequisite to certain damages. I will say it again and again: If you are serious about protection, register early.

10. This discussion of registration as a condition to certain remedies is not to be confused with the general proposition that U.S. works are to be registered before filing an infringement lawsuit. U.S. Copyright Act, 17 U.S.C. § 411(a).

11. U.S. Copyright Act, 17 U.S.C. § 504(c)(2).

12. U.S. Copyright Act, 17 U.S.C. § 504(c)(2).

13. *Playboy Enterprises, Inc. v. Russ Hardenburgh, Inc.,* 982 F. Supp. 503 (N.D. Ohio 1997); *Religious Technology Center v. Netcom On-Line Communication Services, Inc.,* 907 F. Supp. 1361 (N.D. Cal. 1995).

14. U.S. Copyright Act, 17 U.S.C. § 512.

15. For the specific provisions of the statute that apply to faculty websites, see U.S. Copyright Act, 17 U.S.C. § 512(e).

16. Sometimes the content remains because the parties have agreed. For example, YouTube has an interest in keeping many copyrighted materials available, and so it has negotiated with some music production companies to secure licenses to maintain online many of the musical works posted by members of the public. The videos are often a good platform for advertising, and YouTube and the copyright owners can share in the revenues.

17. The copyright policy of the Internet Archive is available here: http://archive.org/about/terms.php. The takedown policy of the HathiTrust is available here: https://www.hathitrust.org/take_down _policy.

18. U.S. Const. amend. XI.

19. The Supreme Court continues to be highly protective of sovereign immunity. It ruled in 2019 that courts in one state are constitutionally obligated to honor the assertion of immunity made by another state. *Franchise Tax Board of California v. Hyatt*, 587 U.S. ___, 139 S. Ct. 1485 (2019). However, the Supreme Court is as of this writing reviewing a court of appeals decision that upheld state immunity in copyright cases. *Allen v. Cooper*, 895 F.3d 337 (4th Cir. 2018), *cert. granted*, 139 S. Ct. 2664 (2019).

20. For the statute granting exclusive jurisdiction to federal courts, *see* 28 U.S.C. § 1338(a).

21. *Chavez v. Arte Publico Press*, 204 F.3d 601 (5th Cir. 2000).

22. The Eleventh Amendment can also prevent infringement lawsuits brought by faculty members against their own universities for the use of their teaching materials. *Nettleman v. Florida Atlantic University Board of Trustees*, 2017 WL 76958 (S.D. Fla. 2017).

23. The *Georgia State Case* is the subject of Chapter 14.

24. Open access, Creative Commons, and other initiatives are examined in Chapter 7 of this book.

PART V

Special Features

MUSIC EXISTS in many forms, including sheet music and sound recordings. This page includes the lyrics and staff notation from a 1922 publication for the song known today as "Happy Birthday to You." Copyright law has many distinctive provisions applicable to music, but the authorship and duration of copyright for this particular song have been litigated under the more familiar principles of law.

CHAPTER 19

MUSIC AND COPYRIGHT

KEY POINTS

- Copyright law often applies distinct rules to musical compositions and sound recordings.
- Many of the exceptions, including the first sale doctrine and the provision for library copying, can apply to music and recordings, subject to detailed conditions.
- The TEACH Act allows performances of music in distance learning, subject to important limitations.
- Section 108 allows libraries to engage in preservation of music and certain uses of some sound recordings.
- Performing rights societies may be helpful for licensing some educational uses of music, but not all.
- Sound recordings were not protected by federal law until February 15, 1972, and the complex law for pre-1972 recordings is explored in the next chapter.

MUSIC HAS BEEN a vital part of the growth of civilization since the earliest recorded history, and it continues to be critical for our understanding of culture and for robust research and teaching. Music also has received a distinct treatment in many respects under copyright law. In many places throughout this book, we can see that the general principles of copyright apply in the same way to all types of works, whether books, software, or music. That general notion is not always true, and American copyright law includes a sizable roster of special laws that apply to only music. Some of these rules for music are of immediate importance to libraries, teaching, and research.

TWO COPYRIGHTS

For most of us, music is something we listen to and enjoy, and it comes to us in a variety of media. Music is embodied in vinyl, cassettes, CDs, MP3s, and more. We might hear it on traditional broadcast radio or be lucky enough to attend a live performance. We download music from websites and stream it from webcasts, Internet radio, and Spotify. From a legal perspective, we need to separate the *musical work* from the *sound recording*. Regardless of the medium, almost any recorded piece of music can typically encompass two basic copyrights.

First, copyright protects the composition, which is also called the "musical work" in the parlance of copyright laws. The law does not specifically define a musical work, but it is well understood to be the composition. A musical work is in many ways akin to a literary work. It is the author's original creativity, and the owner has a variety of fundamental rights to the aspects of the work that are protectable under copyright law. The copyrightable musical work may include lyrics, musical notes, the arrangement, and any accompanying elements.

Second, copyright may also protect the sound recording that captures the singers and musicians performing the work. The law defines a sound recording as a work that results "from the fixation of a series of musical, spoken, or other sounds."[1] A sound recording may capture a performance of the composition, regardless of the medium or format. The recording may be on reel-to-reel tape, cassette, 8-track, digital audiotape, a computer file, or any other mechanism for capturing sounds in the analog or digital realm.

AS WITH all other copyrights, the rights in the sound recording and underlying work will eventually enter the public domain. Consider, for example, some of the greatest operas and symphonies from long ago. Ordinarily, performing and recording a musical work require permission from the copyright owner. If a Mozart masterpiece is in the public domain, no copyright permission is needed to use the composition. A modern recording of the Mozart piece is still a new original work with a new copyright. As a result, the use of that recording may require analysis and application of multiple aspects of copyright.

A sound recording is not always a recording of music. The recording could instead capture spoken words or other sounds—comedy routines, bird calls, White House meetings, and family interviews. The existence of two copyrights applies to more than just music. Library collections frequently include sound recordings of poetry, political speeches, stage plays, and oral histories, not to mention the growing reserves of audiobooks. One person may hold the copyright in the underlying work. Another rights-holder may hold a copyright in the reading, recitation, or performance captured in the recording.

Because the two copyrights are separate, each one will often have a different owner, a different duration of protection, and even a distinct set of legal rights belonging to each copyright owner. Therefore, playing the recording to the public, or digitizing it for a research collection, may well be a use of two copyrights and require consideration of the legal rights of two owners.

A recording engineer, or more likely the recording company, may hold a copyright in the sound recording. The copyright in the composition may still be held by the original composer, or with the passage of time, the rights may have been inherited by or transferred to other parties. Understanding the relationship between musical works and sound recordings is fundamental to protecting the copyrights in the works and to making uses of them under important statutory exceptions to the exclusive rights of ownership.

MUSICAL COMPOSITIONS and sound recordings are today routinely eligible for copyright protection. A new composition is easily original, and it is fixed when noted on paper or played onto a recording. A sound recording of the same musical composition may have originality in the rendition, style, or accompaniment. It, too, is fixed upon making the recording. For more information about these principles, see Chapter 4.

THE ART AND INDUSTRY OF MUSIC

Given some distinct traits of music, Congress has been persuaded over the years to enact for the industry a host of technical and specialized copyright rules. Further, because of distinctive industry practices, various conventions about licensing have reshaped the way we might use or even just enjoy music. These rules can become important in the search for meaningful and lawful ways to use the works in teaching, learning, and scholarship.

Why does the law—and this book—give considerable attention to music? Musical works and recordings have given rise to a legal framework that underpins an entire industry—and that principally protects rights of copyright owners and ostensibly meets the market's craving for tunes. For the music industry, musical works and sound recordings represent engines for creative and economic growth that are increasingly threatened by copyright infringers. For users, musical works and sound recordings have become educational tools of growing importance in library collections and in support of innovative teaching and learning. Music offers a fundamental insight into understanding society and culture. People also simply like music—it can communicate ideas and reveal deeply felt motivations and beliefs.

Live musical performances often require copyright clearance. They can also be great fun, but the experience sometimes can benefit from precautionary earplugs.

TECHNOLOGICAL EVOLUTION AND LEGAL FRAMEWORKS

The law has long had trouble keeping pace with innovations and different forms of copyrightable writings, including art and musical staff notations. Federal copyright law did not apply to music at all until 1831.[2] For decades the law extended to only compositions, even decades after the invention of recording systems. U.S. copyright was finally extended to sound recordings, effective as of February 15, 1972.[3] As is examined in the next chapter, the struggle over pre-1972 recordings has led to development of new state and federal laws.

Issues related to music and recordings have raised some of the most perplexing copyright questions. A century ago, the Supreme Court struggled with the copyright implications of player piano rolls—then a new and challenging technology.[4] Courts need to address issues of digital file sharing[5] and webcasting on Internet radio stations.[6] Some nuances in the law are unclear, some are seemingly contrived, and many are embedded in history and the relationship of music technologies to copyright law.

In general, the law today grants the basic set of rights to the copyright owners of musical works and recordings. Owners have rights of reproduction and distribution of their works. The copyright in musical works includes a general right of public performance. The owner of the sound recording has a performance right, but only in the context of a "digital audio transmission."[7]

As with most works, the copyright laws also carve out various exceptions to owners' rights, such as fair use. If the use fits within the various requirements of an exception, the owner cannot legally prevent the use. While the interplay of rights and exceptions is fundamental to understanding copyright protection

THE FULL definition of sound recordings provides that they are "works that result from the fixation of a series of musical, spoken, or other sounds, but not including the sounds accompanying a motion picture or other audiovisual work, regardless of the nature of the material objects, such as disks, tapes, or other phonorecords, in which they are embodied." U.S. Copyright Act, 17 U.S.C. § 101. Thus, sound recordings exist independently of technology or format definitions and could include tin rolls, reel-to-reel, cassette, wire recorders, MP3 files, and as yet unforeseeable means for recording "musical, spoken, or other sounds."

and rights of use, the rules applied to music are sometimes distinct from general copyright standards. This chapter summarizes several major aspects of copyright law as applied to music, with emphasis on the copyright exceptions of importance to educators and librarians.

SECTION 108: LIBRARY COPYING

Recall from Chapter 17 that Section 108 of the U.S. Copyright Act permits many libraries to copy protected works for a variety of important purposes, including preservation and replacement, interlibrary loan, and private study by patrons. However, Section 108 does not allow libraries to copy *all* works for *all* purposes. The statute by its own terms is sometimes restricted to only certain types of works.

Section 108 is broadest when applied to preservation or replacement of works—provisions that can apply to any type of copyrighted material. By contrast, when libraries are making and delivering copies of works for the user's private study, those provisions of Section 108 do not apply to musical works.[8] Thus, under Section 108, libraries cannot make copies of musical compositions for the patron's study, scholarship, or research.

The limits of Section 108, however, are not a dead end. For example, a desired use may not fall within the parameters of Section 108, but that use may still fit within fair use under Section 107. Specifically, Section 108 may not allow a library to make and deliver a copy of a musical composition, but making and sending that same copy could under the right circumstances constitute fair use. Analyzing the four factors might reveal many opportunities to make use of works beyond the more rigorous limit.

> **UNTIL 1995,** recordings enjoyed no performance rights. Thus, when a recorded work of music was performed for a live audience, through broadcast or any other means, only the owner of the composition had rights—and could demand payment. With the growth of online transmission, Congress in 1995 granted a limited performance right to the owner of the recording. That owner can now have rights to some digital performances, but still not in other contexts, including the familiar terrestrial radio broadcasts. U.S. Copyright Act, 17 U.S.C. § 106(6).

> **MUCH MORE** information about fair use is found in **Chapters 10 through 14** of this book. In conventional analysis, fair use can be a tough doctrine when applied to music. For example, musical works are generally highly creative, tipping the second factor against fair use. A reasonable understanding of music might necessarily require using a substantial portion of the work, affecting the third fair use factor. However, the Supreme Court ruling in the case involving the "Oh, Pretty Woman" song greatly relaxed some of these traditional proscriptions. *Campbell v. Acuff-Rose Music, Inc.*, 510 U.S. 569 (1994).

Further, some parts of Section 108 may not apply to musical works, but they might still permit copying of sound recordings. Indeed, the provisions permitting copies for private study explicitly apply to copies and to phonorecords. Thus, making and delivering a copy of a sound recording could fit neatly within Section 108 if it is a recording of a public domain composition or of a speech or other nonmusical work.[9]

Underscoring the difference between a musical work and a sound recording, consider the following practical applications of Section 108:[10]

- A library wants to make copies of printed sheet music, which is a form of a musical work. Section 108 allows that the library may make copies of music for preservation or replacement but not for private study.[11]
- A library wants to make copies of a sound recording of a performance of a copyrighted musical work. The library may generally copy a sound recording for any of the allowed purposes under Section 108. However, Section 108 permits the library to make a copy of the underlying musical work only for purposes of replacement or preservation.

- A library wants to make copies of sound recordings of musical works, and the underlying composition is in the public domain. The library may make copies of these recordings for any of the purposes within Section 108.
- A library would like to copy a sound recording of something other than music, such as a poetry reading, a political speech, an oral history interview, or nature sounds. Because the copy does not involve a musical work, Section 108 authorizes the library to copy the recording with the nonmusical content.

As a practical matter, the library can institute preservation programs consistent with Section 108 for all recordings. But when a patron requests copies for private study, the library is often limited to recordings of nonmusical works. This awkward distinction is a by-product of Congress's attempt to balance the rights and interests of copyright owners and copyright users. Musical compositions enjoy more protection presumably because copying them for patrons might cause market harm to the music industry. On the other hand, the inability to copy some works for individual study can ultimately reduce the value and usefulness of library collections.

SECTION 109: THE FIRST SALE DOCTRINE

Section 109 is another exception that sometimes applies differently to musical works. Commonly known as the first sale doctrine, this provision limits the copyright owner's ability to control copies—or physical embodiments—of a copyrighted work.[12] For example, someone may own the copyright in a music CD, but the owner of a copy of that CD generally may dispose of that particular copy through any means, including giving it away, selling it, lending it, or even renting it.[13]

Without the first sale doctrine, many common activities, such as selling books or lending them from libraries, could be unlawful distributions of copyrighted works. In the 1980s, the music industry became particularly alarmed at the growth of private businesses renting music CDs to the public. The obvious concern was that, unlike renting a book or many other works, a customer could rent a CD for a brief time and simply and quickly copy it. For much less than a typical purchase price, the customer could upload copies to computers, phones, and other devices. More perplexing for the rightsholder, the customer would then return the disk, making it available for the next customer to copy.[14]

THE LENDING of a sound recording containing a musical work does not enjoy the first sale exception of Section 109 if the lending or rental is for the purpose of "direct or indirect commercial advantage." U.S. Copyright Act, 17 U.S.C. § 109(b)(1)(A). While the commercial uses are barred, the noncommercial uses by libraries and other organizations may continue. Note that the limit on commercial lending applies to only certain works. The law does not bar commercial lending of motion pictures, so your local video store may legally remain in business—although streaming has quickly made most lending of movies obsolete. Of course, other forces come to bear, and the concept of a retail store that lends videos has almost entirely vanished. The last Blockbuster may for the moment be found in Bend, Oregon.

Congress amended the statute to bar the first sale doctrine as it may apply to musical works or sound recordings containing musical works unless the lending is undertaken for "nonprofit purposes" by a nonprofit library or a nonprofit educational institution.[15] *Nonprofit* is a crucial condition for meeting this exception. Although it is not defined in the statute, most academic and public libraries should easily meet this standard. As a result, most non-profit academic libraries may surely continue to keep and lend their collections of sound recordings of music and other types of works.

SECTION 110(2): THE TEACH ACT AND DISTANCE EDUCATION

Chapter 16 of this book offers considerable detail about the TEACH Act, a statutory exception that permits uses of copyrighted works in distance education. An examination of the statute emphasizes that the law applies differently to different types of works. One important distinction in the TEACH Act surrounds the treatment of *dramatic* and *nondramatic* musical works.

Section 110(2) allows the performance of entire nondramatic musical works by transmission in distance learning. By contrast, the law allows performances of dramatic musical works only in "reasonable and limited portions."[16] The distinction between dramatic and nondramatic music enjoys a rich and intriguing history in shaping and applying copyright law, but the statutes have yet to offer an explicit definition of these terms.

> **THE HISTORY** of dramatic and nondramatic works is rich with nuance and rationale from copyright owners. Indeed, the Copyright Act of 1909 (which was replaced in full by the revision act of 1976) included a concept of *dramatico-musical* works and addressed *grand performing rights* as distinguished from *small performing rights*. Moving to today's law, references in statutes and licenses to allowing performances of nondramatic music usually anticipate a simple, unadorned playing of instruments, singing of songs, or performances of the musical work through broadcast on radio or television. The performance often may be live, or it may be made from a preexisting recording.

Understanding the meaning of nondramatic musical works is necessary to application of Section 110(2). We can find some insight from various sources, but generally a work is dramatic if it is meant to be used to perform a story. Dramatic musical works may include opera, Broadway musicals, and ballet.[17] Under that definition, a musical work might be dramatic in one context but nondramatic in another.

Many dramatic songs are also released as nondramatic popular versions, such as "Pinball Wizard," "Mamma Mia," and "Let It Go." As a pop single, each may be considered a nondramatic work and usable in full under the TEACH Act. Each of these songs also has been part of an opera, stage musical, or movie. If included in a course in its dramatic context, that same song might be allowed in only reasonable and limited portions.

While the TEACH Act expressly allows these performances of musical works, it makes no explicit mention of sound recordings. The lack of any language clearly allowing performances of sound recordings can create a dilemma because playing a sound recording is a common and sometimes inevitable means for performing the musical work. You might perform a sound recording, for example, by sliding a disk into a CD player, plopping an LP onto a turntable, or embedding an MP3 file into a website. You are simultaneously performing the underlying musical work. If the educational experience involves listening to the music, the sound recording is essential.

The TEACH Act does offer some hope. Although it may not mention sound recordings, the statute does allow performances of all types of copyrighted works (including sound recordings) at least (once again) in reasonable and limited portions. The interpretation sets up a dilemma for educators. The TEACH Act allows performance of a nondramatic musical work in full, but it allows performance of only portions of a sound recording of it from a CD or any other source.[18]

Therefore, if you are singing or making another live performance of the composition, you may perform the entire work. However, if the performance is from a CD or another sound recording, you will be limited to *portions*. How much is that? The question of portions under the TEACH Act is addressed in Chapter 16 of this book.

Sometimes we use music in ways that the law might not have expected. The patriotic song "My Adored Homeland" is etched into a stone in the shape of Mongolia. The monument reproduces and displays the song and perhaps is a derivative work. It is located near the main plaza in the capital city of Ulaanbaatar.

The awkwardness of the TEACH Act on this point may best be understood by grappling with the unusual history and scope of protection for sound recordings. For example, because federal copyright protection did not even apply to sound recordings until 1972, performances of early recordings might not be infringements of federal law at all.[19] Further, even when Congress granted protection as of 1972, it sharply restricted the performance rights for the recordings. If the recording has no performance rights, then an exception under the TEACH Act is not even needed. However, if the underlying composition is protected, the TEACH Act may be summoned to support education.

PERFORMING RIGHTS SOCIETIES

The performance rights for nondramatic and dramatic musical works have raised other copyright complications. For historical reasons, principally the advent of radio and television broadcasting, the performance of nondramatic musical works has been of growing importance to broadcasters and to copyright owners who ultimately devised licensing collectives to clear permission rights and to allocate requisite royalties to copyright holders.

For many decades, these performing rights societies included the American Society of Composers, Authors and Publishers (ASCAP), Broadcast Music, Inc. (BMI), and the Society of European Stage Authors and Composers (SESAC). Since 2003, SoundExchange has administered the licensing of digital performances. In just recent years, Global Music Rights (GMR) has positioned itself to compete with the more established services. These agencies enjoy a nonexclusive right to license public performance rights in the numerous musical works that each organization represents. Users may search these song lists on the web. If a particular song is on a song list, the quest for permission can then be directed at the appropriate society. If the song is not on a list, then you may return to the customary search for the individual owner of the rights.

Although these licensing societies can greatly streamline the process of securing permissions, they are generally limited to granting rights to make public performances of compositions of nondramatic music. As a result, the licenses allow only public performances and do not address reproduction or distribution rights of the musical works and sound recordings. Thus, in order to reproduce and distribute the musical work or sound recording, you may need to seek separate permission from the copyright owner.

These performing rights societies do not license performance rights in dramatic musical works or performance rights in sound recordings. Users generally will need to secure a license to those works directly from the copyright owner, provided that their uses do not fall under another enumerated exception. Many uses within the library and academic community may fit within one or more exceptions in the Copyright Act, including fair use. On the other hand, many educational institutions purchase annual performance licenses from some of the societies to cover performances of music at sporting events and in other public forums.

> **COLLEGES AND** universities often secure blanket licenses with one or more licensing societies to cover many public performances of nondramatic musical works on campus. For more information, see the websites for some of the most familiar organizations:
>
> - ASCAP: http://www.ascap.com
> - BMI: http://www.bmi.com
> - SESAC: http://www.sesac.com
> - GMR: https://globalmusic rights.com
>
> These organizations usually license only performances of works. If you are making a new recording of an existing song, you may need to contact the Harry Fox Agency at http://www.harryfox.com.

THE FUTURE OF MUSIC

The copyright law for music continues to be in transition. Various bills in Congress have proposed to extend the performance right to sound recordings as fully as the rights for musical compositions, but with no success.[20] Under these proposals, recording artists would share in the payments for broadcasts and other performances of sound recordings. Meanwhile, courts have had occasion to hand down decisions about the scope of protection, similarity of works, and fair use of music and recordings, creating something of a mixed assortment of cases and generating a good deal of debate and confusion about the law.[21]

Regardless of legal developments, the marketplace for music is changing rapidly. New means for lawfully acquiring music continue to proliferate. Amazon, Google, and iTunes have become leading sellers of downloads priced for the mass market. Pandora has become the modern incarnation of request radio, and Spotify has challenged conventions of the industry. YouTube has become a treasure trove of music, and behind the scenes YouTube negotiators have cut deals with the leading music labels to share proceeds from advertising. Meanwhile, Taylor Swift and other artists have fought back for what they argue is a fair share.

> **THE CHANGING** nature of music and technology has led to the creation of new collective licensing societies. For example, SoundExchange (https://www.soundexchange.com) licenses rights in recordings for noninteractive digital transmissions. SoundExchange licenses performances made by webcasting, satellite radio, and other means. It collects and pays royalties for performances on Pandora and Spotify, but the rates and coverage have been much in dispute lately.

These online music sources often include live performances, high-end productions, and simple recordings of favorite and obscure songs. Are they lawfully online? Often the user cannot tell. Some of these innovations in music delivery exist because they fit within the law; others exist with only authorization and permission of the rightsholders. The Internet today is also rich with illicit copies, as well as materials voluntarily and perfectly lawfully posted by rightsholders. The educator, librarian, or other user cannot jump to a sweeping conclusion about the propriety of the material, but each should use good sense and watch for warning signs.

Music may have distinctive law because music has a distinctively important place in our society and culture. We continue to find new aesthetic ventures in music and, in the process, test the limits of copyright. Politicians rely on campaign songs to embrace their spirit. Sampling is a fixture of hip-hop. Shaggy's take on "Angel of the Morning" gives an old standard a fresh feel. Mashups from DJ Earworm and others allow new understandings of existing music. Girl Talk seems to be living voluntarily on the edge between social movement and copyright infringement.

Whether on concert tour or in the classroom, the rules of copyright will steadily collide with the important place that music has in our lives. Composers, performers, producers, lawyers, lawmakers, and consumers are in steady quest for new formulas, new limits, and new possibilities. Meanwhile, librarians work through this maze of law to build collections. Educators struggle with fair use and other means for using recordings and lyrics in research and innovative teaching tools. Also, somewhere deep in an office of most colleges and universities, someone is authorizing annual payment to one or more of the collective licensing agencies for the right to use music at halftime shows and other campus gatherings.

NOTES

This chapter in earlier editions was prepared by Professor Dwayne K. Buttler of the University of Louisville. His contributions continue to inspire and shape this chapter, and I thank him for his important work and lasting influence.

1. U.S. Copyright Act, 17 U.S.C. § 101.
2. Act of February 3, 1831, ch. 16, 4 Stat. 436.
3. Act of October 5, 1971, Pub. L. No. 92-140, 85 Stat. 391, 391–92.
4. *White-Smith Publishing Co. v. Apollo Co.*, 209 U.S. 1 (1908).
5. *Metro-Goldwyn-Mayer Studios Inc. v. Grokster, Ltd.*, 545 U.S. 913 (2005).
6. *Arista Records, LLC v. Launch Media, Inc.*, 578 F.3d 148 (2d Cir. 2009), *cert. denied*, 559 U.S. 929 (2010).
7. U.S. Copyright Act, 17 U.S.C. § 106(6).
8. U.S. Copyright Act, 17 U.S.C. § 108(i).
9. The references to sound recordings in this part of the chapter are generally to recordings made after 1972. The next chapter addresses the problem of pre-1972 recordings. Because many early recordings were protected under *state* copyright, it was not clear at all whether they might have been used in accordance with Section 108 or any of the exceptions in *federal* copyright law.
10. Keep in mind as well that these examples are about only Section 108. Some uses may be allowed if within fair use or another exception or if all aspects of the work are in the public domain.
11. For a detailed examination of some issues of copyright and music preservation, *see* June M. Besek, *Copyright and Related Issues Relevant to Digital Preservation and Dissemination of Unpublished Pre-1972 Sound Recordings by Libraries and Archives* (Washington, DC: Council on Library and Information Resources and Library of Congress, 2009).
12. The first sale doctrine is examined more generally in Chapter 9.
13. U.S. Copyright Act, 17 U.S.C. § 106(3).
14. Application of the first sale doctrine to digital works has been problematic. The Second Circuit in 2018 rejected the application of first sale to a system that would allow transfers of digital files, even if only one usable copy existed at any time. *Capitol Records, LLC v. ReDigi Inc.*, 910 F.3d 649 (2d Cir. 2018), *cert. denied*, 139 S. Ct. 2760 (2019).
15. U.S. Copyright Act, 17 U.S.C. § 109(b)(1)(A).

16. U.S. Copyright Act, 17 U.S.C. § 110(2).

17. In the early traditions of copyright, a dramatic performance of a musical work is an exercise of grand performance rights, while a nondramatic performance is a small right. *See* Melville B. Nimmer & David Nimmer, *Nimmer on Copyright*, § 10.10[E] (New York: Matthew Bender & Co., 2018), 10–98. *See also Robert Stigwood Group, Ltd. v. Sperber*, 457 F.2d 50, 55 n.6 (2d Cir. 1972).

18. At the risk of making the law of music more cumbersome, sound recordings in general do not have a performance right under copyright law. Still, the performance of recorded music may implicate the performance right attached to the underlying musical work. Thus, the TEACH Act and other exceptions become relevant.

19. See the next chapter of this book about new federal law for pre-1972 recordings and the application of the TEACH Act.

20. Performance Rights Act, S. 379, 111th Cong. (2009); H.R. 848, 111th Cong. (2009). The U.S. Copyright Office has continued to support a full performance right for sound recordings, but no such legislation has yet passed. U.S. Copyright Office, *Copyright and the Music Marketplace* (Washington, DC: U.S. Copyright Office and Library of Congress, 2015), 138, https://www .copyright.gov/docs/musiclicensingstudy/copyright-and-the-music-marketplace.pdf.

21. *See*, for example, *Bridgeport Music, Inc. v. Dimension Films*, 410 F.3d 792 (6th Cir. 2005); *Newton v. Diamond*, 388 F.3d 1189 (9th Cir. 2004), *cert. denied*, 545 U.S. 1114 (2005); *Saregama India Ltd. v. Mosley*, 687 F. Supp. 2d 1325 (S.D. Fla. 2009), *aff'd*, 635 F.3d 1284 (11th Cir. 2011).

CHAPTER 20

THE PECULIAR LAW OF PRE-1972 SOUND RECORDINGS

KEY POINTS

- Sound recordings made before February 15, 1972, had no federal copyright protection, but some early foreign recordings had their copyrights restored.
- State law sometimes offered protection for early recordings, but the existence and scope of state protection have been highly uneven.
- In 2018, Congress added an entirely new set of legal rights for pre-1972 recordings, explicitly maintaining fair use and other copyright exceptions.
- The law creates a new exception for noncommercial uses of recordings and other possibilities that can be beneficial for libraries and education.

THE PREVIOUS CHAPTER begins with the fundamental concept that a recording of music will often involve two distinct copyrights—the copyright in the underlying musical composition and a separate copyright in the recording of the performance. The two works are routinely used together. Our ability to enjoy music often depends on listening to a recording, whether listening to a digital or terrestrial broadcast or playing a selection from a smartphone or a vinyl LP. The music in our lives is often intrinsically dependent on the fixation of a performance into a sound recording. The recording may be digital, on vinyl or tape, or launched from a website.

For various reasons, sound recordings have posed a litany of technological, political, economic, and legal challenges for copyright law. Courts and Congress have struggled. The awkward development of the law effectively left sound recordings made before 1972 with no federal copyright protection. State law sometimes has attempted to fill the void, creating a scope of state copyright protection that is often indeterminate and certainly inconsistent across the fifty U.S. states.

In recent years, the economic interests related to early recordings have escalated. Early works have found a new market on specialized radio stations and in movie soundtracks. Recording artists from the 1960s and earlier decades have filed lawsuits asserting rights under that muddled state law regarding broadcast performances of their works on digital radio. Congress stepped into the fray in late 2018 with passage of the Music Modernization Act, crafting an entirely new form of legal protection for pre-1972 recordings. The new law also opened fresh opportunities for researchers, educators, and libraries. This chapter is an overview of the background and current condition of the law of these early sound recordings.

BEFORE 1972: SOMETHING FROM NOTHING

Despite the long history of copyright fundamentals and the historical growth of the scope of copyright protection, sound recording posed a dilemma for lawmakers. The law is often slow to encompass new technologies, and sound recordings were a messy amalgamation of underlying works and derivative rights. They were also not visually perceptible, such as a book or a painting, so they did not fit the model of traditional works. In the decades after their invention, the growth of business interests and the importance of recordings in the marketplace finally led Congress to bring sound recordings under federal copyright protection as of February 15, 1972.[1]

When Congress enacted the full revision of the Copyright Act in 1976, it affirmed the copyrightability of sound recordings but stood by the 1972 effective date for eligibility. The practical result is that sound recordings today do have federal copyright protection, but only if the recordings were made on or after February 15, 1972. Think of the fabulous world of recordings made before 1972: Enrico Caruso, Glenn Miller, Duke Ellington, Patty Page, Elvis Presley, Richie Valens, the Supremes, and the landmark achievements of Aretha Franklin.[2] Those are just examples of music recordings. Sound recordings can also capture speeches, poetry readings, and plays, which means no federal protection for recordings of early radio broadcasts and political rallies.

These recordings made before February 15, 1972, are without copyright protection under U.S. federal law—sort of, and sometimes. A few major nuances are in order. First, keep in mind that this is a rule about the sound recording only and not necessarily about the underlying composition or other content. Thus, if Bob Dylan composes the song and Frankie Valli records it before 1972, the recording may be without federal protection but the underlying musical work is copyrighted.[3] When that recording is played on the radio or sold in copies, the owner of the copyright in the song may have a performance right under federal copyright law.

Second, the lack of federal copyright for pre-1972 recordings originally applied to all sound recordings, but since 1996 most foreign pre-1972 recordings have the benefit of federal copyright protection. As surveyed in Chapter 6, these foreign works had their copyrights restored in 1996 in connection with joining the World Trade Organization. Among the works eligible for restoration were works in the public domain due to "lack of subject matter protection in the case of sound recordings fixed before February 15, 1972."[4] The upshot is that a recording made by the Beach Boys in Los Angeles before 1972 is a U.S. work and without federal protection whereas a recording made by the Beatles in London before 1972 is now most certainly restored. Anyone using the Beatles recording under U.S. law would need to investigate the rights of the performers and others associated with the recording, the rights of the composers, and the rights of their successor owners.[5]

Third, the pre-1972 U.S. recordings were never entirely in the public domain and freely usable without *any* legal constraint. They lacked only

IT GETS even more complicated. While federal copyright protection extends to only recordings made after February 15, 1972, even then Congress did not give the copyright owner of the recording all possible rights. When a new recording of a new song is performed on a conventional radio broadcast, both copyrights are implicated. However, only the composition has a performance right. Only the rightsholder of the underlying musical work will receive a royalty for airplay. By contrast, both the recording and the musical work have rights of reproduction and distribution, so both rightsholders are able to claim a royalty from sales of CDs, downloads, or other copies. The story is still not done. As mentioned in the previous chapter, Congress amended the law in 1995 to grant some performance rights in sound recordings, but with respect to only certain digital audio transmissions. Music lawyers stay busy.

THESE TECHNICAL and detailed rules about foreign works and the preemption of state law seem to have set up at least one major copyright quandary. The Music Modernization Act of 2018 repealed the bar against federal preemption of state law and put in its place a federal system for pre-1972 recordings that is similar to, but not the same as, copyright. To emphasize that distinction, the law now provides that "no sound recording fixed before February 15, 1972 shall be subject to copyright" under the U.S. Copyright Act. U.S. Copyright Act, 17 U.S.C. § 301(c). However, the restoration of foreign works establishes true copyright protection for pre-1972 sound recordings. Is Section 301 on a collision course with the restoration law? Can the restored copyright exist simultaneously with the new quasi-copyright in sound recordings? Sometimes only future litigation can give answers to our legal curiosities.

copyright protection under *federal law*. In the absence of federal copyright, many states have offered legal protection in the form of state copyright or common law copyright. The federal Copyright Act previously had taken great strides to preserve that state law; the statutes before the revision in 2018 specifically mandated that with respect to pre-1972 sound recordings, "any rights or remedies under the common law or statutes of any State shall not be annulled or limited by this title until February 15, 2067."[6] State law has been problematic in many respects. It often lacks specificity about the duration of rights, fails to include a performance right, and neglects the role of exceptions and limitations.

Fourth, with the passage of the Music Modernization Act in late 2018, Congress crafted a new form of federal protection for pre-1972 recordings. The protection is codified in a lengthy Section 1401 of the U.S. Copyright Act, but the legal rights are not technically *copyright*. They fit into a legal zone sometimes called *neighboring rights*. The legal rights apply to all pre-1972 sound recordings, and the term of protection is defined by a series of chronological tranches, based mainly on when the recording was first published. Much of this chapter is devoted to deciphering this new quasi-copyright statute.

The dilemma of pre-1972 recordings has been greatly exacerbated in recent years by the changing marketplace. Many early recordings long have had value, but they have gained new monetary potential with the growth of innovative delivery systems, downloadable distributions, postings on YouTube, digital sampling, and Internet radio.

In the meantime, multiple lawsuits that have been filed around the country tested the application of state copyright laws and exploring whether there might be federal protection in new digital remasters of the earlier analog recordings.[7] Holders of arguable rights in recordings by the Turtles, Jackie Wilson, Johnny Tillotson, Mahalia Jackson, and many other hit makers of the early years of soul and rock have filed actions to test their rights under the laws of different states.

The result has been mixed and even more mixed up. The New York State Court of Appeals (the state's highest court) ruled that New York does have common law protection for recordings, but the state law does not recognize, and never has recognized, a performance right.[8] As a result, playing the early recordings on the radio or Internet is not an infringement in New York. Yet a federal court in California ruled that California state law does include a performance right.[9] The Ninth Circuit has more recently referred the question to the California Supreme Court to resolve.[10] Meanwhile, Flo & Eddie, Inc. has filed a similar lawsuit in Florida.[11]

FLO & EDDIE, Inc. is the holder of rights in many of the early recordings by the Turtles, a band that enjoyed enormous success in the 1960s. The co-owners of the corporation are Howard Kaylan and Mark Volman, two founding members of the Turtles, and they have been touring and enjoying their successful songs for decades. Who could have foreseen that "Happy Together" would be the work that might ultimately test the coordination of federal and state copyright laws? It is indeed one of the famous and valuable songs at the center of the Flo & Eddie litigation that is testing the meaning and scope of copyright protection in various U.S. states.

Litigation on this issue will surely continue for years, and there is no reason to expect that the resulting law will be the same in all states. Indeed, most states have not explicitly adopted any law at all for pre-1972 recordings.[12] The law is therefore highly uncertain and widely variable across state lines, and the implications can be profound and confusing: Does a nationwide webcast of a song require clearance and royalties if received in only certain states? Does a takedown notice as authorized under federal law apply to copyrights that are protected under state law?[13] Can a library build a digital collection of early recordings and rely on the federal rules of copyright expiration and fair use when states fail even to mention these concepts in their laws?

Often advocated as the means for resolving these questions, and for creating some degree of national consistency in copyright law, was the suggestion that Congress extend federal copyright protection to all early recordings. The pre-1972 works would simply be under the same familiar copyright laws. That proposal to federalize early recordings definitely had critics, but it also had important support from the U.S. Copyright Office.[14] By late 2018, Congress had chosen a different path through this maze. It chose not to grant conventional copyright but instead to forge a new genre of legal rights solely for the recordings. In the process, Congress also made clear that the familiar exceptions, such as fair use and the exceptions for libraries, would apply in the new legal milieu—which takes us to the Music Modernization Act of 2018.

MUSIC MODERNIZATION AND LEGAL INNOVATION

In late 2018, Congress enacted a lengthy bill known as the Music Modernization Act (MMA).[15] Much of the attention in the press and among the composers, performers, producers, and others in the industry was on the restructuring of the compulsory licenses for recordings and performances of music sound recordings. These developments were highly significant. They went far in building systems for licensing and collecting royalties on performances of early and new recordings. Of importance to libraries and education, however, the legislation also included a new regime of legal protection for sound recordings made before February 15, 1972, and it explicitly preserved the application of fair use and other exceptions.[16]

The MMA also explicitly carried over multiple exceptions, limitations, and other safeguards for the use of the pre-1972 recordings. Consider these highlights that are now part of the new *Chapter 14* of the U.S. Copyright Act, all of which can prove critical and often beneficial to teaching, research, and information services:

■ The new rights are not denoted as *copyright*, but they come into existence and are subject to terms similar to copyright. Indeed, the rights extend to all *covered activity*, defined as "any activity that the copyright owner of a sound recording would have the exclusive right to do or authorize under section 106 or 602, or that would violate section 1201 or 1202, if the sound recording were fixed on or after February 15, 1972."[17] In other words, the rights applicable to pre-1972 recordings include the basic economic rights of copyright owners as well as the rights created by the DMCA.

ALTHOUGH FEW librarians and educators will need to delve deeply into the provisions about compulsory licensing, one incident of those provisions may prove to be of great service to academia. The legislation mandates the creation of a database of songs with assurance of public access to the metadata at no cost. As it develops, the database should be a means for discerning songs with identical or similar names and at least guiding the user to a copyright claimant for permissions as needed. Of course, the virtue of the database will depend on the quality of the inputs, including the accuracy of information and the rightfulness of the claims of ownership. Technical services librarians will surely see opportunities for shaping the details of each catalog record. The database will adhere to cataloging conventions, including the use of International Standard Recording Codes and International Standard Work Codes for identifying recordings and compositions.

The first movie from the Beatles was released in 1964, along with sound recordings, sheet music, and much more. The compositions were copyrightable from the outset, but not the pre-1972 sound recordings. In 1996 those foreign recordings would presumably have had their copyrights restored. If they were not restored for any reason, the Music Modernization Act would likely have given the sound recordings the new quasi-copyright protection.

- The new rights for sound recordings are subject to many of the exceptions of greatest importance, including fair use. Explicitly applicable to the new legal system for pre-1972 sound recordings are Sections 107 (fair use), 108 (for libraries and archives), 109 (the first sale doctrine), 110 (performances and displays in classroom and distance education), and 112(f) (incidental recording of distance education courses).[18] Each of these statutes already applies in some ways to music and recordings in a distinct manner. Nevertheless, assurance of the survival of these exceptions for pre-1972 sound recordings is a big deal.

- The library exception in Section 108(h), which allows libraries to make extensive uses of many works during their last twenty years of copyright protection, now applies to all sound recordings made before February 15, 1972. Moreover, when applied to these early recordings, the works do not have to be in their last twenty years of protection, sparing libraries the burden of calculating the duration for each work.[19] Other detailed requirements of Section 108(h) are examined as part of the library exceptions in Chapter 17.

FOR AN overview of the economic rights of copyright owners, see Chapter 8 of this book. The DMCA is surveyed in Chapter 22. The DMCA rights include the rights to prevent circumvention of technological protection measures and to act against removal of copyright management information. Notably absent from the list are moral rights. Congress long has been reluctant to apply moral rights to any works, so their absence here is hardly surprising. Because moral rights under Section 106A of the Copyright Act extend to only a narrow class of works of visual arts, it would have to be a most unusual example of a sound recording that could even raise serious questions about moral rights. Perhaps an audible description of artwork for the visually impaired (mentioned in Chapter 9 of this book)? Possible, perhaps, but seemingly improbable.

- The new law carves out a broad exception for *noncommercial uses* of pre-1972 sound recordings.[20] This provision has enormous potential, allowing many uses of the sound recordings, especially for the nonprofit and beneficial objectives of libraries and educational institutions. This statutory section is examined in detail later in the chapter.
- The new form of legal protection expires on a prescribed schedule, depending on the original publication date of the recording. As a general rule, the protection lasts for 95 years from publication plus an additional number of years depending on the year of publication. The new terms may be awkward at times, but they have the effect of sending a wave of sound recordings at the end of most years into the public domain, or at least leaving them free of this federal quasi-copyright.

> This chapter highlights the basics of the Music Modernization Act and the pieces of good news for libraries and education. However, it is worth repeating that the MMA is creating a new form of legal protection, and it is often layered on top of others. It is now perfectly possible, and even common, for a single pre-1972 recording to embody multiple legal rights established under the U.S. Copyright Act. First, the underlying musical composition (or other work) can have copyright protection. Second, the pre-1972 recording can have protection under the MMA. A third possibility is a point of some bewilderment. As mentioned elsewhere in this chapter, some early foreign recordings do have genuine copyright protection, which could well survive enactment of the MMA.

DURATION OF PROTECTION

You might think that a new regime of legal protection would be a great opportunity to start with a clean slate and make simple rules. No such luck. To grant rights for a defined term is to both give those rights and take them away at the end of the term. In establishing the new rules, Congress needed to assure rightsholders that it was not terminating their new protection sooner than the rights that the recording artist might have had under state law, which is now preempted. It avoided that problem by adding a period of years to a conventional copyright term. The result can be a contorted calculation.

Ninety-Five and Then Some

The duration of the new protection starts with the simple and familiar term of 95 years from first publication.[21] That term is analogous to the basic term for early published works, as detailed in Chapter 6. The MMA then adds extra years, called a *transition period*. It does not merely add the same number but instead a different number of years, depending on when the recording was first published. The basic rule is based on the date of *publication*, regardless of when the recording was actually made. The later the publication, the greater the number of added years.[22]

The MMA defines the term of protection in chronological groupings:

- Recordings *published* in 1922 and earlier receive protection to the end of 2021. The practical effect is that works that were already at least 95 years old when the MMA was enacted gained a few years of legal rights. They were spared a prompt conferral to the public domain.
- Recordings *published* between the beginning of 1923 and the end of 1946 receive an additional *five* years of protection. As a result, a work published in 1923 will get 95 years, to the end of 2018, plus *five* years, to the end of 2023. Works published in each of the ensuing years are protected successively to the next year.

> **THESE CATEGORIES** created terms of legal protection based on the date of publication, regardless of the date of creation of the sound recording. For example, consider the last category in the list. It applies to works that were published at any time after the beginning of 1957. The recording may have been made decades before 1957, but it can still be in this category. The *publication* date might be as recent as yesterday, and it can be in this category. If the recording was never published, it is in this category with other 1957 works. But if the recording was created after February 15, 1972, regardless of when or whether it might be published, the Music Modernization Act does not apply. That recording was originally and is today governed by the conventional provisions of the U.S. Copyright Act.

- Recordings *published* between the beginning of 1947 and the end of 1956 receive an additional *fifteen* years of protection. You can see the pattern. A work published in 1947 will get 95 years plus *fifteen* more, out to the end of 2057, and so on.
- Recordings not in any of the foregoing categories are protected until February 15, 2067. This category of course applies to only pre-1972 recordings, but it includes any such works that were *published* anytime after the end of 1956 and any that have never been published. This is the critical provision of the MMA that brings unpublished works under its purview.

That last bullet point has two additional critical implications. First, it has the effect of bringing the entire system of distinct legal protection for pre-1972 sound recordings to a close on February 15, 2067. On that date, the MMA rights end, and these special rules for pre-1972 recordings will become a thing of history. By contrast, the recordings made on and after February 15, 1972, will have conventional copyright protection. The scope and duration of rights for those recordings will be determined by the more standard rules of copyright law. The second major implication is that this last category of duration is not dependent on publication, so it also applies to *unpublished* works from the past.

Unpublished Sound Recordings

That point about *unpublished* works merits a much closer look. While the other duration groupings explicitly base the term of protection on the year of *first publication*, the last category is about any recordings fixed before February 15, 1972, that are not included in any of the preceding categories. The word *published* is not mentioned as a requirement for this specific statutory subsection. That category is therefore about pre-1972 recordings that were *published* anytime in or after 1957. It also is about any recordings made anytime before February 15, 1972, that were *unpublished* as of January 1, 1957, or a later date of creation, and remained unpublished.[23]

Despite some awkward calculations and odd outcomes, application of the MMA provisions to unpublished pre-1972 sound recordings is overall good news for libraries and other institutions working with collections of music, interviews, speeches, oral history projects, and other such recordings. Ordinarily, one might think that the creation of a new layer of legal protection would be unwelcome. The legal system might instead be more constructive if it were to create added certainty and preserve essential exceptions. The MMA expressly incorporates and secures key rights of use, including fair use and Section 108. It also includes a new concept applicable to non-commercial uses (described later in this chapter). These alone open enticing possibilities. The MMA also did some peculiar gyrations with Section 108(h). With some patient understanding, this restructuring of Section 108(h) may have tremendous potential. The scope of possibilities is greatly expanded when applied to unpublished works.

> **THE BASIC** rule of duration for *unpublished* pre-1972 sound recordings is simply that the new form of protection extends until February 15, 2067. The earliest forms of sound recordings include such technological innovations as the phonautograph, invented in 1857, and the paleophone, invented in 1877. Thomas Edison patented the phonograph cylinder in 1878. The unpublished recordings from even those distant times are now protected until February 15, 2067. The earliest recordings that were most probably in the public domain under conventional federal and state laws now seem to have a new federal quasi-copyright for a maximum duration approaching 200 years.

SECTION 108(H) AND PRE-1972 RECORDINGS

Brace yourself for some unusual statutory construction, and some reward for the hard work. Recall that Chapter 17 of this book offers a reticent view of Section 108(h) of the U.S. Copyright Act. That provision created broad possibilities for libraries to use works during their final twenty years of copyright protection. The statute has been an interesting innovation since its enactment in 1998, but its complications and limitations have prevented it from garnering much implementation. Especially vexing has been that Section 108(h) requires calculating the often-elusive copyright duration, and the statute explicitly applies to only published works.

Congress reacted to these constraints in the statute when enacting the MMA, and it made major substantive adjustments in the application of Section 108(h) to pre-1972 recordings. In so doing, Congress may have infused considerable new life into a nearly moribund provision. Keep a handle on this key description of the law: The MMA did not actually amend the existing Section 108(h). The previous language of the statute is unchanged, so do not expect to find any mention of sound recordings in that provision. Instead, the MMA established that when applying Section 108(h) to pre-1972 sound recordings, the clause "during the last 20 years of any term of copyright of a published work" is to be construed as meaning "at any time after the date of enactment of this section."[24]

Pause a moment. This is a major development. Recall that the new law for early recordings is a distinct form of protection, one that is not exactly copyright in a traditional sense. In crafting the law, Congress chose to apply Section 108 and certain other exceptions unchanged. However, when applying Section 108(h), Congress chose to give the statute a new meaning. The choice that Congress made should be particularly welcome to librarians who are building and digitizing collections or using recordings in any other way. By effectively deleting the words *during the last 20 years of any term of copyright of a published work*, Congress removed the requirement that a library must determine when the last twenty years apply, and it removed the confinement of the law to only published works.[25]

The effect may be sweeping. Congress essentially chose that Section 108(h) would potentially apply to any pre-1972 recordings, and the rights under Section 108(h) could be exercised at any time after the law takes effect. The MMA took effect when signed by the president on October 11, 2018. At any time after that date, Section 108(h) may apply to the use of pre-1972 sound recordings, regardless of when they were actually made, without the requirement of calculating and waiting for that final twenty years of protection and without limiting the library services to published works.

To be sure, the other requirements of Section 108(h) still apply, and libraries have some groundwork to complete under the law. Yet by this approach to Section 108(h), Congress has opened the way for libraries and archives to make most uses of pre-1972 sound recordings, for the purposes of preservation, scholarship, or research, subject to a

> **AS AN** example of the potential of the new Section 108(h), consider the collections of oral history sound recordings in many library collections. The original Section 108(h) allows the library to make copies only if the recording had been published and only in the last twenty years of its copyright protection. Few such recordings are published, and they are deteriorating on the shelf long before the copyright clock can count down. The MMA removed both of those requirements when applying the statute to sound recordings. Subject to the various other requirements in the statute, the newly reconstituted Section 108(h) may be a blessing for digitizing, preserving, and using the pre-1972 recordings in the treasured oral history collections.

reasonable investigation of the criteria related to commercial exploitation, assessment of the market, and other requirements in the statute. The possibilities for libraries and archives to digitize and make available either selected items or vast collections of the early recordings appear to be within reach.

NONCOMMERCIAL USES AND REASONABLE SEARCHES

The MMA provides one more opportunity that may prove useful for education and library services. The new law establishes a public right to make certain noncommercial uses of pre-1972 sound recordings without permission from the rightsholder. This provision is relatively broad in scope, offering possibilities beyond the allowed uses of Section 108(h).[26] The noncommercial provision is also relatively specific, perhaps offering a bit more comfort than the flexibilities of fair use.

The basic provision really is fairly simple. The statute allows any person to make any noncommercial use of a pre-1972 sound recording that is not being commercially exploited. Under that rule, libraries could consider building collections of recordings and educators and researchers could include them in teaching and innovative projects. These possibilities may still hold true, but first the law sets a variety of conditions, limits, and definitions:

- The user must make a reasonable and good faith search to determine whether the recording is currently being commercially exploited. The search must include records that rightsholders may file with the Copyright Office and services that offer a "comprehensive set of sound recordings for sale or streaming."[27]
- The person engaging in the noncommercial use must file a notice with the Copyright Office identifying the sound recording and the nature of the use.[28] This mechanism of searching and filing a notice is reminiscent in some respects of an orphan works law, and if it is successful, it could become a model for broader legislation.
- The rightsholder has not, within ninety days after the filing of the user's notice, in turn filed a notice opting out of allowing the noncommercial use.[29]
- The law does not define *noncommercial*, but it does state that recovering costs of reproduction and distribution of recordings does not necessarily render the use commercial. Further, the fact that a user also makes commercial uses of recordings does not necessarily mean that another use cannot be noncommercial.[30]

THE LAW goes an additional distance to protect the rights of use and to encourage filing notices of noncommercial uses with the Copyright Office. The statute affirms that the fact that a user has filed a notice does not in itself affect any of the exceptions in Sections 107, 108, 109, 110, or 112(f) as applied to sound recordings. In other words, if a library or another user chooses to pursue this option for noncommercial uses, it should not be barred from also asserting that fair use or another exception can allow the particular use. U.S. Copyright Act, 17 U.S.C. § 1401(c)(2)(C). The statute later adds that the filing of a notice by the rightsholder to opt out of the use will similarly not "enlarge or diminish" the same exceptions. U.S. Copyright Act, 17 U.S.C. § 1401(c)(5)(B). It may come down to this: The effort by a user to exercise rights under this provision should not be held against the user who might later need to claim protection under one of the exceptions.

Regardless of all other details, the law allows this safe harbor: "A person engaging in a noncommercial use of a sound recording otherwise permitted under this subsection who establishes that the person made a good faith, reasonable search under paragraph (1)(A) without finding commercial exploitation of the sound recording by or under the authority of the rights owner shall not be found to be in violation of subsection (a)."[31] This clause is simultaneously confounding and gratifying. It can override many of the details that could apply under this complicated law, and to some extent it really is simply providing that a user is not in violation of the rights for pre-1972 recordings if the user makes the appropriate search and finds no commercial exploitation.

That safe harbor could well apply in various situations to effectively avoid possible lawsuits and threats of liability:

- The user has conducted the requisite search, but facts later come to light demonstrating that the work was actually being commercially exploited. It is the search that makes the difference, not the later evidence.[32]
- The user has conducted the requisite search, but the user begins activity before filing the notice of use or before it is publicly recorded or before the rightsholder files a notice of opting out. Even if those notices have the cumulative effect of ending the noncommercial use, the interim activity will not be a violation of rights.
- The user has conducted the requisite search, but the process is intrinsically flawed. The searched records might be deficient or in error. The recording might be misidentified. The notice filings could be defective, or they might be submitted by the wrong party or include invalid claims. In the meantime, the use based on a proper search should not create liabilities.[33]

The main function of a legal safe harbor is to provide peace of mind. A safe harbor can encourage honest and good faith application of the law and downplay the risks of litigation and other unwanted outcomes. This safe harbor can serve exactly that role, and the harbor wall that keeps the fleet of noncommercial activity secure and afloat begins with reasonable and good faith searches by the library, educator, or other user.

The safe harbor is one of various virtues of the noncommercial provision, and potentially any person who complies with the requirements can rely on it. While a library or archive may have the option to rely on Section 108(h) instead, the noncommercial exception will sometimes be preferable for its safe harbor and other reasons. For example, Section 108(h) applies to only "preservation, scholarship, or research," and the library may only "reproduce, distribute, display, or perform" the work.[34] By contrast, the noncommercial exception can apply for any purpose and to any activity, from reproduction to remixing, as long as the use is ultimately noncommercial.

CONTROL AND RESPECT

Much as this chapter focuses on the positives for librarians and educators, yet the complications and machinations of the law are hard to avoid. The

---

THE MUSIC Modernization Act creates new rights and borrows some legal fundamentals from the basic structure of copyright law. On the question of identifying the holder of the legal rights, Congress chose to defer to state law. Congress provided that the rightsholder is "the person that has the exclusive right to reproduce a sound recording under the laws of any State" under the law in effect the day before enactment of the MMA. U.S. Copyright Act, 17 U.S.C. § 1401(l)(1). This is a simple and loaded provision. If it works well, it requires determining whether state law applies to the work in question and whether the state law includes a right of reproduction. Because state law is largely preempted by the MMA and because the MMA rights will endure until 2067, we will have an ongoing need to know the law from that day back in 2018 when the MMA took effect. The statute also refers to the law of any state. Taken literally, we need only one state to have relevant law for the entire country. Looking at it another way, we could easily imagine different laws from different states. The MMA does not resolve these quandaries.

Music Modernization Act has done away with some of the clumsy state law, and it has opened vital new possibilities. It offers a path through the legal requirements, although with burdens and costs. Like so much of copyright (and other legal systems), you are not likely to get the benefit of it without considerable effort and deliberate planning. The good news about noncommercial uses or Section 108(h), for example, will come to only those who diligently take control of their pursuits.

These opportunities are also structured in a manner that the effort must be repeated and reapplied for each sound recording. The search required for noncommercial uses is a search with respect to each individual sound recording. The conditions required for application of Section 108(h) must also be evaluated for each work. Mentioned earlier in this chapter is the development of databases of recordings and information about ownership. Enterprising librarians might well develop an analogous database of recordings that are and are not subject to commercial exploitation, easing the search for the next person.

Regardless of whether compliance with the law is complex or streamlined, the MMA is one more example of a general trend in the recent evolution of copyright law. It is principally about the rights and uses of individual works, each considered separately; Congress is not ready to indulge in mass digitization. Copyright law is increasingly detailed and rigorous; Congress is not inclined to enact flexible and fluid principles. Finally, the ability to use the various exceptions and limitations often demands that librarians, educators, and other users follow specific conditions in the statutes. The exceptions also seem to rely regularly on familiar tenets: The law favors the person who heeds the law, respects diverse interests, and makes a reasonable and good faith effort to comply.

NOTES

1. *Goldstein v. California*, 412 U.S. 546 (1973) (acknowledging that recordings gained federal protection starting in 1972, but the states continue to have authority regarding pre-1972 recordings).

2. This list is conspicuously American and is so for a reason. Yet even the Italian Caruso made many of his recordings in the United States. As described elsewhere in this chapter, most foreign recordings from the same era have had their copyrights restored.

3. Bob Dylan wrote and recorded "Don't Think Twice, It's All Right" in 1962, and it was released in 1963. Frankie Valli with the Four Seasons (acting under the pseudonym the Wonder Who?) recorded the song with the title "Don't Think Twice" and released it in 1965.

4. U.S. Copyright Act, 17 U.S.C. § 104A(h)(6)(C)(2).

5. No rule applies without some exception. In this case, not all foreign recordings had their copyrights restored, although the restoration rule does apply to works from most countries, including the long list of countries with which the United States has treaty ties and countries that are the subject of a presidential proclamation. U.S. Copyright Act, 17 U.S.C. § 104A(h)(3).

6. U.S. Copyright Act, 17 U.S.C. § 301(c).

7. A federal district court in California held that a remastering of an analog recording into digital involves choices that are sufficient for the digital version to qualify for copyright protection as a new derivative. The Ninth Circuit reversed on appeal. *ABS Entertainment, Inc. v. CBS Corporation*, 908 F.3d 405 (9th Cir. 2018).

8. *Flo & Eddie, Inc. v. Sirius XM Radio, Inc.*, 28 N.Y.3d 583, 605–06 2016.

9. *Flo & Eddie, Inc. v. Sirius XM Radio, Inc.*, 2014 WL 4725382 (C.D. Cal. 2014).

10. *Flo & Eddie, Inc. v. Pandora Media, Inc.*, 851 F.3d 950 (9th Cir. 2017).

11. *Flo & Eddie, Inc. v. Sirius XM Radio, Inc.*, 827 F.3d 1016 (11th Cir. 2016) (certifying questions about Florida copyright law to the state's supreme court).

12. Program on Information Justice and Intellectual Property, Washington College of Law, American University, *Protection for Pre-1972 Sound Recordings under State Law and Its Impact on Use by*

Nonprofit Institutions: A 10-State Analysis (Washington, DC: Council on Library and Information Resources and Library of Congress, 2009), http://www.loc.gov/static/programs/national-recording -preservation-plan/publications-and-reports/documents/pub146.pdf.

13. *Capitol Records, LLC v. Vimeo, LLC*, 826 F.3d 78, 99 (2d Cir. 2016).

14. U.S. Copyright Office, *Copyright and the Music Marketplace* (Washington, DC: U.S. Copyright Office and Library of Congress, 2015), 140, https://www.copyright.gov/docs/musiclicensingstudy/copyright-and-the-music-marketplace.pdf.

15. The full name of the legislation is the Orrin G. Hatch–Bob Goodlatte Music Modernization Act, named for two retiring members of Congress who introduced the final bills.

16. This portion of the MMA is titled "Classics Protection and Access Act." Earlier proposed legislation carried the cumbersome title "Compensating Legacy Artists for their Songs, Service, and Important Contributions to Society," which conveniently abbreviated to "CLASSICS Act."

17. U.S. Copyright Act, 17 U.S.C. § 1401(l)(1).

18. U.S. Copyright Act, 17 U.S.C. § 1401(f)(1)(A). Other exceptions also apply, but these provisions are of greatest importance to librarians and educators.

19. U.S. Copyright Act, 17 U.S.C. § 1401(f)(1)(B).

20. U.S. Copyright Act, 17 U.S.C. § 1401(c).

21. As a general proposition, the CLASSICS Act adopts the definitions of terms from Section 101 of the U.S. Copyright Act, where the term *publication* is defined. U.S. Copyright Act, 17 U.S.C. § 1401(f)(6)(B).

22. The emphasis is on *publication*, but this chapter does demonstrate how the new law also applies to *unpublished* recordings.

23. Such recordings may have been published anytime after that date or never published at all. Regardless, they are in this category.

24. U.S. Copyright Act, 17 U.S.C. § 1401(f)(1)(B).

25. It bears repeating and emphasizing that these interpretative changes to Section 108(h) are relevant to only the application of the new protection for pre-1972 sound recordings. All other works that are subject to conventional copyright are subject to the terms of Section 108(h) without these changes.

26. Most fundamentally, Section 108(h) may be used by only qualifying libraries and archives. The noncommercial use exception from the MMA may be exercised by any party.

27. U.S. Copyright Act, 17 U.S.C. § 1401(c)(1)(A).

28. U.S. Copyright Act, 17 U.S.C. § 1401(c)(1)(B). The notice must include considerable detail about the use and the search to confirm the absence of commercial exploitation. U.S. Copyright Act, 17 U.S.C. § 1401(c)(3).

29. U.S. Copyright Act, 17 U.S.C. § 1401(c)(1)(C).

30. U.S. Copyright Act, 17 U.S.C. § 1401(c)(2).

31. U.S. Copyright Act, 17 U.S.C. § 1401(c)(4)(A).

32. Not clear under the law is what happens if a search shows no commercial exploitation but the rightsholder later begins exploiting the work. Would a user have to cease activity?

33. The MMA includes penalties for persons who knowingly make invalid claims. U.S. Copyright Act, 17 U.S.C. § 1401(c)(6).

34. U.S. Copyright Act, 17 U.S.C. § 108(h)(1).

COPYRIGHT, ARCHIVES, AND UNPUBLISHED MATERIALS

KEY POINTS

- Unpublished works can include manuscripts, photographs, computer programs, e-mails, business memos, and a wide variety of materials.
- Congress eliminated the perpetual common law copyright protection that previously applied, and unpublished works are today subject to federal copyright protection.
- In general, the duration of protection for unpublished works is the same as for other works, meaning that the copyrights in unpublished works from long ago could have expired.
- Fair use can apply to unpublished works, but it usually applies narrowly as compared to other types of works.
- Some other provisions of the U.S. Copyright Act, notably Section 108, include distinctive rules applicable to unpublished works.

UNPUBLISHED WORKS CAN range from historical manuscripts to modern research findings and computer programming. In many instances, copyright law applies a distinctive set of rules to such works, often resulting in tighter controls on their use. Sometimes the reasons for the law are built on sound policies of confidentiality or privacy. The author of private correspondence and journals may have extraordinary need for greater control over writings that disclose confidences. Memoranda in business files may contain trade secrets. Many computer programs may be selectively utilized or licensed, never meant for wide distribution or publication. Other unpublished works are simply not quite ready for full disclosure. They may be drafts of articles or raw film footage not yet refined into the final published version. Special protection for these works is sometimes easy to justify.

The history of copyright law includes important precedent for distinctive treatment of unpublished materials. Today, the rights of copyright owners include rights of reproduction and more. Some cases have referenced a "right of first publication."[1] Control over when a work would reach the market and be openly disclosed was generally safeguarded for the author's benefit. If the author clearly meant for the drafts to reach a limited group of readers, a court will likely apply a tight construction of fair use.[2]

The logic of these developments is fairly simple. Concerns about confidentiality often lead to greater protection and hence usually a more constrained allowance of fair use or other public rights of use. Whether that explanation is valid or not, it has shaped copyright law in several respects, generally resulting in greater protection for unpublished works. This chapter focuses on a few aspects of current copyright law specifically applicable to unpublished works, and that are of particular importance to librarians, educators, and researchers.

DURATION OF PROTECTION

Before 1978, unpublished works were not protected under federal copyright law at all. The application of federal statutory copyright protection began to apply only upon publication of the book, music, or other work. If the work was published with a proper copyright notice, then statutory protection would apply for a period of years. If the publication lacked the requisite notice, the work immediately entered the public domain.

Up to the time of publication, however, the work enjoyed the so-called common law copyright protection. This protection was not part of federal law, but the rights were instead generally recognized and enforced under state law. Common law protection applied automatically, and one of its most significant traits was that it lasted indefinitely. More bluntly, it would last in perpetuity—forever—as long as the work remained unpublished. The author might have been dead for centuries, but the copyright lived on.

Common law copyright posed serious challenges for anyone working with unpublished materials, such as the biographer needing to quote from letters and diaries or wanting to reprint a family snapshot. The legal protection was strong, and even letters from centuries ago still had valid copyrights.

Archival collections are found in many different forms, holding diverse content, in a wide range of institutions. Libraries frequently hold collections of unpublished works. Museums and other cultural organizations collect the archives of authors, artists, and others. National and local governments commonly establish archives to preserve the history and heritage of the land.

Chapter 6 of this book details the rules and terms of copyright duration. Before 1978, the federal statutory copyright protection began with a term of twenty-eight years that was renewable. With changes in the law and extensions of protection, the protection today for works published before 1978 is a maximum of 95 years. The law of duration is more complicated than any one rule can reflect. Moreover, Congress in 2018 created an entirely new form of legal protection akin to copyright for sound recordings made before February 15, 1972. The Music Modernization Act includes a truly distinct calculation of duration, along with exceptions that may be important to archives that have collections of recordings of music, speeches, interviews, or any other subject. This new law is examined in Chapter 20 of this book.

With the full revision of the U.S. Copyright Act, effective January 1, 1978, Congress brought an end to much of the problem. Congress abolished common law copyright and brought all eligible works—published or not—under federal copyright protection.[3] Moreover, Congress eliminated the perpetual protection and applied the basic terms of protection to new and old works that are unpublished.[4] For the first time in American history, the copyrights to unpublished works could now expire. For the first time, researchers could anticipate that unpublished materials—including diaries, letters, survey responses, e-mail correspondence, manuscripts, photographs, art, or software—would eventually enter the public domain and become available for unrestricted use.

Still, Congress did not make the law easy. To understand the duration rules for unpublished works, we still need to separate works created before and after the beginning of 1978. For unpublished works created since that date, we can apply the general rules of duration:

- For works created by individual authors, the copyright lasts for the life of the author plus 70 years.[5]
- In the case of works made for hire, the duration for unpublished works is generally 120 years from the date of creation. If the work is eventually published, the copyright duration will be the lesser of either 120 years from creation or 95 years from publication.[6]

What about unpublished works from before 1978? Even works from the earliest years of American history? Congress laid down the basic proposition that the general, current duration rules apply to those materials as well, although Congress postponed application of those rules until January 1, 2003.[7] As of that date, a wealth of unpublished materials entered the public domain for the first time. For example:

WORKS MADE for hire include a work prepared by an employee within the scope of his or her employment or a work by an independent contractor that is specially commissioned by an employer. The full definition of a *work made for hire* is more complex, and the implications are significant. The details are examined in Chapter 7 of this book. The duration rules that apply to works made for hire also apply to anonymous and pseudonymous works. Many unpublished works routinely lack a clear identification of authors. The works might be scribbles, missives, snapshots, scrapbooks, or other cryptic products.

- Your archive may include letters and diaries written by Thomas Jefferson (died in 1826), Frederick Douglass (died in 1895), or Louisa May Alcott (died in 1888). Because the writers had been deceased for more than 70 years, the copyright for their unpublished works lapsed on January 1, 2003. You may reprint the materials in full and upload them into a digital library without copyright restriction.
- You are writing the history of Mega Corporation, and you have files of memos written by company founders in the nineteenth century. If the writings are works for hire and are more than 120 years old, they are no longer under copyright protection.

- You are planning to publish a book about the Civil War and want to include a set of photographs from the era, but you cannot identify the photographer. If the unpublished works are indeed anonymous, the copyright expired after 120 years from the date of creation.[8]

Again, Congress did not make the law quite so simple. At least one more important twist in this law remains. Congress postponed the new law—as applied to unpublished materials—until 2003 in order to give rightful copyright owners an opportunity to find and benefit from copyright protection. Copyright owners by that time were typically family members or others who had received the copyright through transfer or inheritance. In the years leading to 2003, Congress offered an important inducement to owners: Find and publish the works before 2003, make them available to the public, and the law will reward you with an additional forty-five years of legal rights.[9]

Consider this actual example. Samuel Clemens, more famous as Mark Twain, died in 1910. A previously unpublished chapter of his novel *Adventures of Huckleberry Finn* was discovered in the 1990s. A new edition of *Huckleberry Finn* was published in 2001 with the missing chapter integrated into the full book.[10] The original portions, published in 1884, entered the public domain decades ago and remain there. An unpublished chapter, however, would ordinarily have expired in 1980, seventy years after Twain's demise. But because the chapter was published before the end of 2002, the one chapter gained an additional forty-five years of copyright protection, to the end of 2047.

Researchers accordingly must be watchful of two common possibilities. First, you might find a manuscript or other seemingly unpublished work from the past, but before you can conclude that it is in the public domain, you need to research whether in fact it might have been published in the meantime. Second, you may find a published work from the distant past, such as an eighteenth-century novel, but some pieces of it may have been added more recently and enjoy protection under copyright law.

> **THE MARK TWAIN** Foundation holds the rights to many writings of Twain, who died in 1910. In addition to the clever publication of a missing chapter, the foundation also arranged for the first publication of Twain's autobiography in 2001, allowing the copyright to avoid expiration until 2047. Although a popular and moderately priced book version of his autobiography was published in 2010, the version published in 2001 was a microfilm set of the manuscript and related letters with a price tag of $50,000. It did not matter that few copies would ever sell; the content captured on the microfilm was in fact published, and the copyright extended. Sheri Qualters, "A Creative Approach to Preserving Copyright for Twain Autobiography," *National Law Journal*, November 11, 2010.

FAIR USE OF UNPUBLISHED WORKS

A series of court rulings through the past two decades has established a relatively narrow application of fair use to unpublished works. The issue has been of enormous importance to the software industry and other parties whose works are often kept unpublished and are worth enormous amounts of money. Yet most judicial decisions have been about the use of letters, diaries, and other resources central to the writing of history and biography. When courts ruled in the late 1980s that biographers may not be within fair use when making customary quotations from letters written by J. D. Salinger and L. Ron Hubbard, researchers expressed alarm.[11]

Congress responded in 1992 by adding this sentence to the fair use statute: "The fact that a work is unpublished shall not itself bar a finding of fair use if such finding is made upon consideration of all the above factors."[12] Congress was striving to dissuade the courts from making a complete bar on fair use for unpublished works, and the effort appeared to work. Subsequent cases have allowed authors to make limited quotations from the journal of Richard Wright and the manuscripts of Marjorie Kinnan Rawlings.[13]

ANOTHER COMMON wrinkle in the use of historical and archival materials is that copyrights expire on different dates in different countries. A recent biography of the artist Piet Mondrian was published in Europe, where his copyrights had expired at the beginning of 2015. European copyrights generally expire 70 years after the death of the author. By contrast, U.S. law would apply that same rule for unpublished works while granting 95 years of protection for many published works. Because some of Mondrian's published works were still under protection in the United States, copyright law reportedly has caused a delay in the American release of the new book. Nina Siegal, "As Artworks Enter Public Domain, Rules Remain Confusing," *The New York Times*, March 13, 2015.

While fair use has found new meaning in the context of unpublished works, that meaning remains somewhat circumscribed. In all of the cases, courts have tipped the *nature* factor firmly against a finding of fair use, reasoning that the unpublished nature of the materials means that they merit greater protection. Courts have built these principles on a presumption that letters, diaries, and other manuscripts may include private information, and stronger protection allows the copyright owner to choose whether, when, and how to make the works publicly available.

The recent cases were provoked by a decision from the U.S. Supreme Court involving the use of quotations from the manuscript of President Gerald Ford's memoirs. The court ruled that the quotations were not within the limits of fair use in large part because the memoirs were not yet published. The court articulated a "right of first publication" and held that fair use applies narrowly when it could effectively erode the author's ability to choose when to publish or even whether to publish the materials at all.[14] Highly influential to the court was the fact that the publisher intended to release the work in the near future and the unapproved publication directly affected the market for licensing excerpts to a popular magazine.

The following cases illustrate the evolution of the fair use law for unpublished works.

Salinger v. Random House, Inc., 811 F.2d 90 (2d Cir. 1987)

Random House was preparing to publish a biography of the famous and reclusive author J. D. Salinger. The book was to include quotations from private correspondence available to researchers in various manuscript collections. Salinger wrote the letters, and recipients had donated the materials to libraries at Harvard, Princeton, and other universities. The lower court had ruled that the limited quotations and paraphrases were within fair use, but the court of appeals disagreed, circumscribing sharply the application of fair use to unpublished materials. The court seemed particularly moved by the apparent personal or confidential nature of the letters as well as their literary qualities. These considerations affected all four of the factors.

IN 1985, the U.S. Supreme Court ruled in *Harper & Row Publishers, Inc. v. Nation Enterprises*, 471 U.S. 539 (1985), that fair use applied narrowly to an unpublished book manuscript in order to preserve the "right of first publication." Recall from Chapter 8 that copyright owners have certain rights set forth in Section 106 of the Copyright Act. The right of first publication is not among them. Where did the Supreme Court find this right? It long had been a feature of the common law of copyright as applied to unpublished materials. Although the U.S. Copyright Act preempts the common law, the Supreme Court relied on the concept and breathed life into what could have been a moribund doctrine.

Purpose: The court agreed that the purpose of the use was criticism, scholarship, or research. Any of these purposes would favor a finding of fair use, even in the context of a book that will likely be published and sold for commercial gain. On the other hand, the court gave no special leniency for biographers who may customarily depend on quoting from private letters to tell an important story.

Nature: On this factor, the court succinctly and firmly leaned against fair use for unpublished materials.

Amount: The court also held the biographer to a highly restrictive standard, finding that many of the quotations used more of Salinger's expression than was "necessary to disseminate the facts." The court appeared to be deeply influenced by the literary qualities of Salinger's letters, finding infringements even when the quotations were limited to just phrases and even paraphrasing of the originals.

Effect: The court relied on testimony about the monetary value of the letters, or the possibility that Salinger or his successors may choose to publish them in the future, to conclude that quotations in a published biography could harm those speculative markets.

> **DESPITE A** narrow construction of fair use applied to private letters and similar materials, some interesting examples continue to brush the limits of fair use. For example, when several letters written by J. D. Salinger to a former romantic acquaintance were sold at auction, sizable excerpts appeared in the *New York Times.* The newspaper also quoted heavily from letters by Thomas Pynchon, another reclusive author, when they were added to the research collections of the Pierpont Morgan Library. For more information about these issues and related examples, see Kenneth D. Crews, "Fair Use of Unpublished Works: Burdens of Proof and the Integrity of Copyright," *Arizona Law Journal* 31 (Spring 1999): 1–93.

Sundeman v. *The Seajay Society, Inc.,* 142 F.3d 194 (4th Cir. 1998)

The *Salinger* decision suggested that the unpublished nature of the work could greatly influence the analysis of all the fair use factors. Researchers began to see in *Salinger* nearly a total elimination of fair use for unpublished works. *Sundeman,* however, reveals that much had changed in the law by the late 1990s. Today, this case is an important reminder that reasonable, limited, scholarly uses of unpublished materials may well be within fair use.

The *Sundeman* decision involved the use of significant quotations from a manuscript by the author Marjorie Kinnan Rawlings. A researcher at a nonprofit foundation selected quotations from the unpublished manuscript and included those quotations in an analytical presentation delivered to a scholarly society. Turning to the four factors, the court ruled that the researcher was acting within fair use.

Purpose: Her use was scholarly and transformative, and it provided criticism and comment on the original manuscript. All of these purposes worked in favor of fair use. The court especially noted that repurposing the excerpts from the original novel to the context of scholarly criticism was a transformative use.

Nature: The court relied on a long series of cases to resolve that the unpublished nature of the work "militates against" fair use. On the other hand, the court pointed to the new language in the fair use statute and emphasized that the use of unpublished works may still be within the law.[15]

Amount: The amount used was consistent with the purpose of scholarly criticism and commentary, and the use did not take "the heart of the work," as has been important in other cases. The court was also not concerned that the amount copied was between 4 percent and 6 percent of the original work.

Effect: The court found no evidence that the presentation displaced any market for publishing the original work, and a presentation at a scholarly conference may in fact have increased demand for the full work.

The Current Trend

These cases reflect the trend away from an apparent per se bar on fair use for unpublished works. When Congress added the language about unpublished works, it was striving to eliminate any notion of a complete bar on fair use. In other rulings, courts have found fair use when a biographer quoted from the personal journals of Richard Wright and when an author of a critical study printed excerpts from rap lyrics written by Eminem before he found fame.[16] Fair use does apply to unpublished works today, and it often will allow brief or moderate quotations, as are customary for research in history, biography, and many other disciplines.[17]

The tomb of author Richard Wright is located in Père Lachaise Cemetery, Paris, France.

LIBRARY PRESERVATION AND OTHER STATUTORY EXCEPTIONS

Recall from Chapter 9 that the Copyright Act includes numerous statutory exceptions to the rights of owners. A few of them have some implications for the use of unpublished works. Most notable is Section 108, which allows most libraries to make limited copies of copyrighted works for specific purposes (see Chapter 17 of this book). One of those purposes is preservation programs, and here the statute outlines a distinctive application to preservation copies of unpublished materials. The rules are not necessarily more rigorous than the rules applicable to published works. They are just different.

BY DETAILING Section 108 as applicable to preservation of unpublished works, Congress was laying out a distinctive scope of user rights for different works. In many other statutory exceptions, however, the law does not specify whether the works used may be published or unpublished. For example, Sections 110(1) and 110(2) address displays and performances of works in the classroom and in distance education. By not stipulating that the work must be published, the law apparently applies equally to the use of unpublished works. For more information about Section 108, see Chapter 17. For more about Section 110, see Chapter 16.

When librarians make preservation copies of published works, they must search the market for a replacement before making a new copy. The rule is logical: As long as the work is still published and reasonably available, libraries should be ready to buy replacements rather than make their own. By contrast, if the work is unpublished, no such market exists. The unpublished work, however, may be personal or confidential. Consequently, the library may make the preservation copy, but sometimes might choose to retain it in the library only for research and study—and not for wide dissemination.

Congress created one more possibility under Section 108 that may be important for archives. Section 108(h) is a broad right for libraries and archives to make many uses of some published works during the last twenty years of their copyright protection. The Music Modernization Act of 2018 applied Section 108 to pre-1972 sound recordings, and specifically when applying subsection 108(h), the law drops the requirement of calculating the last twenty years and the limitation to published works. Archives with collections of published and unpublished sound recordings may find the newly reinterpreted statute to be enormously supportive of preservation, access, and other important services. The new law is explored in Chapter 20.

DEEDS OF ACQUISITION

Many of the complications and unwelcome constrains of copyright can be alleviated through good management and thoughtful terms of acquisition. Preparing deeds of gift or purchase has been fundamental to acquiring and managing archival collections. The basic function of such a deed is to document the transfer of title to physical or digital works, assuring that the intent of the parties is clear and that the archives in fact has obtained ownership to the works free from any competing claims.[18]

As a transfer of ownership, the deed document can be little more than a simple statement describing the transaction. However, if the collection is complex, if it includes materials from diverse authors and sources, and if the donor's rights are dubious, the instrument of transfer can evolve into a lengthy agreement. The archive may need contractual warranties about ownership title and indemnifications against any third-party claims. If the collection is especially valuable or the materials controversial, sensitive, or scandalous, the archive may need added assurances. With each new issue, the agreement becomes lengthier, but the added terms can be essential for protecting the archive and its investment.

The deed of gift or acquisition agreement can also be a tool for clarifying many of the copyright issues, although not always for the better. An agreement can create further burdens on the usefulness of the collection or make the materials more easily available. Agreements often impose added restrictions beyond copyright, such as barring any uses for a period of years or hampering the materials with added requirements and consents before they can be used. On the other hand, an agreement can be the ideal means for redefining more clearly and simply some of the nettlesome rules that can hinder the use and value of an archival collection. The contract can be an opportunity to overcome the uncertainties of fair use and Section 108 and redefine when materials may be digitized for preservation or research and even made available online.

Acquisition agreements can go further, waiving some restrictions in copyright law and even permitting the archive to place Creative Commons or other licenses on the materials. An agreement might provide for the transfer of the copyright in the materials to the archives, allowing the archives to make decisions about managing the legal rights. Not all donors will be ready to make that move, but where appropriate, a transfer can immediately streamline the institution's ability to make the collection available to researchers and the public.

The archivist charged with the duty to negotiate and draft terms of acquisition is in an influential position to ease the way through many of the copyright issues. No one set of terms will be right for every collection or every donor, but the archivist who is aware of the alternatives and possibilities can shape the negotiations and attempt to secure the most favorable terms. The astute archivist will also know that one set of contractual terms may not be enough for even a single collection. The donor can negotiate copyright terms with respect to only the copyrights that the donor owns or controls. An archival collection usually includes content from multiple authors and sources. In the end, the archivist or researcher must still turn to copyright law and permissions to determine the proper uses of various items in any given collection.

PROMOTING PROGRESS

This chapter is an overview of discrete aspects of copyright law applicable to unpublished materials. These examples provide important demonstrations of the underlying principles and functions of copyright. Copyright law serves two pragmatic purposes: to protect creative works and to facilitate beneficial uses of those works by the public. Those purposes are often in conflict with each other. Through the past two centuries, Congress has steadily reevaluated the tension and has struck new legal articulations of a balance.

When applied to unpublished materials, the law sometimes establishes a distinct balance, reflecting the particular interests of copyright owners and the singular importance of unpublished materials for research, education, and other pursuits. When Congress eliminated perpetual copyright protection for manuscripts or applied a limited fair use to personal diaries, it strove to achieve the overarching goal of copyright law—to promote the progress of science and learning. In that spirit, Congress has moved away from rigid and absolute bars on uses of unpublished works. Instead, the law has migrated toward a bit of flexibility and ultimately a fresh rethinking and recalibration of the rights of owners and users and the interests of the public in accessing and learning from the extraordinary materials in archival collections.

NOTES

1. *Harper & Row Publishers, Inc. v. Nation Enterprises,* 471 U.S. 539 (1985); *Estate of Martin Luther King, Jr., Inc. v. CBS, Inc.,* 194 F.3d 1211 (11th Cir. 1999).

2. By contrast, if the work is unpublished because the market interest in the work is slim, a court may not construe fair use narrowly for that unpublished work. *Corbello v. DeVito,* 262 F. Supp. 3d 1056 (D. Nev. 2017) (currently on appeal to the Ninth Circuit).

3. U.S. Copyright Act, 17 U.S.C. § 301(a).

4. U.S. Copyright Act, 17 U.S.C. §§ 302–304.

5. In the case of works created by joint authors, the copyright lasts through the life of the last of the authors to die plus 70 more years. U.S. Copyright Act, 17 U.S.C. § 302.

6. U.S. Copyright Act, 17 U.S.C. § 302(c).

7. U.S. Copyright Act, 17 U.S.C. § 303.

8. U.S. Copyright Act, 17 U.S.C. § 302(c).

9. U.S. Copyright Act, 17 U.S.C. § 303.

10. Mark Twain, *Adventures of Huckleberry Finn,* ed. Victor Fisher & Lin Salamo, with Walter Blair, ill. E.W. Kemble & John Harley (Berkeley: University of California Press, 2001).

11. *Salinger v. Random House, Inc.,* 811 F.2d 90 (2d Cir. 1987); *New Era Publications International v. Henry Holt & Co., Inc.,* 695 F. Supp. 1493 (S.D.N.Y. 1988), *aff'd,* 873 F.2d 576 (2d Cir. 1989).

12. Fair Use and Unpublished Works Act, Pub. L. No. 102-492, 106 Stat. 3145 (1992) (codified at 17 U.S.C. § 107).

13. *Wright v. Warner Books, Inc.,* 953 F.2d 731 (2d Cir. 1991); *Sundeman v. The Seajay Society, Inc.,* 142 F.3d 194 (4th Cir. 1998).

14. *Harper & Row Publishers, Inc. v. Nation Enterprises,* 471 U.S. 539 (1985).

15. A court that recently applied fair use to an unpublished doctoral dissertation found that the second factor weighed against the fair use claim of a university library that had added the dissertation to its collections. *Diversey v. Schmidly,* 738 F.3d 1196 (10th Cir. 2013).

16. *Wright v. Warner Books, Inc.,* 953 F.2d 731 (2d Cir. 1991); *Shady Records, Inc. v. Source Enterprises, Inc.,* 371 F. Supp. 2d 394 (S.D.N.Y. 2005).

17. Courts continue to weigh the second factor against fair use for unpublished works, especially when the use is not transformative and the works have creative elements. *Monge v. Maya Magazines, Inc.*, 688 F.3d 1164 (9th Cir. 2012).

18. For a most thoughtful overview of many of these issues, *see* April M. Hathcock, "From Dusty Boxes to Data Bytes: Acquiring Rights to Special Collections in the Digital Age," *The Reading Room* 1 (Spring 2016): 22–34, http://readingroom.lib.buffalo.edu/PDF/vol1-issue2/From-Dusty -Boxes-to-Data-Bytes.pdf.

CHAPTER 22

ANTICIRCUMVENTION AND DIGITAL RIGHTS MANAGEMENT

KEY POINTS

- In 1998 Congress enacted a prohibition against circumvention of technological protection systems.
- Access to and use of many works is controlled by digital rights management systems; circumventing DRM measures may be unlawful.
- DRM poses continued challenges for educators, librarians, and others seeking to access and use materials that are subject to controls and terms of license agreements.
- Court rulings may have tempered some concerns that the prohibition would undercut fair use and other opportunities.
- Regulatory exceptions allow some circumvention of protection systems, notably to copy short portions of motion pictures for educational purposes.

MANY COPYRIGHTED WORKS of all types are sold and distributed online, on disks, or through other media and often require a password or other technological key to gain access to the stored content. The protection system may be a password to enter a database or a code on a disk to allow watching a movie on a PC, a Mac, or another platform. Your uses of the works themselves may be perfectly legal and expected; you might be exercising fair use or just watching a movie stored on the disk. But breaking that lock to access the copyrighted work can nevertheless be a violation of the anticircumvention provisions of the U.S. Copyright Act.

Why would a copyright owner place the content behind some form of technological lock? There are many reasons. The lock can be a form of control, allowing owners to target sales of specific works. The version of a movie sold on disk in the United States might be different from the version sold in Asia. Access to databases is sometimes sold by the minute; password control can be a way of calculating the bill. Access controls can also identify whether you might be an authorized user and possibly inhibit unauthorized reproduction and distribution.

These controls and restrictions can be an anathema to education and librarianship. The ability to control access and prevent uses of copyrighted materials can undercut fair use and other lawful acts. It can interfere with even simple and lawful viewing or reading of digital materials on different platforms. This law against circumvention of technological protection systems has been a mixed blessing, to be most generous.

The United States was among the first countries to enact the new prohibition in its copyright statutes. The U.S. government championed the idea in the 1990s, and it was included in a copyright treaty adopted by the World Intellectual Property Organization in 1996.[1] In the following years, many countries began to implement the treaty and adopt the prohibition against bypassing or circumventing technological controls on access to or use of copyrighted works.

Technological controls can be highly esoteric or simple and familiar. For example, many commercial DVDs or Blu-ray disks have embedded code, allowing a movie to be viewed on only certain equipment. That form of market control may be beneficial to the rightsholders, but the method is also enormously controversial. Viewing the film may be lawful, but the anticircumvention law means that breaking code just to watch a movie is a potential legal violation.

> **THE DIGITAL** Millennium Copyright Act, enacted October 28, 1998, is a lengthy and complex piece of legislation that modified copyright law in several important respects. It included protections for online service providers (see Chapter 18), established rights for designs of boat hulls, created limited immunity for computer repair services, and launched initiatives leading to the TEACH Act for distance learning (see Chapter 16).

The anticircumvention law is implicated in increasingly diverse situations, from hacking into a computer or database to jailbreaking a smart phone for loading unauthorized apps. The law of anticircumvention is contentious in the marketplace of ideas, in the courts, and in legislatures. Given the pressure to accede to international treaties, dozens of countries now have enacted some form of a law prohibiting the circumvention of technological protection measures that block access to copyrighted works.[2] The underlying copyrighted works may be movies, text, images, software code, or anything else.

The U.S. Congress enacted anticircumvention statutes in 1998 as part of the Digital Millennium Copyright Act. When crafting the anticircumvention provisions, Congress made a broad analogy, comparing the act of breaking codes or bypassing controls as the equivalent of "breaking into a locked room in order to obtain a copy of a book."[3] Congress was in large part addressing perceptions of widespread piracy of digital works due to "the ease with which digital works can be copied and distributed worldwide virtually instantaneously" through the Internet.[4]

Copyright owners may benefit from the new law, but educators and librarians have wondered whether these provisions will ultimately redefine access to and lawful uses of copyrighted works. Debates have provoked questions about the survival of fair use and other long-standing principles of copyright law. Section 1201 of the Copyright Act sets forth the basic law, which may potentially alter fundamental activities, such as library services, research, website development, distance education, and Internet access, thus imposing enormous challenges for higher education.

A RELATED provision of the DMCA creates another type of violation. Section 1202 of the Copyright Act now protects the integrity of "copyright management information," such as the title of a work, the name of its author and the copyright owner, and the terms and conditions for using the work. Removing a copyright notice or removing the names of authors from any work could be a violation if the removal conceals or allows an infringement of the copyright to that work. U.S. Copyright Act, 17 U.S.C. § 1202. This provision fits specifically with licensing of the content. If a work is made available to a user with conditions and restrictions in a license agreement, the stripping away of any restrictions printed or embodied on the work itself can be a copyright violation. The prohibition against removal of an author's name is somewhat akin to the moral right of attribution.

THE MEANING OF ANTICIRCUMVENTION

Section 1201 creates various new potential legal liabilities. The main provision states simply, "No person shall circumvent a technological measure that effectively controls access to" a copyrighted work.[5] For example, the law would ostensibly prohibit hacking through a password interface on a database or bypassing encrypted controls on a CD or DVD or other medium. The statute further bars circumvention of measures that effectively control the exercise of an owner's rights in his or her copyrighted works, such as reproducing and distributing copyrighted works.[6]

In addition, Section 1201 prohibits the manufacture, distribution, or importation of a "technology, product, service, device, component, or part thereof" that is primarily designed or produced for the purpose of circumventing a technological measure.[7] In other words, not only is circumvention unlawful, but the making and distribution of software or other equipment for circumventing controls can also be a violation.

Access and even reproduction and use of works may be restricted in many ways. For example, some museums ban or limit photography of their exhibitions. The reasons vary greatly—to protect works, to encourage ticket sales, or to meet the requirements of owners lending their valuable works for display.

EARLY LITIGATION OF THE DMCA

In the two decades since enactment of the DMCA, the anticircumvention law has developed in perhaps surprising and unexpected directions. The earliest enforcement actions were widely reported in the news and debated in academic circles, although the courts ultimately did not at first make extensive rulings on the substantive meaning of the anticircumvention law.

The Prosecution of Elcomsoft and Dmitry Sklyarov

One of the first cases involving an alleged violation of the DMCA was a criminal case brought against Dmitry Sklyarov, a Russian immigrant, and Elcomsoft, an affiliated company. Sklyarov and Elcomsoft were charged with distributing software that could enable users to bypass the encryption technology used to protect Adobe electronic books. They faced a variety of criminal charges, including conspiracy to traffic in technological systems that were designed and marketed primarily to circumvent measures protecting a right of a copyright owner (pursuant to Section 1201(b)(1)(C)). Sklyarov was released from federal custody after entering into an agreement with the United States Attorney. In late 2002, a jury acquitted Elcomsoft of criminal copyright charges.[8]

> **POSSIBLE SANCTIONS** for violating Sections 1201 or 1202 can be hefty. Civil remedies may include injunctive relief, impoundment and modification or destruction of infringing items, statutory or actual damages, and disgorgement of profits and attorneys' fees. Willful criminal violations can lead to enormous fines and lengthy prison terms. U.S. Copyright Act, 17 U.S.C. §§ 1203 & 1204. Libraries, archives, and educational institutions are exempt from criminal liability, and they enjoy some limits on civil penalties if they did not reasonably believe that they were violating the law. The law offers some protection, but librarians and educators are still expected to stay within the law.

Professor Felten and the Music Challenge

Professor Edward Felten of Princeton University responded to a public challenge from the Secure Digital Music Initiative (SDMI), inviting experts to analyze the security of an SDMI digital watermark copy-prevention system. Felten and his research team successfully found a means to circumvent the SDMI technological controls. When Felten sought to publish his findings, he faced legal threats from SDMI. The claim was that under the DMCA, his research paper was a circumvention device because it purported to describe how the SDMI technology works. The Electronic Freedom Foundation supported Professor Felten and initiated legal action in federal court, asking the court to declare that publishing a research paper is not a violation of the DMCA. When the music industry dropped its threats against Felten, the court dismissed his case.

The Felten and Sklyarov cases did not result in elaborate rulings about the substantive merits, but other situations have led to litigation and interpretive rulings from various courts. Although these cases seem to have little direct relevance to librarians and educators, they do offer important insights into the meaning of the law and its possible application in future situations.

> **IN THE** *Elcomsoft Case*, the act of circumvention was specifically intended to allow application of software that could enable a user to transfer the book to another computer, to make a print or backup copy, or to hear or audibly read the e-books. In an interesting development, the regulations from the Librarian of Congress, summarized later in this chapter, now offer an exception to the anticircumvention law for purposes of making an e-book audible. Thus, while the DMCA appeared to have a stringent effect in its early years, later developments have tempered its consequences.

DECISIONS FROM THE COURTS

Litigation surrounding the meaning and application of Section 1201 has expanded steadily through the years. Some of the earliest cases, following enactment of the DMCA, are landmarks that tell much about the fundamentals of the anticircumvention law. The following cases continue to offer insights about the law's potential meaning for educators and librarians.

Universal City Studios, Inc. v. Reimerdes

A group of movie studios sought an injunction under the DMCA, charging the defendants with sharing software that could enable users to view DVD movies on different operating systems.[9] Each DVD included a content scrambling system (CSS) that permitted the film to be played, but not copied, on only certain players that incorporated the plaintiffs' licensed decryption technology. The CSS, therefore, was a means for controlling access to the copyrighted content on the disk. The defendants' website included a link to other sites where users could find and download DeCSS software. That program allowed users to circumvent the CSS protective system and to view the film on other DVD players. Once they circumvented the CSS, users could also copy the motion picture and not merely view it.

> **MOTION PICTURE** companies brought another case against RealNetworks, the maker of popular software for viewing online films. The court ruled that the product RealDVD violated the law by trafficking in devices that enabled consumers to decrypt antidescrambling software on DVDs. The court found a violation of the law against trafficking, even though the private copying of a film by a consumer may be fair use. The court noted, however, that fair use could apply to circumvention claims asserted against the actual copying. *RealNetworks, Inc. v. DVD Copy Control Association*, 641 F. Supp. 2d 913 (N.D. Cal. 2009).

The court found the defendants had violated the anticircumvention law by making DeCSS available on their website. The violation was also rooted in providing software that would enable users to simply watch the movie, a perfectly legal activity. The court may have been influenced by the fact that the DVDs could be copied once they were accessed using DeCSS. Nevertheless, the defendants' use of systems to access, and not necessarily copy, locked material was the actual violation. This case demonstrates that the anticircumvention law can prevent even lawful activities if the user must bypass technological controls to reach the needed content.

Chamberlain Group, Inc. v. Skylink Technologies, Inc.

While the *Reimerdes* decision appeared to establish a far-reaching right for copyright owners—perhaps allowing them to assert copyright infringement against users who bypass access controls under nearly any circumstance—the *Chamberlain* decision tempered that view in important respects.[10] The court made clear that the access right was confined to situations in which access was unauthorized. The court placed the burden on the copyright owner to prove that the user accessed the copyrighted work for a purpose that was not authorized by the owner or by law. That is, in order for a violation of the DMCA to occur, the user's ultimate purpose of circumventing the technological measure must be to gain access to, or make use of, the copyrighted work in some unlawful or unauthorized manner.

THE RELATIVELY easy access to the code in the garage door opener also raised the question of whether the technological control effectively controls access to the copyrighted work. One court has held that the practical ability of anyone to retrieve the operating code in computer printers meant that the encryption methods did not effectively restrict access. *Lexmark International, Inc. v. Static Control Components, Inc.*, 387 F.3d 522 (6th Cir. 2004). Similarly, the fact that a software program was accessed without authority is also not a violation if the owner sold or licensed copies that could be retrieved without use of the software key. *Storage Technology Corporation v. Custom Hardware Engineering & Consulting, Ltd.*, 2006 WL 1766434 (D.Mass. 2006).

The factual context of the case reveals much about the new law—and it makes the odd revelation that garage doors have something in common with library research. Skylink manufactured a universal remote control that could operate garage door openers made by various companies, including openers made by Chamberlain. Chamberlain charged that Skylink's device violated Section 1201, asserting that for Skylink's remote to function, it had to circumvent copyrighted computer codes embedded in Chamberlain's equipment. The court disagreed, finding that owners of Chamberlain's openers necessarily have access to the codes in order for the opener to function properly—through the use of a remote control. Moreover, nothing in the garage door opener itself, or in the customer agreement, barred access. Therefore, when Skylink accessed the codes, it was not engaged in any unlawful use of the copyrighted work.

This case offers an important interpretation of Section 1201 that may have profound and positive consequences for anyone concerned about possible far-reaching effects of the law. The court in *Chamberlain* turned to the statutory definition of *circumvent* and noted that it included an explicit reference to *unauthorized* access. The court accordingly ruled that a circumvention under Section 1201 can occur only when the ultimate access is one that is not authorized by law and creates a copyright violation, or it is at least *reasonably related* to a violation of the owner's reproduction rights or other rights under the Copyright Act.[11] The court also underscored that the DMCA should not be used to erode fair use or other sanctioned activities; thus, bypassing the technological controls for lawful ends may not be a violation of Section 1201.[12]

Chamberlain goes far to take much of the threat out of Section 1201. The court's fresh reconsideration of the law is built on solid reasoning and good public policy. The court's interpretations also fit nicely with the normal functioning of software in such things as garage door openers. As we use these devices, we deploy the software with the simple click of a button. Normal operations pose little realistic opportunity to copy the software or make other improper use of it.

Chamberlain further emphasizes that the situation in *Reimerdes* was quite different. While users of the DVDs in *Reimerdes* might only have watched the movie—a lawful activity—the circumvention of the controls also enabled users to copy the movie. Accordingly, bypassing codes for unlawful ends, such as unauthorized reproduction, could remain a violation of the DMCA under the reasoning of both *Reimerdes* and *Chamberlain*.

EXCEPTIONS FOR LIBRARIES AND EDUCATION

Amidst uncertainties surrounding the effects of the anticircumvention law, Congress sought to alleviate some concerns by creating several complex exceptions to the law. A few of them are specifically for the benefit of higher education. Some exceptions were enacted as part of the original DMCA and are secured in federal statutes; other exceptions are created periodically by regulations from the Librarian of Congress.

> **THE U.S. COPYRIGHT ACT** provides this definition: "[T]o 'circumvent a technological measure' means to descramble a scrambled work, to decrypt an encrypted work, or otherwise to avoid, bypass, remove, deactivate, or impair a technological measure, without the authority of the copyright owner." U.S. Copyright Act, 17 U.S.C. § 1201(a)(3)(A).

> **THE ANTICIRCUMVENTION** law includes a few additional exceptions for purposes such as accessing information for law enforcement (Section 1201(e)). Of interest to some scholars is a provision allowing reverse engineering of programs to create interoperability with other programs (Section 1201(f)). Another provision allows researchers to decrypt security codes, for the purpose of identifying and analyzing flaws and vulnerabilities (Section 1201(g)). Each of these statutes is rigorous and narrow and should be used only with meticulous care.

Statutory Exceptions

Upon enactment of the DMCA, Congress carved out for libraries the authority to circumvent technological protections if the purpose is to access and review the protected work "solely in order to make a good faith determination of whether to acquire a copy of that work."[13] Like most exceptions to anticircumvention, this one is qualified by multiple detailed conditions. In addition to the narrow and meticulous construction of the exception, a library is subject to serious legal penalties if it utilizes the exception but is later determined by a court to have misapplied the law.[14] One has to seriously evaluate in each situation whether the benefits of attempting to use this exception will outweigh accompanying risks of possible liability.

Perhaps the biggest drawback of the exception is its practical difficulty. The exception may be used only to review copyrighted works with an eye toward possible purchase; many reputable vendors will allow such a review or sampling without hesitation. Ultimately, anyone using the exception is proposing to hack through the password or other protective system. Few reputable libraries might have a hacker readily available to crack the lock to commercial databases. Many database producers also kindly provide short-term access to prospective buyers, leaving the statute as perhaps little more than a statement of policy or a bargaining chip.

Regulatory Exceptions

The Librarian of Congress has the authority to issue periodic exceptions to the anticircumvention law. During the initial two years after enactment, and every three years thereafter, the Librarian of Congress, upon recommendation of the Register of Copyrights, is required

UNDER THE terms of Section 1201(a)(1)(C) of the U.S. Copyright Act, the Librarian of Congress is directed to develop new regulatory exceptions every three years. The first round was issued in 2000, with subsequent regulations every three years since. The most recent regulations, issued in October 2018, were the seventh triennial round of rulemaking. Each round is a new opportunity for educators, librarians, and any other interested parties to gather evidence and to urge the Librarian of Congress to craft new exceptions that meet real and important needs. Readers should consider preparing for the next round in 2021, and every three years thereafter.

to conduct proceedings to examine and review the effect of the DMCA on the availability and use of copyrighted works, notably for education and libraries. Specifically, the Librarian of Congress is empowered to identify particular classes of works and to identify particular users who would be "adversely affected" if the restrictions of the law prevented their making "noninfringing uses" of those works.[15]

Each triennial round of rulemaking is legally in force for only three years unless the regulations are renewed. For example, the regulatory exceptions from 2012 expired in 2015 unless the Librarian of Congress renewed them. With most rounds, the Librarian has renewed some, allowed others to lapse, and added new exceptions. If an exception lapses, the activity that was perfectly lawful one year may be a violation today. To provide some relief and continuity for users, the Copyright Office instituted in 2018 a streamlined method for reviewing current regulations. Upon finding little public objection, the Copyright Office signaled early its intention to renew in October 2018 all existing regulatory exceptions.[16]

Still, the exact language of the regulations has changed, and anyone using these rules needs to carefully check for the current provisions. Each year the regulations grow longer and more elaborate in their scope and application. The task for the U.S. Copyright Office similarly has become steadily more daunting. The office's initial foray into the process in the year 2000 was modest in retrospect. The Copyright Office received 392 public comments to evaluate. In the rulemaking in 2015, the office received nearly 40,000 comments from interested members of the public.[17]

With each round, the Copyright Office ultimately drafts proposals that are sent to the Librarian of Congress, who has the authority to promulgate them as legally enforceable regulations. The issues have become bigger and more contentious. In 2009, the process was stalled several months as the Copyright Office and the Librarian of Congress sparred over one recommended exception. In 2014, Congress stepped into the process and enacted a bill that replaced one of the regulations with its own preferred way of dealing with jailbreaking telephones.[18]

The latest round of regulations was issued in October 2018.[19] The current regulations might fill several pages in a book such as this one, and they will remain in effect until the next rulemaking, due in October 2021. The current regulations address a variety of specific circumstances when a user is allowed to circumvent the protection measures for exactly defined uses of motion pictures, literary works, and computer software.

IN 2009 the Copyright Office recommended against a regulation that would have allowed a person who is blind or has other disabilities from enabling a read-aloud function on e-book readers. The Librarian of Congress supported that exception, leading to a delay in issuing final regulations. A similar provision has continued to be part of the subsequent rulemakings. The current version can be found at 37 C.F.R. § 201.40(b)(3).

Some of the regulatory exceptions are immediately relevant to uses by educators and librarians. Other exceptions apply to documentary filmmakers, to automobile repair services, to video gamers, to the needs of blind persons, and to consumers just looking for compatible telephone service. This chapter will not reprint or examine all of the regulations, but it will look instead at a few of them as examples.

Educational Uses of Motion Pictures

The regulations include a series of provisions that allow circumvention of the protection systems on motion pictures. One set of exceptions allows broad uses for the purpose of criticism or comment. Another series of exceptions applies for educational purposes. These regulations are generally prefaced with a variety of general conditions and elaborations:

- The exceptions apply to motion pictures as defined in the Copyright Act, including television shows and videos.
- The motion picture must have been lawfully made and acquired on a DVD or Blu-ray disk or via digital transmission, each with CSS or certain other technological protections.
- The person exercising the exception must be engaged in noninfringing uses of the copyrighted works. In other words, the regulation might allow the circumvention, but the user still needs to confirm that the ultimate use of the content is lawful under fair use, permission, or other grounds.
- The circumvention must be undertaken solely to make use of *short portions* of the motion pictures. These amounts are not defined, leaving users to make reasonable judgments.

With those prefatory conditions, two of the regulatory exceptions allow circumvention for education on terms as follows:[20]

> (A) By college and university faculty and students or kindergarten through twelfth-grade (K–12) educators and students (where the K–12 student is circumventing under the direct supervision of an educator), including of accredited general educational development (GED) programs, for the purpose of criticism, comment, teaching, or scholarship. . . .

On the one hand, the range of educators and students who can use this provision is extensive. The latest rulemaking has greatly opened the possibilities. On the other hand, as with most copyright rules, the law also sets significant conditions and requirements. In this instance, the use must be subject to the various prefatory conditions listed earlier, and the educational purpose needs to be specifically related to criticism, comment, teaching, or scholarship.

This regulatory exception is also subject to a technological restriction. In general, the content may be decrypted and copied by means of only screen-capture technology. The user has the option to deploy other technological means if the user reasonably believes "that non-circumventing alternatives are unable to produce the required level of high-quality content. . . ." The regulation recognizes that the quality of the copy may make an important difference to teaching and other pursuits, and so it allows a user under some conditions to go beyond simple screen-capture options. That option does not apply to this next exception:

> (C) By educators and participants in nonprofit digital and media literacy programs offered by libraries, museums, and

> **WHEN THE** Copyright Office proposed the regulatory exceptions in October 2018, it also released an explanatory report offering important insights into the new provisions. That report and other background materials can be found at https://www.copyright.gov/1201/2018/. When the Copyright Office makes the next round of proposals in late 2021, it will most assuredly issue similar materials.

> **IN A** report accompanying the 2015 proposed regulations, the Copyright Office explicitly declined to define *short portions*, concluding that the office "suggests that the 'short portions' limitation provides useful guidance as to what is generally likely to be a fair use in these contexts without imposing a wholly inflexible rule as to length." U.S. Copyright Office, *Section 1201 Rulemaking* (Washington, DC: U.S. Copyright Office, Library of Congress, 2015), 70, https://cdn.loc.gov/copyright/1201/2018/2018_Section_1201_Acting_Registers_Recommendation.pdf.

THE REGULATORY exceptions reprinted in full in this chapter may be found in the *Code of Federal Regulations*, Title 37, Section 201.40(b). In addition to regulatory exceptions examined elsewhere in this chapter, provisions that are especially relevant to libraries, education, and other readers of this book include the following:

- Section 201.40(b)(1)(i): Use of motion pictures for criticism and comment in connection with making documentary films, noncommercial videos, and other specified pursuits
- Section 201.40(b)(2): Use of motion pictures at educational institutions to add captions or other enhancements to serve the needs of students with disabilities
- Section 201.40(b)(12)(ii): Preservation of video games in the form of computer programs, by an eligible library, archives, or museum
- Section 201.40(b)(13)(i): Preservation of computer programs, or digital materials that are dependent on a computer program for access, by an eligible library, archives, or museum

Remember, each of these exceptions includes extensive detail, usually narrowing its application to exact types of works, specific users, and other requirements.

other nonprofit entities with an educational mission, in the course of face-to-face instructional activities, for the purpose of criticism or comment, except that such users may only circumvent using screen-capture technology that appears to be offered to the public as enabling the reproduction of motion pictures after content has been lawfully acquired and decrypted.

Let's deconstruct some of the language in the preceding two clipped excerpts from the regulations:

- The first provision explicitly applies to circumvention undertaken by college and university faculty members, educators, and students. Primary and secondary schools may also benefit from it. The second provision reaches across many types of organizations, but the use must be for media literacy programs. Although the language is specific, it seems reasonable that authorized users could rely on the services of technology specialists, librarians, and others acting on their behalf.
- Both provisions apply to uses for educational purposes. *Education* is not defined, and the language makes no requirement about structured courses or programs. The first provision seems to narrow the permitted purposes by adding that the use must be for "criticism, comment, teaching, or scholarship." The second of the two provisions mentions "instructional activities," imitating the broad scope of some educational uses allowed under Section 110(1) of the Copyright Act.
- The regulations often require or anticipate that the circumvention is to be made by screen-capture technology. The Copyright Office is anticipating the situation where, for example, a DVD is lawfully acquired and played, with the audiovisual images appearing on a screen. In that event, the images on the screen may be captured for educational uses. However, copies by screen capture can often be grainy or otherwise ill-suited for many needs.
- When screen capture is inadequate, in the reasonable estimation of the educator or other user, the second of the two provisions would allow the user to employ other methods to circumvent and reproduce a work in order to secure copies of proper quality. That option to pursue better methods also applies to the regulation for MOOCs, examined later in this chapter.

The structure of these regulations follows a pattern that appears in other copyright exceptions. It applies to only certain works, in this case motion pictures. It applies for only certain purposes. The quantity is usually limited. The ultimate use of the copyrighted material must be lawful. These barriers are used to limit applicability of the exceptions, to reduce the risks of misuse of the works, and to safeguard much of the commercial market for the original work.

Like many of the recent statutory developments in copyright law, the language of the regulations is highly precise and narrow in application, and they leave a few terms for interpretation. The statutes and the regulations are outcomes of a public vetting, with multiple opportunities for interested parties to try to shape the final result. The quest for a meaningful copyright rule that leaves leading stakeholders reasonably satisfied often leads to a not wholly satisfactory result.

MOOCs and Motion Pictures

A somewhat similar regulation applies to the development of MOOCs. While some elements of the regulation repeat language from the preceding example, you can also find a few concepts borrowed from the TEACH Act. Circumvention is allowed for noninfringing uses of short portions of motion pictures for educational purposes on the following terms:[21]

> (B) By faculty of massive open online courses (MOOCs) offered by accredited nonprofit educational institutions to officially enrolled students through online platforms (which platforms themselves may be operated for profit), in film studies or other courses requiring close analysis of film and media excerpts, for the purpose of criticism or comment, where the MOOC provider through the online platform limits transmissions to the extent technologically feasible to such officially enrolled students, institutes copyright policies and provides copyright informational materials to faculty, students, and relevant staff members, and applies technological measures that reasonably prevent unauthorized further dissemination of a work in accessible form to others or retention of the work for longer than the course session by recipients of a transmission through the platform, as contemplated by 17 U.S.C. 110(2). . . .

The reference in this regulation to Section 110(2) is the TEACH Act, a statutory exception principally applicable to distance learning.[22] The TEACH Act was enacted by Congress in 2002, with the outlook that it could facilitate limited uses of copyrighted works in online and distance education. One could argue that the Copyright Office was wise to coordinate the regulation with the terms of a related statute. Once an institution comports with the TEACH Act, it should be able to fairly easily apply this regulation to related circumventions.

On the other hand, many institutions have found the TEACH Act's requirements to be cumbersome and sometimes prohibitively restrictive. Note carefully that the regulation is not requiring educational institutions to comply with the TEACH Act overall, and the elements that are carried over into this regulation are not among that statute's most problematic terms. Compliance with this regulation seems reasonably feasible. Further, because the regulation also requires that the ultimate use of the copyrighted work must be noninfringing, which might well mean that the user is already conforming to the TEACH Act or another opportunity allowed under copyright law.

> **THE TEACH** Act is examined in detail in **Chapter 16** of this book. Like the regulation for MOOCs, compliance with the TEACH Act calls for a variety of technological protections. The TEACH Act goes much further and requires adoption of copyright policies, distribution of copyright information to students, and maintenance of tight limits on the uses of different types of copyrighted works.

> **THE REGULATION** examined here applies to only uses of motion pictures in MOOCs. Unfortunately, no other regulation explicitly applies to other works or uses in other forms of online or distance education. Why would the exception be so limited? Perhaps the most logical reason is that if a regulation were applicable to educational uses in general or encompassed all types of works, it could displace the statutory allowance that Congress and the courts have crafted in the TEACH Act, fair use, or other copyright principles. Further, the existing regulation can apply only if the ultimate use is noninfringing. Thus, the user still needs to evaluate other copyright exceptions and limitations. It is also possible that only a limited exception will survive the political and economic pressures that come to bear as the Copyright Office drafts regulations. The office as a practical matter is going to focus its energies on issues with strong public interest and about which diverse stakeholders are generally coming to agreement.

Making Use of the Exceptions

Like so much of copyright law, the anticircumvention exceptions are a mixed blessing. They are exceptions to only the prohibitions on cracking the protection system. These provisions do not themselves permit other uses of the underlying copyrighted works—although they often convey a strong suggestion that the described uses are lawful. These exceptions are also hard-won, as conflicting perspectives and interests converge during the policy review in Washington, DC.

The exceptions may allow something important and beneficial to occur, but they also bring responsibilities and possible liabilities to anyone seeking to exercise the legal provisions. The details matter. Here is one possibility for how the exceptions for education (reprinted and examined in detail earlier in this chapter) might work:

SCENARIO

Professor Salah teaches world history and would like to create for her teaching a selection of materials that demonstrate historical subjects in popular culture. The exceptions for educational uses apply to any college or university faculty member or student, so Professor Salah certainly appears to be within the scope. She wants to know when she can circumvent to retrieve copyrighted works and include them in her course.

The relevant educational exception applies specifically to motion pictures, and Professor Salah can use the exception only if she is ultimately making use of short portions of motion pictures for the purpose of criticism, comment, teaching, or scholarship, as well as for the purpose of education. Her ultimate use of the motion picture must also be noninfringing. If she is using too much or some other type of work, she falls outside the boundaries of the regulatory exception.

Once Professor Salah has met all of the foregoing conditions, she may then circumvent the protection specifically with a screen-capture technology in order to copy portions of the motion picture. If she is teaching film studies or other courses that require close analysis of the motion picture, she may then be able to crack the CSS or other similar code in order to obtain higher quality reproductions of the film.

Even at that, the regulation really does not provide that the actual copying and subsequent uses of the movie clips are lawful; this exception speaks to only the circumvention. However, the use of short movie clips, for these limited purposes, may well be within fair use. After lawfully circumventing, Professor Salah would do well to go back to the four factors of fair use and make a freshly reasoned decision about just the copying. She might even find solace in the TEACH Act.

Some educators will be discouraged by the details and limits in the exceptions. Yet the exceptions do provide a safe zone from liability, and they ultimately allow educators to bypass the code that would otherwise bar all copying and even mere access. Moreover, after Professor Salah has worked through the specifics, she may be well positioned to assert fair use. Properly deployed, the exceptions can be an enormous benefit for her and her students. She might assemble film clips for study, incorporate them into a class wiki, and bring them into her classroom teaching. Without meaningful exceptions, the anticircumvention law would be a barrier to even these proper and beneficial uses of copyrighted works.

THE OUTLOOK FOR LIBRARIES AND EDUCATION

The purpose of the general anticircumvention law, at Section 1201 of the Copyright Act, is to allow owners to control many uses of copyrighted works. The purpose of the exceptions is to permit reasonable and beneficial uses of the protected works. The two features of the law work together, we trust, to both protect copyrighted works and advance the public interest in education, research, and library services. The legal protection against circumvention also sets the stage for asserting contractual restrictions on access and use of materials.

Libraries routinely enter into agreements for the acquisition of copyrighted works that are stored behind a password control or another technological restriction. The rightholders offering the database or other materials may be willing to allow access and use, but only on agreed terms. For example, libraries long have purchased hard-copy journals, made them widely available to the public, and allowed multiple readers to benefit from the works and to make fair use of them. Those same journals are now widely accessed through online databases, with restricted access and separate terms of use.

The contract becomes the source for the rules applied to those copyrighted materials; the contract can supersede the rights and exceptions detailed in the law. Libraries and their patrons may have online access only on the terms of the license agreement with the publishers (the digital rights management). Under those conditions, copyright owners have the ability to define who may access the databases and to restrict and impose conditions or fees for each use.

BECAUSE ACCESS to content is increasingly subject to the terms of license agreements, the librarian or other professional responsible for negotiating and approving licenses may be the most important member of the organization. That person is in a position to determine whether users will have access to content at all and the terms on which the materials may be used.

The practical results of these controls are new constraints on the utility of library resources. Owners can deny access to users who do not assent to all stipulated restrictions or narrowly limit access to certain users. Owners may set restrictions that attempt to curtail public access, fair use, and other virtues of copyright law. Indeed, licenses commonly define how the materials may be used for such purposes as interlibrary loans, and access is routinely limited to *authorized users*, defined in different ways under different agreements.

The rights and exceptions related to anticircumvention set up a new range of opportunities and duties for individual owners and users, and for their publishers and educational institutions. When Professor Salah simply wants to make use of an education exception exactly as intended, she faces a need to learn and apply the rules, and her university may need to determine whether to make the needed software and equipment available to her—and whether to protect her if she commits a copyright transgression.

Nevertheless, technological protections and the need to manage them are of growing importance in education and librarianship. Consider these familiar situations, each of which could be a legal violation if no exception applies:

- A user may be able to use or adjust the controls of a DVD player in order to watch films from disks that have region code restrictions. Private viewing of copyrighted films is not a copyright violation. Bypassing the region code could be considered a circumvention.
- A disk with software or other copyrighted works might have encoded restrictions preventing their use on certain computer brands. Even if no one is making copies or altering the underlying work, adjusting the code to allow loading the software onto the buyer's home computer could be a violation.
- A library may need to make a preservation copy of a digital work, consistent with Section 108 of the Copyright Act. The end use is clearly permitted under the law, but it might still be a circumvention.

> **"REGION CODES"** are often embedded within DVD movies and computer game disks and even the gaming systems and disk players themselves to restrict use of the work to a designated region of the world. A buyer of a DVD in Europe, for example, would often be blocked from playing that disk in a machine purchased in North America. In *Sony Computer Entertainment America Inc. v. Gamemasters*, 87 F. Supp. 2d 976 (N.D. Cal. 1999), the defendant created a "Game Enhancer" that allowed users of a Sony PlayStation to play games on machines that were not from the designated region. The court held that enabling users to bypass territory codes was a form of circumventing access controls. Because the simple act of using a disk from another country is not a violation of U.S. law, one has to wonder if a court would still find a violation in the aftermath of the *Chamberlain* decision from 2004.

Maybe these uses would be allowed under a future regulatory exception. The Copyright Office considers the exceptions anew every three years. This allows them new opportunities to consider possibilities. The *Chamberlain* decision, examined earlier in this chapter, suggests that circumvention may not be a violation at all if the final use of the copyrighted work is not itself infringing. That possibility could rescue some of the uses on the previous list. In the meantime, to make any lawful uses of works that are stored behind technological controls, the earnest educator, librarian, or other user still has to make the decision—and have the know-how—to circumvent whatever controls exist. That honest user must be ready to decide whether the circumvention is within the law.

NOTES

1. The WIPO Copyright Treaty of 1996, at art. 11, calls for countries to enact "adequate legal protection . . . against the circumvention of effective technological measures. . . ." The full text of the treaty and the growing list of signatory countries may be found at https://www.wipo.int/treaties/en/ip/wct/.
2. As of this writing, more than 100 countries are signatories to the WIPO Copyright Treaty, which provides for anticircumvention.
3. The Digital Millennium Copyright Act, 105th Cong., 2d Sess., H. Doc. 551, at 17–18 (1998).
4. The Digital Millennium Copyright Act, 105th Cong., 2d Sess., S. Doc. 190, at 8 (1998).
5. U.S. Copyright Act, § 1201(a)(1)(A).
6. U.S. Copyright Act, § 1201(b).
7. U.S. Copyright Act, §§ 1201(a)(2) & (b).
8. In the *Elcomsoft Case*, the court also upheld the constitutionality of the anticircumvention provisions. *United States v. Elcom Ltd.*, 203 F. Supp. 2d 1111 (N.D. Cal. 2002).

9. *Universal City Studios, Inc. v. Reimerdes*, 111 F. Supp. 2d 294 (S.D.N.Y. 2000), *aff'd sub nom Universal City Studios v. Corley*, 273 F.3d 429 (2d Cir. 2001).

10. *Chamberlain Group, Inc. v. Skylink Technologies, Inc.*, 381 F.3d 1178 (Fed. Cir. 2004).

11. Another court has stated broadly that "courts generally have found a violation of the DMCA only when the alleged access was intertwined with a right protected by the Copyright Act." *Storage Technology Corporation v. Custom Hardware Engineering & Consulting, Inc.*, 421 F.3d 1307, 1318 (Fed. Cir. 2005).

12. Not all courts have accepted the conclusion that an act of circumvention must have some connection to an infringement of the copyright owner's rights. *See MDY Industries, LLC v. Blizzard Entertainment, Inc.*, 629 F.3d 928, 950 (9th Cir. 2010). The Ninth Circuit also ruled that the owner of a movie disk does not have the right to circumvent in order to access and simply watch the film. *See Disney Enterprises, Inc. v. VidAngel, Inc.*, 869 F.3d 848, 863 (9th Cir. 2017).

13. U.S. Copyright Act, 17 U.S.C. § 1201(d).

14. U.S. Copyright Act, 17 U.S.C. § 1201(d)(3).

15. U.S. Copyright Act, 17 U.S.C. §§ 1201(a)(1)(C)–(D).

16. The renewal was not exactly verbatim, but instead the new regulations were drafted in a manner such that the substance of the 2018 rules embodied the substance of the previous round.

17. U.S. Copyright Office, *Section 1201 of Title 17: A Report of the Register of Copyrights* (Washington, DC: U.S. Copyright Office and Library of Congress, 2017), 25, https://www
.copyright.gov/policy/1201/section-1201-full-report.pdf.

18. Senate Bill 517, Unlocking Consumer Choice and Wireless Competition Act, 113th Cong., 2d sess. (2014). Because regulations lapse and are revised every three years, this congressional tinkering with the regulations was superseded by the 2015 rulemaking.

19. 37 C.F.R. § 201.40.

20. 37 C.F.R. § 201.40(b)(1)(ii).

21. 37 C.F.R. § 201.40(b)(1)(ii)(B).

22. The TEACH Act is codified at U.S. Copyright Act, 17 U.S.C. § 110(2). It is examined in detail in Chapter 16 of this book.

COPYRIGHT AND THE WORLD

Foreign Law and Foreign Works

KEY POINTS

- Although copyrighted works may originate in other countries, when they are inside the United States, apply U.S. law to most works and most uses.
- Many of the same principles of copyright that apply to domestic U.S. works also apply to works from most foreign countries.
- Yet there are major differences in even the fundamental principles that could prove important in some instances.
- Application of U.S. domestic law sometimes requires applying the law of another country.
- Courts in the United States and elsewhere sometimes need to analyze and apply the law of a foreign country in order to decide a copyright case.

THE CONCEPT OF *international copyright law* is founded on the many treaties and other multinational instruments that create an obligation of signatory countries to shape and implement their domestic laws according to specific international norms and requirements. Chapter 3 of this book demonstrates how U.S. domestic law is largely shaped by that international system. This chapter, by contrast, offers a look at *foreign copyright law*. Foreign law is the law of another country, whatever its source or terms. A full understanding of American copyright law, the focus of this book, occasionally necessitates delving into the domestic law of other countries. Similarly, other countries sometimes need to turn to American law as they apply their own copyright laws. This chapter breaks the national borders of copyright law and closes with a reminder that laws and countries do not act in isolation. Library services and education are not strictly defined by political boundaries and fences, and neither is copyright law.

Consider again the adage repeated throughout this book: When in the United States, apply U.S. copyright law. Most of this book is built on that presumed truth. But the familiar adage is not necessarily so. At various times the domestic law of the United States explicitly calls for applying the law of another country. These instances are not common and may seldom arise in one's career with copyright. Nevertheless, these meticulous points of law demonstrate that even national law does not operate in a simple vacuum. We are not alone in the world in our pursuits, in our adventures, and in our copyright analyses.

NATIONAL BORDERS AND COPYRIGHT

Consider that basic tenet of copyright law in more universal terms: The domestic law of any country is the fundamental copyright law that applies within the boundaries and jurisdiction of that country. This principle applies regardless of where the work originated. Thus, regardless of whether the book, movie, software, or art originated domestically or in any other country, once that work is located in the United States, American law applies to determine ownership, duration, fair use, and much more. Like so many rules of copyright, even this international principle has exceptions and variations. Yet the precept remains a starting point for most situations, and this chapter references back to it repeatedly.

What is the source of this guiding doctrine? In the construct of contemporary copyright law, the source is the same Berne Convention that was a focus of much of Chapter 3.[1] The protection of foreign works has been a core objective of the Berne Convention and many other international agreements for decades. In the parlance of treaty language, the doctrine of *national treatment* establishes the requirement that each member country give nationals (i.e., authors and other rightsholders) from any other member country at least the same rights under copyright that the country gives to its own nationals. The Berne Convention sets the standard firmly and simply: "Authors shall enjoy, in respect of works for which they are protected under this Convention, in countries of the Union other than the country of origin, the rights which their respective laws do now or may hereafter grant to their nationals. . . ."[2]

The World Trade Organization agreement on intellectual property moves away from identical protection to the possibility that a country might actually provide greater protection for works of foreign nationals: A member country must offer rights for foreign works that are "no less favorable than that it accords to its own nationals with regard to the protection of intellectual property. . . ."[3] It is perfectly possible for a country to give greater protection to foreign works than the country gives to its own works—and the United States does in fact give a few greater rights to some foreign works. Such variations and nuances in the law, however, do not dispel the broad principle of protection for one another's works.

FOREIGN WORKS AND U.S. LAW

The Copyright Act of the United States demonstrates how the fundamental principles apply, although not always consistently or logically. The U.S. act, by its own explicit terms, does in fact apply to works from most or even all countries, but it does not offer the same protection to all types of works from all countries. For example, unpublished works from any country of the world can enjoy protection under U.S. law inside the United States. Published works, however, are protected only if they have a *point of attachment* that qualifies them for protection; for example, if on the date of first publication, one or more of the authors is a national or domiciliary of the United States or a country that is a party to a copyright treaty with the United States. That rule alone encompasses all but a few countries of the world.[4]

U.S. COPYRIGHT law gives greater protection to foreign works than it gives to its own domestic works in various ways, including the following:

- Only foreign works, although not all foreign works, are eligible to have their copyrights restored if they entered the public domain for failure to comply with U.S. formalities and other reasons. Restoration is surveyed in Chapter 6.
- Copyright ordinarily must be registered with the U.S. Copyright Office before filing an infringement claim, but that requirement applies to only U.S. works and not to foreign works. See Chapter 6.
- The Copyright Act excludes works of the U.S. government from copyright protection, but it holds open the prospect of copyright for works created by foreign governments. See Chapter 5.

THE U.S. COPYRIGHT ACT applies only within the boundaries and other jurisdictions of the United States, starting with the fifty states and the District of Columbia. It also applies in Puerto Rico, Guam, the Northern Marianas, American Samoa, the U.S. Virgin Islands, and a dozen or so other locations. Inside these geographic bounds, U.S. law grants protection to unpublished works, regardless of the author's nationality or domicile. American law also protects published works that have some point of attachment to the United States, for example:

- At least one author is a national or domiciliary of the United States.
- At least one author is a national or domiciliary of a treaty party or is a stateless person residing anywhere in the world.
- The work was first published in the United States or a treaty party.
- If a sound recording, it was first fixed in a treaty party.
- If an architectural work, it is located in the United States or a treaty party.
- The work was first published by the United Nations or the Organization of American States or any of their agencies.

A *treaty party* is any country that is a member, with the United States, of at least one international copyright agreement. Only a few countries are not members of any of the copyright agreements, and even then the U.S. president has authority to issue a proclamation that grants reciprocal protection of copyrights. U.S. Copyright Act, 17 U.S.C. § 104. The list of countries whose works might be outside the reach of U.S. law is short: Eritrea, Ethiopia, Iran, Iraq, Nauru, Palau, San Marino, Somalia, and South Sudan. Circular 38A, titled *International Copyright Relations of the United States*, is a publication of the Copyright Office showing the international copyright treaties that each country of the world has joined.

Once the work is found to qualify for protection under U.S. law and the work is located within U.S. jurisdiction, we return to the basics: Apply U.S. law. It is U.S. law that will determine the rights of the owner and the exceptions; it is U.S. law that will determine the duration of protection and the terms for enforcement. Because the United States is a member of the Berne Convention and other treaties, that law must include the treaty requirement of *national treatment*. These principles have the practical effect of creating a more harmonized copyright law around the world, making the law more predictable and reliable as authors, publishers, educators, and libraries buy, use, develop, sell, and share works in multiple countries.

COPYRIGHT QUESTIONS AND FOREIGN VARIATIONS

So far this chapter has been emphasizing that the U.S. law of copyright applies inside this country. That principle is definitely true, but sometimes a bit of foreign law creeps into the copyright evaluation. Consider a most common situation: You are at your college library inside the United States, and you find a book that was originally written and published in India. The book is perfect for your teaching and research needs, and you would like to scan a few pages and incorporate them into your website and other projects. What are the rules of copyright that apply? The answer begins with application of U.S. law, but it is possible that you might have to dip into the law of India as well.

The ensuing questions are a revisit to the basic tenets of copyright, with variations on the answers demonstrating the different treatment for foreign works under U.S. law. However, start with the threshold question: Does a published work from India even have copyright protection under U.S. law? The answer is clearly *yes* in most cases. A published work is protected in the United States if it is first published in a country that is a signatory to one of several different copyright treaties with the United States. India is a signatory to the Berne Convention and other agreements. Even if the work was published elsewhere and at least one of the authors was a national or domiciliary of a treaty party such as India, the work could be protected under U.S. law. If the work was unpublished, it would have protection under U.S. law regardless of the country of origin.[5] Application of even most fundamental rules can require research into the background of the authors and the facts and circumstances surrounding the creation and publication of the work.

Question 1: Does the book meet the eligibility requirements for copyright protection?

Chapter 4 offers the general rule that copyright protection applies to original works of authorship that are fixed in any tangible medium of expression. We would apply the same rule to the book from India.

- *Foreign variation I:* If the book is a governmental work, the outcome could be completely different for a foreign work. The U.S. Copyright Act places in the public domain works of the U.S. government. As elaborated in Chapter 5 of this book, that exclusion from copyright applies to only works prepared by an officer or employee of the federal government.[6] The statute does not apply to works prepared by a foreign government. As a result, the governmental publication from India may well have a copyright that is recognized under American law, whether or not the government of India wants to bother enforcing it in the United States.
- *Foreign variation II:* If the work in question is a sound recording, instead of a book, we might have a considerably different outcome. Although U.S. law did not apply federal copyright protection to sound recordings until 1972, U.S. copyright as of 1996 restores copyright in pre-1972 recordings if they originated from most foreign countries.[7] This retroactive application of the law is rooted in the same treaty requirements that led to restoration of many other expired works—the subject of the next question.

Question 2: How long does the copyright last?

Chapter 6 details the complex rules of copyright duration. Those same rules generally apply to foreign works located in the United States, including the general protection for life of the author plus 70 years.

- *Foreign variation I:* Recall from Chapter 6 that previous U.S. law required that published works include a formal copyright notice and that the copyright be renewed after twenty-eight years. Because of these requirements, many domestic and foreign works entered the public domain for failure to comply. The restoration of copyrights, as detailed in Chapter 6, means that some early works that had been in the public domain, because of the formalities, were brought back under copyright protection in 1996. U.S.

> **THE MUSIC** Modernization Act of 2018, explored in Chapter 20, created a new regime of legal protection—technically not copyright, but similar—for sound recordings made before February 15, 1972. The new law applies to domestic and foreign works, but the law created an unanswered question about whether it replaces the restoration of true copyright protection for pre-1972 works or if the restored rights continue. If foreign recordings are brought under the new MMA protection, then the law for foreign and domestic works will be generally the same. However, if foreign pre-1972 recordings are governed by true copyright law, while the domestic counterparts are under the new MMA protection, then we will find substantial variations in legal treatment throughout the litany of copyright questions and principles.

THE GENERAL principle of granting the same term of protection for foreign works could be upended by applying the *rule of the shorter term*. That rule provides that a country may generally apply its duration rules to foreign works, but if the duration of copyright in the work's country of origin is shorter, then the shorter term will apply. For example, Germany has adopted the rule. Germany's basic copyright term is life plus 70 years. A foreign work located in Germany will generally have that full protection. However, Canada adheres to the shorter term of life plus 50 years. As a result, the Canadian work will have protection under German copyright law, but the protection in Germany will expire when the shorter term of Canadian law reaches an end. The rule of the shorter term is allowed, but not required, under the Berne Convention. The United States has not adopted it. Thus, the Canadian work gets the full 70 years in the United States.

works remain in the public domain. The foreign copyrights were restored only if the works had not yet entered the public domain under the law of the country of origin. As a result, to apply this rule from an American statute, one has to actually research and apply the law of India or another relevant country.[8]

- *Foreign variation II:* Two rulings from the Ninth Circuit Court of Appeals, which technically apply in only the several Western states, have held that the duration of copyright in foreign works does not begin until the work is published in the United States. Thus, although the book *Bambi, a Life in the Woods* was first published in Austria in 1923 without a copyright notice, the court ruled that the U.S. term of statutory protection did not begin until 1926, when the book was republished with a notice consistent with American law.[9] This decision effectively granted a theoretically perpetual common law protection in the United States for a foreign book, for however many years pass before its publication in the United States. This decision has been harshly critiqued, but it also has been affirmed somewhat begrudgingly in a second ruling from the same court.[10]

Question 3: Who is the copyright owner?

Chapter 7 outlines the conditions of ownership and work made for hire. Most principles of ownership that apply to the domestic book also apply to the Indian book.

- *Foreign variation:* American courts have sometimes looked to the law of the country of origin to determine ownership.[11] Few countries have a concept quite like the American doctrine of work made for hire. If we apply the law of the country of origin, we could easily have a situation where the work would be for hire under U.S. law, but it is not a work made for hire under the law of the country of origin. Bringing foreign law into the equation could completely flip the determination of ownership.[12]

Question 4: What are the rights of the owner?

Chapter 8 itemizes the various rights of the copyright owner, and those will indeed largely run true for domestic as well as foreign works.

- *Foreign variation:* The restoration of foreign copyrights, described earlier, had some subtle and sometimes bizarre implications for the distribution rights. Chapter 9 describes the first sale or exhaustion principle that allows a specific copy of a work to be further transferred without violating the copyright owner's distribution rights. Under a byzantine statutory clause, it seems that first sale does not apply to some copies of works that had been produced while the work was in the public domain before its copyright restoration. As a result, those particular copies may in fact not be further sold or even loaned by libraries. The copyright owner of the restored rights could theoretically bar the downstream transactions.[13]

Question 5: Is the use within fair use or another exception?

Multiple chapters of this book offer detailed views of the copyright exceptions and their application in various circumstances. Whatever fair use might mean, it applies on its face to the foreign book in the same manner that it would apply to the American book.[14]

- *Foreign variation:* At last, the foreign variations on this question may be few and only by implication.[15] The odd twist on the doctrine of exhaustion, mentioned earlier, is a rare example of foreign works being called out explicitly for a distinct application of a copyright exception. The flexibility of fair use might mean that it could apply differently when considering the use of a foreign book, perhaps because of limited marketability in the United States, but the conclusion would be reached based on the same four factors in the statute and their interpretation by the courts.[16]

Question 6: How is the copyright enforced?

Copyright law gives the owner automatic legal rights that may be asserted in many ways and enforced through legal action.

- *Foreign variation:* While formalities to copyright protection are banished under the Berne Convention, American law still requires registration as a precondition to filing a lawsuit.[17] However, to avoid charges that U.S. law violates Berne by imposing a formality on foreign works, the registration requirement applies to only U.S. works.[18] Enforcement of copyright protection for foreign works, as opposed to American works, in U.S. courts is therefore one significant step easier. Recall from Chapter 18 that registration with the U.S. Copyright Office is also a precondition to certain remedies, including statutory damages and attorneys' fees. That registration requirement applies equally to domestic and foreign works.[19]

In light of these copyright questions and complications, one has to ask whether the general tenet about applying U.S. law really eases application of copyright law. For almost all common needs, the answer is yes. Think about the scenario of the book from India. If you were to apply U.S. law for most or all of the copyright questions, you would likely reach the right answer to most and sometimes all of the basic copyright questions.

The general tenet, however, has a necessary corollary that potentially compounds the complexities of copyright: When in India, apply the law of India, even if the book originated in the United States. That may seem harmless and logical, and it probably is for the most part. However, in a networked world, where copyrighted works are uploaded, downloaded, shared, sold, and remixed across multiple jurisdictions, the applicable law becomes at best multitudinous and at worst obtuse and indecipherable. For the work that enters the jurisdiction of diverse countries, whether shipped in a box or transmitted from a web server, that one work can theoretically be governed simultaneously by the copyright laws of all countries affected.[20]

COURTS AND THE CHOICE OF LAW

To only a limited extent have courts started to unravel the complications of international copyright and seek specific answers. Of course, the dilemma in the quest for answers is that they are determined by the copyright law of the jurisdiction of the court. For example, a French court applied its principles of law to conclude that American copyright law applies to the question of making works available from a California web server, but French courts had jurisdiction because the works were accessible in France.[21] At the same time, if the work is downloaded and utilized by someone in France, you can be sure that French law would apply to the end user's activities.

The applicable jurisdiction also determines the extent of any infringement and the monetary remedies that might be due. An American court found that a motion picture was infringed in the United States and distributed unlawfully domestically and internationally. In calculating the harm to the copyright owner, and hence the dollars due by the infringer, the court looked to only sales that occurred inside the boundaries of the United States. If the infringing sales transpired outside the country, that nation's law and courts would make the final determination of infringement and calculation of damages due.[22]

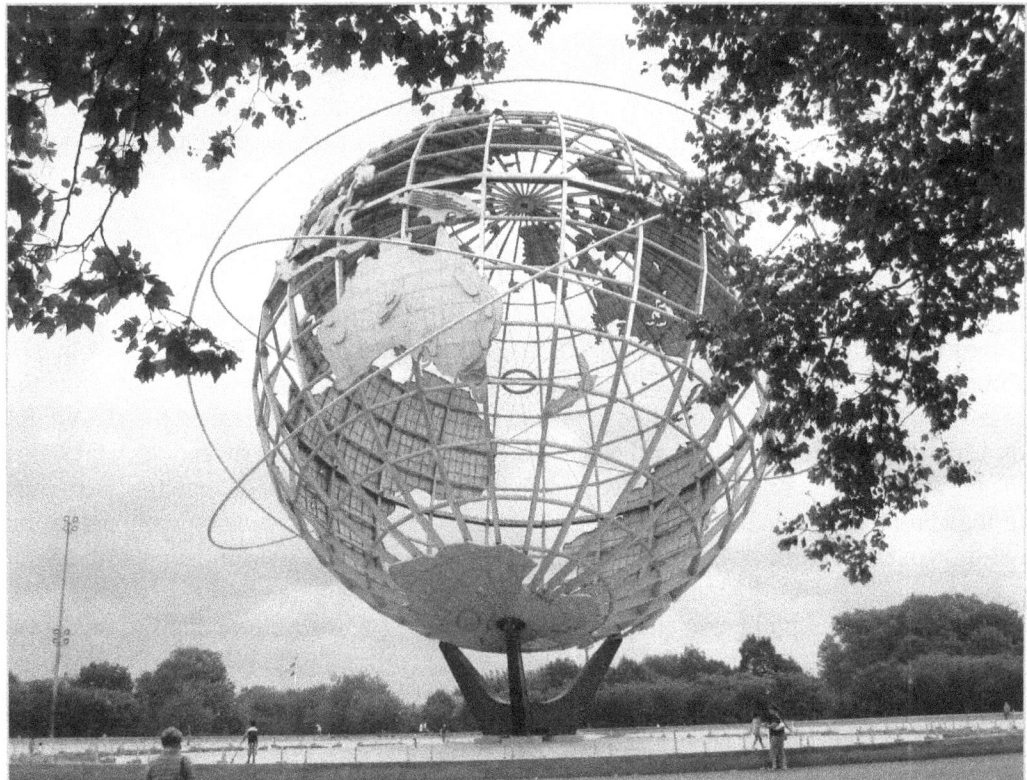

The Unisphere Globe was designed by Gilmore D. Clarke for the World's Fair of 1964, and it stands today in its original location in Flushing Meadows, in the Borough of Queens, New York City. It reminds us that the world really does come together on occasion. It is also a copyrightable sculpture.

FOREIGN LAW AND DOMESTIC DECISIONS

Think again to the foundational rule: When in the United States, apply U.S. law. The series of questions offered earlier illustrates that adage. The points reiterate core propositions about domestic law applied to domestic and foreign works, but they are deceptively simple. Foreign law finds its way into many aspects of domestic copyright law. Indeed, in all areas of the law, courts find themselves applying the law of another country. It may not be routine, but it is not uncommon in the courts of the United States and elsewhere.

As a delightful example, a court in London in the United Kingdom decided a case involving the alleged infringement of a film recording of a Beatles concert.[23] The concert was held in the United States, and obviously the original film footage was made and released in the United States. A British documentarian included clips of the concert footage in a new documentary motion picture; an infringement occurred in the United States when the documentary was released there.

A significant complication for the litigation, however, was that a party accused of infringement was in the United Kingdom, and therefore the British courts had jurisdiction over the defendant. The result was that the case was heard and decided in a courthouse in London, although the British court needed to apply American law to assess the alleged infringements occurring in the United States. The question of infringement was more than whether the use included reproduction and other rights of the owner. That part of the claim was easy. Under U.S. law, infringement also depends on whether the defendant acted within fair use. The British court, in deciding a copyright case between British parties, turned to the American law of fair use to resolve the legal dispute.[24]

Fair use does not exist in U.K. copyright. The judge had no formal experience or training in fair use, and any reader indulging this far into this book knows that fair use fills much more than a few chapters. The court allowed both parties to present expert testimony from American copyright specialists to help educate the judge about fair use. The court handed down its decision, with a somewhat formidable and insightful understanding of that quirky niche of American jurisprudence.[25]

U.S. COURTS AND FOREIGN LAW

American courts make comparable applications of foreign law. The Second Circuit Court of Appeals heard a case involving the alleged infringement of Russian newspapers.[26] As in the case of the Beatles concert, the alleged infringement occurred in the United States. A point of dispute, however, was whether the plaintiff bringing the case even owned the copyrights in question. The newspapers were prepared and first published in Russia, but they were used in the United States. While American law applied to the use, Russian law applied to the question of copyright ownership. After determining that Russian law applied, the American court allowed expert testimony about the meaning of the foreign law.

If this were a simple case about one person creating one article or another work, the answer about ownership might be the same under the laws of most countries. But this case was about newspaper articles written by multiple contributors and assembled into issues of the paper by an editor and a publisher. National laws sometimes offer specialized law for different types of works—in this case, Russia has a rule for newspapers. The court found that under the copyright law of Russia, the "authors of newspaper articles retain the copyright in their articles unless there has been a contractual assignment to their employer or some specific provision of law provides that the author's rights vest in the employer."[27] The court relied on the experts to help it understand the nuances and vagaries of Russian law.

EPILOGUE

As this copyright venture turns to a confluence of Russia, the Beatles, and expert witnesses in the courtroom, it seems like a good opportunity to reflect and wrap up with a worldwide view. This chapter is about the reach of the law and the imperfection of national borders. The examples about the incorporation of foreign law into domestic court rulings and statutes tell us that we cannot live in isolation. Although we will continue relying on principles about law and national borders, those rules are no longer absolute. Even if the domestic law ended completely at the frontier with the next country, we know that our books and commodities, our Internet transmissions and broadcast signals, and our knowledge and creativity grow only when we are able to move with considerable fluidity and ease through transit checkpoints.

We need to understand something about foreign and international copyright for many reasons. The law of the United States, and that of any other country, is increasingly becoming a mix of nationalities. Our systems of education, libraries, publishing, entertainment, and information sharing are nearly impossible to confine to one country. Finally, we need to learn about the laws of other jurisdictions because they have something to share. Influential developments in the law often come from directives in the European Union or in treaties negotiated in Geneva. Good ideas, worthy of consideration and borrowing, can come from any part of the world.

A recurring theme of this book is that we may not all become experts in copyright, but we need to learn enough to be responsible citizens. We need to respect the copyrights of others and know how to meaningfully exercise our rights under fair use and other exceptions. We need to recognize that we are all copyright owners and consequently become good stewards of our own legal rights—and know when to assert rights and when to share them. We also need to know the international legal context, so we can watch change emerge and blossom around the planet. Finally, becoming a witness to copyright in an international context empowers each of us to be a global partner and contributor as we work with copyright principles to promote progress and foster boundless creativity and borderless knowledge.

NOTES

1. Berne Convention for the Protection of Literary and Artistic Works, https://www.wipo.int/treaties/en/ip/berne/.

2. Berne Convention, art. 5(1).

3. TRIPS, art. 3(1). The WTO is based on a series of agreements, including an instrument called Agreement on Trade-Related Aspects of Intellectual Property Rights, better known as TRIPS. The full text is available as Annex 1C at https://www.wto.org/english/docs_e/legal_e/legal_e.htm.

4. The accompanying text box offers some details about works protected by U.S. law as well as the short list of countries whose works are outside the protective reach of American law.

5. U.S. Copyright Act, 17 U.S.C. § 104. As is so often true, the statute offers many more details and possibilities.

6. U.S. Copyright Act, 17 U.S.C. § 105.

7. The extension of federal copyright to early recordings was a result of the restoration requirement. However, in October 2018, Congress passed the Music Modernization Act, which granted a quasi-copyright protection to pre-1972 recordings. This new law, explored in Chapter 20, raises a serious question about whether it supersedes the restored foreign protection.

8. To make it trickier, you specifically need to apply the law of the other country as it existed in 1996 or other year when the U.S. established copyright ties. You cannot simply apply today's law. Rarely is such legal information realistically and reliably available for any country. U.S. Copyright Act, 17 U.S.C. § 104A(h).

9. *Twin Books Corp. v. Walt Disney Co.*, 83 F.3d 1162 (9th Cir. 1996).

10. *Societe Civile Succession Guino v. Renoir*, 549 F.3d 1182 (9th Cir. 2008).

11. See the discussion later in this chapter regarding the Russian newspapers.

12. The determination of work made for hire not only affects ownership but also can change the duration of the copyright, and it can mean the barring of moral rights under U.S. law. If foreign law is therefore used to determine whether a work is for hire, that foreign law can profoundly shape many aspects of the legal protection for the work in question.

13. U.S. Copyright Act, 17 U.S.C. § 109(a). I feel bad just shedding a little light on this strange provision. It usually goes unnoticed, and it would be nearly impossible to enforce. Because of the odd categories of works that are and are not subject to this rule, it is perfectly possible or even likely that two identical books could be subject to opposite rules based upon the exact timing of when each was produced. Enough said.

14. The meaning of fair use and the four factors is explored in some depth in Chapters 10 through 14 of this book.

15. Worth mentioning, because of their central importance to librarians and educators, are the exceptions applicable to noncommercial or library uses of pre-1972 sound recordings. They are detailed in Chapter 20, and as noted, the pre-1972 law for foreign and domestic works may vary significantly.

16. Just to get highly technical, the exceptions generally apply to copyrighted works. Therefore, foreign works that have had their copyrights restored are then subject to the various exceptions.

17. Chapters 6 and 18 offer some insights about this requirement and a 2019 decision from the U.S. Supreme Court.

18. U.S. Copyright Act, 17 U.S.C. § 411(a). *United States work* is defined in Section 101, and it includes works first published in the United States or, in the case of unpublished works, works for which all of the authors are nationals or residents of the United States.

19. U.S. Copyright Act, 17 U.S.C. § 412.

20. Don't forget to be practical. We all know that works are posted online each day in seemingly limitless quantities, and they are not under assault from every country in the world with Internet connections. Be reasonable.

21. *La Société des Auteurs des arts visuels et de L'image Fixe (SAIF) v. Google France, S.A.R.L., and Google Inc.*, Cour d'appel [CA] [regional court of appeal] Paris, 1e ch., Jan. 26, 2011.

22. In a case involving the Beatles movie *Yellow Submarine*, the court in *Subafilms, Ltd. v. MGM-Pathé Communications Co.*, 24 F.3d 1088 (9th Cir. 1994) (en banc), held that U.S. copyright law does not apply if the infringements occurred outside the United States, even if the activities were authorized by individuals inside the United States.

23. The parties did litigate in U.S. courts with respect to the enforcement of rights and the distribution of the film in the United States. *Ace Arts, LLC v. Sony/ATV Music Publishing, LLC*, 56 F. Supp. 3d 436 (S.D.N.Y. 2014).

24. *Sony/ATV Music Publishing, LLC v. WPMC Limited*, [2015] EWHC (Ch) 1853 (UK High Court of Justice, Case No. HC-2012-000143).

25. The litigation continues. In 2018, the producer of the documentary film filed a new case in a U.S. court seeking a declaratory judgment that the producer has the right to use the concert film footage, either because some of it is public domain or the production is within fair use.

26. *Itar-Tass Russian News Agency v. Russian Kurier, Inc.*, 153 F.3d 82 (2d Cir. 1998).

27. *Id.* at 85.

CHAPTER 24

PERMISSION, LICENSING, AND OPEN ACCESS

KEY POINTS

- No permission is needed if your work is in the public domain or if your use is within fair use or another exception.
- Permission for some works may be available through a collective licensing agency.
- Many works are available under Creative Commons and other simplified licensing arrangements.
- Contacting a copyright owner and drafting a permission letter can involve a careful strategy.
- You still have options with orphan works and after reaching a dead end in your quest for permission.

THIS BOOK HAS been overwhelmingly about the law of copyright. It has surveyed the rights of owners and the limitations on those rights, all as established in the statutes, court rulings, and other sources of the law. This system of rights and exceptions is intended to serve and maintain a balance between copyright owners and the public. However, not all planned uses of copyrighted works will fit neatly into the statutory construct. Sometimes we need to step outside the legal formula either to redefine the rights an owner might choose to assert or to seek a license—or permission—when the planned use is not covered by the statutory exceptions.

This chapter offers a conceptual overview of licenses and their role in the copyright system, with a step-by-step process for obtaining permission to use copyrighted works. This chapter provides insights for streamlining the process and strategies for dealing with problems that commonly occur when making permission requests.

Opening portions of this chapter offer guidance and strategies for securing permissions directly from the author or other rightsholder, but consent to use a copyrighted work can come in many forms. For example, the availability of multitudes of works through open access, and specifically the rapid expansion of works with Creative Commons licenses, is effectively a grant of permission from the rightsholders to make those works publicly available and to give advance permission for extensive uses of the works without needing to locate and contact anyone.

Keeping an ordered perspective is important. Permission is necessary only if the work is in fact protected by copyright. At least for copyright purposes, you don't need to seek permission for the use of facts or of works that are in the public domain. You don't need permission if your use is within fair use or another exception. You also don't need to seek individual permission if a Creative Commons or other license already permits your use.

LICENSED WORKS

Many uses of copyrighted works in education and research are subject to advance license agreements. For example, numerous colleges and universities have standard agreements with ASCAP and other collective licensing agencies for the public performance of music. These licenses might generally cover marching bands at football games, academic assemblies, and other campus events. Libraries enter into numerous license agreements for the acquisition of research databases and vast collections of electronic books, periodicals, films, and many other works. The library agreements permit various uses—often beyond the basics of reading and downloading a copy for personal study.

One of these licenses may well serve your needs and your project. However, the permitted uses under these licenses are often narrowly defined, and the terms of the agreements themselves are too often filed away in offices where they are simply not reasonably available for review and scrutiny.

> **AS WITH** the entire book, **this chapter** is almost exclusively about copyright. You may or may not need permission to use a work because of copyright issues. However, even if the work is in the public domain or the use does not require copyright permission for any other reason, you might still need permission on some other account. For example, reprinting the document might violate a person's privacy or a nation's security interest. Your use of a photograph might implicate the right of publicity of the celebrity or other person captured in the image. An archival collection or oral history interview might have been contributed to the library's collection with the requirement that researchers obtain consent from donors or family members for any uses.

CREATIVE COMMONS LICENSES

The licensing system of Creative Commons was introduced in Chapter 7 as an innovation in ownership concepts. In this chapter, CC deserves attention as a vital means for quickly and easily securing permission. CC licenses come in many forms, and one of the most generous is the CC-BY license. It requires only that you give attribution to the author when using the work. With that attribution, you can proceed to use the work for any purpose—including copying and selling it—while keeping all the money. You may also revise the work, incorporate it into your multimedia project, and build new learning materials, audiovisual works, and even competing products. A CC license can be extraordinarily broad and generous, if the rightsholder so desires. CC is also an instrumental component of the open access movement.

Many authors opt to limit the uses by choosing one of the other CC licenses. Many academic writers might select a license that limits you to noncommercial uses, and some authors choose the covenant of *no derivatives*. CC licenses are specific to each work. If the license on a particular work is broad enough to cover your needs, then you can quickly move ahead with your project. CC licenses also foster the proliferation of open educational resources, digital repositories, and many collections of publicly available materials.

> **RIGHTSHOLDERS MAY** use the CC0 license to disclaim any copyright interests and to place works in the public domain. Many museums long had asserted rights in their photographic images of artworks. Increasingly, prominent museums are placing collections of their photographic images of public domain works online for unrestricted downloading, with the assurance of a CC0 license. The Metropolitan Museum of Art joined the trend by announcing that 375,000 images are now available for free downloads from the museum website. For the Met's policy and more, visit http://www.metmuseum.org/openaccess.

If the copyright owner has made the work easily available, you need to do your part by respecting the grant. For example, most CC licenses at least require attribution. When you use text, photographs, and other works under such a CC license, be sure to include a footnote or other form of citation with attribution to the author or other source. The work itself, alongside the CC license statement, may include a preferred form of attribution. Use it. Giving attribution to the source is a gesture of respect, and it is usually essential to intellectual honesty.

Failing to give attribution can be a breach of the CC terms. If you have not complied with the CC terms, you are not within the requirements of the license, and you likely will lose all the benefits of Creative Commons. You may find yourself striving to justify your use on other grounds or facing a demand from the copyright owner for a potentially hefty fee for uses outside the CC construct. In other words, if you do not adhere to the license, you might default to a straightforward infringement.

STEPS IN THE PERMISSION PROCESS

Specify the Work and the Planned Use

The first step in obtaining permission to use a copyrighted work is to identify precisely the work in question and your planned uses of it. When selecting a work, stay flexible and consider substitutions that may meet your needs. Copyright owners are free to deny permission requests or require a licensing fee that may be outside your budget. Also, finding and eliciting a response from copyright owners can sometimes prove difficult or impossible. Having multiple works to draw upon will improve your chances of success.

YOU DO not need to seek or secure permission if your use is within fair use or another exception. Study the exceptions summarized in **Chapter 9** of this book. The fundamental point of the exceptions is that the public may use the works without permission and without incurring liability. Seeking permission may at times be good courtesy. From another perspective, seeking permission for activity within fair use not only is unnecessary but may be counterproductive.

In addition, stay flexible about your precise uses of the work. For example, you might have a great plan to digitize photos and make them available on a website. The owner may object to broad access and require limitations. Similarly, the owner may oppose the making of digital copies but will allow print versions of the works. Explore alternatives with the owner as necessary.

Similarly, stay flexible about the particular work you want to use. Sometimes you absolutely have to use a specific work of art or a landmark journal article. However, if permission to use that great street scene of Paris is not easily available or comes at high price, keep in mind that Paris is a beautiful city; many other photographs are available, and many of them have CC or other easy licenses.

Determine Whether Permission Is Necessary

Permission may not be necessary for many reasons, but a common reason is that the work is not protected by copyright at all. A work may be in the public domain for a myriad of reasons.[1] If it is, you may use it freely and without copyright restrictions. Early research concerning the copyright status of a work can save considerable time and money.

Permission is also not necessary if you are within fair use or another exception to the rights of copyright owners. Even so, you might find yourself requesting permission simply as a courtesy or to find a more comfortable solution to a close call about fair use. Seeking permission when it is not clearly necessary can backfire. The copyright owner is now apprised of your project and may object to your use or set an unaffordable fee. Seeking permission is good and important, but not in every instance.

Finally, the copyright owner may have already granted permission for your particular use. The original work may include a statement of permission or a Creative Commons license.[2] Often libraries purchase videos and other works with a license to use them in educational performances. Sometimes colleges and universities acquire full-text databases under contracts that permit a variety of educational uses. A little checking can spare you the burden of tracking down the copyright owner.

Identify and Contact the Copyright Owner

You can determine the identity of the copyright owner through several methods. It is best to start with the work itself because it may include a copyright notice indicating the original claimant of the copyright. Although the copyright notice is a good place to start your investigation, remember that copyright ownership may have been transferred to another person or entity, leaving some notices out-of-date and inaccurate. Nevertheless, the name on the work is the obvious place to start. Searches of directories, newspapers, and Internet sources will often turn up the publisher or the author or the author's heirs.

The records at the U.S. Copyright Office may be helpful in determining the copyright owner. Copyright owners seeking the fullest protection of their works will often register claims with the Copyright Office. Registration, however, is not a prerequisite for protection, so the public records are hardly complete.[3] Also, the Copyright Office may list one party as the owner, but that original owner may have since transferred the copyright to a new owner, with no recordation of the change. Again, documents at the Copyright Office can be incomplete and outdated.

All too often the quest for the copyright owner is akin to a detective venture. The original author may have transferred the copyright to a publisher. That publisher may have sold its assets, including copyrights, to another company. In other cases, the original author may have retained the copyright but died and left the estate, including copyrights, to an assortment of family members. Sometimes you just have to persevere and indulge in a series of telephone calls to authors, editors, and family members.

Some copyright owners have eased the search. They may act through various collective licensing agencies that serve as agents for multiple copyright owners. Publishers of books and journals often use the Copyright Clearance Center. Some musical works are licensed through agencies such as ASCAP or BMI. If an organization represents the copyright owner, it may offer a license directly to you. In other instances, the organization may put you in direct contact with the owner. Licenses through these agencies are often available by submitting the request and paying the licensing fee online. Licensing directly from the author or rightsholder can still be an option, and often it is faster and less expensive.

REQUESTING PERMISSION does not preclude a later decision to rely instead on fair use. In many fair use cases, permission was initially sought but not granted. One might think that the denial of permission should weigh against fair use. In fact, courts rule otherwise in order to not discourage users from making an honest effort to seek permission when it may be warranted. *Campbell v. Acuff-Rose Music, Inc.,* 510 U.S. 569, 585 n.18 (1994).

THE U.S. COPYRIGHT OFFICE'S records may be searched to help determine the copyright status of works and the identity of the copyright claimant. Filings made in and after 1978 may be searched for online at https://www.copyright.gov. The Copyright Office will conduct searches for a fee. For many years, the Copyright Office published a printed directory of registrations and renewals, which can also assist with finding the names of copyright claimants. Issues of the *Catalog of Copyright Entries* from 1923 through 1977 are now scanned and available through Google. See http://books.google.com/googlebooks/copyrightsearch.html. Additional resources are gathered at this site from the University of Pennsylvania: https://onlinebooks.library.upenn.edu/cce/. Copies of the Catalog from as early as 1891 are also available from the Internet Archive. See https://archive.org/details/copyrightrecords.

MANY TOOLS are available to help identify rightsholders. Resources include these databases from the University of Texas:

- WATCH: Writers and Authors and Their Copyright Holders, http://norman.hrc.utexas .edu/watch/
- FOB: Firms Out of Business, http://norman.hrc.utexas.edu/watch/fob.cfm

These databases are hardly complete—there are more publishers and authors in the world than anyone could ever gather in one database. However, these resources offer a great place to start some searches. A search for the prominent author Philip Roth can lead you to his agent. A search for the publisher Henry Holt can let you know that the company was acquired as part of the Macmillan Group.

Large publishers and television networks sometimes have their own permission departments to handle requests. These departments may be contacted via an e-mail address available on the company's website. Many of these departments offer standard permission request forms that you may complete and submit through traditional mail or online.

THE COPYRIGHT Clearance Center can help expedite some licensing processes. Through its website, you may request permission to make certain uses of thousands of works, including books, magazines, journal articles, newsletters, and dissertations. Permission fees are paid directly to the Copyright Clearance Center and are then forwarded to the appropriate copyright owners. The Copyright Clearance Center's website is https://www.copyright.com. The use of ASCAP, BMI, and other music licensing agencies is examined in Chapter 19.

Draft a Permission Request

Ultimately, you often need to contact copyright owners directly, either by e-mail or through the postal service. An advance telephone call will often assure that you are writing to the proper owner. That call may also signal whether the permission will likely be forthcoming.

As you prepare the permission letter, consider choosing one of two strategies for drafting your request:

1. *Specific request:* Many copyright owners insist on a detailed request, and the permission will be limited accordingly. For example, if you request permission to make print copies of a work during the next semester of your course, the permission will not cover digital scans, posting the item to the course website, or using it in subsequent semesters. Copyright owners often require elaborate information to determine fees or whether to grant permission at all. Omitting pertinent information in your request may delay permission.

WHENEVER POSSIBLE, seek to secure grants of permission in writing. Oral permission may be allowed under the law, but a written and signed document will be important in case of any misunderstandings between you and the copyright owner. A model permission letter is included as Appendix F of this book.

2. *General request:* Sometimes a little generality in your permission request can be helpful. Open-ended and broad language may offer more flexibility to meet your changing needs. For example, if you anticipate using the work in repeated semesters for various

projects, you might ask for broad rights to "use the work in connection with my teaching." Accordingly, you might not specify such matters as

- a termination date for the permission,
- a maximum number of students using the work,
- the medium by which you will share the work (i.e., electronic or print), and
- the specific nature of the use (i.e., distance education or face-to-face teaching).

One obvious downside of this strategy is that the copyright owner may ask for more information or may insist on adding such limits or conditions to the permission. Any back-and-forth negotiation will lead to delays.

> **THE TERMS** of your licensing agreement are limited by only your imagination and the willingness of the parties to reach agreement. Contemplate all your possible uses—present and future—and request permission accordingly.

Whatever method or means you use to secure permission, you ought to be ready to address these important points:

- *What:* Cite the precise work and the exact portion of the work you wish to use. The fee to use a portion of a work may be less than the fee for the use of an entire work. For text works, include the exact pages, sections, or chapters you plan to use. For sound recordings and audiovisual works, include a detailed description of the portion and length you wish to use.
- *Who:* The person granting the permission is the *licensor*, but you must consider carefully who should be the *licensee*. If you are working on a project individually, then the permission might be in your name. If you have coauthors, you might ask for a grant of permission to "us" and list the names. Be careful with permissions for book projects and other publications. If the permissions are in the name of the publisher, what happens if you change publishers? You might need to start the permission process anew. You will often be best served by having the permission granted to you personally, giving you the flexibility to work with other publishers now and in the future.
- *When:* The copyright owner may want to know when and for how long you plan on using the work. Some owners may be wary of granting permission for extended periods of time or for dates far in the future. For teaching uses, don't hesitate to ask for multiple semesters. For a publication project, extend the request to translations and future editions. You bear little risk in asking.
- *Why:* The purpose of your use may be critical to determining the licensing fee or whether permission is granted at all. Owners tend to be more supportive of nonprofit classroom uses, but if you are planning to include the material in a publication or on an open website, you will likely need to offer those details.
- *How:* The proliferation of alternatives for using copyrighted works has caused many owners to insist on detailed plans. You might have to specify whether you are making classroom handouts or sending the materials to a commercial printer for duplication. Some owners will want to know if you will deliver the works electronically and if your course management system is password protected.
- *How much:* The price that copyright owners will charge for use of their works is difficult, if not impossible, to estimate. Some licensing fees will be exorbitant and cost prohibitive, yet other copyright owners may be happy

to grant permission at little or no cost. You usually just have to ask. Owners may base fees on the type of use or the number of people who may have access to their works. You should be ready to provide the details as best you can.

ORPHAN WORKS AND THE DEAD END OF PERMISSION QUESTS

Too often, your effort to secure permission reaches a dead end. That disappointing conclusion may take many forms: You never find the copyright owner; the copyright owner never responds to your request; the licensing fee is prohibitive; or the copyright owner denies permission altogether. Dead ends are common and can be extremely frustrating. Copyrighted works of indeterminate ownership, or with owners that can no longer be found, are often called *orphans*. Orphan works lead to confusion, and they even have been the subject of proposed legislation in Congress. For now, at least, U.S. law offers no specific solution to the problem of orphan works or other dead ends. Instead, you might consider these strategies:

- *Return to fair use.* The fair use analysis that you conducted before seeking permission should have been based in part on the potential effect that your use would have on the market for the work. Reaching a dead end may suggest that your use will cause little or no harm to the market for licensing the work. Armed with this new information, a new fair use analysis may now have a different result.
- *Replace the planned work with alternative materials.* Substitute works may satisfy your needs. Look for works in the public domain or works for which permission is more likely to be forthcoming. Also, consider creating your own work and avoid having to ask for permission altogether.
- *Alter your planned use of the work.* Some copyright owners will deny certain types of use or permission to copy large portions of a work. Revise your plans to accommodate the owner's requirements. For example, request to use a smaller portion of

Air New Zealand has made reasonable inquiries to try and identify who owns the copyright of the images and footage that appear in this exhibition. If you think you are the owner of any rights in any images, please contact us at Brand Manager, Air New Zealand, Private Bag 92007, Auckland 1010, and we will endeavour to reach a suitable arrangement with you.

The permissions system is far from perfect. Sometimes we have to do our best and accept what we can find.

CHAPTER 18 includes an overview of the risks and liabilities of copyright infringement. That chapter also describes some important protection for educators and librarians who are acting in good faith. One practical point to emphasize here is that liabilities may be limited if the work is not registered with the Copyright Office. Some users may also have added protections if they conduct a good faith application of fair use.

the work, or deliver the work to students via a password-protected system rather than a public website.

■ *Conduct a risk-benefit analysis.* Sometimes you face the difficult need to assess whether using the work is worth the risk of stirring legal claims. Your assessment should carefully weigh a number of variables, including the importance of using a particular work in your project, how openly exposed your use of the work will be, and the thoroughness of your investigation and the diligence of your attempts to request permission. Undertaking such an analysis should be done with caution. The effort can pose serious legal and ethical quandaries. Educators and librarians may want to consider notifying supervisors or asking legal counsel to assist in such an analysis. Unfortunately, copyright owners are often elusive, leaving users to face such difficult decisions.

> THE EUROPEAN Union and a small number of other countries have enacted copyright law attempting to address the problem of orphan works. The EU approach is to require a diligent search of sources to find a rightful owner. Once a work is determined to be an orphan in one country, it is deemed to be an orphan in all twenty-eight EU countries. Other countries with related legislation include Canada and South Korea. The exception of noncommercial uses in the new law for pre-1972 sound recordings may become a model for broader orphan works legislation. See the discussion of the Music Modernization Act in Chapter 20.

LEARNING FROM EXPERIENCE

If you are regularly tracking down permissions to use copyrighted works, you will start to see some patterns, and you will begin to predict (at least roughly) how certain rightsholders are likely to reply. Some reply quickly and generously; some never respond at all. Others impose a litany of conditions, while the next will send you to the Copyright Clearance Center or other agent. The first lesson from experience is that copyright owners have a wide range of habits and inclinations. One approach does not fit all.

Imagine you are seeking permissions from a wide range of rightsholders for a diversity of familiar projects. You might be building a website or planning to publish a new book. You might be gathering teaching materials for a course or launching a multimedia resource on a topic of interest. Here are some strategies and insights that might help you avoid frustrations and save time:

■ *Reach out early by phone or e-mail.* You can write the best permission letter possible and send it to the most well-meaning copyright owner, but it can still end up in the inbox of endless ordeals. You want some action. Prepare the letter, but first send a polite message of introduction to be sure you have found the right person and to see if the rightsholder has a preferred form.

■ *Embrace authors.* You might be seeking permission to reproduce a published article or book chapter, and often authors have transferred those copyrights to the publishers. Don't assume that is true. Many authors today are retaining their rights, and you can often have great success contacting authors first. The author is often able to verify ownership or refer you to the publisher. Moreover, if you

> WATCH FOR layers of copyrights and, as a result, layers of permissions. An earlier text box highlighted the different legal constraints—particularly privacy and security interests—that might apply to a work. In addition, a single work might embody multiple copyrights and an array of claimants. Consider the rights associated with a clip from a musical motion picture. A list of rightsholders might have a legitimate claim to some aspect of the clip. The production company can have rights in the visuals of the film. The composer may hold rights in the musical work. The recording artist of the song or the label might lay claim to the underlying master recording. Competing claimants might assert a performance right for the film or the music. The persons depicted in the film might have rights of publicity with respect to the use of their images, names, and voices. Comprehensive clearance can be foreboding and often elusive.

ONE MORE reality check: Expect anything; don't get frustrated. You might have to write and call multiple times to get a response. You can reach agreement one day, only to have the rightsholder ask for a few more conditions the next day. Sometimes a rightsholder will refuse to grant permission until you have approval from yet other parties. The permission may come with burdensome requirements for acknowledging the claim in your publication or a requirement to pay a percentage of royalties you might receive. Be prepared to negotiate. You will need to decide at each stage whether to proceed with your use as planned, accept the conditions, or push back with diplomatic negotiations.

have to contact the publisher, it always feels good to mention to the publisher that the author supports your use.

- *Contemplate joint owners.* If you are seeking a nonexclusive license to use a work with joint copyright ownership, you usually need permission from only one of the copyright owners. However, you might reach out to two or three or more authors for various reasons: You might get a reply from only one, or you might want to extend the courtesy of letting all authors know you appreciate their work. On the downside, you might discover that the joint owners are deep in disputes with one another. Permissions all around might help you avoid getting caught up in that clamor.

- *Think about heirs.* People die. Companies get bought out and absorbed. Sometimes you need to do some detective work to find family members or successor companies. You might be lucky and find a newspaper article or obituary with all the needed information. In other cases you have to do some research. When you find that grandchild or other successor, reach out with a phone call or e-mail to gracefully begin the conversation. A diplomatic chat can be very effective for explaining the importance of the work and why granting permission would be a good thing.

- *Money is unpredictable.* Some licensors have an inflexible fee schedule, and others can set prices on the fly. For many nonprofit educational uses that are not published or posted to the web, fees are often waived. If the permission requires a fee and you cannot swing it, don't hesitate to send a request for a waiver. On the other hand, if the fee is fair and modest, consider paying it. Sometimes authors need an income too.

- *Collective licensors can be a challenge.* Large organizations that represent multitudes of rightsholders have a lot of people to keep happy. As a result, their license terms can be highly cautious and exceedingly elaborate. Be sure to read the pages of fine print. Read all the conditions and requirements. They can be cumbersome, and they sometimes unload potential risks back onto the user. Don't accept the deal if it is not right for you.

- *Collective licenses are not required.* If you reach out to one of the collective licensors and for any reason you are not satisfied, you may always still contact the author, publisher, or other rightsholder directly. In fact, you may always make that contact first. The copyright owner may well have chosen to license through a collective agency, but ordinarily that agreement is not exclusive.

- *Watch for limits.* Some permissions come with defined limits. A major newspaper might give permission for reproductions in only North America. A film producer might allow uses for only three years. Watch carefully and decide if those limits are acceptable for your needs. Feel free to negotiate.

- *Don't do it all at once.* If your project requires a long list of permissions, reach out to copyright owners in stages. For example, if you need permission from three different film producers about three different films, make initial contact with only one. That one exchange will probably give you insights for revising your permission letter, reworking your use of the film clips, and anticipating terms and prices. Learning as you go will make the process easier and more successful.
- *Follow your instincts.* If all seems right and the permissions are signed and in order, you are probably fine. On the other hand, if something in the reply from a publisher or the comments from an author suggests that you might not have contacted the right party, follow up with polite questions. You want to be reasonably sure that you have a valid permission in hand, and the higher the profile and the more important your project, the more certain you want to be.
- *Keep copies.* Set up paper and electronic files of your permission letters and all related correspondence. Be sure to keep copies with signatures, or at least retain the e-mails that grant permission. Those e-mails can be as important as any other legal document. Similarly, keep notes about the sources you checked, including evidence that you could not find a legitimate rightsholder or that you found the work with a CC license that met your needs.

The virtue of flexibility has been advanced many times in this book. When it comes to permissions, be flexible about the selection of materials and how you might use them. When you run into complications or high costs, your flexibility can rescue the project. Patience is also a virtue. Most permission requests are usually wrapped up in several days or a few weeks. You should get started early in your project because some permissions may be stalled for months. Patience is also essential as you try to convince reluctant rightsholders that your project is worthy of their support.

NOTES

1. Some works are not eligible for copyright protection (see Chapter 5 of this book), while other works may be in the public domain due to expiration of the copyrights (see Chapter 6).

2. For a brief discussion of Creative Commons, see Chapter 7 of this book.

3. Registration may not be required to have copyright protection, but it still offers several benefits to the copyright owner. For more about registration, see Chapter 6.

APPENDIX A

SELECTED PROVISIONS FROM THE U.S. COPYRIGHT ACT

CONGRESS OF THE United States has the constitutional power to enact copyright statutes. The earliest federal copyright legislation dates to 1790, and Congress has revised the Copyright Act at various times since then. In 1976, Congress made the most recent complete revision of the federal copyright statutes, which took effect on January 1, 1978. Current law is therefore often referred to as the Copyright Act of 1976. However, Congress has amended the Copyright Act of 1976 on many occasions. Some of the changes have been minor; others have been profound and complicated.

This appendix reprints selected provisions from the current U.S. Copyright Act. The statutes are selected principally because of their relevance to the issues covered by this book. For example, readers will find here the statutes related to the rights of owners and the statutes on fair use and other exceptions relevant to librarianship and education. The language in brackets is commentary provided by the author of this book.

The full text of the U.S. Copyright Act is available from many sources. The website of the U.S. Copyright Office includes a link to the full Copyright Act as well as links to individual bills and to helpful explanations of copyright law (such as the circulars and other materials). Visit that website at https://www.copyright.gov.

PROVISIONS FROM THE U.S. COPYRIGHT ACT

- Section 101. Definitions
- Section 102. Subject matter of copyright: In general
- Section 103. Subject matter of copyright: Compilations and derivative works
- Section 105. Subject matter of copyright: United States Government works
- Section 106. Exclusive rights in copyrighted works
- Section 106A. Rights of certain authors to attribution and integrity
- Section 107. Limitations on exclusive rights: Fair use
- Section 108. Limitations on exclusive rights: Reproduction by libraries and archives
- Section 109. Limitations on exclusive rights: Effect of transfer of particular copy or phonorecord
- Section 110. Limitations on exclusive rights: Exemption of certain performances and displays

- Section 121. Limitations on exclusive rights: Reproduction for blind or other people with disabilities
- Section 121A. Limitations on exclusive rights: Reproduction for blind or other people with disabilities in Marrakesh Treaty countries
- Section 504. Remedies for infringement: Damages and profits
- Section 1201. Circumvention of copyright protection systems
- Section 1401. Unauthorized use of pre-1972 sound recordings

Section 101. Definitions

[The importance of the definitions should not be overlooked. For example, Section 105 states that a work of the U.S. government is not protected by copyright. To determine the reach of that provision, one must look to the definition of a "work of the United States Government" in Section 101. Nothing in Section 105 itself will tell the reader to look to the definitions; anyone working with the Copyright Act must be familiar with the words and concepts that are defined in the code and remember to research them. To make the matter more interesting, some provisions of the Copyright Act include their own definitions of selected terms, apart from the definitions in Section 101. For example, this appendix includes Section 110, which includes some definitions. The following definitions are only selected excerpts from Section 101 as may be especially relevant to the scope of this book.—Kenneth D. Crews]

An "anonymous work" is a work on the copies or phonorecords of which no natural person is identified as author.

An "architectural work" is the design of a building as embodied in any tangible medium of expression, including a building, architectural plans, or drawings. The work includes the overall form as well as the arrangement and composition of spaces and elements in the design, but does not include individual standard features.

"Audiovisual works" are works that consist of a series of related images which are intrinsically intended to be shown by the use of machines or devices such as projectors, viewers, or electronic equipment, together with accompanying sounds, if any, regardless of the nature of the material objects, such as films or tapes, in which the works are embodied.

The "Berne Convention" is the Convention for the Protection of Literary and Artistic Works, signed at Berne, Switzerland, on September 9, 1886, and all acts, protocols, and revisions thereto.

A "collective work" is a work, such as a periodical issue, anthology, or encyclopedia, in which a number of contributions, constituting separate and independent works in themselves, are assembled into a collective whole.

A "compilation" is a work formed by the collection and assembling of preexisting materials or of data that are selected, coordinated, or arranged in such a way that the resulting work as a whole constitutes an original work of authorship. The term "compilation" includes collective works.

A "computer program" is a set of statements or instructions to be used directly or indirectly in a computer in order to bring about a certain result.

"Copies" are material objects, other than phonorecords, in which a work is fixed by any method now known or later developed, and from which the work can be perceived, reproduced, or otherwise communicated, either directly or with the aid of a machine or device. The term "copies" includes the material object, other than a phonorecord, in which the work is first fixed.

"Copyright owner", with respect to any one of the exclusive rights comprised in a copyright, refers to the owner of that particular right.

A work is "created" when it is fixed in a copy or phonorecord for the first time; where a work is prepared over a period of time, the portion of it that has been fixed at any particular time constitutes the work as of that time, and where the work has been prepared in different versions, each version constitutes a separate work.

A "derivative work" is a work based upon one or more preexisting works, such as a translation, musical arrangement, dramatization, fictionalization, motion picture version, sound recording, art reproduction, abridgment, condensation, or any other form in which a work may be recast, transformed, or adapted. A work consisting of editorial revisions, annotations, elaborations, or other modifications, which, as a whole, represent an original work of authorship, is a "derivative work".

A "digital transmission" is a transmission in whole or in part in a digital or other non-analog format.

To "display" a work means to show a copy of it, either directly or by means of a film, slide, television image, or any other device or process or, in the case of a motion picture or other audiovisual work, to show individual images nonsequentially.

A work is "fixed" in a tangible medium of expression when its embodiment in a copy or phonorecord, by or under the authority of the author, is sufficiently permanent or stable to permit it to be perceived, reproduced, or otherwise communicated for a period of more than transitory duration. A work consisting of sounds, images, or both, that are being transmitted, is "fixed" for purposes of this title if a fixation of the work is being made simultaneously with its transmission.

A "joint work" is a work prepared by two or more authors with the intention that their contributions be merged into inseparable or interdependent parts of a unitary whole.

"Literary works" are works, other than audiovisual works, expressed in words, numbers, or other verbal or numerical symbols or indicia, regardless of the nature of the material objects, such as books, periodicals, manuscripts, phonorecords, film, tapes, disks, or cards, in which they are embodied.

"Motion pictures" are audiovisual works consisting of a series of related images which, when shown in succession, impart an impression of motion, together with accompanying sounds, if any.

To "perform" a work means to recite, render, play, dance, or act it, either directly or by means of any device or process or, in the case of a motion picture or other audiovisual work, to show its images in any sequence or to make the sounds accompanying it audible.

A "performing rights society" is an association, corporation, or other entity that licenses the public performance of nondramatic musical works on behalf of copyright owners of such works, such as the American Society of Composers, Authors and Publishers (ASCAP), Broadcast Music, Inc. (BMI), and SESAC, Inc.

"Phonorecords" are material objects in which sounds, other than those accompanying a motion picture or other audiovisual work, are fixed by any method now known or later developed, and from which the sounds can be perceived, reproduced, or otherwise com-municated, either directly or with the aid of a machine or device. The term "phonorecords" includes the material object in which the sounds are first fixed.

"Pictorial, graphic, and sculptural works" include two-dimensional and three-dimen-sional works of fine, graphic, and applied art, photographs, prints and art reproductions, maps, globes, charts, diagrams, models, and technical drawings, including architectural plans. Such works shall include works of artistic craftsmanship insofar as their form but not their mechanical or utilitarian aspects are concerned; the design of a useful article, as defined in this section, shall be considered a pictorial, graphic, or sculptural work only if, and only to the extent that, such design incorporates pictorial, graphic, or sculptural features that can be identified separately from, and are capable of existing independently of, the utilitarian aspects of the article.

A "pseudonymous work" is a work on the copies or phonorecords of which the author is identified under a fictitious name.

"Publication" is the distribution of copies or phonorecords of a work to the public by sale or other transfer of ownership, or by rental, lease, or lending. The offering to distribute copies or phonorecords to a group of persons for purposes of further distribution, public performance, or public display, constitutes publication. A public performance or display of a work does not of itself constitute publication.

To perform or display a work "publicly" means—

> (1) to perform or display it at a place open to the public or at any place where a substantial number of persons outside of a normal circle of a family and its social acquaintances is gathered; or
> (2) to transmit or otherwise communicate a performance or display of the work to a place specified by clause (1) or to the public, by means of any device or process, whether the members of the public capable of receiving the performance or display receive it in the same place or in separate places and at the same time or at different times.

"Sound recordings" are works that result from the fixation of a series of musical, spoken, or other sounds, but not including the sounds accompanying a motion picture or other audiovisual work, regardless of the nature of the material objects, such as disks, tapes, or other phonorecords, in which they are embodied.

A "transfer of copyright ownership" is an assignment, mortgage, exclusive license, or any other conveyance, alienation, or hypothecation of a copyright or of any of the exclusive rights comprised in a copyright, whether or not it is limited in time or place of effect, but not including a nonexclusive license.

To "transmit" a performance or display is to communicate it by any device or process whereby images or sounds are received beyond the place from which they are sent.

A "treaty party" is a country or intergovernmental organization other than the United States that is a party to an international agreement.

The "United States", when used in a geographical sense, comprises the several States, the District of Columbia and the Commonwealth of Puerto Rico, and the organized territories under the jurisdiction of the United States Government.

For purposes of section 411, a work is a "United States work" only if—

> (1) in the case of a published work, the work is first published—
>> (A) in the United States;
>> (B) simultaneously in the United States and another treaty party or parties, whose law grants a term of copyright protection that is the same as or longer than the term provided in the United States;
>> (C) simultaneously in the United States and a foreign nation that is not a treaty party; or

    (D) in a foreign nation that is not a treaty party, and all of the authors of the work are nationals, domiciliaries, or habitual residents of, or in the case of an audiovisual work legal entities with headquarters in, the United States;

(2) in the case of an unpublished work, all the authors of the work are nationals, domiciliaries, or habitual residents of the United States, or, in the case of an unpublished audiovisual work, all the authors are legal entities with headquarters in the United States; or

(3) in the case of a pictorial, graphic, or sculptural work incorporated in a building or structure, the building or structure is located in the United States.

A "work of visual art" is—

(1) a painting, drawing, print or sculpture, existing in a single copy, in a limited edition of 200 copies or fewer that are signed and consecutively numbered by the author, or, in the case of a sculpture, in multiple cast, carved, or fabricated sculptures of 200 or fewer that are consecutively numbered by the author and bear the signature or other identifying mark of the author; or

(2) a still photographic image produced for exhibition purposes only, existing in a single copy that is signed by the author, or in a limited edition of 200 copies or fewer that are signed and consecutively numbered by the author.

A work of visual art does not include—

(A) (i) any poster, map, globe, chart, technical drawing, diagram, model, applied art, motion picture or other audiovisual work, book, magazine, newspaper, periodical, data base, electronic information service, electronic publication, or similar publication;

      (ii) any merchandising item or advertising, promotional, descriptive, covering, or packaging material or container;

      (iii) any portion or part of any item described in clause (i) or (ii);

(B) any work made for hire; or

(C) any work not subject to copyright protection under this title.

A "work of the United States Government" is a work prepared by an officer or employee of the United States Government as part of that person's official duties.

A "work made for hire" is—

(1) a work prepared by an employee within the scope of his or her employment; or

(2) a work specially ordered or commissioned for use as a contribution to a collective work, as a part of a motion picture or other audiovisual work, as a translation, as a supplementary work, as a compilation, as an instructional text, as a test, as answer material for a test, or as an atlas, if the parties expressly agree in a written instrument signed by them that the work shall be considered a work made for hire. For the purpose of the foregoing sentence, a "supplementary work" is a work prepared for publication as a secondary adjunct to a work by another author for the purpose of introducing, concluding, illustrating, explaining, revising, commenting upon, or assisting in the use of the other work, such as forewords, afterwords, pictorial illustrations, maps, charts, tables, editorial notes, musical arrangements, answer material for tests, bibliographies, appendixes, and indexes, and an "instructional text" is a literary, pictorial, or graphic work prepared for publication and with the purpose of use in systematic instructional activities.

[The definition of a "work made for hire" includes some additional language specifying that paragraph (2) of the definition shall not be interpreted with reference to a congressional bill from 1999 that added "sound recordings" to the list but was quickly repealed in 2000. The law develops in some peculiar ways.—*Author*]

Section 102. Subject matter of copyright: In general

(a) Copyright protection subsists, in accordance with this title, in original works of authorship fixed in any tangible medium of expression, now known or later developed, from which they can be perceived, reproduced, or otherwise communicated, either directly or with the aid of a machine or device. Works of authorship include the following categories:

(1) literary works;
(2) musical works, including any accompanying words;
(3) dramatic works, including any accompanying music;
(4) pantomimes and choreographic works;
(5) pictorial, graphic, and sculptural works;
(6) motion pictures and other audiovisual works;
(7) sound recordings; and
(8) architectural works.

(b) In no case does copyright protection for an original work of authorship extend to any idea, procedure, process, system, method of operation, concept, principle, or discovery, regardless of the form in which it is described, explained, illustrated, or embodied in such work.

Section 103. Subject matter of copyright: Compilations and derivative works

(a) The subject matter of copyright as specified by section 102 includes compilations and derivative works, but protection for a work employing preexisting material in which copyright subsists does not extend to any part of the work in which such material has been used unlawfully.

(b) The copyright in a compilation or derivative work extends only to the material contributed by the author of such work, as distinguished from the preexisting material employed in the work, and does not imply any exclusive right in the preexisting material. The copyright in such work is independent of, and does not affect or enlarge the scope, duration, ownership, or subsistence of, any copyright protection in the preexisting material.

Section 105. Subject matter of copyright: United States Government works

Copyright protection under this title is not available for any work of the United States Government, but the United States Government is not precluded from receiving and holding copyrights transferred to it by assignment, bequest, or otherwise.

Section 106. Exclusive rights in copyrighted works

Subject to sections 107 through 122, the owner of copyright under this title has the exclusive rights to do and to authorize any of the following:

(1) to reproduce the copyrighted work in copies or phonorecords;

(2) to prepare derivative works based upon the copyrighted work;

(3) to distribute copies or phonorecords of the copyrighted work to the public by sale or other transfer of ownership, or by rental, lease, or lending;

(4) in the case of literary, musical, dramatic, and choreographic works, pantomimes, and motion pictures and other audiovisual works, to perform the copyrighted work publicly;

(5) in the case of literary, musical, dramatic, and choreographic works, pantomimes, and pictorial, graphic, or sculptural works, including the individual images of a motion picture or other audiovisual work, to display the copyrighted work publicly; and

(6) in the case of sound recordings, to perform the copyrighted work publicly by means of a digital audio transmission.

Section 106A. Rights of certain authors to attribution and integrity

(a) Rights of Attribution and Integrity.—Subject to section 107 and independent of the exclusive rights provided in section 106, the author of a work of visual art—

(1) shall have the right—

  (A) to claim authorship of that work, and
  (B) to prevent the use of his or her name as the author of any work of visual art which he or she did not create;

(2) shall have the right to prevent the use of his or her name as the author of the work of visual art in the event of a distortion, mutilation, or other modification of the work which would be prejudicial to his or her honor or reputation; and

(3) subject to the limitations set forth in section 113(d), shall have the right—

  (A) to prevent any intentional distortion, mutilation, or other modification of that work which would be prejudicial to his or her honor or reputation, and any intentional distortion, mutilation, or modification of that work is a violation of that right, and
  (B) to prevent any destruction of a work of recognized stature, and any intentional or grossly negligent destruction of that work is a violation of that right.

(b) Scope and Exercise of Rights.—Only the author of a work of visual art has the rights conferred by subsection (a) in that work, whether or not the author is the copyright owner. The authors of a joint work of visual art are coowners of the rights conferred by subsection (a) in that work.

(c) Exceptions.—(1) The modification of a work of visual art which is the result of the passage of time or the inherent nature of the materials is not a distortion, mutilation, or other modification described in subsection (a)(3)(A).

(2) The modification of a work of visual art which is the result of conservation, or of the public presentation, including lighting and placement, of the work is not a destruction, distortion, mutilation, or other modification described in subsection (a)(3) unless the modification is caused by gross negligence.

(3) The rights described in paragraphs (1) and (2) of subsection (a) shall not apply to any reproduction, depiction, portrayal, or other use of a work in, upon, or in any connection with any item described in subparagraph (A) or (B) of the

definition of "work of visual art" in section 101, and any such reproduction, depiction, portrayal, or other use of a work is not a destruction, distortion, mutilation, or other modification described in paragraph (3) of subsection (a).

(d) Duration of Rights.—(1) With respect to works of visual art created on or after the effective date set forth in section 610(a) of the Visual Artists Rights Act of 1990, the rights conferred by subsection (a) shall endure for a term consisting of the life of the author.

(2) With respect to works of visual art created before the effective date set forth in section 610(a) of the Visual Artists Rights Act of 1990, but title to which has not, as of such effective date, been transferred from the author, the rights conferred by subsection (a) shall be coextensive with, and shall expire at the same time as, the rights conferred by section 106.

(3) In the case of a joint work prepared by two or more authors, the rights conferred by subsection (a) shall endure for a term consisting of the life of the last surviving author.

(4) All terms of the rights conferred by subsection (a) run to the end of the calendar year in which they would otherwise expire.

(e) Transfer and Waiver.—(1) The rights conferred by subsection (a) may not be transferred, but those rights may be waived if the author expressly agrees to such waiver in a written instrument signed by the author. Such instrument shall specifically identify the work, and uses of that work, to which the waiver applies, and the waiver shall apply only to the work and uses so identified. In the case of a joint work prepared by two or more authors, a waiver of rights under this paragraph made by one such author waives such rights for all such authors.

(2) Ownership of the rights conferred by subsection (a) with respect to a work of visual art is distinct from ownership of any copy of that work, or of a copyright or any exclusive right under a copyright in that work. Transfer of ownership of any copy of a work of visual art, or of a copyright or any exclusive right under a copyright, shall not constitute a waiver of the rights conferred by subsection (a). Except as may otherwise be agreed by the author in a written instrument signed by the author, a waiver of the rights conferred by subsection (a) with respect to a work of visual art shall not constitute a transfer of ownership of any copy of that work, or of ownership of a copyright or of any exclusive right under a copyright in that work.

Section 107. Limitations on exclusive rights: Fair use

Notwithstanding the provisions of sections 106 and 106A, the fair use of a copyrighted work, including such use by reproduction in copies or phonorecords or by any other means specified by that section, for purposes such as criticism, comment, news reporting, teaching (including multiple copies for classroom use), scholarship, or research, is not an infringement of copyright. In determining whether the use made of a work in any particular case is a fair use the factors to be considered shall include—

(1) the purpose and character of the use, including whether such use is of a commercial nature or is for nonprofit educational purposes;

(2) the nature of the copyrighted work;

(3) the amount and substantiality of the portion used in relation to the copyrighted work as a whole; and

(4) the effect of the use upon the potential market for or value of the copyrighted work.

The fact that a work is unpublished shall not itself bar a finding of fair use if such finding is made upon consideration of all the above factors.

Section 108. Limitations on exclusive rights: Reproduction by libraries and archives

(a) Except as otherwise provided in this title and notwithstanding the provisions of section 106, it is not an infringement of copyright for a library or archives, or any of its employees acting within the scope of their employment, to reproduce no more than one copy or phonorecord of a work, except as provided in subsections (b) and (c), or to distribute such copy or phonorecord, under the conditions specified by this section, if—

(1) the reproduction or distribution is made without any purpose of direct or indirect commercial advantage;

(2) the collections of the library or archives are (i) open to the public, or (ii) available not only to researchers affiliated with the library or archives or with the institution of which it is a part, but also to other persons doing research in a specialized field; and

(3) the reproduction or distribution of the work includes a notice of copyright that appears on the copy or phonorecord that is reproduced under the provisions of this section, or includes a legend stating that the work may be protected by copyright if no such notice can be found on the copy or phonorecord that is reproduced under the provisions of this section.

(b) The rights of reproduction and distribution under this section apply to three copies or phonorecords of an unpublished work duplicated solely for purposes of preservation and security or for deposit for research use in another library or archives of the type described by clause (2) of subsection (a), if—

(1) the copy or phonorecord reproduced is currently in the collections of the library or archives; and

(2) any such copy or phonorecord that is reproduced in digital format is not otherwise distributed in that format and is not made available to the public in that format outside the premises of the library or archives.

(c) The right of reproduction under this section applies to three copies or phonorecords of a published work duplicated solely for the purpose of replacement of a copy or phonorecord that is damaged, deteriorating, lost, or stolen, or if the existing format in which the work is stored has become obsolete, if—

(1) the library or archives has, after a reasonable effort, determined that an unused replacement cannot be obtained at a fair price; and

(2) any such copy or phonorecord that is reproduced in digital format is not made available to the public in that format outside the premises of the library or archives in lawful possession of such copy.

For purposes of this subsection, a format shall be considered obsolete if the machine or device necessary to render perceptible a work stored in that format is no longer manufactured or is no longer reasonably available in the commercial marketplace.

(d) The rights of reproduction and distribution under this section apply to a copy, made from the collection of a library or archives where the user makes his or her request or from that of another library or archives, of no more than one article or other contribution to a copyrighted collection or periodical issue, or to a copy or phonorecord of a small part of any other copyrighted work, if—

    (1) the copy or phonorecord becomes the property of the user, and the library or archives has had no notice that the copy or phonorecord would be used for any purpose other than private study, scholarship, or research; and

    (2) the library or archives displays prominently, at the place where orders are accepted, and includes on its order form, a warning of copyright in accordance with requirements that the Register of Copyrights shall prescribe by regulation.

(e) The rights of reproduction and distribution under this section apply to the entire work, or to a substantial part of it, made from the collection of a library or archives where the user makes his or her request or from that of another library or archives, if the library or archives has first determined, on the basis of a reasonable investigation, that a copy or phonorecord of the copyrighted work cannot be obtained at a fair price, if—

    (1) the copy or phonorecord becomes the property of the user, and the library or archives has had no notice that the copy or phonorecord would be used for any purpose other than private study, scholarship, or research; and

    (2) the library or archives displays prominently, at the place where orders are accepted, and includes on its order form, a warning of copyright in accordance with requirements that the Register of Copyrights shall prescribe by regulation.

(f) Nothing in this section—

    (1) shall be construed to impose liability for copyright infringement upon a library or archives or its employees for the unsupervised use of reproducing equipment located on its premises: *Provided,* That such equipment displays a notice that the making of a copy may be subject to the copyright law;

    (2) excuses a person who uses such reproducing equipment or who requests a copy or phonorecord under subsection (d) from liability for copyright infringement for any such act, or for any later use of such copy or phonorecord, if it exceeds fair use as provided by section 107;

    (3) shall be construed to limit the reproduction and distribution by lending of a limited number of copies and excerpts by a library or archives of an audiovisual news program, subject to clauses (1), (2), and (3) of subsection (a); or

    (4) in any way affects the right of fair use as provided by section 107, or any contractual obligations assumed at any time by the library or archives when it obtained a copy or phonorecord of a work in its collections.

(g) The rights of reproduction and distribution under this section extend to the isolated and unrelated reproduction or distribution of a single copy or phonorecord of the same material on separate occasions, but do not extend to cases where the library or archives, or its employee—

    (1) is aware or has substantial reason to believe that it is engaging in the related or concerted reproduction or distribution of multiple copies or phonorecords of the same material, whether made on one occasion or over a period of time, and whether intended for aggregate use by one or more individuals or for separate use by the individual members of a group; or

    (2) engages in the systematic reproduction or distribution of single or multiple copies or phonorecords of material described in subsection (d): *Provided,* That nothing in this clause prevents a library or archives from participating in interlibrary arrangements that do not have, as their purpose or effect, that the

library or archives receiving such copies or phonorecords for distribution does so in such aggregate quantities as to substitute for a subscription to or purchase of such work.

(h) (1) For purposes of this section, during the last 20 years of any term of copyright of a published work, a library or archives, including a nonprofit educational institution that functions as such, may reproduce, distribute, display, or perform in facsimile or digital form a copy or phonorecord of such work, or portions thereof, for purposes of preservation, scholarship, or research, if such library or archives has first determined, on the basis of a reasonable investigation, that none of the conditions set forth in subparagraphs (A), (B), and (C) of paragraph (2) apply.

(2) No reproduction, distribution, display, or performance is authorized under this subsection if—

(A) the work is subject to normal commercial exploitation;
(B) a copy or phonorecord of the work can be obtained at a reasonable price; or
(C) the copyright owner or its agent provides notice pursuant to regulations promulgated by the Register of Copyrights that either of the conditions set forth in subparagraphs (A) and (B) applies.

(3) The exemption provided in this subsection does not apply to any subsequent uses by users other than such library or archives.

(i) The rights of reproduction and distribution under this section do not apply to a musical work, a pictorial, graphic or sculptural work, or a motion picture or other audiovisual work other than an audiovisual work dealing with news, except that no such limitation shall apply with respect to rights granted by subsections (b) and (c), or with respect to pictorial or graphic works published as illustrations, diagrams, or similar adjuncts to works of which copies are reproduced or distributed in accordance with subsections (d) and (e).

Section 109. Limitations on exclusive rights: Effect of transfer of particular copy or phonorecord

(a) Notwithstanding the provisions of section 106(3), the owner of a particular copy or phonorecord lawfully made under this title, or any person authorized by such owner, is entitled, without the authority of the copyright owner, to sell or otherwise dispose of the possession of that copy or phonorecord. Notwithstanding the preceding sentence, copies or phonorecords of works subject to restored copyright under section 104A that are manufactured before the date of restoration of copyright or, with respect to reliance parties, before publication or service of notice under section 104A(e), may be sold or otherwise disposed of without the authorization of the owner of the restored copyright for purposes of direct or indirect commercial advantage only during the 12-month period beginning on—

(1) the date of the publication in the Federal Register of the notice of intent filed with the Copyright Office under section 104A(d)(2)(A), or
(2) the date of the receipt of actual notice served under section 104A(d)(2)(B), whichever occurs first.

(b)(1)(A) Notwithstanding the provisions of subsection (a), unless authorized by the owners of copyright in the sound recording or the owner of copyright in a computer program (including any tape, disk, or other medium embodying such program), and in the case of a sound recording in the musical works embodied therein, neither the owner of a particular phonorecord nor any person in possession of a particular copy of a computer program (including any tape, disk, or other medium embodying such program), may, for the purposes of direct or indirect commercial advantage, dispose of, or authorize the disposal of, the possession of that phonorecord or computer program (including any tape, disk, or other medium embodying such program) by rental, lease, or lending, or by any other act or practice in the nature of rental, lease, or lending. Nothing in the preceding sentence shall apply to the rental, lease, or lending of a phonorecord for nonprofit purposes by a nonprofit library or nonprofit educational institution. The transfer of possession of a lawfully made copy of a computer program by a nonprofit educational institution to another nonprofit educational institution or to faculty, staff, and students does not constitute rental, lease, or lending for direct or indirect commercial purposes under this subsection.

(B) This subsection does not apply to—

    (i)   a computer program which is embodied in a machine or product and which cannot be copied during the ordinary operation or use of the machine or product; or

    (ii)   a computer program embodied in or used in conjunction with a limited purpose computer that is designed for playing video games and may be designed for other purposes.

(C) Nothing in this subsection affects any provision of chapter 9 of this title.

(2) (A) Nothing in this subsection shall apply to the lending of a computer program for nonprofit purposes by a nonprofit library, if each copy of a computer program which is lent by such library has affixed to the packaging containing the program a warning of copyright in accordance with requirements that the Register of Copyrights shall prescribe by regulation.

(B) Not later than three years after the date of the enactment of the Computer Software Rental Amendments Act of 1990, and at such times thereafter as the Register of Copyrights considers appropriate, the Register of Copyrights, after consultation with representatives of copyright owners and librarians, shall submit to the Congress a report stating whether this paragraph has achieved its intended purpose of maintaining the integrity of the copyright system while providing nonprofit libraries the capability to fulfill their function. Such report shall advise the Congress as to any information or recommendations that the Register of Copyrights considers necessary to carry out the purposes of this subsection.

(3) Nothing in this subsection shall affect any provision of the antitrust laws. For purposes of the preceding sentence, "antitrust laws" has the meaning given that term in the first section of the Clayton Act and includes section 5 of the Federal Trade Commission Act to the extent that section relates to unfair methods of competition.

(4) Any person who distributes a phonorecord or a copy of a computer program (including any tape, disk, or other medium embodying such program) in violation of paragraph (1) is an infringer of copyright under section 501 of this title and is subject to the remedies set forth in sections 502, 503, 504, 505, and 509. Such violation shall not be a criminal offense under section 506 or cause such person to be subject to the criminal penalties set forth in section 2319 of title 18.

(c) Notwithstanding the provisions of section 106(5), the owner of a particular copy lawfully made under this title, or any person authorized by such owner, is entitled, without the authority of the copyright owner, to display that copy publicly, either directly or by the projection of no more than one image at a time, to viewers present at the place where the copy is located.

(d) The privileges prescribed by subsections (a) and (c) do not, unless authorized by the copyright owner, extend to any person who has acquired possession of the copy or phonorecord from the copyright owner, by rental, lease, loan, or otherwise, without acquiring ownership of it.

(e) Notwithstanding the provisions of sections 106(4) and 106(5), in the case of an electronic audiovisual game intended for use in coin-operated equipment, the owner of a particular copy of such a game lawfully made under this title, is entitled, without the authority of the copyright owner of the game, to publicly perform or display that game in coin-operated equipment, except that this subsection shall not apply to any work of authorship embodied in the audiovisual game if the copyright owner of the electronic audiovisual game is not also the copyright owner of the work of authorship.

Section 110. Limitations on exclusive rights: Exemption of certain performances and displays

Notwithstanding the provisions of section 106, the following are not infringements of copyright:

(1) performance or display of a work by instructors or pupils in the course of face-to-face teaching activities of a nonprofit educational institution, in a classroom or similar place devoted to instruction, unless, in the case of a motion picture or other audiovisual work, the performance, or the display of individual images, is given by means of a copy that was not lawfully made under this title, and that the person responsible for the performance knew or had reason to believe was not lawfully made;

(2) except with respect to a work produced or marketed primarily for performance or display as part of mediated instructional activities transmitted via digital networks, or a performance or display that is given by means of a copy or phonorecord that is not lawfully made and acquired under this title, and the transmitting government body or accredited nonprofit educational institution knew or had reason to believe was not lawfully made and acquired, the performance of a nondramatic literary or musical work or reasonable and limited portions of any other work, or display of a work in an amount comparable to that which is typically displayed in the course of a live classroom session, by or in the course of a transmission, if—

(A) the performance or display is made by, at the direction of, or under the actual supervision of an instructor as an integral part of a class session offered as a regular part of the systematic mediated instructional activities of a governmental body or an accredited nonprofit educational institution;

(B) the performance or display is directly related and of material assistance to the teaching content of the transmission;

(C) the transmission is made solely for, and, to the extent technologically feasible, the reception of such transmission is limited to—

(i) students officially enrolled in the course for which the transmission is made; or

(ii)   officers or employees of governmental bodies as a part of their official duties or employment; and

(D)   the transmitting body or institution—

(i)   institutes policies regarding copyright, provides informational materials to faculty, students, and relevant staff members that accurately describe, and promote compliance with, the laws of the United States relating to copyright, and provides notice to students that materials used in connection with the course may be subject to copyright protection; and

(ii)   in the case of digital transmissions—

(I)   applies technological measures that reasonably prevent—

(aa)   retention of the work in accessible form by recipients of the transmission from the transmitting body or institution for longer than the class session; and

(bb)   unauthorized further dissemination of the work in accessible form by such recipients to others; and

(II)   does not engage in conduct that could reasonably be expected to interfere with technological measures used by copyright owners to prevent such retention or unauthorized further dissemination;

[The remainder of Section 110 creates exceptions, generally allowing performance and displays of works, but only under specific conditions and for specific types of users. Among the users who have the benefit of these provisions are religious organizations, restaurants, horticultural organizations, and blind and handicapped persons. Section 110 continues with the following language, applicable to the Section 110(2) about distance education.—Kenneth D. Crews]

In paragraph (2), the term "mediated instructional activities" with respect to the performance or display of a work by digital transmission under this section refers to activities that use such work as an integral part of the class experience, controlled by or under the actual supervision of the instructor and analogous to the type of performance or display that would take place in a live classroom setting. The term does not refer to activities that use, in 1 or more class sessions of a single course, such works as textbooks, course packs, or other material in any media, copies or phonorecords of which are typically purchased or acquired by the students in higher education for their independent use and retention or are typically purchased or acquired for elementary and secondary students for their possession and independent use.

For purposes of paragraph (2), accreditation—

(A)   with respect to an institution providing post-secondary education, shall be as determined by a regional or national accrediting agency recognized by the Council on Higher Education Accreditation or the United States Department of Education; and

(B)   with respect to an institution providing elementary or secondary education, shall be as recognized by the applicable state certification or licensing procedures.

For purposes of paragraph (2), no governmental body or accredited nonprofit educational institution shall be liable for infringement by reason of the transient or temporary storage of material carried out through the automatic technical process of a digital transmission of the performance or display of that material as authorized under paragraph (2). No such material stored on the system or network controlled or operated by the transmitting body or institution under this paragraph shall be maintained on such system or network in a manner ordinarily accessible to anyone other than anticipated recipients. No such copy shall be maintained on the system or network in a manner ordinarily accessible to such anticipated recipients for a longer period than is reasonably necessary to facilitate the transmissions for which it was made.

Section 121. Limitations on exclusive rights: Reproduction for blind or other people with disabilities

(a) Notwithstanding the provisions of section 106, it is not an infringement of copyright for an authorized entity to reproduce or to distribute in the United States copies or phonorecords of a previously published, literary work or of a previously published musical work that has been fixed in the form of text or notation if such copies or phonorecords are reproduced or distributed in accessible formats exclusively for use by eligible persons.

(b) (1) Copies or phonorecords to which this section applies shall—

    (A) not be reproduced or distributed in the United States in a format other than an accessible format exclusively for use by eligible persons;

    (B) bear a notice that any further reproduction or distribution in a format other than an accessible format is an infringement; and

    (C) include a copyright notice identifying the copyright owner and the date of the original publication.

  (2) The provisions of this subsection shall not apply to standardized, secure, or norm-referenced tests and related testing material, or to computer programs, except the portions thereof that are in conventional human language (including descriptions of pictorial works) and displayed to users in the ordinary course of using the computer programs.

(c) Notwithstanding the provisions of section 106, it is not an infringement of copyright for a publisher of print instructional materials for use in elementary or secondary schools to create and distribute to the National Instructional Materials Access Center copies of the electronic files described in sections 612(a)(23)(C), 613(a)(6), and section 674(e) of the Individuals with Disabilities Education Act that contain the contents of print instructional materials using the National Instructional Material Accessibility Standard (as defined in section 674(e)(3) of that Act), if—

  (1) the inclusion of the contents of such print instructional materials is required by any State educational agency or local educational agency;

  (2) the publisher had the right to publish such print instructional materials in print formats; and

  (3) such copies are used solely for reproduction or distribution of the contents of such print instructional materials in accessible formats.

(d) For purposes of this section, the term—

  (1) "accessible format" means an alternative manner or form that gives an eligible person access to the work when the copy or phonorecord in the accessible format is used exclusively by the eligible person to permit him or her to have access as feasibly and comfortably as a person without such disability as described in paragraph (3);

  (2) "authorized entity" means a nonprofit organization or a governmental agency that has a primary mission to provide specialized services relating to training,

education, or adaptive reading or information access needs of blind or other persons with disabilities;

(3) "eligible person" means an individual who, regardless of any other disability—

   (A) is blind;
   (B) has a visual impairment or perceptual or reading disability that cannot be improved to give visual function substantially equivalent to that of a person who has no such impairment or disability and so is unable to read printed works to substantially the same degree as a person without an impairment or disability; or
   (C) is otherwise unable, through physical disability, to hold or manipulate a book or to focus or move the eyes to the extent that would be normally acceptable for reading; and

(4) "print instructional materials" has the meaning given under section 674(e)(3)(C) of the Individuals with Disabilities Education Act.

Section 121A. Limitations on exclusive rights: Reproduction for blind or other people with disabilities in Marrakesh Treaty countries

(a) Notwithstanding the provisions of sections 106 and 602, it is not an infringement of copyright for an authorized entity, acting pursuant to this section, to export copies or phonorecords of a previously published literary work or of a previously published musical work that has been fixed in the form of text or notation in accessible formats to another country when the exportation is made either to—

(1) an authorized entity located in a country that is a Party to the Marrakesh Treaty; or
(2) an eligible person in a country that is a Party to the Marrakesh Treaty,

if prior to the exportation of such copies or phonorecords, the authorized entity engaged in the exportation did not know or have reasonable grounds to know that the copies or phonorecords would be used other than by eligible persons.

(b) Notwithstanding the provisions of sections 106 and 602, it is not an infringement of copyright for an authorized entity or an eligible person, or someone acting on behalf of an eligible person, acting pursuant to this section, to import copies or phonorecords of a previously published literary work or of a previously published musical work that has been fixed in the form of text or notation in accessible formats.

(c) In conducting activities under subsection (a) or (b), an authorized entity shall establish and follow its own practices, in keeping with its particular circumstances, to—

(1) establish that the persons the authorized entity serves are eligible persons;
(2) limit to eligible persons and authorized entities the distribution of accessible format copies by the authorized entity;
(3) discourage the reproduction and distribution of unauthorized copies;
(4) maintain due care in, and records of, the handling of copies of works by the authorized entity, while respecting the privacy of eligible persons on an equal basis with others; and
(5) facilitate effective cross-border exchange of accessible format copies by making publicly available—

    (A) the titles of works for which the authorized entity has accessible format copies or phonorecords and the specific accessible formats in which they are available; and

    (B) information on the policies, practices, and authorized entity partners of the authorized entity for the cross-border exchange of accessible format copies.

(d) Nothing in this section shall be construed to establish—

    (1) a cause of action under this title; or

    (2) a basis for regulation by any Federal agency.

(e) Nothing in this section shall be construed to limit the ability to engage in any activity otherwise permitted under this title.

(f) For purposes of this section—

    (1) the terms "accessible format", "authorized entity", and "eligible person" have the meanings given those terms in section 121; and

    (2) the term "Marrakesh Treaty" means the Marrakesh Treaty to Facilitate Access to Published Works by Visually Impaired Persons and Persons with Print Disabilities concluded at Marrakesh, Morocco, on June 28, 2013.

Section 504. Remedies for infringement: Damages and profits

(a) In General.—Except as otherwise provided by this title, an infringer of copyright is liable for either—

    (1) the copyright owner's actual damages and any additional profits of the infringer, as provided by subsection (b); or

    (2) statutory damages, as provided by subsection (c).

(b) Actual Damages and Profits.—The copyright owner is entitled to recover the actual damages suffered by him or her as a result of the infringement, and any profits of the infringer that are attributable to the infringement and are not taken into account in computing the actual damages. In establishing the infringer's profits, the copyright owner is required to present proof only of the infringer's gross revenue, and the infringer is required to prove his or her deductible expenses and the elements of profit attributable to factors other than the copyrighted work.

(c) Statutory Damages.—

    (1) Except as provided by clause (2) of this subsection, the copyright owner may elect, at any time before final judgment is rendered, to recover, instead of actual damages and profits, an award of statutory damages for all infringements involved in the action, with respect to any one work, for which any one infringer is liable individually, or for which any two or more infringers are liable jointly and severally, in a sum of not less than $750 or more than $30,000 as the court considers just. For the purposes of this subsection, all the parts of a compilation or derivative work constitute one work.

    (2) In a case where the copyright owner sustains the burden of proving, and the court finds, that infringement was committed willfully, the court in its discretion may increase the award of statutory damages to a sum of not more than $150,000. In a case where the infringer sustains the burden of proving, and the court finds, that such infringer was not aware and had no reason to

believe that his or her acts constituted an infringement of copyright, the court in its discretion may reduce the award of statutory damages to a sum of not less than $200. The court shall remit statutory damages in any case where an infringer believed and had reasonable grounds for believing that his or her use of the copyrighted work was a fair use under section 107, if the infringer was: (i) an employee or agent of a nonprofit educational institution, library, or archives acting within the scope of his or her employment who, or such institution, library, or archives itself, which infringed by reproducing the work in copies or phonorecords; or (ii) a public broadcasting entity which or a person who, as a regular part of the nonprofit activities of a public broadcasting entity (as defined in subsection (g) of section 118) infringed by performing a published nondramatic literary work or by reproducing a transmission program embodying a performance of such a work.

Section 1201. Circumvention of copyright protection systems

(a) Violations Regarding Circumvention of Technological Measures.—

(1) (A) No person shall circumvent a technological measure that effectively controls access to a work protected under this title. The prohibition contained in the preceding sentence shall take effect at the end of the 2-year period beginning on the date of the enactment of this chapter.

(B) The prohibition contained in subparagraph (A) shall not apply to persons who are users of a copyrighted work which is in a particular class of works, if such persons are, or are likely to be in the succeeding 3-year period, adversely affected by virtue of such prohibition in their ability to make noninfringing uses of that particular class of works under this title, as determined under subparagraph (C).

[Section 1201 continues with details about the authority of the Librarian of Congress to create exceptions to the anticircumvention provision. The statute also includes lengthy and elaborate statutory exceptions, some of which are examined in the text of this book.—*Kenneth D. Crews*]

Section 1401. Unauthorized use of pre-1972 sound recordings

(a) In General.—

(1) Unauthorized Acts.—Anyone who, on or before the last day of the applicable transition period under paragraph (2), and without the consent of the rights owner, engages in covered activity with respect to a sound recording fixed before February 15, 1972, shall be subject to the remedies provided in sections 502 through 505 and 1203 to the same extent as an infringer of copyright or a person that engages in unauthorized activity under chapter 12.

(2) Term of Prohibition.—

(A) In General.—The prohibition under paragraph (1)—

(i) subject to clause (ii), shall apply to a sound recording described in that paragraph—
(I) through December 31 of the year that is 95 years after the year of first publication; and
(II) for a further transition period as prescribed under subparagraph (B)

of this paragraph; and

    (ii)   shall not apply to any sound recording after February 15, 2067.

  (B) Transition Periods.—

    (i)   Pre-1923 Recordings.—In the case of a sound recording first published before January 1, 1923, the transition period described in subparagraph (A)(i)(II) shall end on December 31 of the year that is 3 years after the date of enactment of this section.

    (ii)   1923–1946 Recordings.—In the case of a sound recording first published during the period beginning on January 1, 1923, and ending on December 31, 1946, the transition period described in subparagraph (A)(i)(II) shall end on the date that is 5 years after the last day of the period described in subparagraph (A)(i)(I).

    (iii)   1947–1956 Recordings.—In the case of a sound recording first published during the period beginning on January 1, 1947, and ending on December 31, 1956, the transition period described in subparagraph (A)(i)(II) shall end on the date that is 15 years after the last day of the period described in subparagraph (A)(i)(I).

    (iv)   Post-1956 Recordings.—In the case of a sound recording fixed before February 15, 1972, that is not described in clause (i), (ii), or (iii), the transition period described in subparagraph (A)(i)(II) shall end on February 15, 2067.

  (3) Rule of Construction.—For the purposes of this subsection, the term "anyone" includes any State, any instrumentality of a State, and any officer or employee of a State or instrumentality of a State acting in the official capacity of the officer or employee, as applicable.

(b) Certain Authorized Transmissions and Reproductions.—A public performance by means of a digital audio transmission of a sound recording fixed before February 15, 1972, or a reproduction in an ephemeral phonorecord or copy of a sound recording fixed before February 15, 1972, shall, for purposes of subsection (a), be considered to be authorized and made with the consent of the rights owner if—

  (1) the transmission or reproduction would satisfy the requirements for statutory licensing under section 112(e)(1) or section 114(d)(2), or would be exempt under section 114(d)(1), as the case may be, if the sound recording were fixed on or after February 15, 1972; and

  (2) the transmitting entity pays the statutory royalty for the transmission or reproduction pursuant to the rates and terms adopted under sections 112(e) and 114(f), and complies with other obligations, in the same manner as required by regulations adopted by the Copyright Royalty Judges under sections 112(e) and 114(f) for sound recordings that are fixed on or after February 15, 1972, except in the case of a transmission that would be exempt under section 114(d)(1).

(c) Certain Noncommercial Uses of Sound Recordings That Are Not Being Commercially Exploited.—

  (1) In General.—Noncommercial use of a sound recording fixed before February 15, 1972, that is not being commercially exploited by or under the authority of the rights owner shall not violate subsection (a) if—

    (A) the person engaging in the noncommercial use, in order to determine whether the sound recording is being commercially exploited by or under the authority of the rights owner, makes a good faith, reasonable search for, but does not find, the sound recording—

(i)   in the records of schedules filed in the Copyright Office as described in subsection (f)(5)(A); and

(ii)   on services offering a comprehensive set of sound recordings for sale or streaming;

(B)   the person engaging in the noncommercial use files a notice identifying the sound recording and the nature of the use in the Copyright Office in accordance with the regulations issued under paragraph (3)(B); and

(C)   during the 90-day period beginning on the date on which the notice described in subparagraph (B) is indexed into the public records of the Copyright Office, the rights owner of the sound recording does not, in its discretion, opt out of the noncommercial use by filing notice thereof in the Copyright Office in accordance with the regulations issued under paragraph (5).

(2) Rules of Construction.—For purposes of this subsection—

(A)   merely recovering costs of production and distribution of a sound recording resulting from a use otherwise permitted under this subsection does not itself necessarily constitute a commercial use of the sound recording;

(B)   the fact that a person engaging in the use of a sound recording also engages in commercial activities does not itself necessarily render the use commercial; and

(C)   the fact that a person files notice of a noncommercial use of a sound recording in accordance with the regulations issued under paragraph (3)(B) does not itself affect any limitation on the exclusive rights of a copyright owner described in section 107, 108, 109, 110, or 112(f) as applied to a claim under subsection (a) of this section pursuant to subsection (f)(1)(A) of this section.

(3) Notice of Covered Activity.—Not later than 180 days after the date of enactment of this section, the Register of Copyrights shall issue regulations that—

(A)   provide specific, reasonable steps that, if taken by a filer, are sufficient to constitute a good faith, reasonable search under paragraph (1)(A) to determine whether a recording is being commercially exploited, including the services that satisfy the good faith, reasonable search requirement under paragraph (1)(A) for purposes of the safe harbor described in paragraph (4)(A); and

(B)   establish the form, content, and procedures for the filing of notices under paragraph (1)(B).

(4) Safe Harbor.—

(A)   In General.—A person engaging in a noncommercial use of a sound recording otherwise permitted under this subsection who establishes that the person made a good faith, reasonable search under paragraph (1)(A) without finding commercial exploitation of the sound recording by or under the authority of the rights owner shall not be found to be in violation of subsection (a).

    (B) Steps Sufficient but Not Necessary.—Taking the specific, reasonable steps identified by the Register of Copyrights in the regulations issued under paragraph (3)(A) shall be sufficient, but not necessary, for a filer to satisfy the requirement to conduct a good faith, reasonable search under paragraph (1)(A) for purposes of subparagraph (A) of this paragraph.

(5) Opting Out of Covered Activity.—

    (A) In General.—Not later than 180 days after the date of enactment of this section, the Register of Copyrights shall issue regulations establishing the form, content, and procedures for the rights owner of a sound recording that is the subject of a notice under paragraph (1)(B) to, in its discretion, file notice opting out of the covered activity described in the notice under paragraph (1)(B) during the 90-day period beginning on the date on which the notice under paragraph (1)(B) is indexed into the public records of the Copyright Office.

    (B) Rule of Construction.—The fact that a rights holder opts out of a noncommercial use of a sound recording by filing notice thereof in the Copyright Office in accordance with the regulations issued under subparagraph (A) does not itself enlarge or diminish any limitation on the exclusive rights of a copyright owner described in section 107, 108, 109, 110, or 112(f) as applied to a claim under subsection (a) of this section pursuant to subsection (f)(1)(A) of this section.

(6) Civil Penalties for Certain Acts.—

    (A) Filing of Notices of Noncommercial Use.—Any person who willfully engages in a pattern or practice of filing a notice of noncommercial use of a sound recording as described in paragraph (1)(B) fraudulently describing the use proposed, or knowing that the use proposed is not permitted under this subsection, shall be assessed a civil penalty in an amount that is not less than $250, and not more than $1000, for each such notice, in addition to any other remedies that may be available under this title based on the actual use made.

    (B) Filing of Opt-Out Notices.—

        (i)   In General.—Any person who files an opt-out notice as described in paragraph (1)(C), knowing that the person is not the rights owner or authorized to act on behalf of the rights owner of the sound recording to which the notice pertains, shall be assessed a civil penalty in an amount not less than $250, and not more than $1,000, for each such notice.

        (ii) Pattern or Practice.—Any person who engages in a pattern or practice of making filings as described in clause (i) shall be assessed a civil penalty in an amount not less than $10,000 for each such filing.

    (C) Definition.—For purposes of this paragraph, the term "knowing"—

        (i)   does not require specific intent to defraud; and

        (ii) with respect to information about ownership of the sound recording in question, means that the person—

            (I) has actual knowledge of the information;

(II)   acts in deliberate ignorance of the truth or falsity of the information; or

(III) acts in grossly negligent disregard of the truth or falsity of the information.

[Section 1401(d) details the licensing of public performances of pre-1972 sound recordings, including payments to collective licensing organizations.—*Kenneth D. Crews*]

(e) Preemption with Respect to Certain Past Acts.—

(1) In General.—This section preempts any claim of common law copyright or equivalent right under the laws of any State arising from a digital audio transmission or reproduction that is made before the date of enactment of this section of a sound recording fixed before February 15, 1972, if—

(A) the digital audio transmission would have satisfied the requirements for statutory licensing under section 114(d)(2) or been exempt under section 114(d)(1), or the reproduction would have satisfied the requirements of section 112(e)(1), as the case may be, if the sound recording were fixed on or after February 15, 1972; and

(B) either—

(i)   except in the case of a transmission that would have been exempt under section 114(d)(1), not later than 270 days after the date of enactment of this section, the transmitting entity pays statutory royalties and provides notice of the use of the relevant sound recordings in the same manner as required by regulations adopted by the Copyright Royalty Judges for sound recordings that are fixed on or after February 15, 1972, for all the digital audio transmissions and reproductions satisfying the requirements for statutory licensing under sections 112(e)(1) and 114(d)(2) during the 3 years before that date of enactment; or

(ii) an agreement voluntarily negotiated between the rights owner and the entity performing the sound recording (including a litigation settlement agreement entered into before the date of enactment of this section) authorizes or waives liability for any such transmission or reproduction and the transmitting entity has paid for and reported such digital audio transmission under that agreement.

(2) Rule of Construction for Common Law Copyright.—For purposes of paragraph (1), a claim of common law copyright or equivalent right under the laws of any State includes a claim that characterizes conduct subject to that paragraph as an unlawful distribution, act of record piracy, or similar violation.

(3) Rule of Construction for Public Performance Rights.—Nothing in this section may be construed to recognize or negate the existence of public performance rights in sound recordings under the laws of any State.

(f) Limitations on Remedies.—

(1) Fair Use; Uses by Libraries, Archives, and Educational Institutions.—

(A) In General.—The limitations on the exclusive rights of a copyright owner described in sections 107, 108, 109, 110, and 112(f) shall apply to a claim under subsection (a) with respect to a sound recording fixed before February 15, 1972.

(B) Rule of Construction for Section 108(h).—With respect to the application of section 108(h) to a claim under subsection (a) with respect to a sound recording fixed before February 15, 1972, the phrase "during the last 20 years of any term of copyright of a published work" in such section 108(h) shall be construed to mean at any time after the date of enactment of this section.

(2) Actions.—The limitations on actions described in section 507 shall apply to a claim under subsection (a) with respect to a sound recording fixed before February 15, 1972.

(3) Material Online.—Section 512 shall apply to a claim under subsection (a) with respect to a sound recording fixed before February 15, 1972.

(4) Principles of Equity.—Principles of equity apply to remedies for a violation of this section to the same extent as such principles apply to remedies for infringement of copyright.

(5) Filing Requirement for Statutory Damages and Attorneys' Fees.—

   (A) Filing of Information on Sound Recordings.—

      (i) Filing Requirement.—Except in the case of a transmitting entity that has filed contact information for that transmitting entity under subparagraph (B), in any action under this section, an award of statutory damages or of attorneys' fees under section 504 or 505 may be made with respect to an unauthorized use of a sound recording under subsection (a) only if—

         (I) the rights owner has filed with the Copyright Office a schedule that specifies the title, artist, and rights owner of the sound recording and contains such other information, as practicable, as the Register of Copyrights prescribes by regulation; and

         (II) the use occurs after the end of the 90-day period beginning on the date on which the information described in subclause (I) is indexed into the public records of the Copyright Office.

      (ii) Regulations.—Not later than 180 days after the date of enactment of this section, the Register of Copyrights shall issue regulations that—

         (I) establish the form, content, and procedures for the filing of schedules under clause (i);

         (II) provide that a person may request that the person receive timely notification of a filing described in subclause (I); and

         (III) set forth the manner in which a person may make a request under subclause (II).

   (B) Filing of Contact Information for Transmitting Entities.—

      (i) Filing Requirement.—Not later than 30 days after the date of enactment of this section, the Register of Copyrights shall issue regulations establishing the form, content, and procedures for the filing of contact information by any entity that, as of the date of enactment of this section, performs a sound recording fixed before February 15, 1972, by means of a digital audio transmission.

(ii)   Time Limit on Filings.—The Register of Copyrights may accept filings under clause (i) only until the 180th day after the date of enactment of this section.

(iii) Limitation on Statutory Damages and Attorneys' Fees.—

   (I)   Limitation.—An award of statutory damages or of attorneys' fees under section 504 or 505 may not be made against an entity that has filed contact information for that entity under clause (i) with respect to an unauthorized use by that entity of a sound recording under subsection (a) if the use occurs before the end of the 90-day period beginning on the date on which the entity receives a notice that—

      (aa) is sent by or on behalf of the rights owner of the sound recording;

      (bb) states that the entity is not legally authorized to use that sound recording under subsection (a); and

      (cc) identifies the sound recording in a schedule conforming to the requirements prescribed by the regulations issued under subparagraph (A)(ii).

   (II) Undeliverable Notices.—In any case in which a notice under subclause (I) is sent to an entity by mail or courier service and the notice is returned to the sender because the entity either is no longer located at the address provided in the contact information filed under clause (i) or has refused to accept delivery, or the notice is sent by electronic mail and is undeliverable, the 90-day period under subclause (I) shall begin on the date of the attempted delivery.

(C) Section 412.—Section 412 shall not limit an award of statutory damages under section 504(c) or attorneys' fees under section 505 with respect to a covered activity in violation of subsection (a).

(6) Applicability of Other Provisions.—

(A) In General.—Subject to subparagraph (B), no provision of this title shall apply to or limit the remedies available under this section except as otherwise provided in this section.

(B) Applicability of Definitions.—Any term used in this section that is defined in section 101 shall have the meaning given that term in section 101.

(g) Application of Section 230 Safe Harbor.—For purposes of section 230 of the Communications Act of 1934 (47 U.S.C. 230), subsection (a) shall be considered to be a "law pertaining to intellectual property" under subsection (e)(2) of such section 230.

(h) Application to Rights Owners.—

(1) Transfers.—With respect to a rights owner described in subsection (l)(2)(B)—

(A) subsections (d) and (e) of section 201 and section 204 shall apply to a transfer described in subsection (l)(2)(B) to the same extent as with respect to a transfer of copyright ownership; and

(B) notwithstanding section 411, that rights owner may institute an action with respect to a violation of this section to the same extent as the owner of an exclusive right under a copyright may institute an action under section 501(b).

(2) Application of Other Provisions.—The following provisions shall apply to a rights owner under this section to the same extent as any copyright owner:

(A) Section 112(e)(2).
(B) Section 112(e)(7).
(C) Section 114(e).
(D) Section 114(h).

(i) Ephemeral Recordings.—An authorized reproduction made under this section shall be subject to section 112(g) to the same extent as a reproduction of a sound recording fixed on or after February 15, 1972.

(j) Rule of Construction.—A rights owner of, or featured recording artist who performs on, a sound recording under this chapter shall be deemed to be an interested copyright party, as defined in section 1001, to the same extent as a copyright owner or featured recording artist under chapter 10.

(k) Treatment of States and State Instrumentalities, Officers, and Employees.—Any State, and any instrumentality, officer, or employee described in subsection (a)(3), shall be subject to the provisions of this section in the same manner and to the same extent as any nongovernmental entity.

(l) Definitions.—In this section:

(1) Covered Activity.—The term "covered activity" means any activity that the copyright owner of a sound recording would have the exclusive right to do or authorize under section 106 or 602, or that would violate section 1201 or 1202, if the sound recording were fixed on or after February 15, 1972.

(2) Rights Owner.—The term "rights owner" means—

(A) the person that has the exclusive right to reproduce a sound recording under the laws of any State, as of the day before the date of enactment of this section; or

(B) any person to which a right to enforce a violation of this section may be transferred, in whole or in part, after the date of enactment of this section, under—

(i) subsections (d) and (e) of section 201; and
(ii) section 204.

APPENDIX B

COPYRIGHT CHECKLIST: FAIR USE

INTRODUCTION

This checklist for fair use is intended to serve two fundamental purposes. First, it should help educators, librarians, and others to focus on factual circumstances that are important to the evaluation of fair use as it may apply in a given set of circumstances. A reasonable fair use analysis is based on four factors set forth in the fair use provision of copyright law, Section 107 of the U.S. Copyright Act. The application of those factors depends on the particular facts of your situation; changing one or more facts may alter the outcome of the analysis. The checklist is based on the four factors and judicial decisions interpreting and applying them.

A second purpose of the checklist is to provide an important means for recording your decision-making process. Maintaining a record of your fair use analysis could be critical to establishing your reasonable and good faith attempts to apply fair use to meet your educational objectives. Section 504(c)(2) of the U.S. Copyright Act offers some protection for educators and librarians who act in good faith. Once you have completed your application of fair use to a particular need, keep your completed checklist in your files for future reference.

As you use the checklist and apply it to your situation, you might often check more than one box in each column and even check boxes across columns. Some checked boxes will *favor fair use*, and others may *oppose fair use*. A key concern is whether you are acting reasonably in checking any given box; the ultimate concern is whether the cumulative weight of the factors favors or opposes fair use. The checklist is a guide; you still need to bring your knowledge and reasonable perspective to the task.

The checklist for fair use originated in 1998 as a task undertaken by Kenneth Crews, while then on the faculty of Indiana University, working closely with Dwayne Buttler in the university's Copyright Management Center. Since then, many colleges, universities, libraries, primary and secondary schools, companies, governmental organizations, and others have adopted and used it. Some users have accepted it without change; others have revised and adapted it to distinct needs. The version here is revised in small measure from the original. As with all advice and information about fair use, you should look closely at whether it serves your particular needs and whether you should make any changes.

COPYRIGHT CHECKLIST: FAIR USE

Name: _____ Date: _____ Project: _____

Institution: _____ Prepared by: _____

PURPOSE

Favoring Fair Use

- ☐ Teaching (including multiple copies for classroom use)
- ☐ Research
- ☐ Scholarship
- ☐ Nonprofit educational institution
- ☐ Criticism
- ☐ Comment
- ☐ News reporting
- ☐ Transformative use
  (alters the original work in a creative manner)
- ☐ Transformative use
  (uses the work for a purpose other than the original purpose)
- ☐ Restricted access (for only students or other appropriate group)
- ☐ Parody

Opposing Fair Use

- ☐ Commercial activity
- ☐ Profiting from the use
- ☐ Straight reproduction (copying without modification)
- ☐ Nontransformative use
- ☐ Entertainment
- ☐ Bad-faith behavior
- ☐ Denying credit to original author

NATURE

Favoring Fair Use

- ☐ Published work
- ☐ Factual or nonfiction based
- ☐ Important to favored educational objectives

Opposing Fair Use

- ☐ Unpublished work
- ☐ Highly creative work (art, music, novels, films, plays)
- ☐ Fiction
- ☐ Consumable work (e.g., worksheets and standard exam forms)

AMOUNT

Favoring Fair Use

- ☐ Small quantity
- ☐ Portion used is not central or significant to entire work
- ☐ Amount is tailored to meet the educational or other favored purpose

Opposing Fair Use

- ☐ Large portion or whole work used beyond the favored purpose
- ☐ Portion used could interfere with a reasonable market for the use (e.g., multiple chapters from a single book)
- ☐ Portion used is central to work or "heart of the work"

EFFECT

Favoring Fair Use

- ☐ User owns lawfully acquired or purchased copy of original work
- ☐ Few or modest number of copies made
- ☐ No significant effect on the market or potential market for copyrighted work
- ☐ No similar product marketed by the copyright holder
- ☐ Lack of a reasonable licensing mechanism for the work and the intended use

Opposing Fair Use

- ☐ Straight copying that is not transformative
- ☐ Portion used could interfere with a reasonable market for the use or derivatives (e.g., multiple chapters from a single book)
- ☐ Reasonably available licensing mechanism for the use of the copyrighted work
- ☐ Affordable permission available for using work
- ☐ Numerous copies made
- ☐ Posted to the Internet or otherwise made widely accessible
- ☐ Repeated or long-term use

APPENDIX C

COPYRIGHT CHECKLIST:
THE TEACH ACT AND DISTANCE EDUCATION

THE TECHNOLOGY, EDUCATION and Copyright Harmonization Act of 2002, better known as the TEACH Act, brought the enactment of a statutory provision allowing educators to use copyrighted works in distance education. The statute, Section 110(2) of the U.S. Copyright Act, carves out an exception to the rights of copyright owners, and it is sharply limited in many ways in order to protect the interests of rightsholders. In order to apply the TEACH Act, educators must meet several requirements. The responsibilities created by the TEACH Act will most likely be distributed among different persons or groups within any one educational institution, and this checklist should be used as an aid to organize and ensure complete compliance with the TEACH Act for each copyrighted work included in the distance education transmission. All requirements must be satisfied in order to fit uses within this statute.

The statute anticipates that the performances and displays may be original or even live uses of existing works. For example, the instructional content may include live concert recitals or poetry readings. The performances and displays may also be made from existing versions. For example, the content might include a clip from a motion picture or from a recorded performance of a musical work. In copyright parlance, a *phonorecord* is the material object or physical embodiment of the recording of sounds. Within the stated limits, the TEACH Act allows uses of copyrighted phonorecords, and the Music Modernization Act of 2018 explicitly applied Section 110(2) to pre-1972 sound recordings that are subject to the new form of legal protection.

If any particular use does not fit the requirements of the TEACH Act, educators may still pursue possibilities under fair use or other exceptions in the copyright law, or they may obtain permission or a license from the copyright owner.

Please complete and retain a copy of this form in connection with each copyrighted work considered for your distance education course.

Your Name: _____

Educational Institution: _____

Course or Project: _____

Today's Date: _____

Prepared by: _____

I. TEACH ACT REQUIREMENTS THAT ARE LIKELY THE RESPONSIBILITY OF INSTRUCTORS

☐ (A) The transmission is of any of the following:

- a performance of a nondramatic literary work; or
- a performance of a nondramatic musical work; or
- a performance of any other work, including dramatic works and audiovisual works, but only in "reasonable and limited portions"; or
- a display in an amount comparable to that which is typically displayed in the course of a live classroom session.

☐ (B) The work is not marketed primarily for performance or display as part of a digitally transmitted mediated instructional activity.

☐ (C) The work to be used is not a textbook, coursepack, or other material in any media, copies or phonorecords of which are typically purchased or acquired by students for their independent use and retention.

☐ (D) The performance or display is:

- made by, at the direction of, or under the actual supervision of an instructor "as an integral part of a class session offered as a regular part of the systematic mediated instructional activities" of the institution; and
- directly related and of material assistance to the teaching content of the transmission; and
- an integral part of a class session offered as a regular part of the "systematic mediated instructional activities" of the institution.

☐ (E) The performance or display is given by means of a copy or phonorecord that was not lawfully made and acquired under U.S. copyright law, and the institution knows or has reason to believe that it was not lawfully made and acquired.

☐ (F) If the work to be used is to be converted from print or another analog version to digital format:

- the amount of the work converted is no greater than the amount that can lawfully be used for the course; and
- no digital version of the work is available to the institution, or the digital version available to the institution has technological protection that prevents its lawful use for the course.

II. TEACH ACT REQUIREMENTS THAT ARE LIKELY THE RESPONSIBILITY OF THE INSTITUTION

☐ (A) The institution for which the work is transmitted is an accredited nonprofit educational institution or is a governmental body.

☐ (B) The institution has instituted policies regarding copyright.

☐ (C) The institution has provided information materials to faculty, students, and relevant staff members that describe and promote U.S. copyright laws.

☐ (D) The institution has provided notice to students that materials used in connection with the course may be subject to copyright protection.

☐ (E) The transmission of the content is made "solely for . . . students officially enrolled in the course for which the transmission is made," and to the extent technologically feasible, the reception of such transmission is limited to such students.

☐ (F) The transmission may also be made by a governmental body "solely for . . . officers or employees of governmental bodies as a part of their official duties or employment," and to the extent technologically feasible, the reception of such transmission is limited to such officers or employees.

III. TEACH ACT REQUIREMENTS THAT ARE LIKELY THE RESPONSIBILITY OF INFORMATION TECHNOLOGISTS

☐ (A) Technological measures have been taken to reasonably prevent:

- retention of the work in accessible form by students for longer than the class session; and

- unauthorized further dissemination of the work in accessible form by such recipients to others.

☐ (B) The institution has not engaged in conduct that could reasonably be expected to interfere with technological measures used by copyright owners to prevent retention or dissemination of their works.

☐ (C) The materials will be stored on a system or network in a manner that is ordinarily not accessible to anyone other than anticipated recipients.

☐ (D) The materials will be maintained on the system or network in a manner ordinarily accessible for a period no longer than is reasonably necessary to facilitate the transmissions for which they were made.

☐ (E) Any copies or phonorecords made for the purpose of transmitting the work are retained and used solely by the institution for purposes of Section 110(2).

APPENDIX D

COPYRIGHT CHECKLIST FOR LIBRARIES: COPIES FOR PRESERVATION OR REPLACEMENT

THIS CHECKLIST APPLIES to the reproduction of a copyrighted work by a library or archives for the purpose of replacement of a published work or for preservation or security of an unpublished work. It is principally an articulation of the elements of Sections 108(b) and 108(c) of the U.S. Copyright Act. Upon meeting the following requirements, the library or archives may make up to three (3) copies or phonorecords of a work. In copyright parlance, a *phonorecord* is the material object or physical embodiment of the recording of sounds. Within the stated limits, Section 108 allows some uses of copyrighted phonorecords, and the Music Modernization Act of 2018 explicitly extends Section 108 to uses of pre-1972 sound recordings that are subject to the new form of legal protection.

The copies are to become part of the library collection; this checklist therefore does not apply to making copies from the collection for an individual user to keep. The person making the copy at the library or archives should complete and retain this checklist to document compliance with Section 108 of the U.S. Copyright Act. If the library or archives finds that the planned copying does not fit the requirements of Section 108, the institution may still pursue possibilities under fair use or another exception in the copyright law, or it may obtain permission or a license from the copyright owner.

Library or Archives: _____ Date: _____

Citation or Description of Materials Copied: _____

_____

REQUIREMENTS OF THE LIBRARY OR ARCHIVES

☐   (1) The collection of the library or archives meets one of the following descriptions: (a) It is open to the public; or (b) It is available not only to researchers affiliated with the institution, but also to others doing research in a specialized field.

☐   (2) The reproduction must not be made with any purpose of direct or indirect commercial advantage.

☐   (3) The reproduction must include one of the following copyright notices: (a) The copyright notice appearing on the original work to be copied; or (b) If no such notice can be found on the work to be copied, a legend stating that the work may be protected by copyright law.

REQUIREMENTS OF AN UNPUBLISHED WORK TO BE COPIED

☐   (4) The work is reproduced for one of the following purposes: (a) Solely for preservation and security; or (b) Deposit for research use in another library or archives fitting the description of Item 1 of this checklist.

☐   (5) The work to be copied is currently in the collections of the library or archives making the reproduction.

☐   (6) Copies or phonorecords made in digital format are not made available to the public in that format outside the premises of the library or archives (other than the copy that may be deposited in another library—see Item 4(a) of this checklist).

REQUIREMENTS OF A PUBLISHED WORK TO BE COPIED

☐   (7) The work is reproduced in order to replace a work that is:

▪   damaged; or

▪   deteriorating; or

▪   lost; or

▪   stolen; or

▪   in a format that has become obsolete. A format is considered obsolete if the machine or device necessary to view the work stored in that format is no longer manufactured or reasonably available in the commercial marketplace.

☐   (8) The library or archives has, after a reasonable effort, determined that an unused replacement cannot be obtained at a fair price.

☐   (9) Copies or phonorecords made in digital format are not made available to the public in that format outside the library or archives premises.

APPENDIX E

COPYRIGHT CHECKLIST FOR LIBRARIES: COPIES FOR PRIVATE STUDY

THIS CHECKLIST APPLIES to the reproduction of a copyrighted work by a library or archives for purposes of giving that copy to an individual user. It is principally an articulation of the elements of Sections 108(d) and 108(e) of the U.S. Copyright Act. If all requirements are met, the library or archives may lawfully make a single copy or phonorecord of a work to fulfill a user's individual request for the material. In copyright parlance, a *phonorecord* is the material object or physical embodiment of the recording of sounds. Within the stated limits, Section 108 allows some uses of copyrighted phonorecords, and the Music Modernization Act of 2018 explicitly extends Section 108 to uses of pre-1972 sound recordings that are subject to the new form of legal protection.

The person making the copy at the library or archives should complete and retain this checklist to document compliance with Section 108 of the Copyright Act. If the library or archives finds that the planned copying does not fit the requirements of Section 108, the institution may still pursue possibilities under fair use or another exception in the copyright law, or it may obtain permission or a license from the copyright owner.

User Request for Copy: Yes _____   No _____   Date: _____

Library or Archives: _____

Citation or Description of Materials Copied: _____

REQUIREMENTS OF THE LIBRARY OR ARCHIVE

☐ (1) The collection of the library or archives meets one of the following descriptions: (a) It is open to the public; or (b) It is available not only to researchers affiliated with the institution, but also to others doing research in a specialized field.

☐ (2) The reproduction must not be made with any purpose of direct or indirect commercial advantage.

☐ (3) The reproduction must include one of the following copyright notices: (a) The copyright notice appearing on the original work to be copied; or (b) If no such notice can be found on the work to be copied, a legend stating that the work may be protected by copyright law.

☐ (4) The library or archives prominently displays a copyright warning, in accordance with requirements of the Register of Copyrights, at the place where orders are accepted and on its order form.

REQUIREMENTS OF THE WORK TO BE COPIED

☐ (5) The copied work is made from the collection of the library or archives where the user makes the request or from the collections of another library or archives (such as through interlibrary loan).

☐ (6)The copied work is either: (a) The entire work or a substantial part of a work if, after a reasonable investigation, the library or archives has determined that a copy or phonorecord of the work cannot be obtained at a fair price; or (b) No more than one article or contribution to a collection or periodical issue or a small part of any other work.

☐ (7) The work that is copied may be either published or unpublished, and the work may be one of the following:

- textual work;

- sound recording, including a pre-1972 recording (a recording of music may be subject to the restriction on the use of the musical composition—see below);

- audiovisual works dealing with news; or

- pictures and graphics published as illustrations, diagrams, or similar adjuncts to an allowed work (e.g., photograph included in an article).

The work copied may NOT be any of the following:

- musical works (musical composition, such as sheet music or a recorded version of a song);

- pictorial, graphic, or sculptural works (but "adjunct" images are allowed—see above); or

- motion pictures or audiovisual works (but "news" audiovisual works are allowed—see above).

REQUIREMENTS FOR THE COPY

☐ (8) The library or archives has had no notice that the copy or phonorecord will be used for any purpose other than private study, scholarship, or research.

☐ (9) The copy or phonorecord becomes the property of the individual user.

APPENDIX F

MODEL LETTER FOR PERMISSION REQUESTS

THE FOLLOWING LETTER is offered as guidance for drafting letters to copyright owners when permission to use the work is necessary. Chapter 24 of this book offers some guidance and tips for preparing an effective permission letter. Naturally, the letter should be revised to meet your particular needs. This example letter is relatively simple, and it should be a suitable start for most requests related to teaching, scholarly publications, and other academic work. An actual signed letter is generally preferable, but in common situations an exchange of e-mails is sufficient. Where the risks are high or the investment steep, an instructor or a librarian may want to consult with counsel and add protective clauses, such as warranties and indemnifications.

Draft and send permission letters with a strategic plan. Investigate or reach out to the copyright owner in advance to be sure you are contacting the right person who is prepared to reply. Include in the letter a request for all uses you realistically anticipate, whether uses in multiple semesters or reprinting in subsequent editions. Stay flexible and be ready with alternatives if the permission is not forthcoming.

Keep a record of your calls, letters, and e-mails as you seek permissions. Always keep a copy of the letters or e-mails in a permanent file.

Today's Date
Your Contact Information
(Address, E-mail, Telephone)
Name and Address of Addressee

Dear _____ :

I am requesting permission to reprint pages _____ through _____ of the following work: *Combustible Copyright*, written by Anson J. Pyre, and published by ABC Originals in 2010. I believe that your company, XYZ Reprints, is currently the holder of the copyright, because the original book states that copyright is held in the name of the publisher, and my research indicates that XYZ Reprints acquired ABC Originals in 2015. If you do not currently hold the right to grant this permission, please let me know, and please direct me to the current rightsholder.

This request is for permission to include the above content as required reading for an online course titled "Hot Copyright" that I will be teaching initially during Fall Semester 20___ at Blaise University, where I serve on the faculty. The current arrangement is for this reading to be accessible to only students enrolled in the course by password access from a university server. This request is for a nonexclusive, irrevocable, and royalty-free permission, and it is not intended to interfere with other uses of the same work by you. Because of changing technologies, I am also requesting permission to use the materials in electronic or other media in connection with future versions of my course in later academic terms. I hope that you will support this educational use. I intend to include a full citation to the work with the readings or other acknowledgment as you might request.

I would greatly appreciate your prompt permission. If you require any additional information, please do not hesitate to contact me. I can be reached at the contact information above.

I am sending this letter by e-mail attachment. I ask that you please sign a copy and return a fully signed copy to me by mail or e-mail attachment.

Sincerely,

Wanda W. Wonderproject

Permission is hereby granted for the use of the material as described above:

Signature: _____   Name & Title: _____

Company/Affiliation: _____   Date: _____

ABOUT THE AUTHOR

KENNETH D. CREWS is an attorney, an author, a professor, and an international copyright consultant. Much of his work has centered on copyright issues of importance to libraries, education, research, and publishing. Dr. Crews has been a professor of law, business, and library science, and he established the nation's first university-based copyright office, at Indiana University, where he also held a tenured law professorship. Crews was later recruited to create a similar office at Columbia University in New York City and to serve on the faculty of Columbia Law School. He studied history at Northwestern University and law at Washington University in St. Louis. Dr. Crews earned MLS and PhD degrees from UCLA's School of Library and Information Science. He resides in Los Angeles, California, and has been an invited speaker on college and university campuses and at conferences in nearly every U.S. state and on six continents. He was the first recipient of the L. Ray Patterson Copyright Award from the American Library Association and received the Mark T. Banner Award from the American Bar Association.

Photo credit: Ajaya Subedi/Social Science Baha (https://soscbaha.org/).

INDEX

Page numbers in italic refer to information found solely in text boxes and sidebars.

#

5Pointz building, 36, 79, 190n8

300 (motion picture), *77*

A

academia

  considerations for authors in, 65–67, 189

  institutional policies for, 10–11, 67–70, 144–146, 156–157, 161–162

  sample scenarios in, 6–11, 115–123, 237–238

  See also education

academic libraries. *See* libraries

accreditation

  determination of, 274

  TEACH Act and, 161–162, 291

acquisition, deeds of, 224

Acuff-Rose Music, Inc., Campbell v., *105*, *110*, 111n9, 112n16, *116*, 146n12, *198*, *254*

Aereo, Inc., American Broadcasting Companies, Inc. v., *77*

Agreement on Guidelines for Classroom Copying, *119*, 128–129, 132–133, *133*, 144

agreements, for publication, 61, 63, 64, 66, 68, 69, 71n23

American Broadcasting Companies, Inc. v. Aereo, Inc., *77*

American Geophysical Union v. Texaco Inc., *109*, *115*

American Library Association (ALA) guidelines, 129

American Society for Testing and Materials v. Public.Resource .Org, Inc., *42*

American Society of Composers, Authors and Publishers (ASCAP), 201, *202*, 252, 254, 263

amount, as fair use factor, 97–99, *103*, 107–108, 116–118, 121, 143, 154, 288

analog, converting from, 166

anticircumvention law. *See* Digital Millennium Copyright Act (DMCA)

appeals, courts of, 17–18, 133, 137–144, 207, 221, 245, 248

architectural works, 27, 37, 88, 91n18, 262

archives

  checklists for, 293–296

  deeds of acquisition and, 224

  Section 108 and, 169–180, 223–224, 269–271

  Section 108(h) and, 176–177, 209, 211–215, 216n26, 223–224

  types of, *218*

  WIPO issues and, 29–30

art, visual works of, 31n12, 36, *73*, 78–79, 190n8, 265, 267–268. *See also* photographs

artists

  moral rights of, 31n12, *73*, 78–79, 190n8, 267–268

  nonhuman, lack of rights for, 33, 62

  performance rights of, 79–80, *198*, 201–202, 204n17–20, 206

Association of American Publishers (AAP), 138–139

Association of Art Museum Directors (AAMD), *128*

attorneys, help from, 11–12

attribution, failing to give, *40*, 253

authors, ownership by. *See* ownership of copyright

Authors Guild v. Google, Inc., *108*

B

Basic Books, Inc. v. Kinko's Graphics Corp., 107, 113–114, 118–119, 124n2, 184, 186

Berne Convention, 25–27, *28*, 29, 30n4, *52*, 242, 246, 262

Bill Graham Archives v. Dorling Kindersley Ltd., *117*, 120, 157n7

www.ingramcontent.com/pod-product-compliance
Lightning Source LLC
Chambersburg PA
CBHW061932260326
41798CB00034B/404